RADIANT

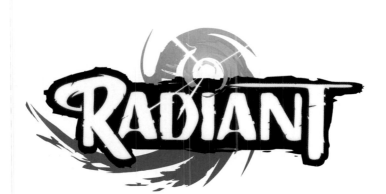

TONY VALENTE

CONTENTS

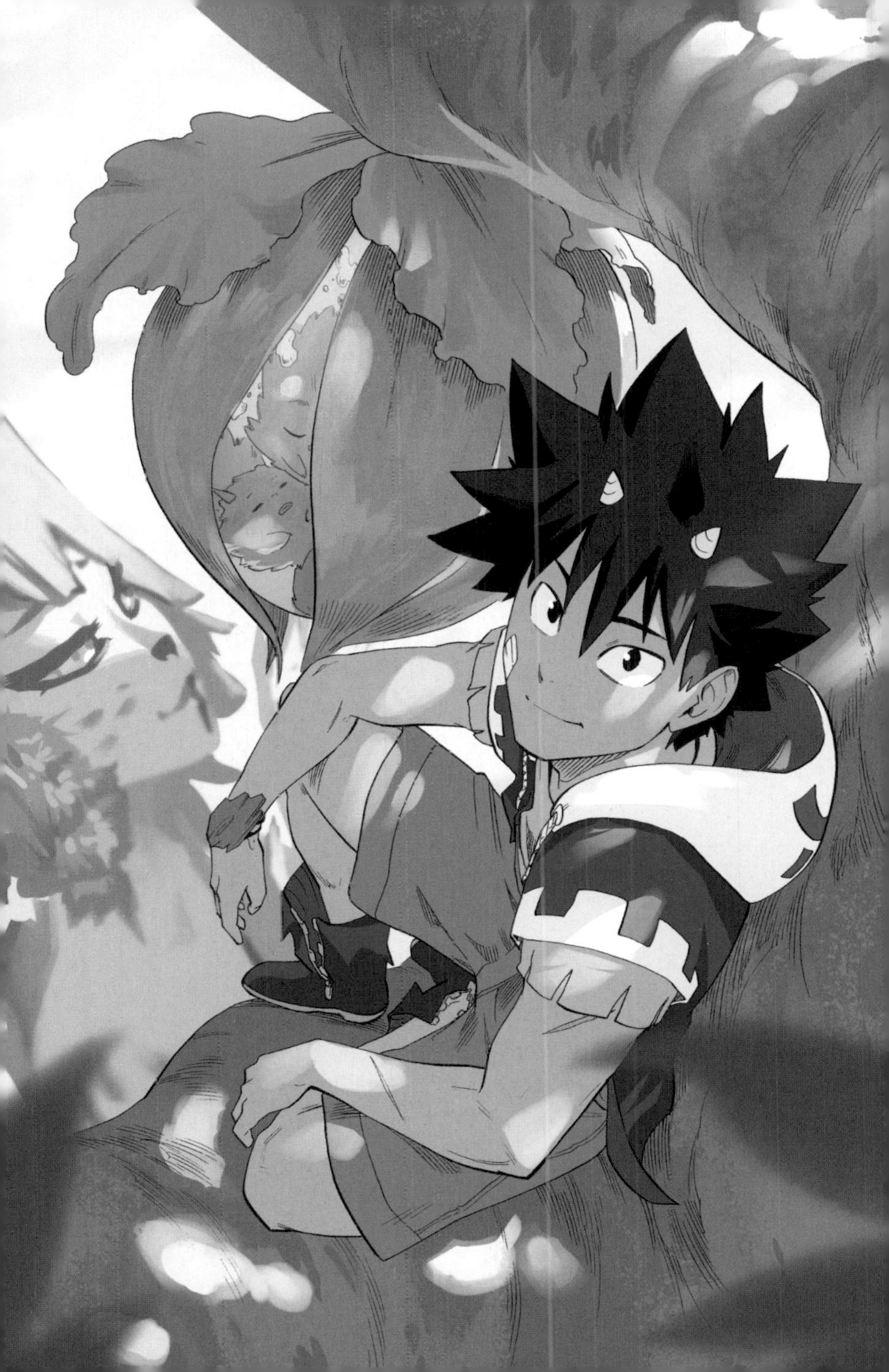

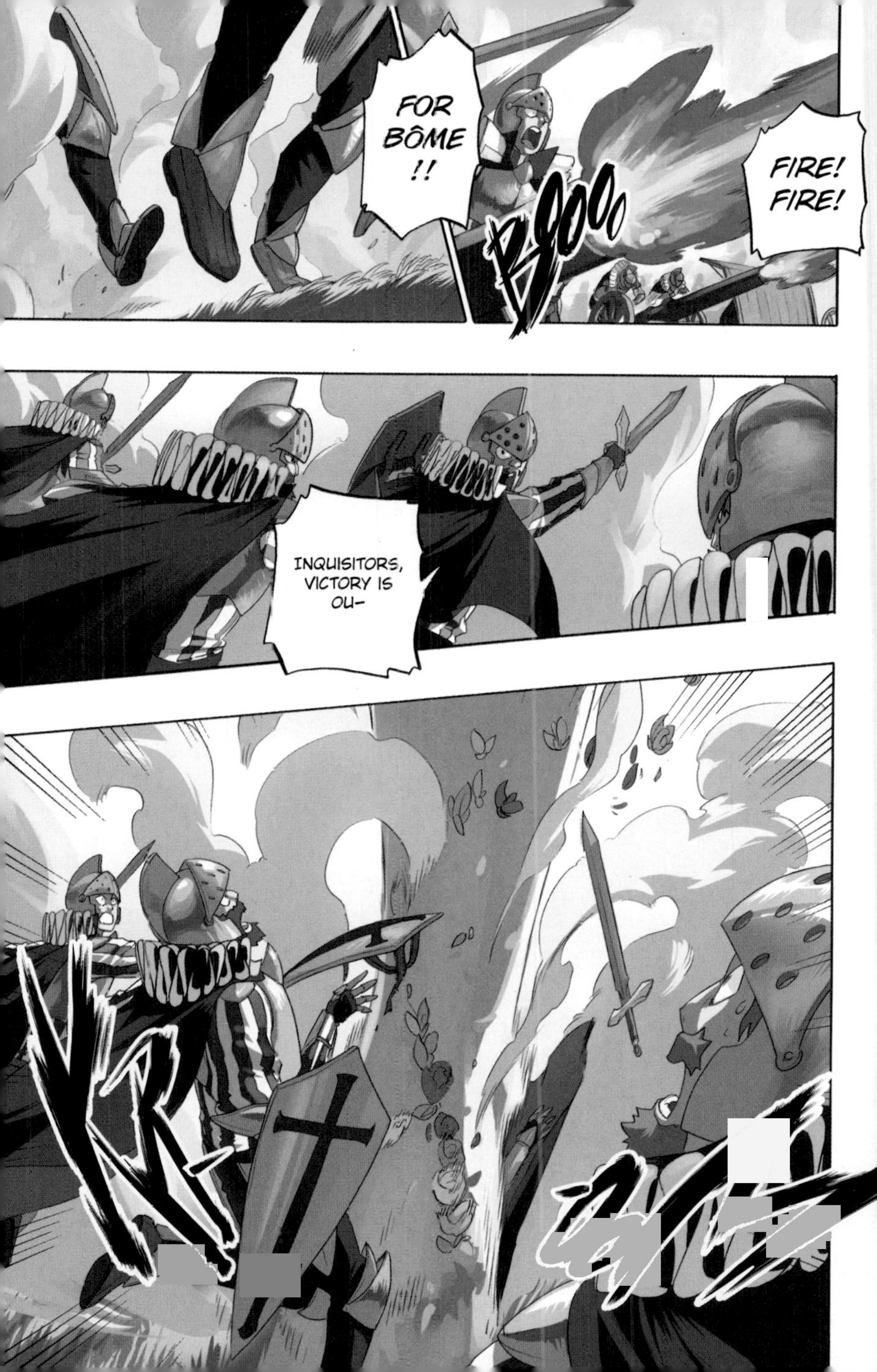
FIRE! FIRE!
FOR BÔME !!
INQUISITORS, VICTORY IS OU–

Chapter 61

Mordred

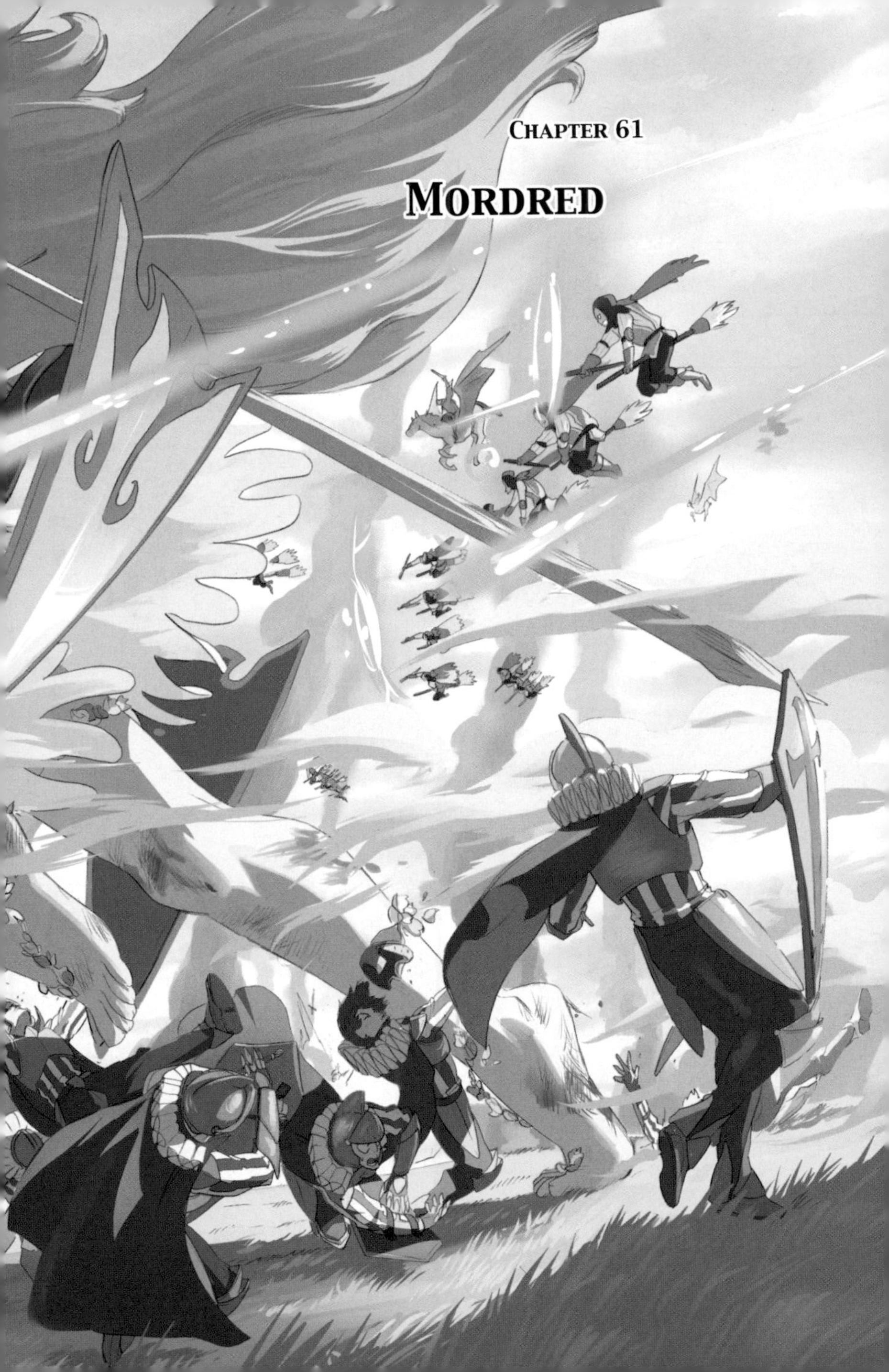

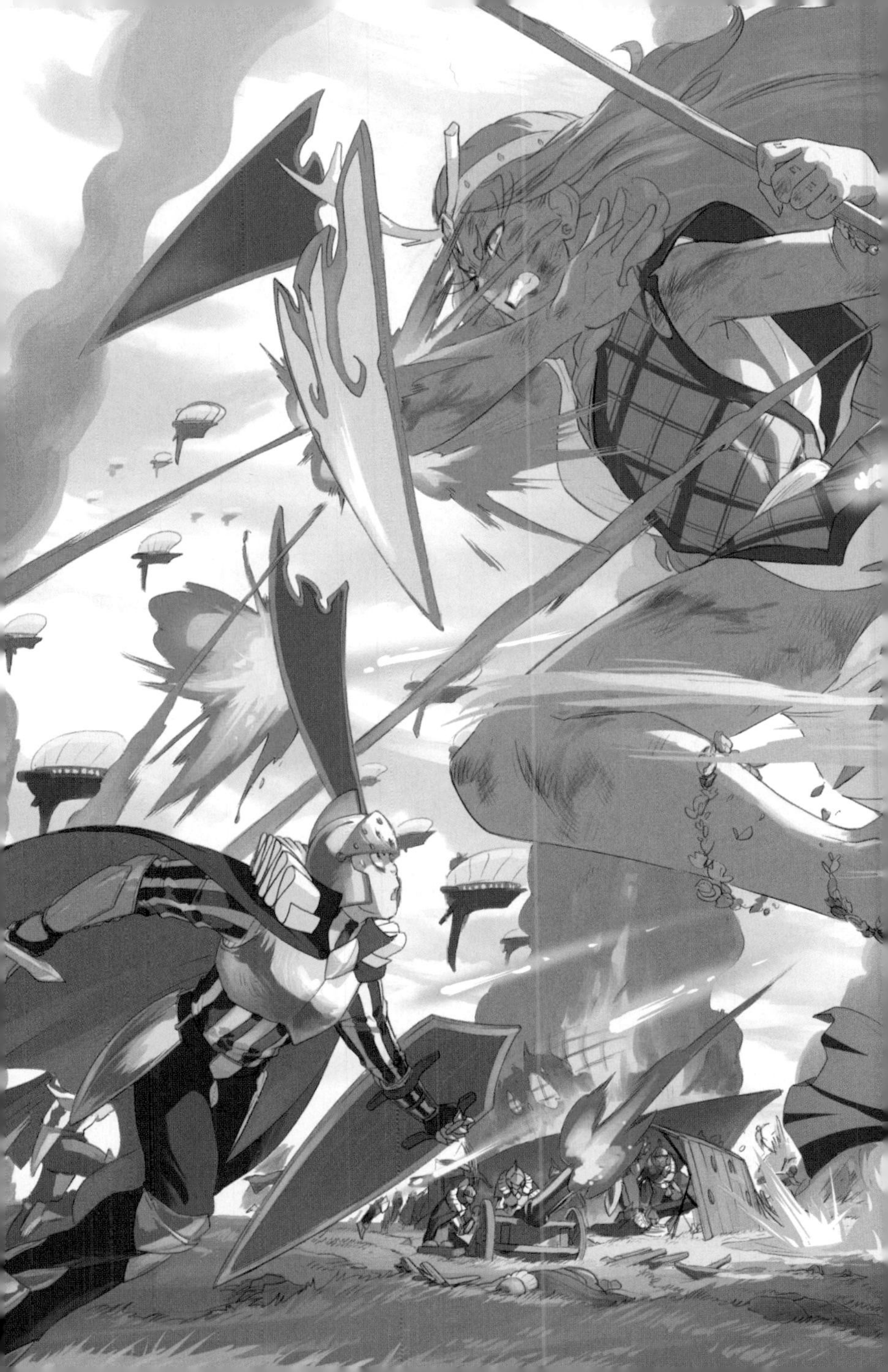

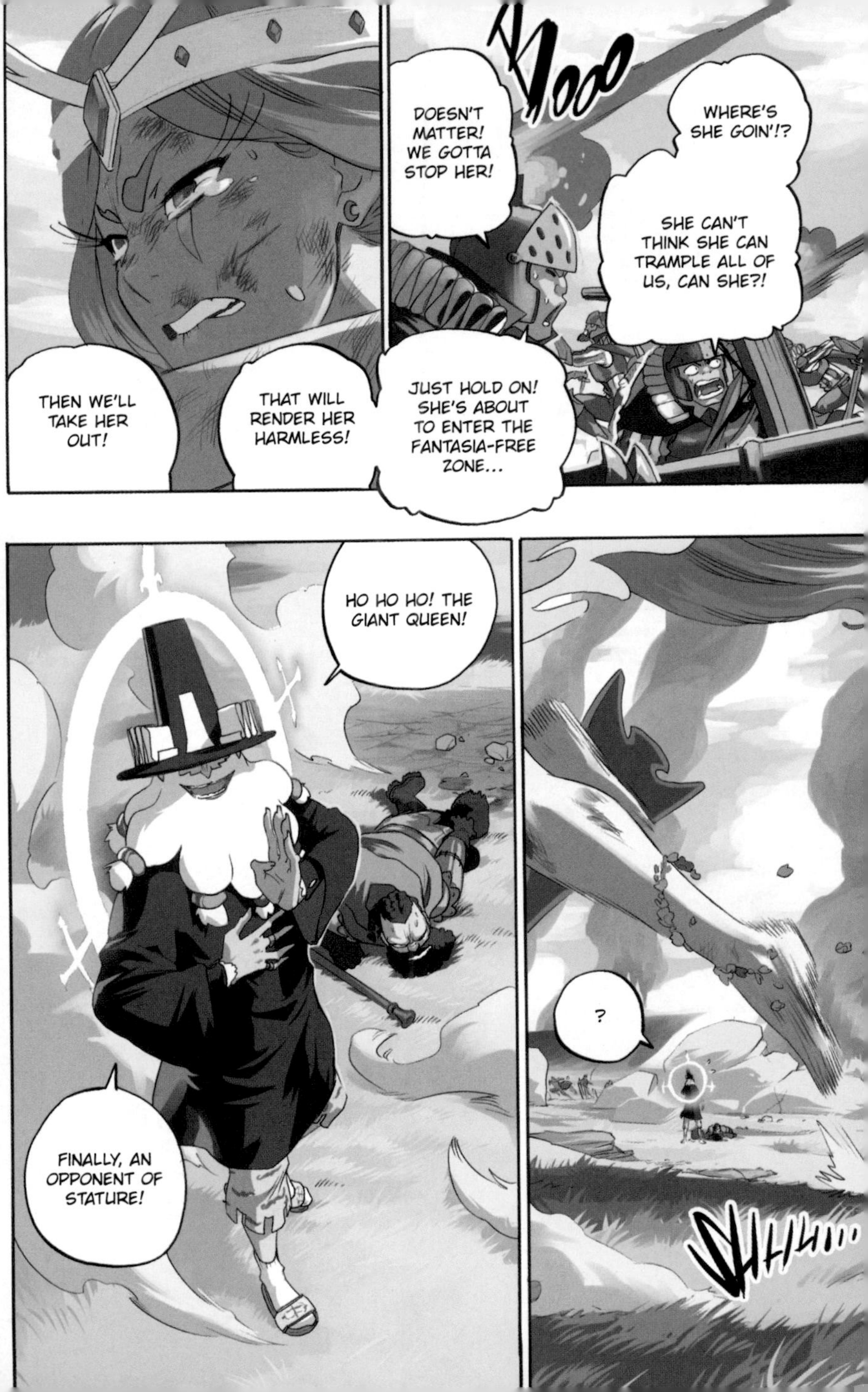
WHERE'S SHE GOIN'!?
SHE CAN'T THINK SHE CAN TRAMPLE ALL OF US, CAN SHE?!
DOESN'T MATTER! WE GOTTA STOP HER!
JUST HOLD ON! SHE'S ABOUT TO ENTER THE FANTASIA-FREE ZONE...
THAT WILL RENDER HER HARMLESS!
THEN WE'LL TAKE HER OUT!
?
HO HO HO! THE GIANT QUEEN!
FINALLY, AN OPPONENT OF STATURE!

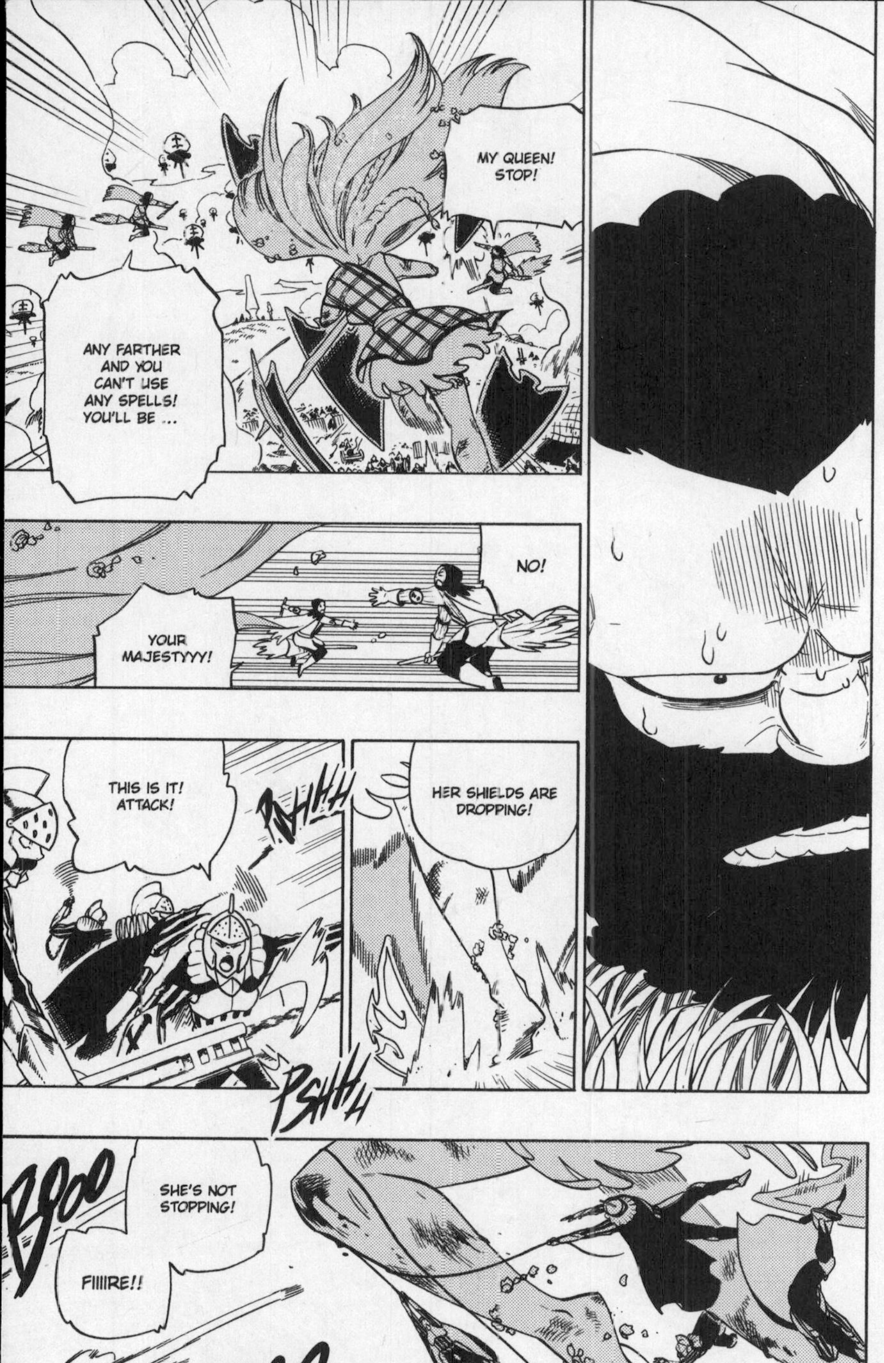
MY QUEEN! STOP!
ANY FARTHER AND YOU CAN'T USE ANY SPELLS! YOU'LL BE ...
NO!
YOUR MAJESTYYY!
HER SHIELDS ARE DROPPING!
THIS IS IT! ATTACK!
PSHH
PSHH
SHE'S NOT STOPPING!
FIIIRE!!
BOOO
BOOO

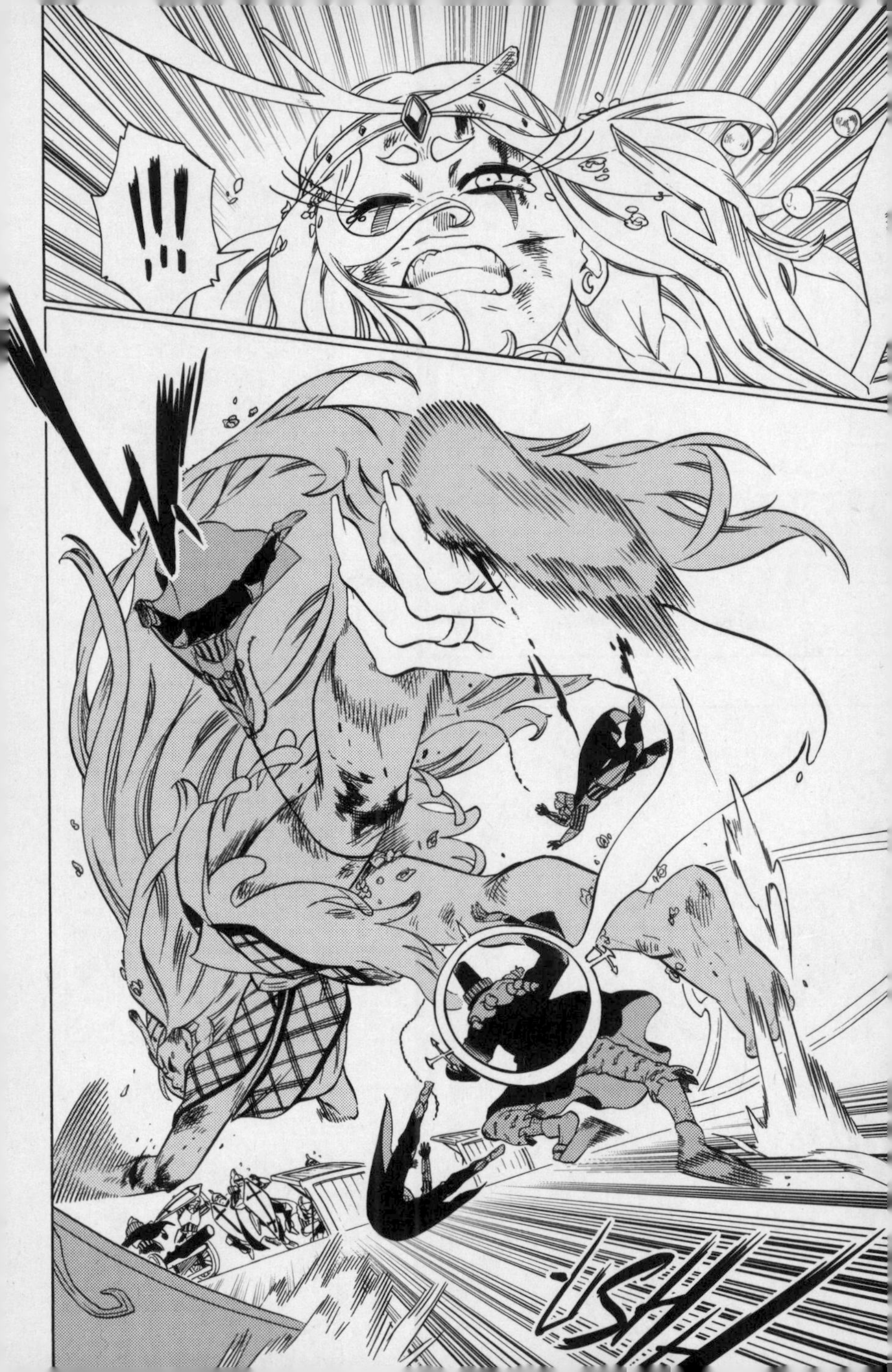
!!!

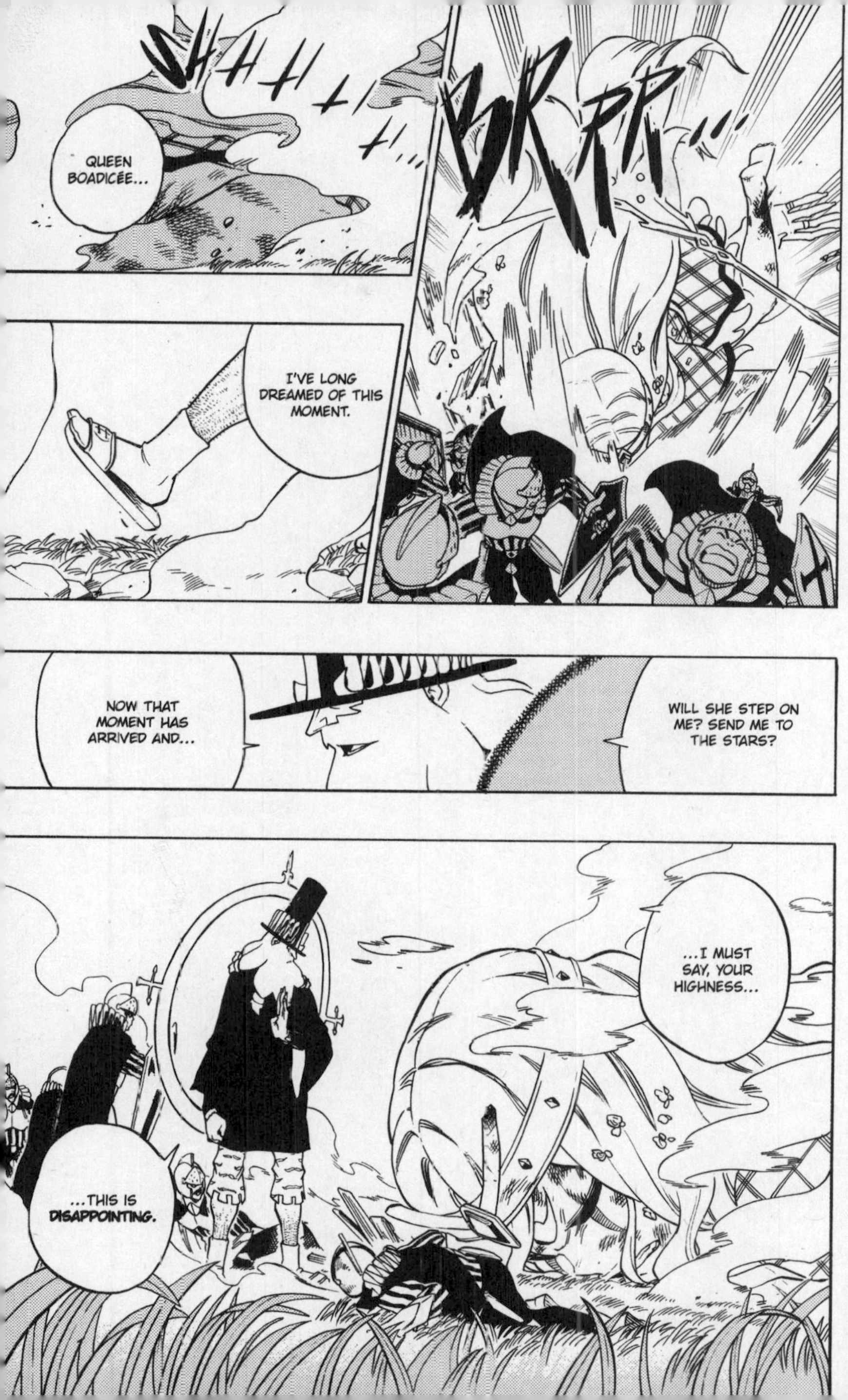
BRRR...
SHHH...
QUEEN BOADICÉE...
I'VE LONG DREAMED OF THIS MOMENT.
WILL SHE STEP ON ME? SEND ME TO THE STARS?
NOW THAT MOMENT HAS ARRIVED AND...
...I MUST SAY, YOUR HIGHNESS...
...THIS IS **DISAPPOINTING.**

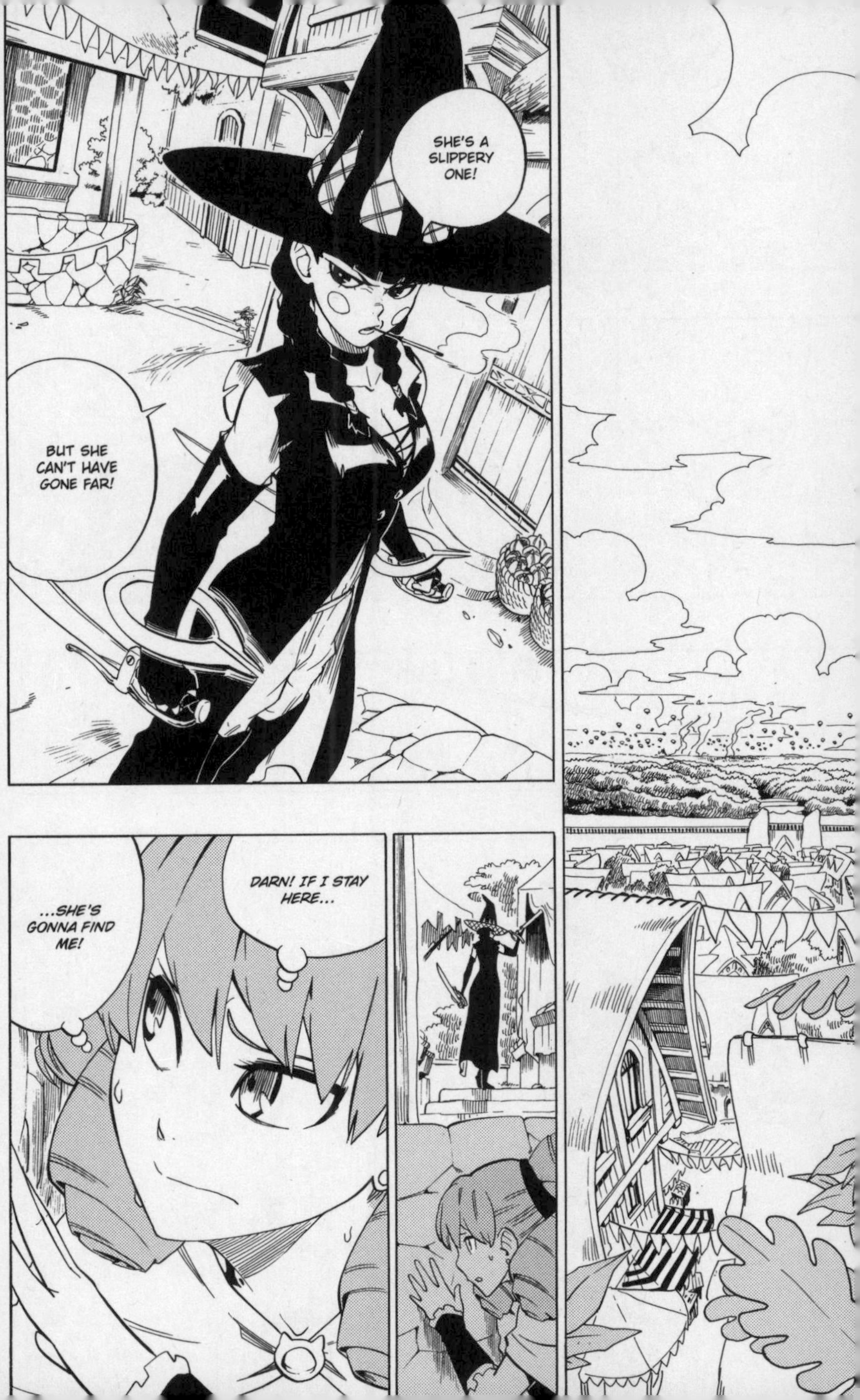
SHE'S A SLIPPERY ONE!
BUT SHE CAN'T HAVE GONE FAR!
DARN! IF I STAY HERE...
...SHE'S GONNA FIND ME!

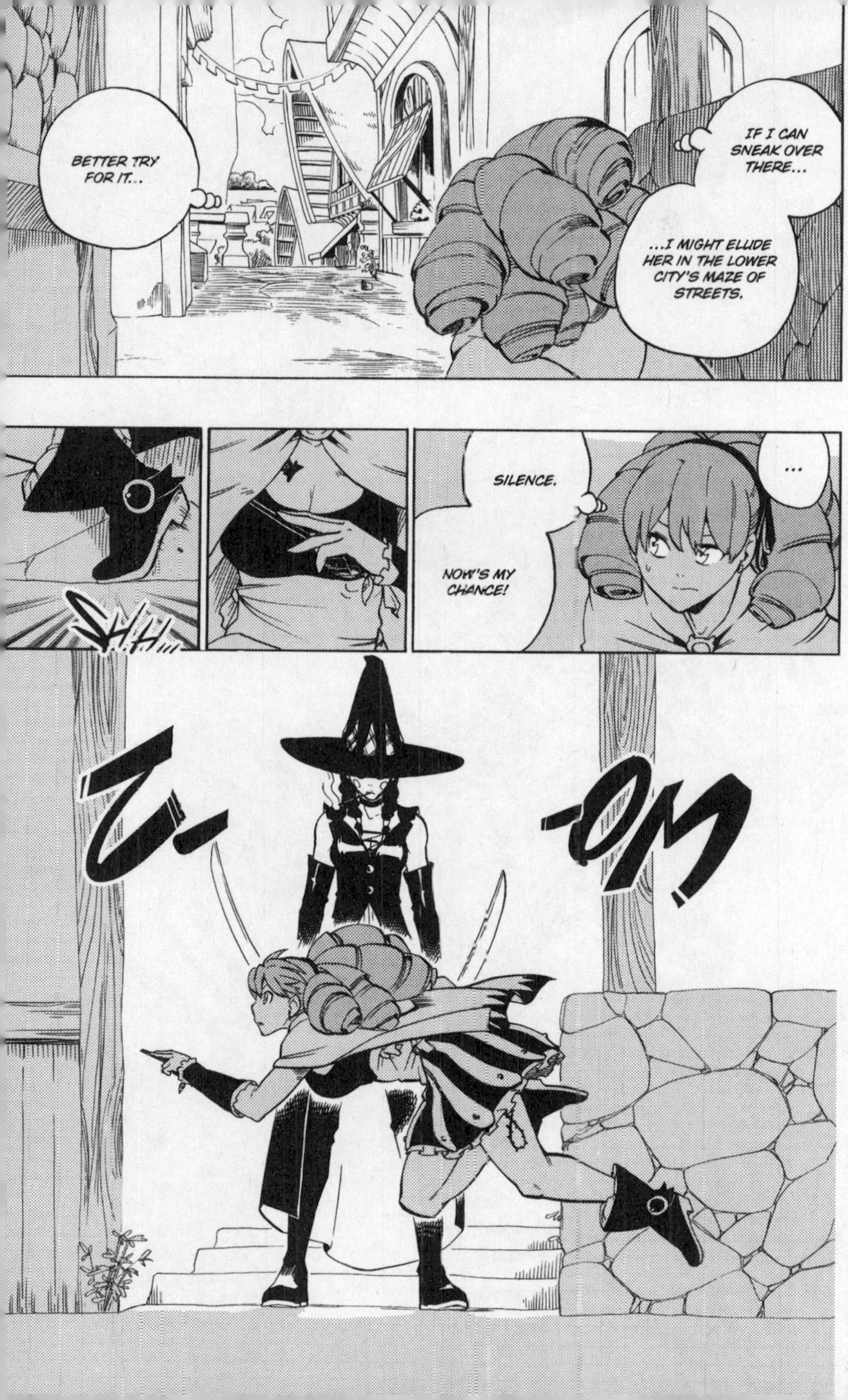
IF I CAN SNEAK OVER THERE...
...I MIGHT ELUDE HER IN THE LOWER CITY'S MAZE OF STREETS.
BETTER TRY FOR IT...
...
SILENCE.
NOW'S MY CHANCE!
SHH...
Z-
-OM

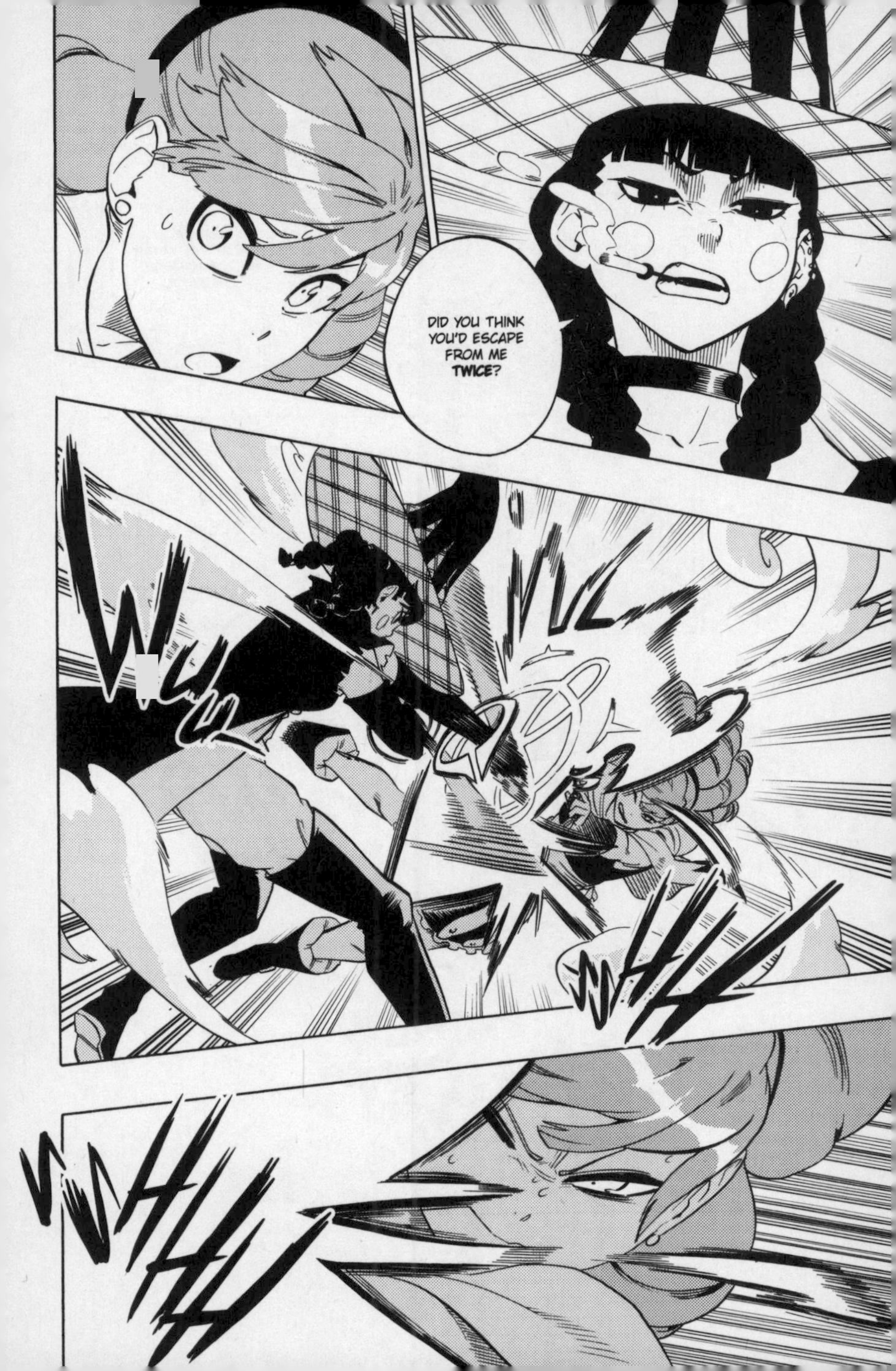
DID YOU THINK YOU'D ESCAPE FROM ME TWICE?

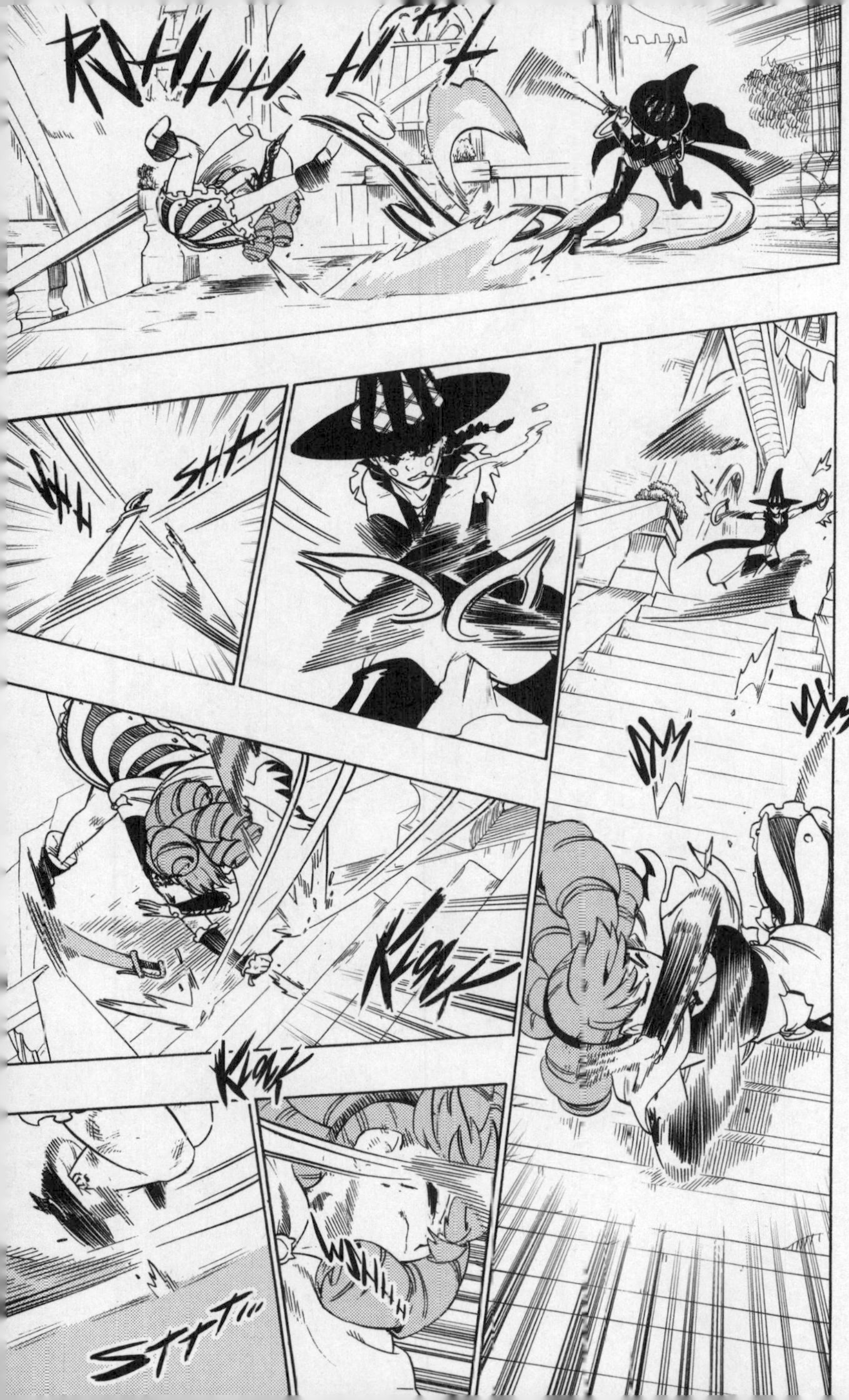
RSHHHH
KLONK
KLONK
STTT...

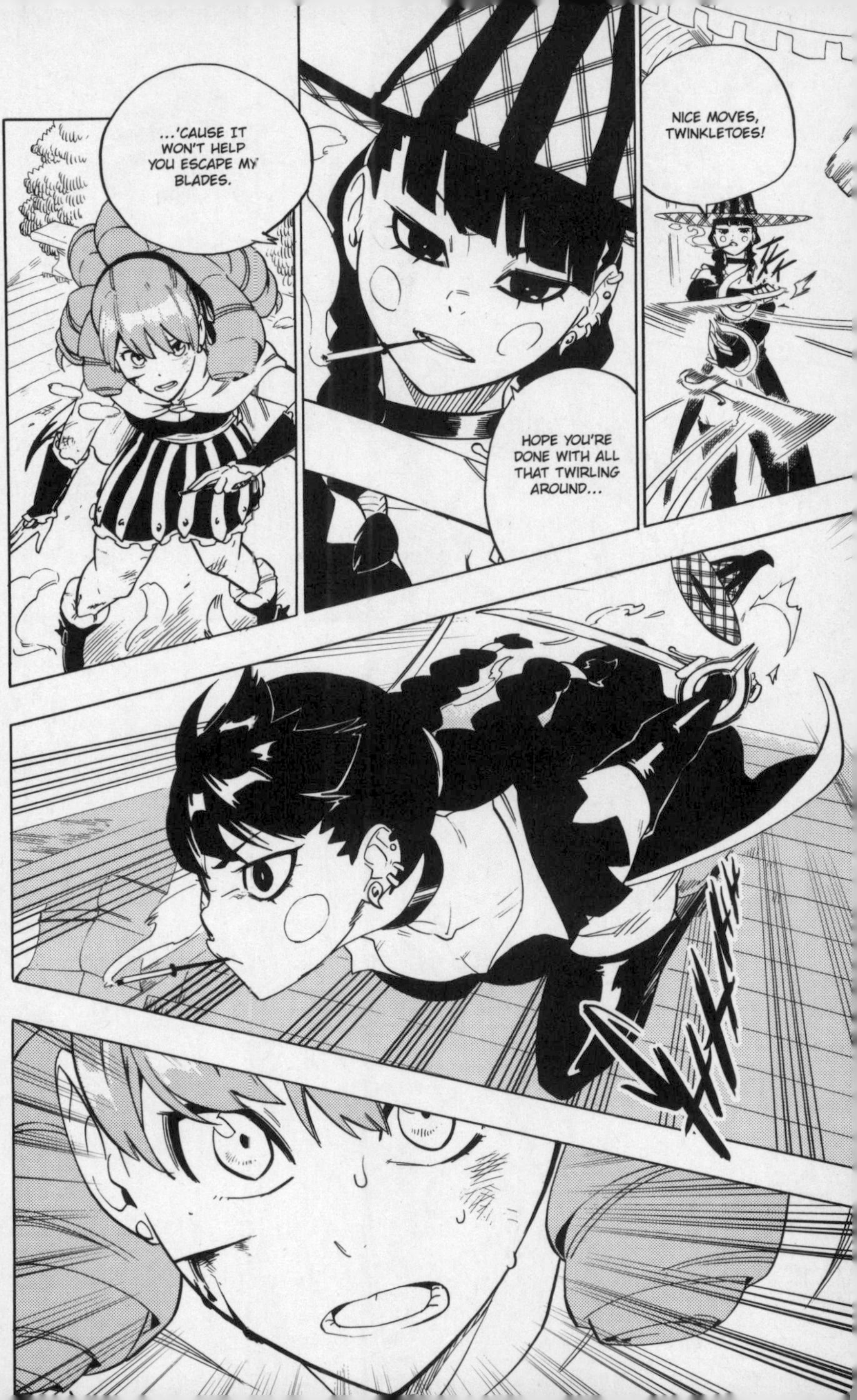
NICE MOVES, TWINKLETOES!
HOPE YOU'RE DONE WITH ALL THAT TWIRLING AROUND...
...'CAUSE IT WON'T HELP YOU ESCAPE MY BLADES.

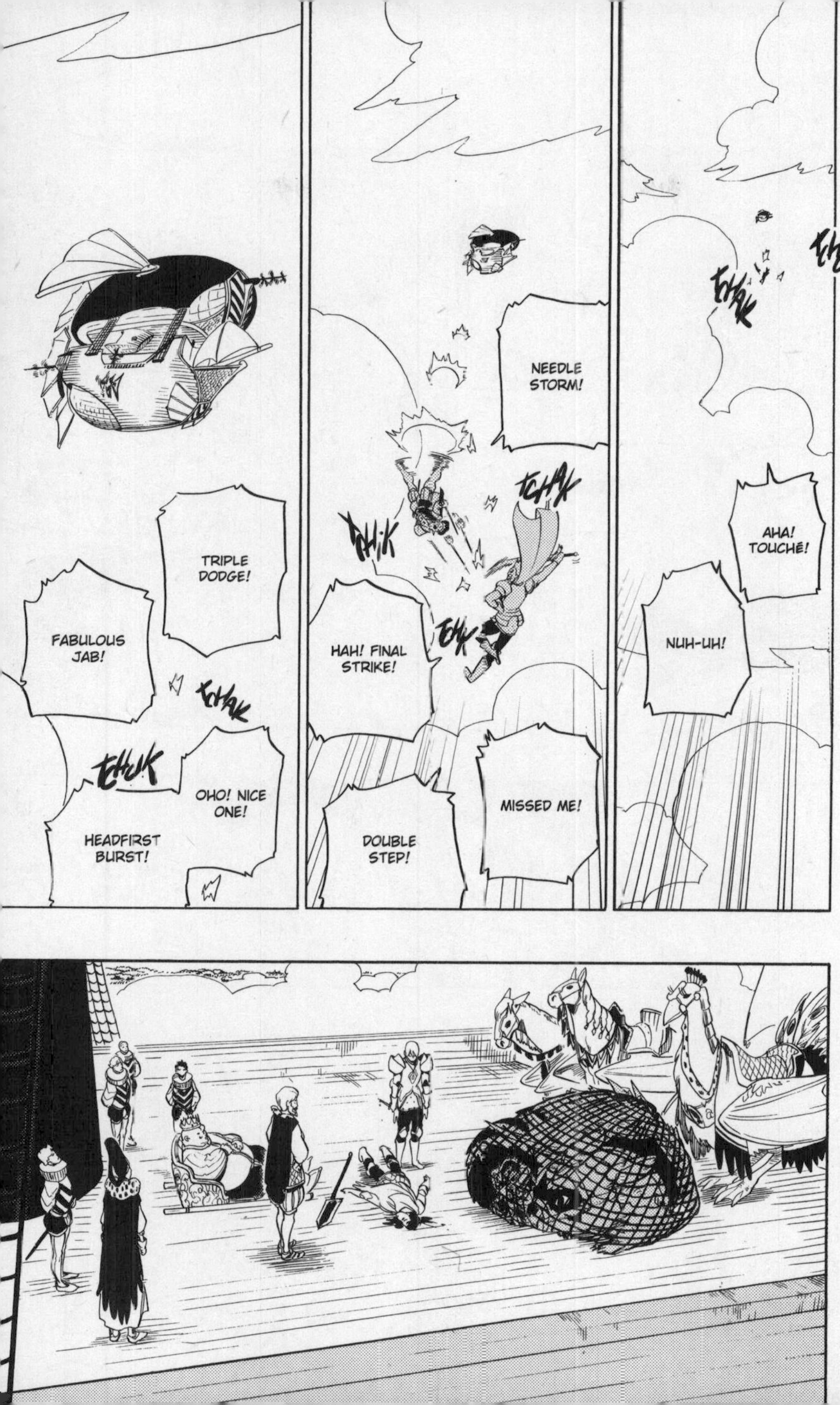
TCHOK
TCHAK
AHA! TOUCHÉ!
NUH-UH!
NEEDLE STORM!
TCHAK
TCHIK
HAH! FINAL STRIKE!
TCHK
MISSED ME!
DOUBLE STEP!
TRIPLE DODGE!
FABULOUS JAB!
TCHAK
OHO! NICE ONE!
TCHUK
HEADFIRST BURST!

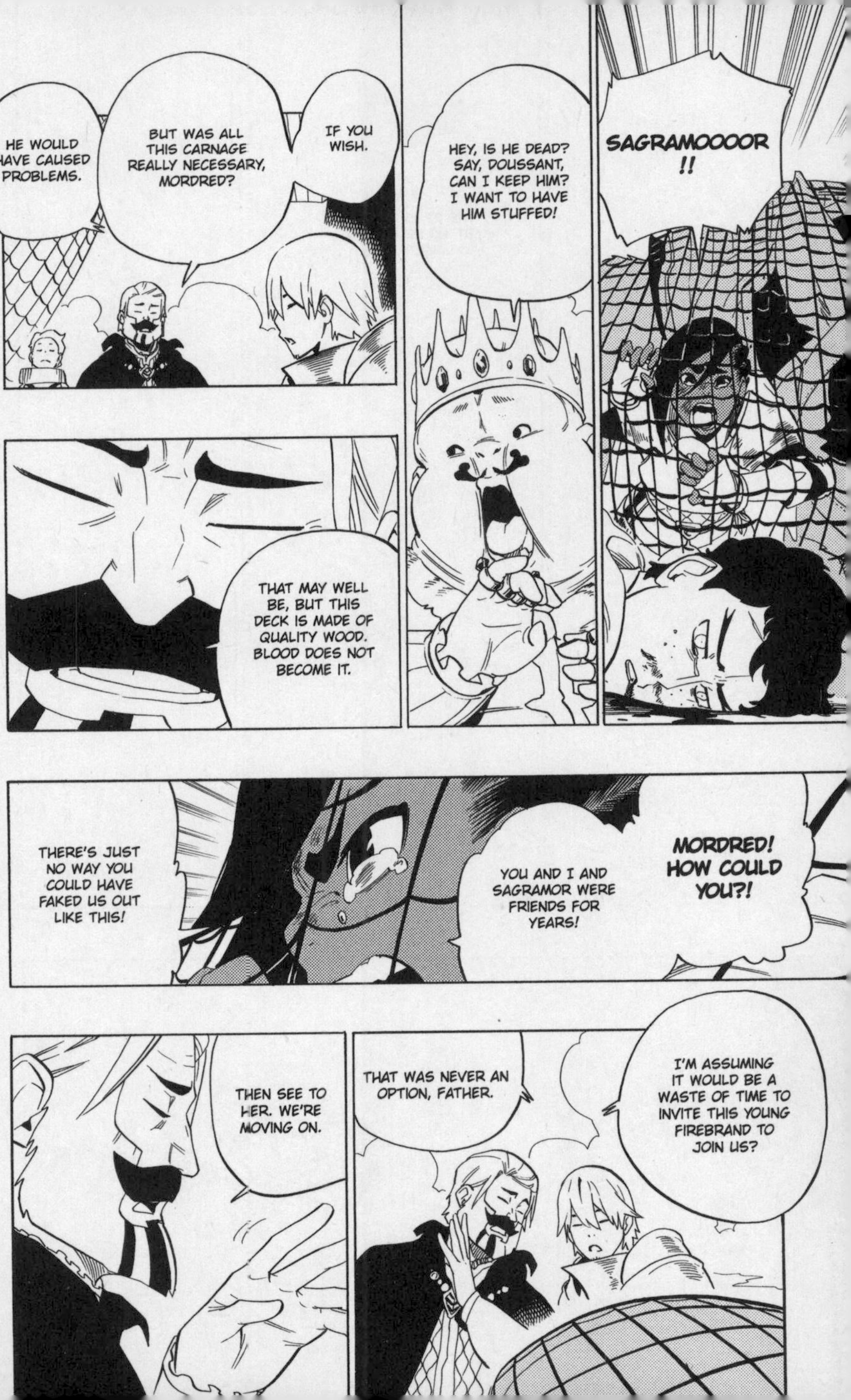
SAGRAMOOOOR !!
HEY, IS HE DEAD? SAY, DOUSSANT, CAN I KEEP HIM? I WANT TO HAVE HIM STUFFED!
IF YOU WISH.
BUT WAS ALL THIS CARNAGE REALLY NECESSARY, MORDRED?
HE WOULD HAVE CAUSED PROBLEMS.
THAT MAY WELL BE, BUT THIS DECK IS MADE OF QUALITY WOOD. BLOOD DOES NOT BECOME IT.
MORDRED! HOW COULD YOU?!
YOU AND I AND SAGRAMOR WERE FRIENDS FOR YEARS!
THERE'S JUST NO WAY YOU COULD HAVE FAKED US OUT LIKE THIS!
I'M ASSUMING IT WOULD BE A WASTE OF TIME TO INVITE THIS YOUNG FIREBRAND TO JOIN US?
THAT WAS NEVER AN OPTION, FATHER.
THEN SEE TO HER. WE'RE MOVING ON.

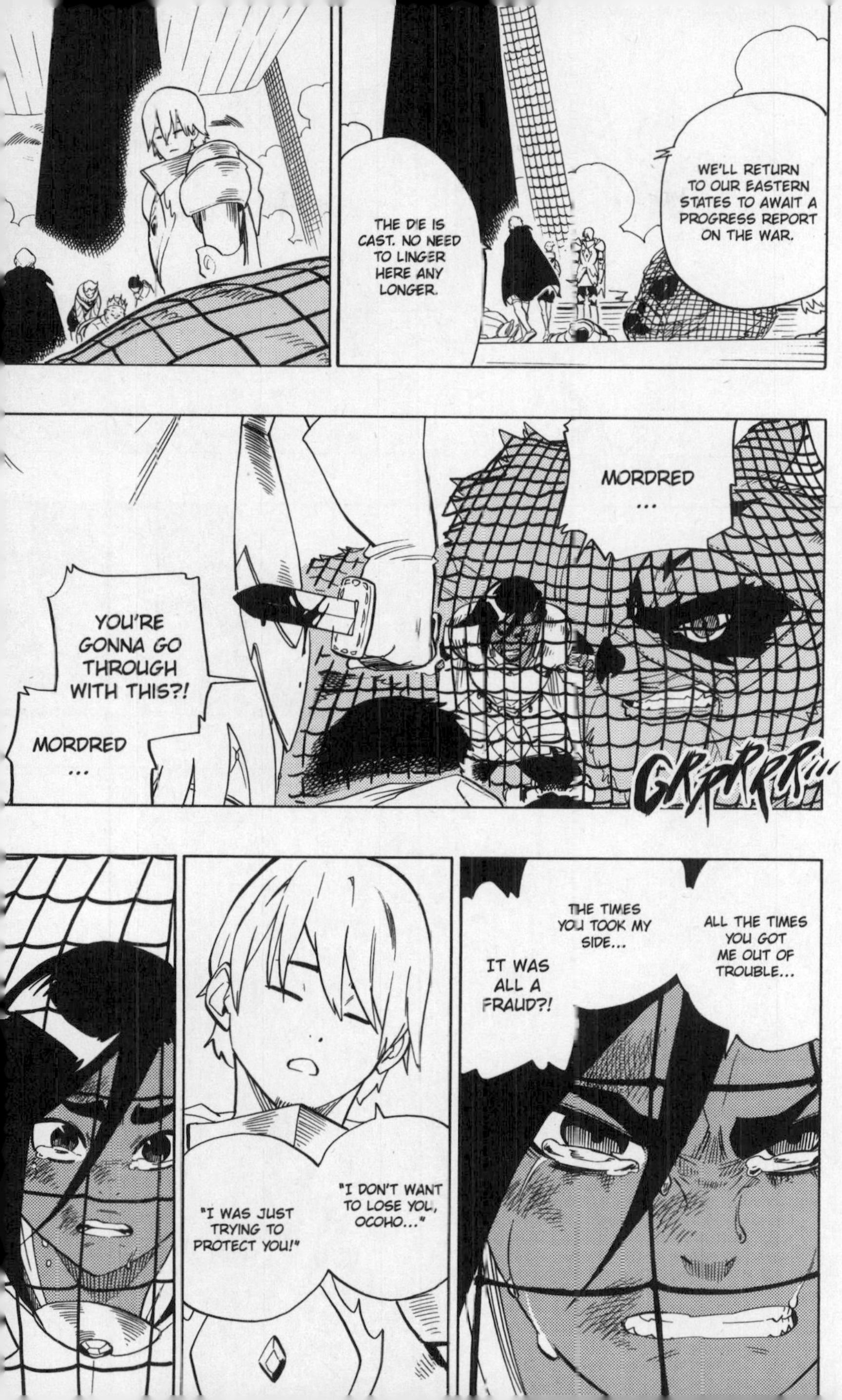
WE'LL RETURN TO OUR EASTERN STATES TO AWAIT A PROGRESS REPORT ON THE WAR.
THE DIE IS CAST. NO NEED TO LINGER HERE ANY LONGER.
MORDRED ...
GRRRRR!!
YOU'RE GONNA GO THROUGH WITH THIS?!
MORDRED ...
ALL THE TIMES YOU GOT ME OUT OF TROUBLE...
THE TIMES YOU TOOK MY SIDE...
IT WAS ALL A FRAUD?!
"I DON'T WANT TO LOSE YOU, OCOHO..."
"I WAS JUST TRYING TO PROTECT YOU!"

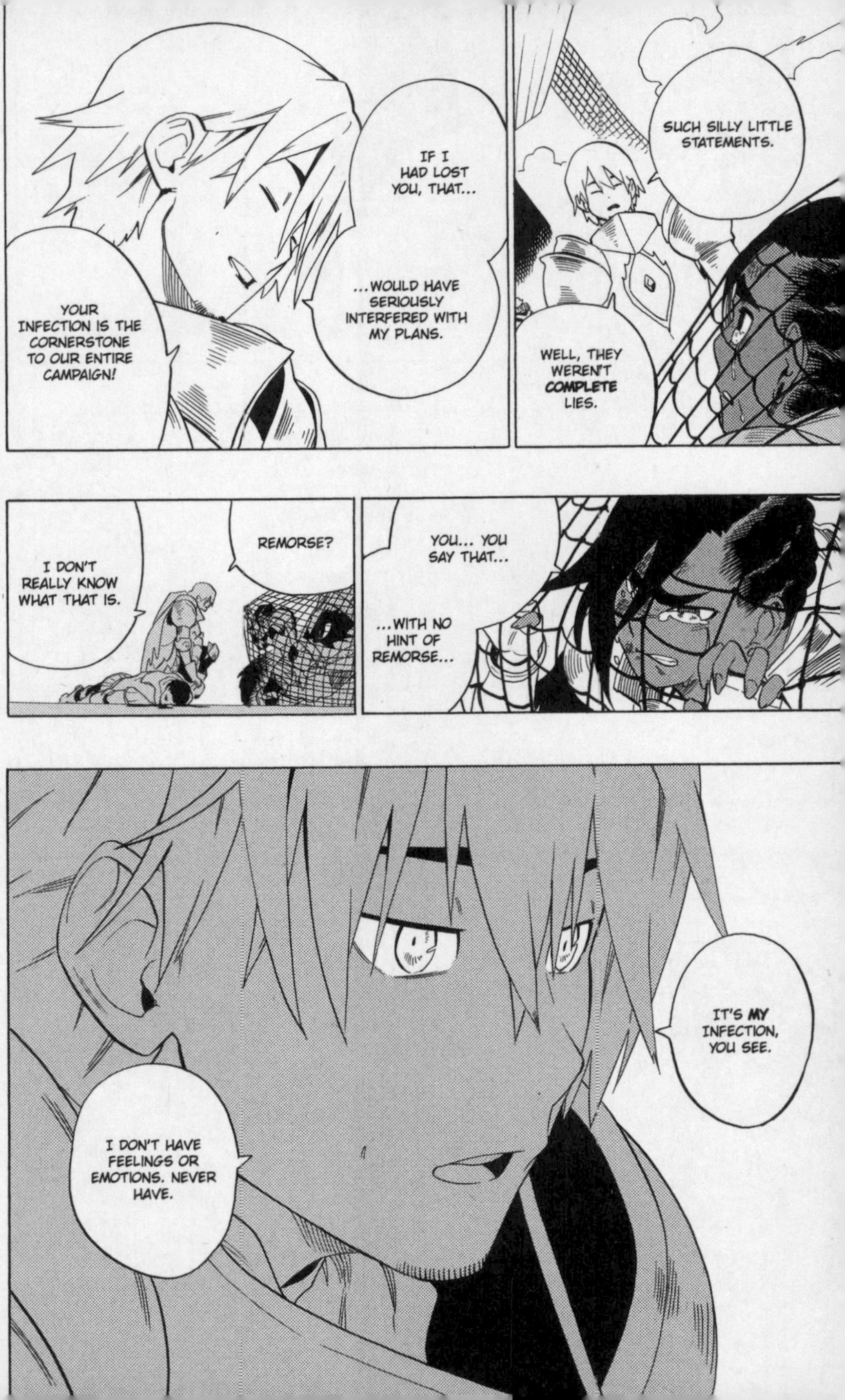
SUCH SILLY LITTLE STATEMENTS.
WELL, THEY WEREN'T **COMPLETE** LIES.
IF I HAD LOST YOU, THAT...
...WOULD HAVE SERIOUSLY INTERFERED WITH MY PLANS.
YOUR INFECTION IS THE CORNERSTONE TO OUR ENTIRE CAMPAIGN!
YOU... YOU SAY THAT...
...WITH NO HINT OF REMORSE...
REMORSE?
I DON'T REALLY KNOW WHAT THAT IS.
IT'S **MY** INFECTION, YOU SEE.
I DON'T HAVE FEELINGS OR EMOTIONS. NEVER HAVE.

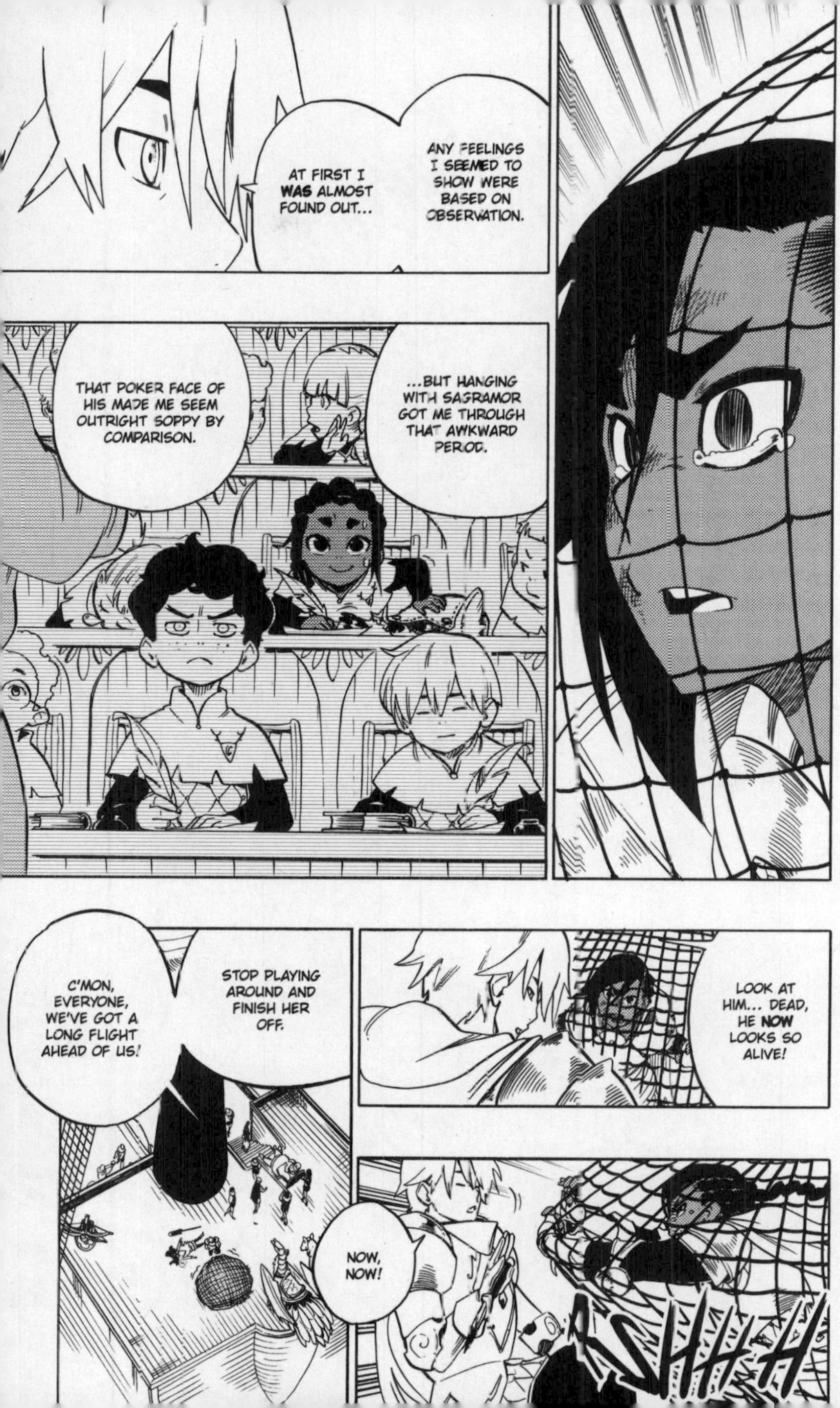
ANY FEELINGS I SEEMED TO SHOW WERE BASED ON OBSERVATION.
AT FIRST I **WAS** ALMOST FOUND OUT...
...BUT HANGING WITH SAGRAMOR GOT ME THROUGH THAT AWKWARD PEROD.
THAT POKER FACE OF HIS MADE ME SEEM OUTRIGHT SOPPY BY COMPARISON.
LOOK AT HIM... DEAD, HE **NOW** LOOKS SO ALIVE!
NOW, NOW!
SHHH
STOP PLAYING AROUND AND FINISH HER OFF.
C'MON, EVERYONE, WE'VE GOT A LONG FLIGHT AHEAD OF US!

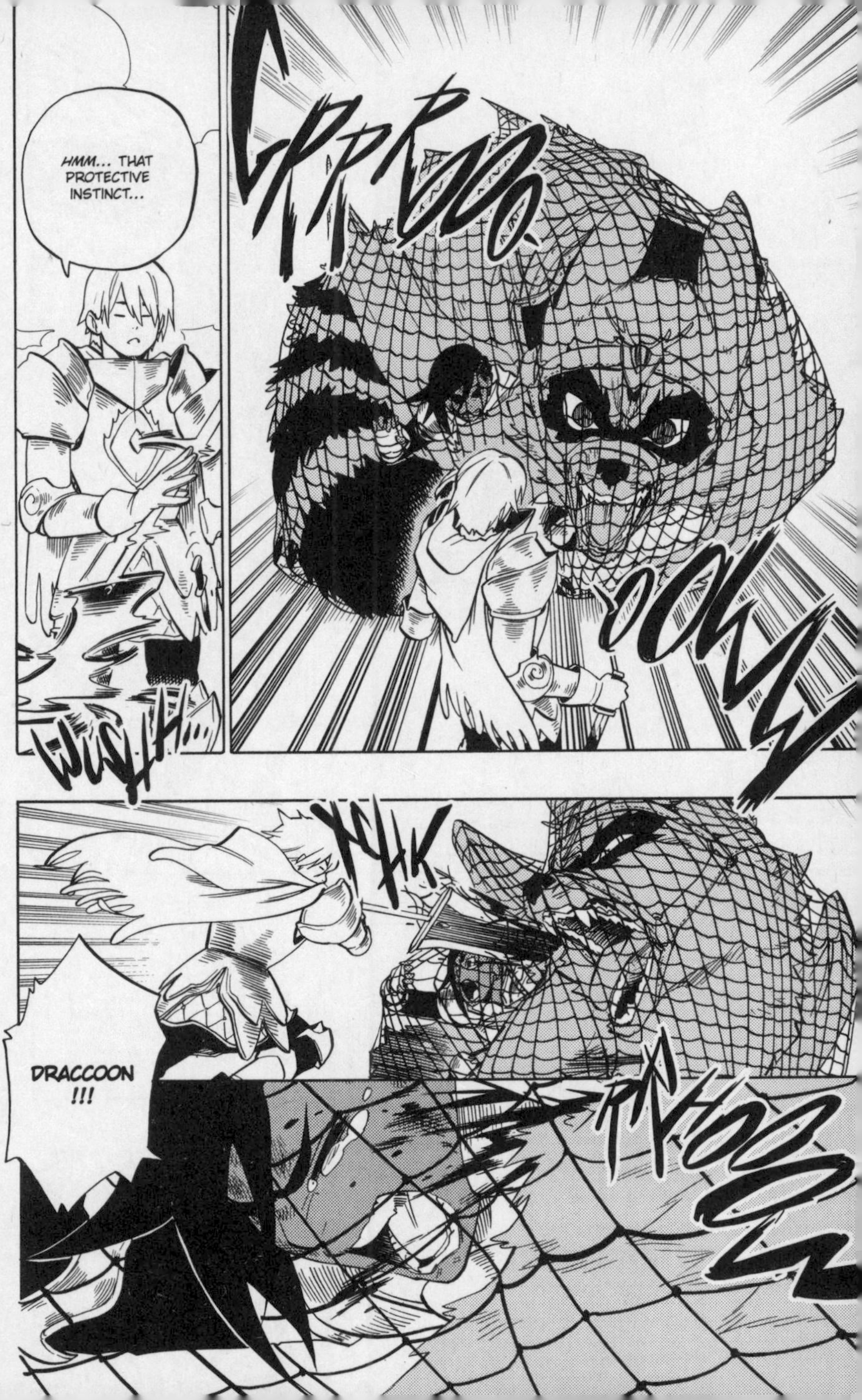
HMM... THAT PROTECTIVE INSTINCT...
DRACCOON !!!

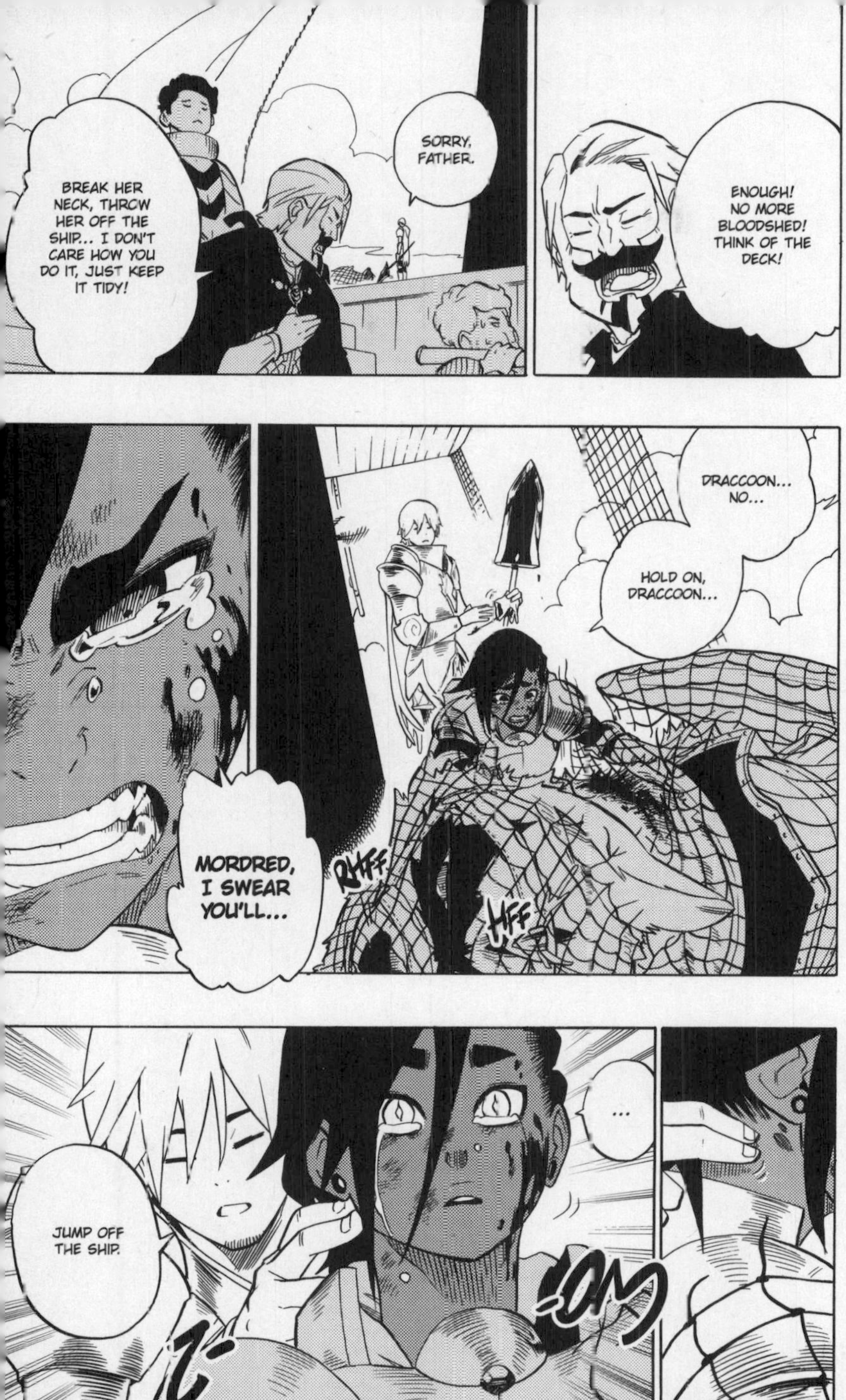
ENOUGH! NO MORE BLOODSHED! THINK OF THE DECK!
SORRY, FATHER.
BREAK HER NECK, THROW HER OFF THE SHIP... I DON'T CARE HOW YOU DO IT, JUST KEEP IT TIDY!
DRACCOON... NO...
HOLD ON, DRACCOON...
HFF
RHFF
MORDRED, I SWEAR YOU'LL...
...
JUMP OFF THE SHIP.

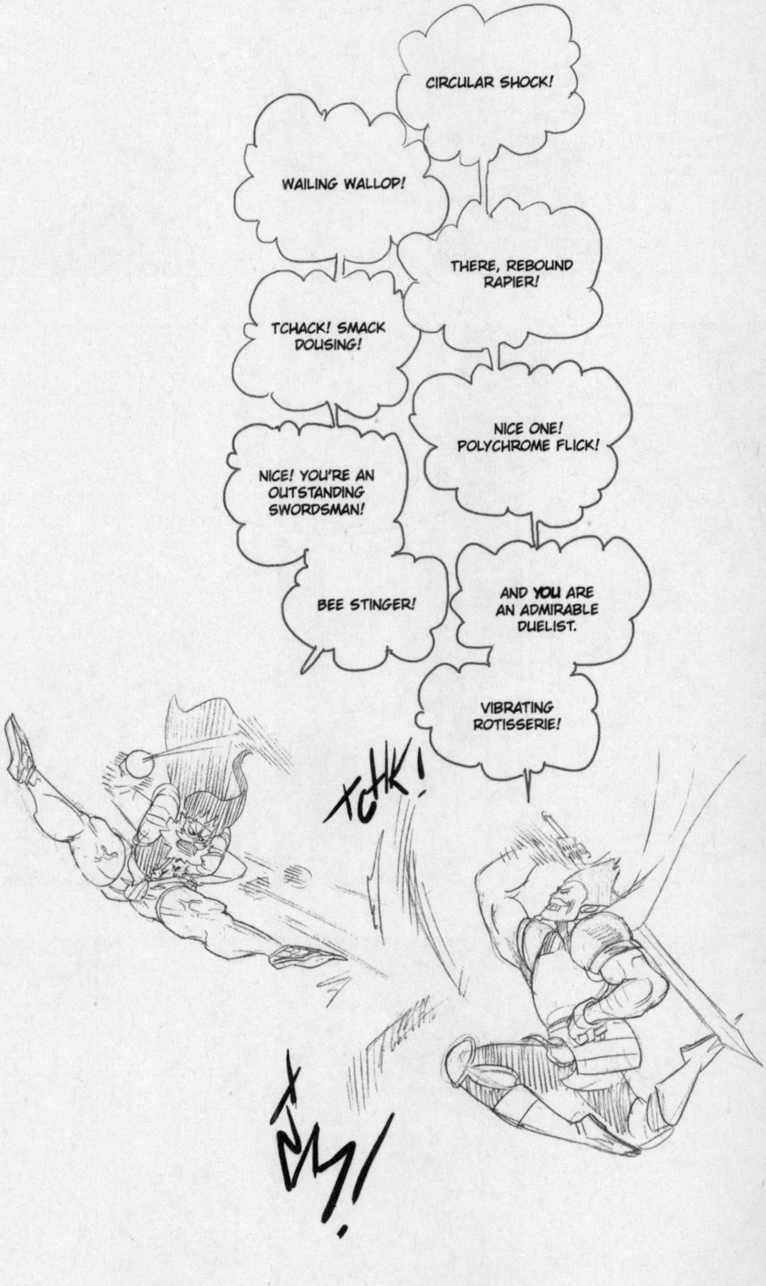
CIRCULAR SHOCK!
WAILING WALLOP!
THERE, REBOUND RAPIER!
TCHACK! SMACK DOUSING!
NICE ONE! POLYCHROME FLICK!
NICE! YOU'RE AN OUTSTANDING SWORDSMAN!
AND YOU ARE AN ADMIRABLE DUELIST.
BEE STINGER!
VIBRATING ROTISSERIE!
TCHK!

CHAPTER 62

THE CAPTURED QUEEN

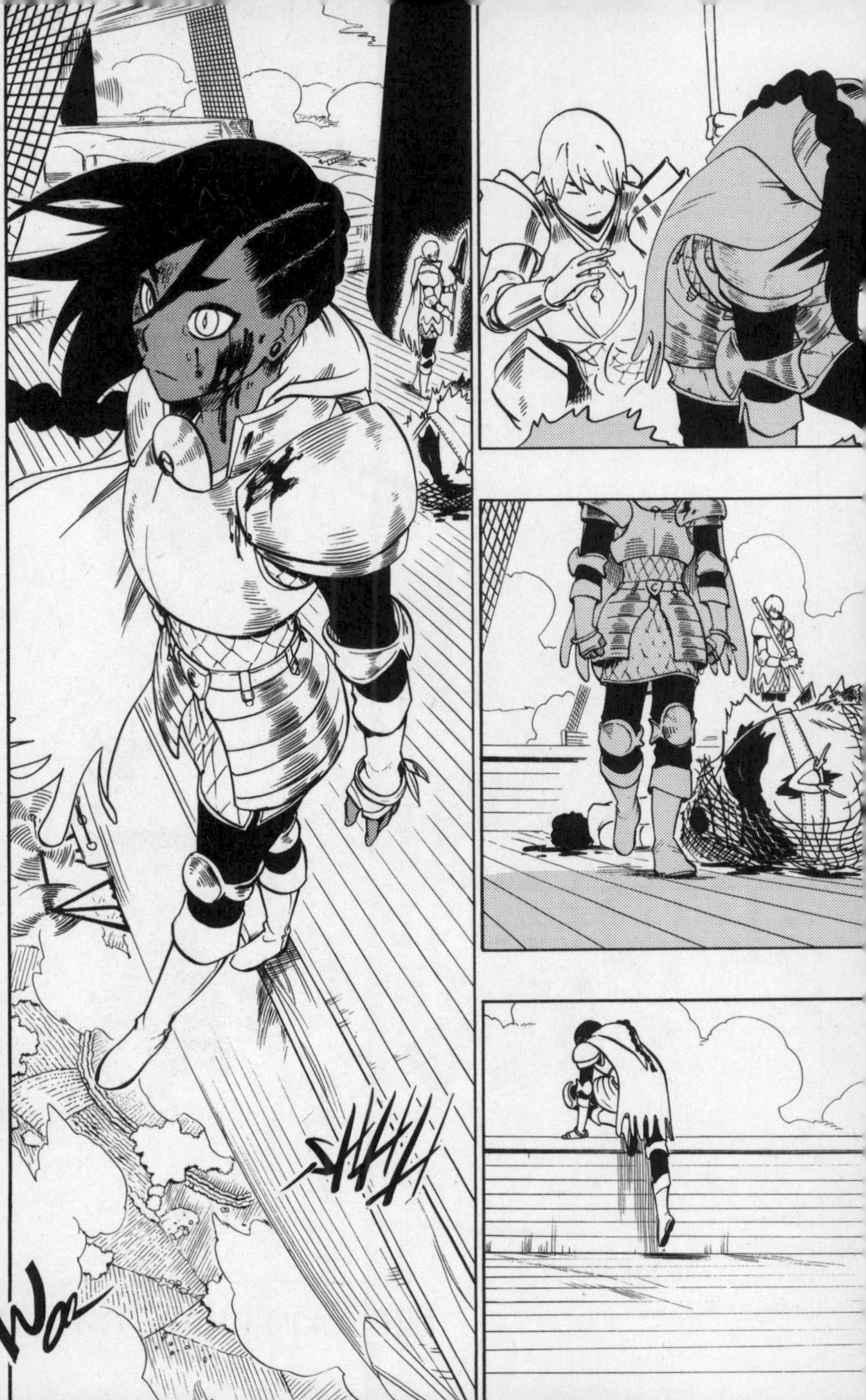
Waa

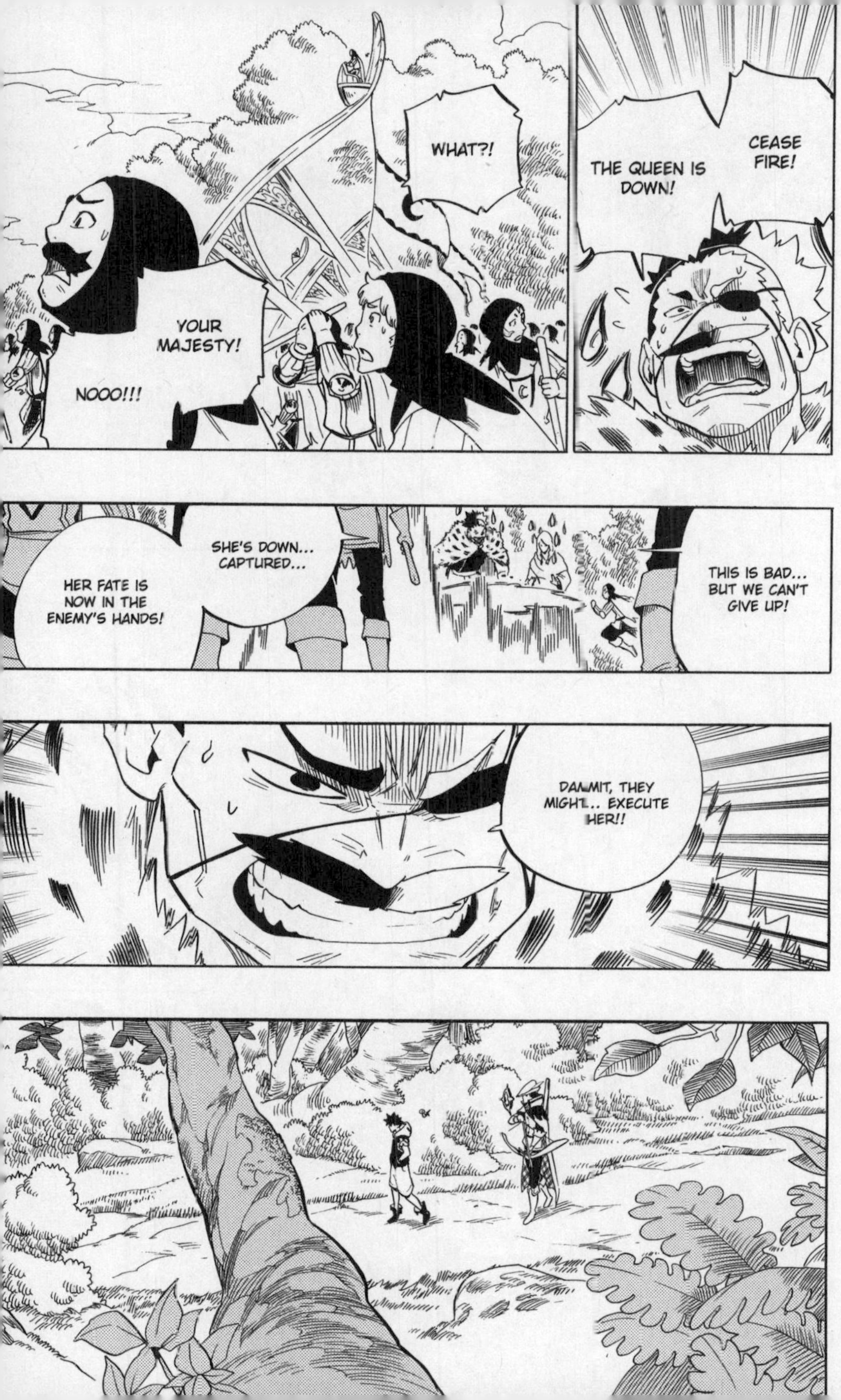
CEASE FIRE!
THE QUEEN IS DOWN!
WHAT?!
YOUR MAJESTY!
NOOO!!!
THIS IS BAD... BUT WE CAN'T GIVE UP!
SHE'S DOWN... CAPTURED...
HER FATE IS NOW IN THE ENEMY'S HANDS!
DAMMIT, THEY MIGHT... EXECUTE HER!!

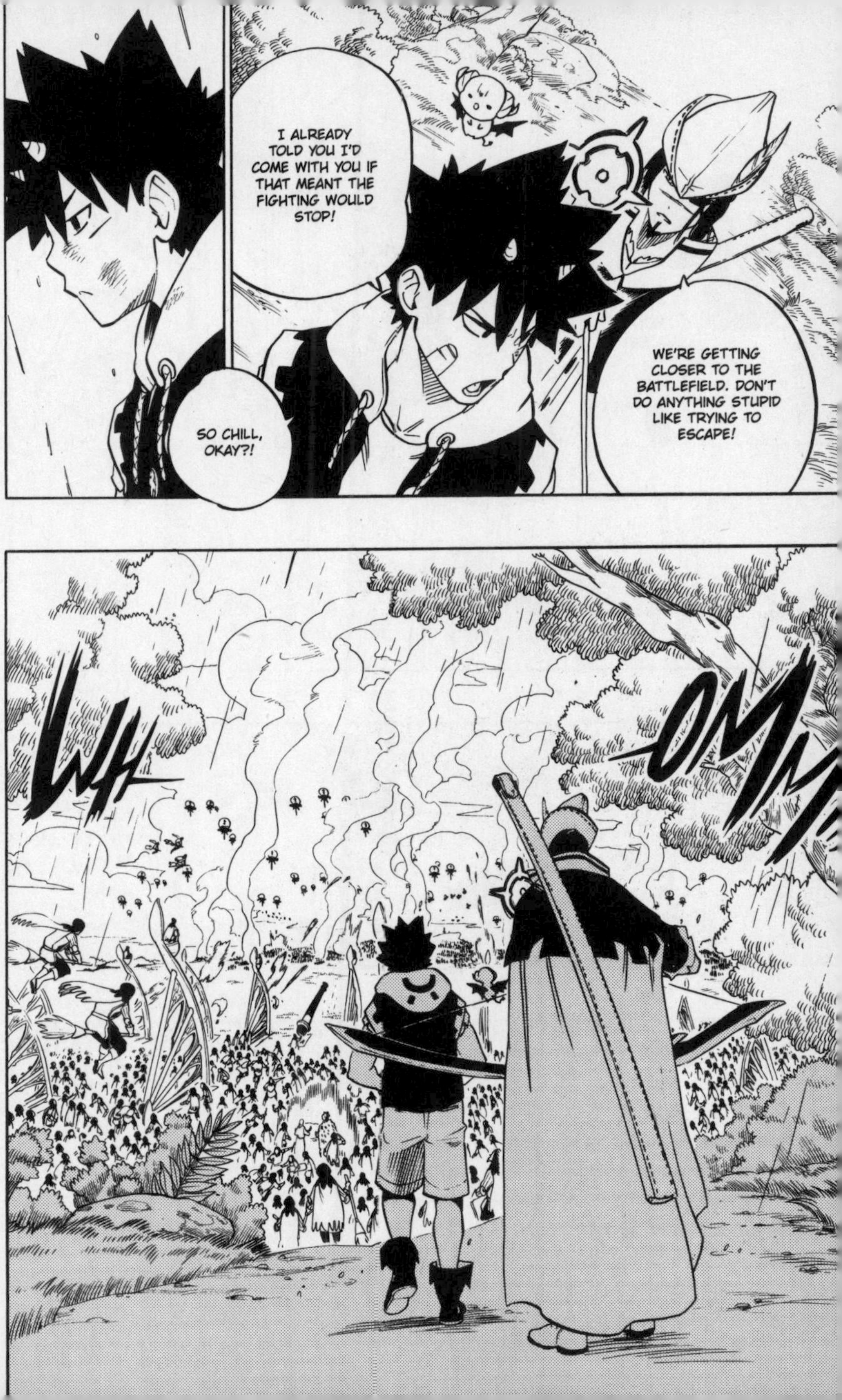
WE'RE GETTING CLOSER TO THE BATTLEFIELD. DON'T DO ANYTHING STUPID LIKE TRYING TO ESCAPE!
I ALREADY TOLD YOU I'D COME WITH YOU IF THAT MEANT THE FIGHTING WOULD STOP!
SO CHILL, OKAY?!
WH
OMM

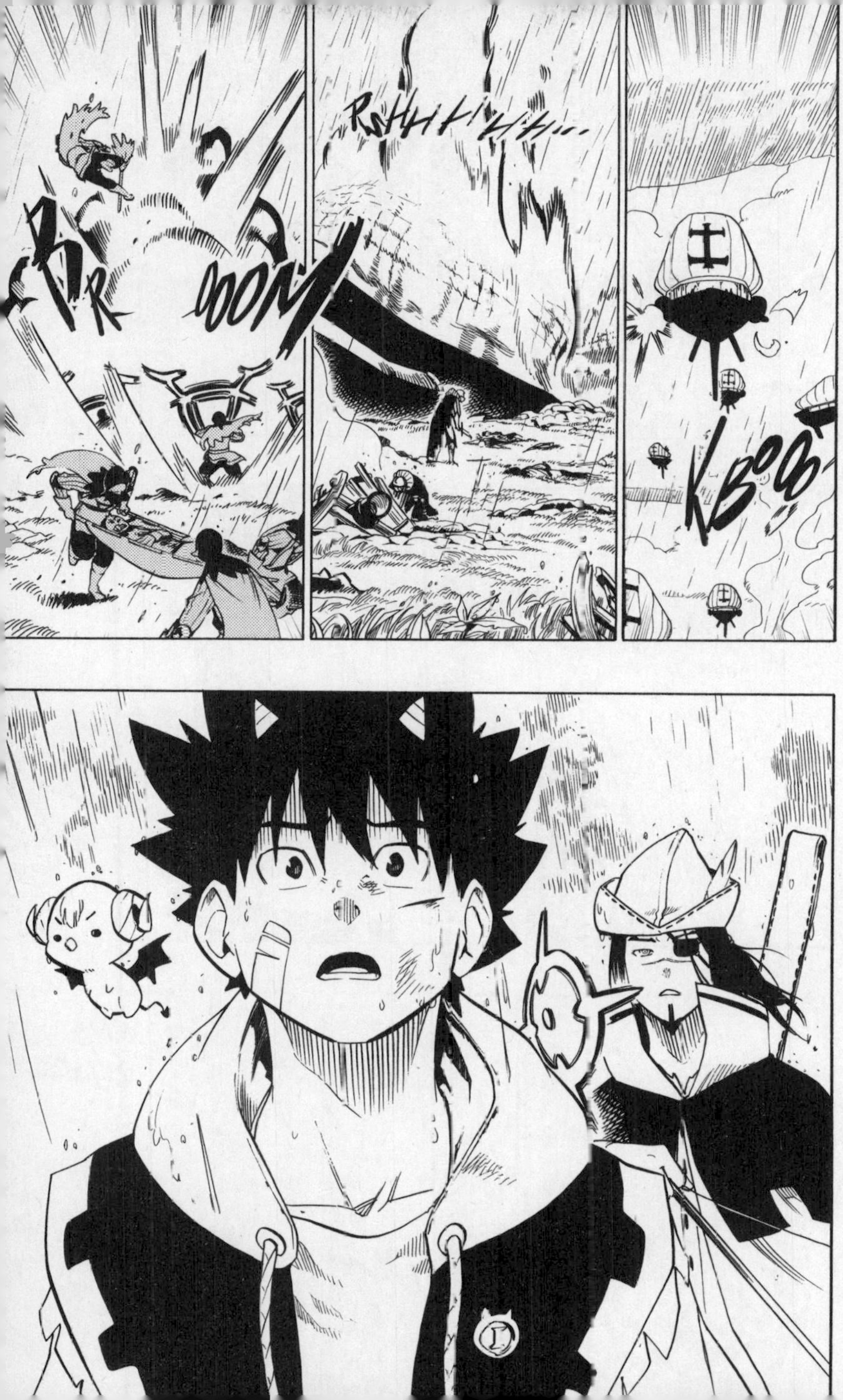
KBOOO
RSHHHHHH...
BRROOOM

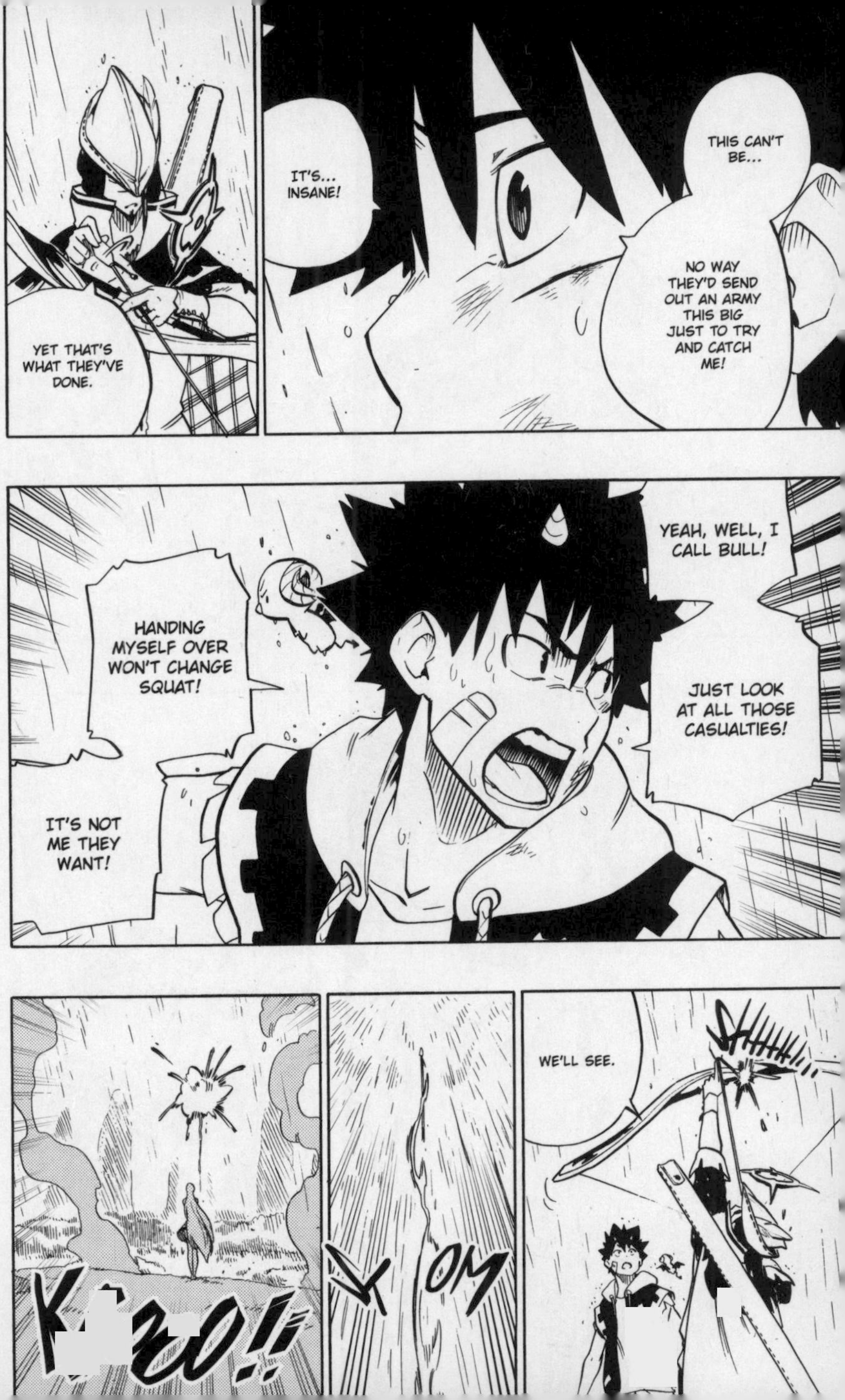
THIS CAN'T BE...
IT'S... INSANE!
NO WAY THEY'D SEND OUT AN ARMY THIS BIG JUST TO TRY AND CATCH ME!
YET THAT'S WHAT THEY'VE DONE.
YEAH, WELL, I CALL BULL!
JUST LOOK AT ALL THOSE CASUALTIES!
HANDING MYSELF OVER WON'T CHANGE SQUAT!
IT'S NOT ME THEY WANT!
WE'LL SEE.

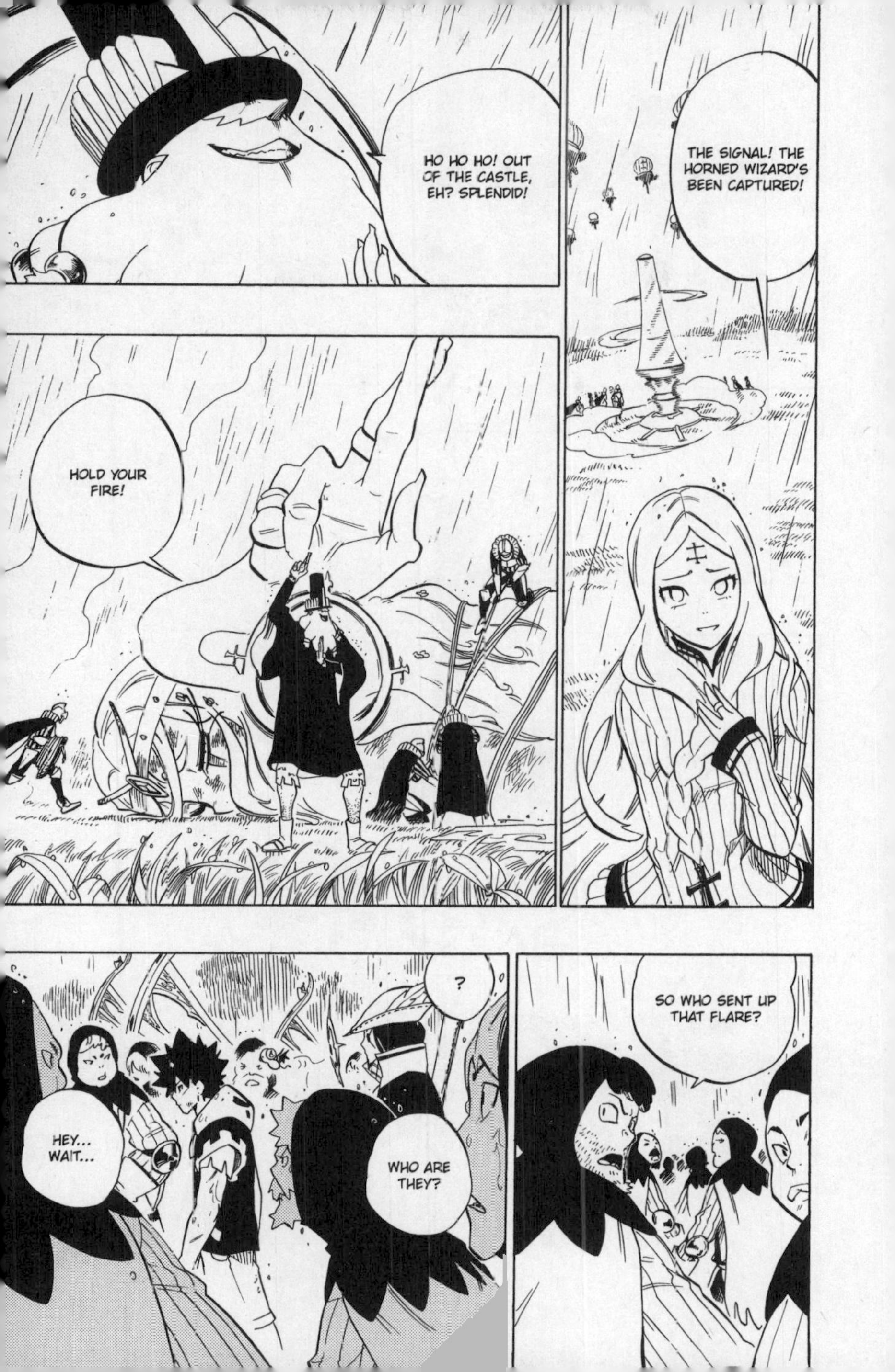
THE SIGNAL! THE HORNED WIZARD'S BEEN CAPTURED!
HO HO HO! OUT OF THE CASTLE, EH? SPLENDID!
HOLD YOUR FIRE!
SO WHO SENT UP THAT FLARE?
?
WHO ARE THEY?
HEY... WAIT...

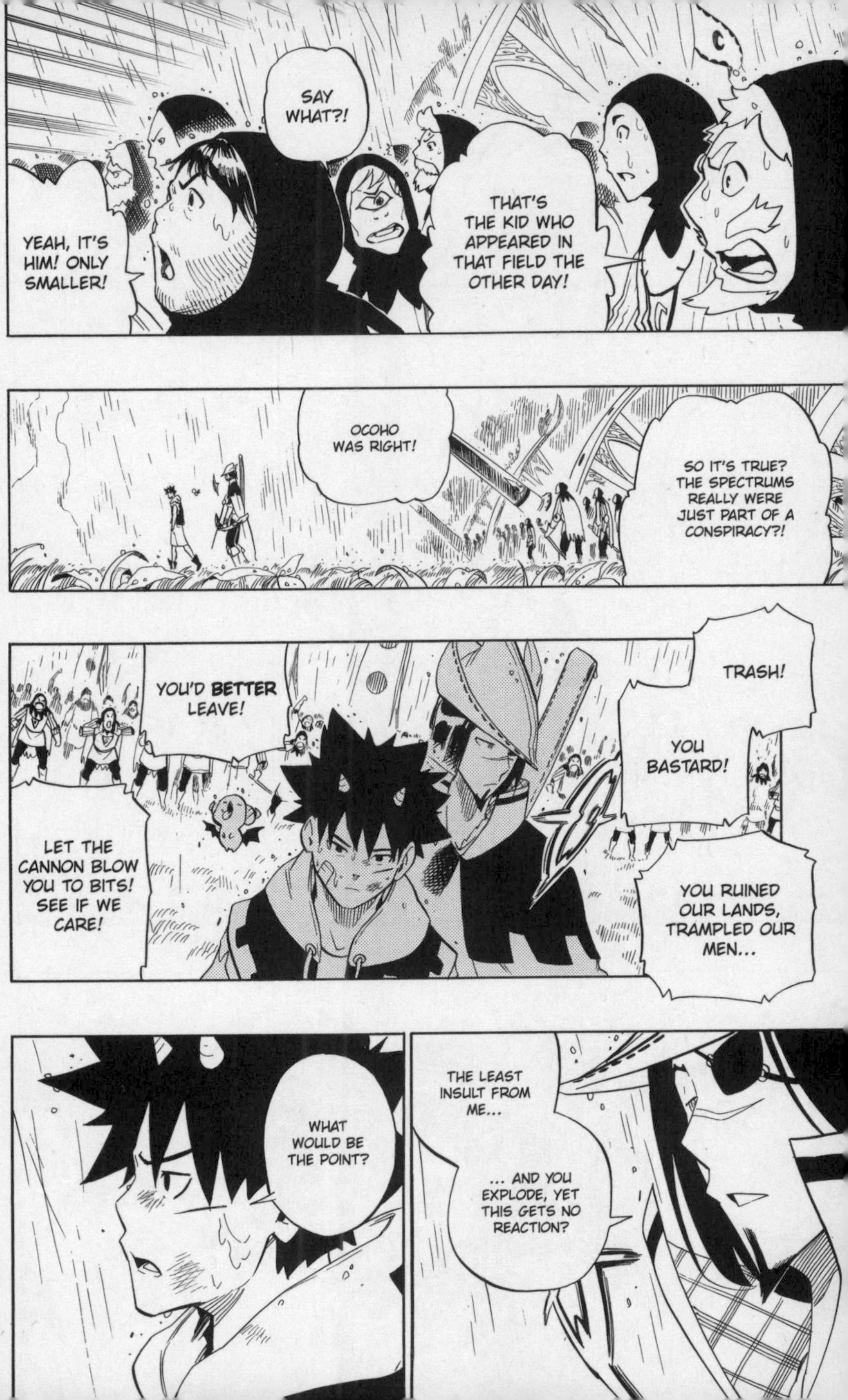
THAT'S THE KID WHO APPEARED IN THAT FIELD THE OTHER DAY!
SAY WHAT?!
YEAH, IT'S HIM! ONLY SMALLER!
SO IT'S TRUE? THE SPECTRUMS REALLY WERE JUST PART OF A CONSPIRACY?!
OCOHO WAS RIGHT!
TRASH!
YOU BASTARD!
YOU RUINED OUR LANDS, TRAMPLED OUR MEN...
YOU'D **BETTER** LEAVE!
LET THE CANNON BLOW YOU TO BITS! SEE IF WE CARE!
THE LEAST INSULT FROM ME...
... AND YOU EXPLODE, YET THIS GETS NO REACTION?
WHAT WOULD BE THE POINT?

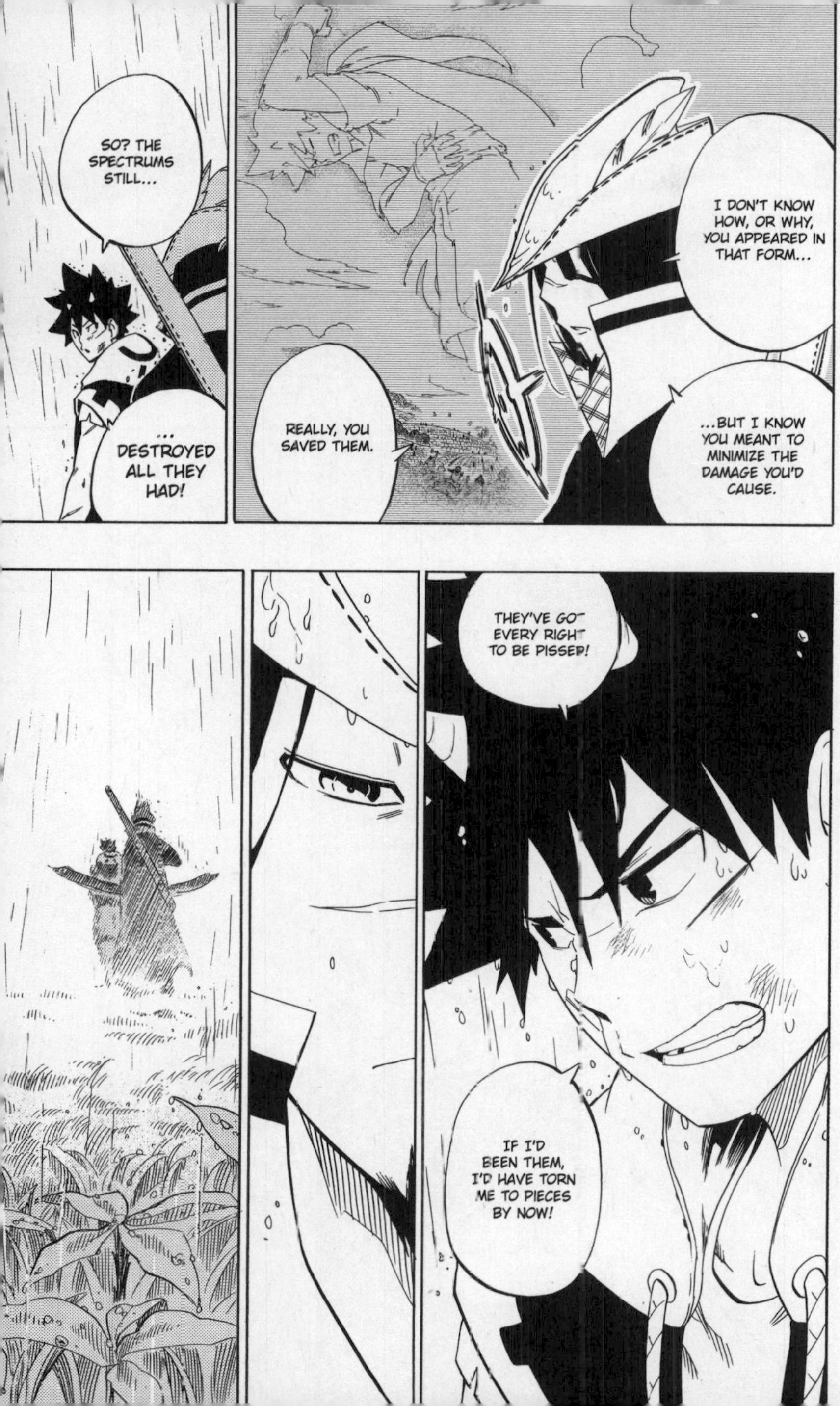
I DON'T KNOW HOW, OR WHY, YOU APPEARED IN THAT FORM...
...BUT I KNOW YOU MEANT TO MINIMIZE THE DAMAGE YOU'D CAUSE.
REALLY, YOU SAVED THEM.
SO? THE SPECTRUMS STILL...
...DESTROYED ALL THEY HAD!
THEY'VE GOT EVERY RIGHT TO BE PISSED!
IF I'D BEEN THEM, I'D HAVE TORN ME TO PIECES BY NOW!

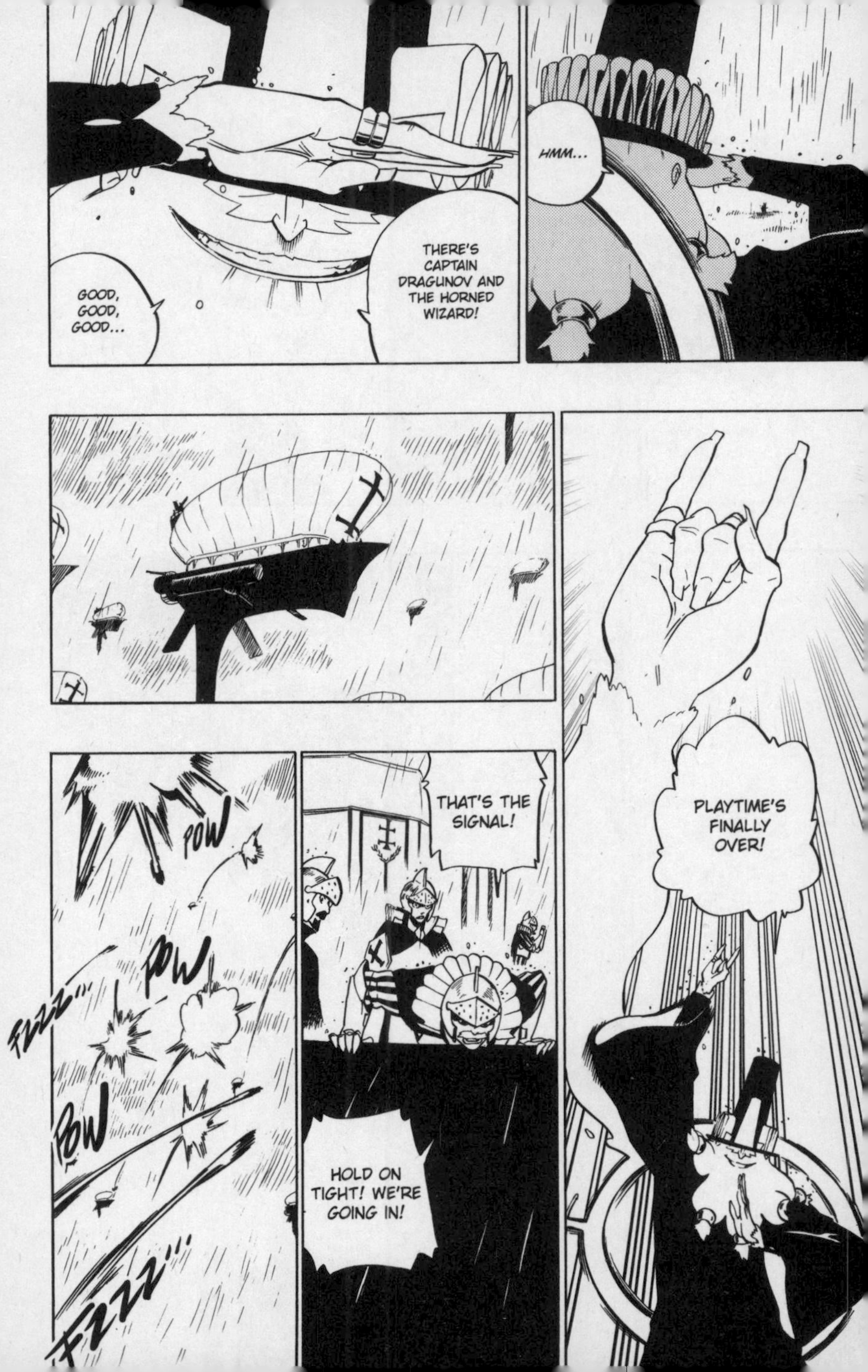
HMM...
THERE'S CAPTAIN DRAGUNOV AND THE HORNED WIZARD!
GOOD, GOOD, GOOD...
PLAYTIME'S FINALLY OVER!
THAT'S THE SIGNAL!
HOLD ON TIGHT! WE'RE GOING IN!
POW
POW
FZZZ...
POW
FZZZ...

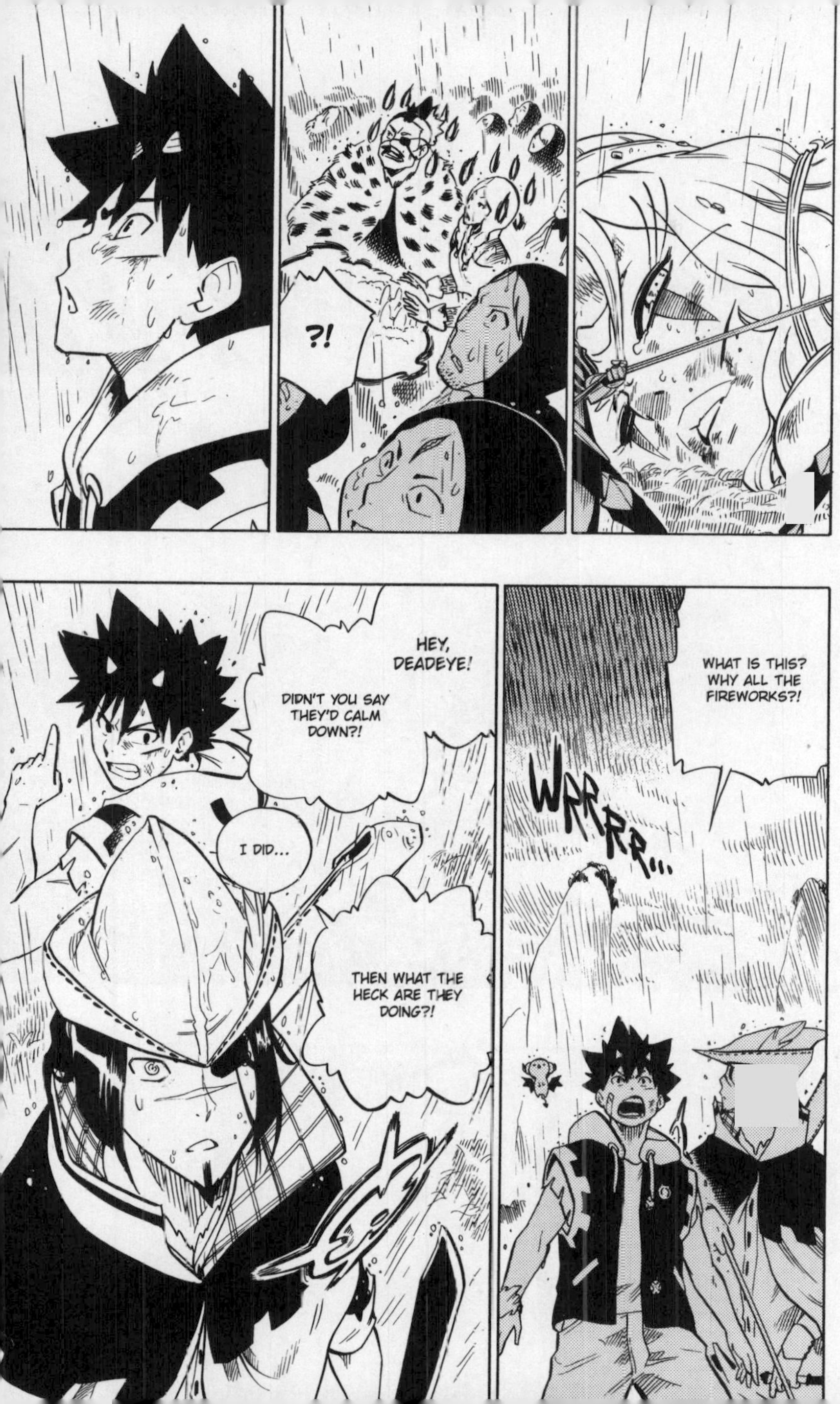
?!
WHAT IS THIS? WHY ALL THE FIREWORKS?!
WRRRRR...
HEY, DEADEYE!
DIDN'T YOU SAY THEY'D CALM DOWN?!
I DID...
THEN WHAT THE HECK ARE THEY DOING?!

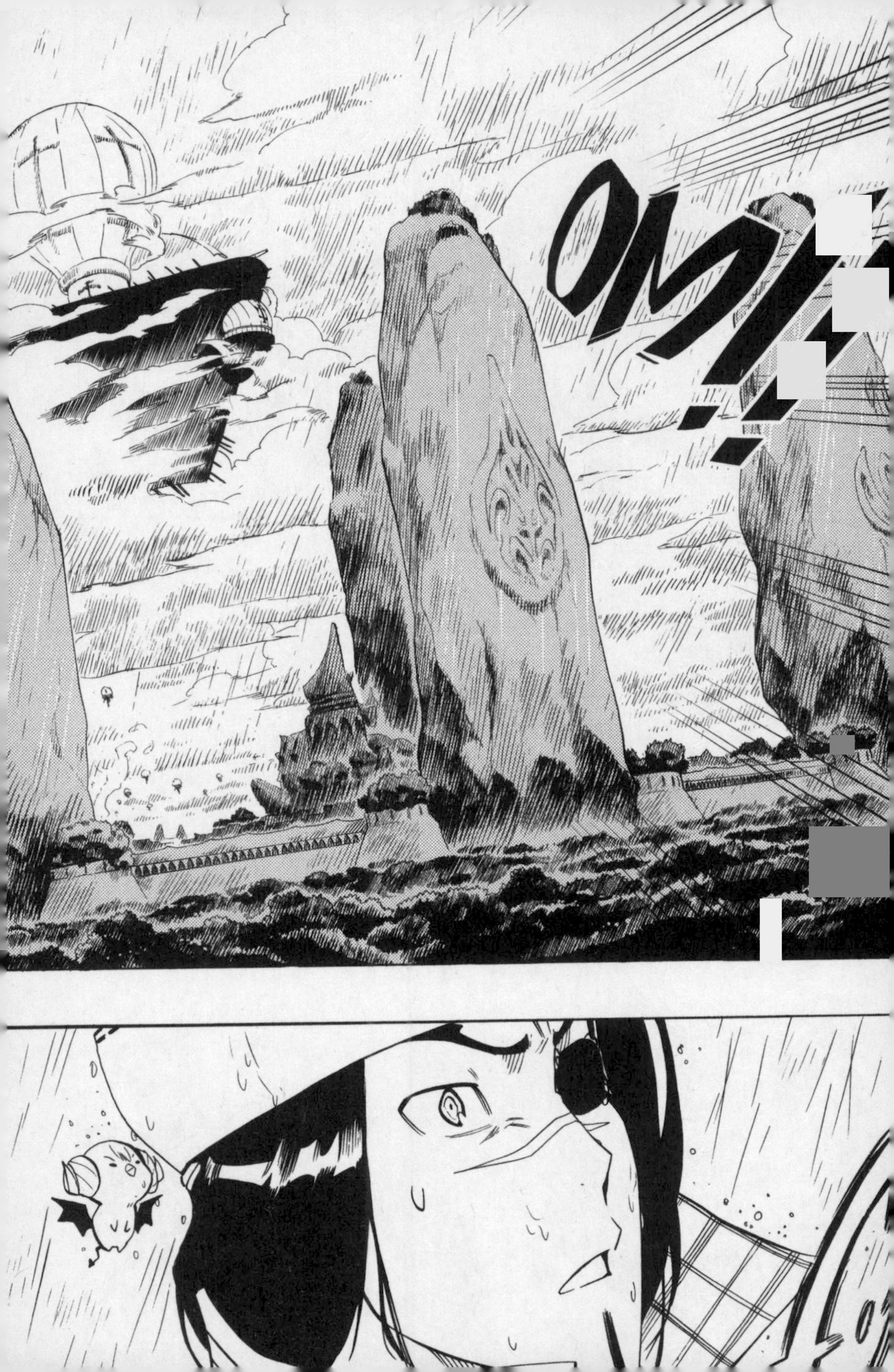
OM!!

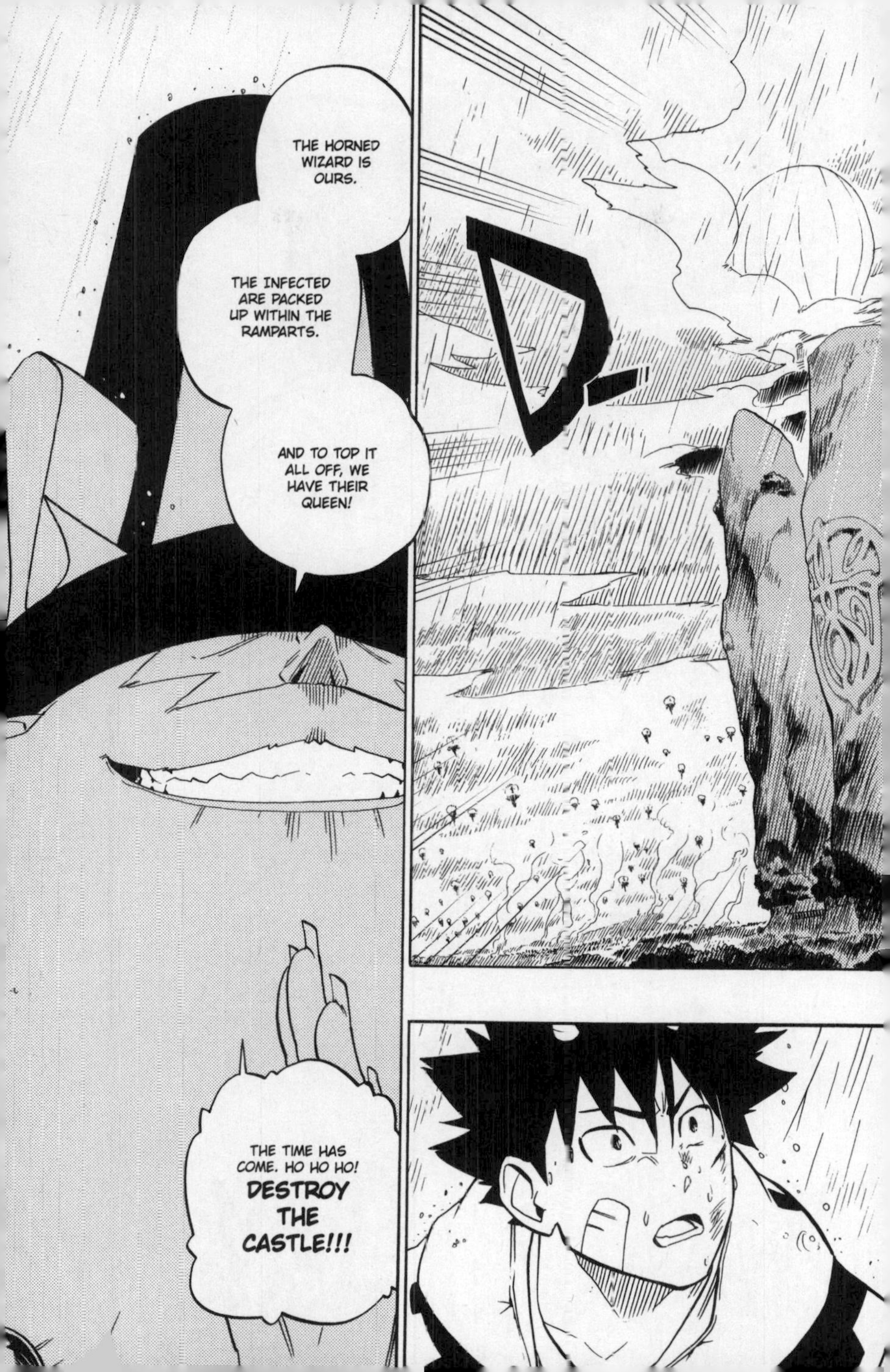
THE HORNED WIZARD IS OURS.
THE INFECTED ARE PACKED UP WITHIN THE RAMPARTS.
AND TO TOP IT ALL OFF, WE HAVE THEIR QUEEN!
THE TIME HAS COME. HO HO HO! DESTROY THE CASTLE!!!

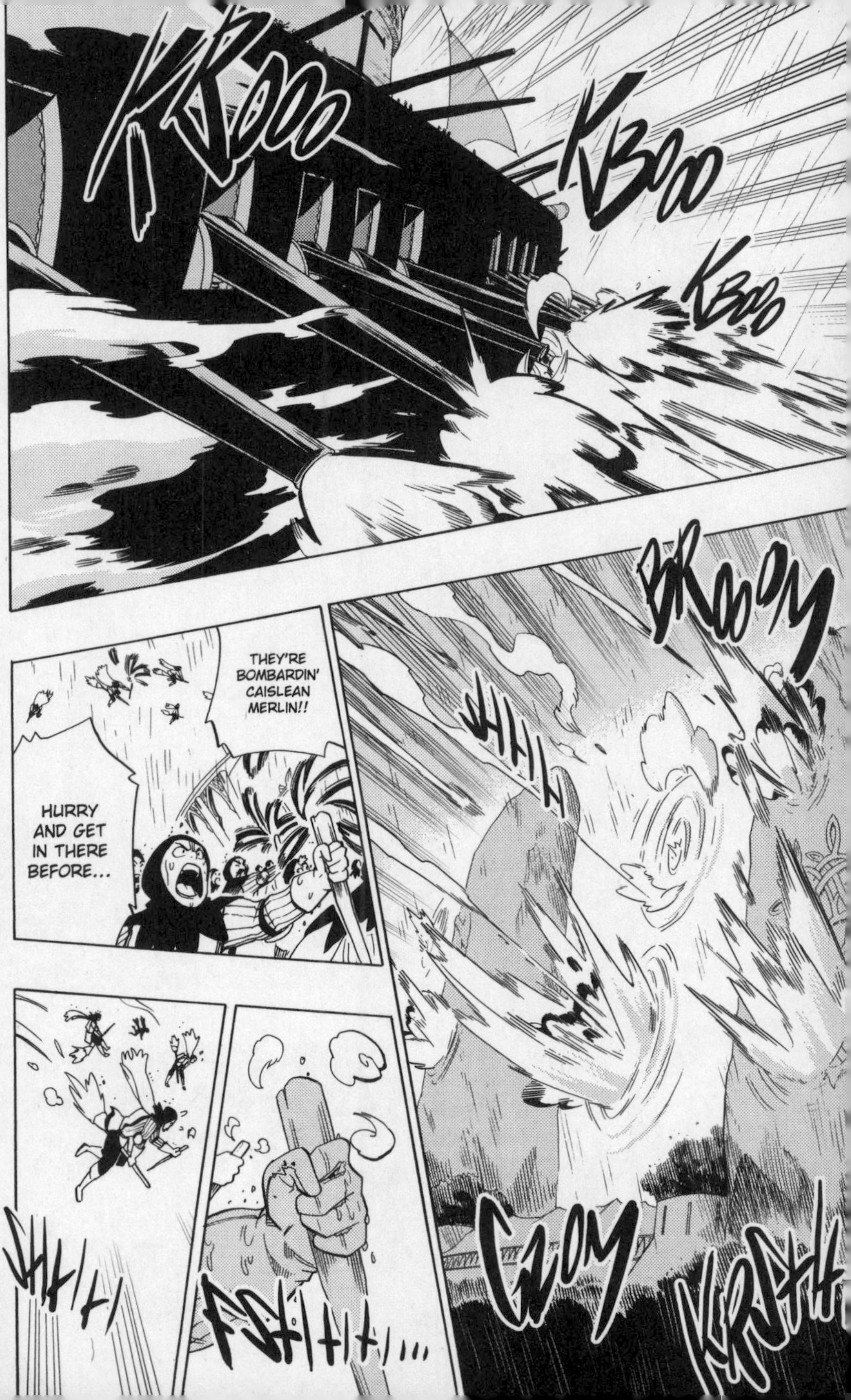
THEY'RE BOMBARDIN' CAISLEAN MERLIN!!
HURRY AND GET IN THERE BEFORE...

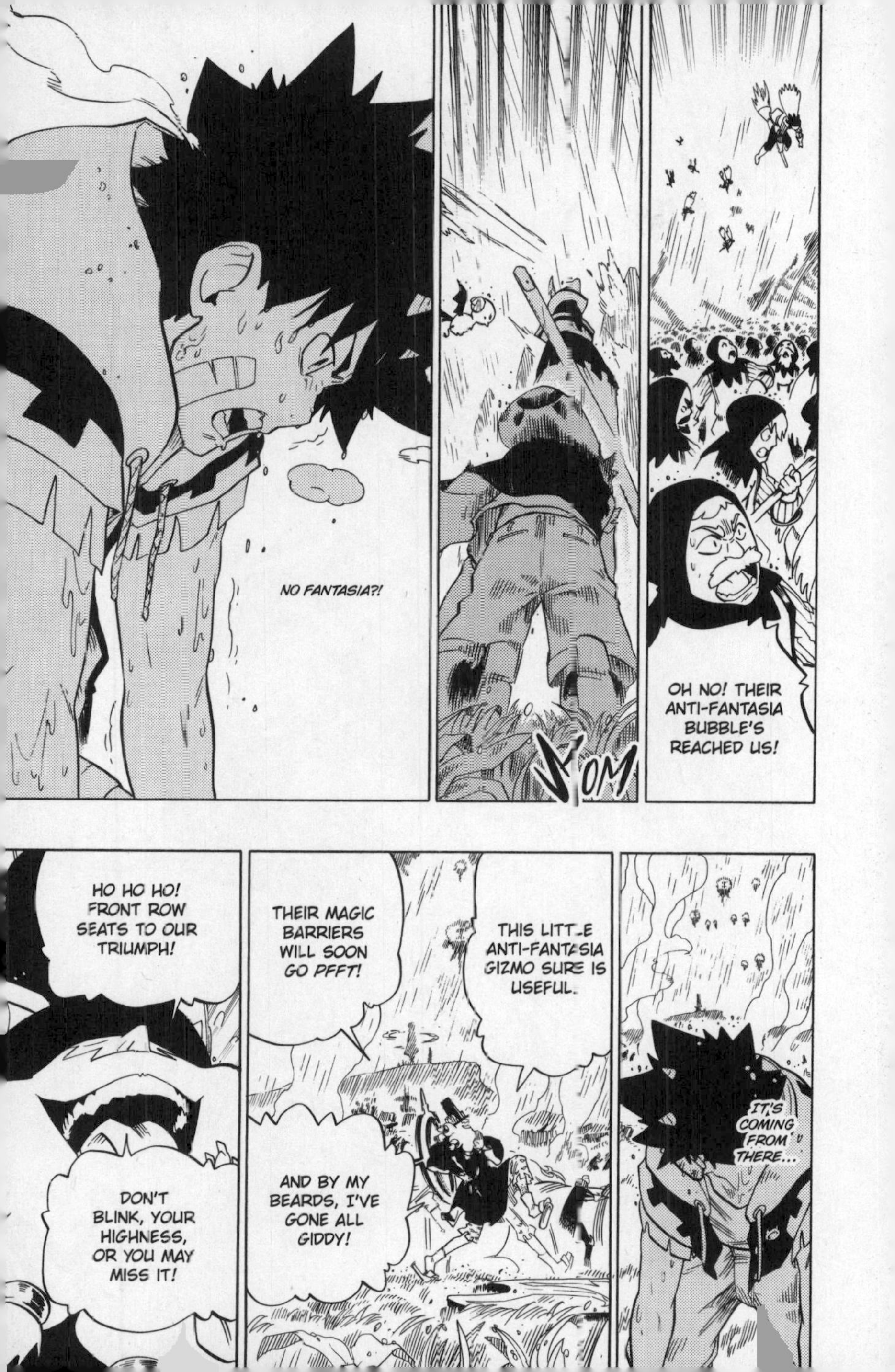
OH NO! THEIR ANTI-FANTASIA BUBBLE'S REACHED US!
NO FANTASIA?!
IT'S COMING FROM THERE...
THIS LITTLE ANTI-FANTASIA GIZMO SURE IS USEFUL.
THEIR MAGIC BARRIERS WILL SOON GO PFFT!
AND BY MY BEARDS, I'VE GONE ALL GIDDY!
HO HO HO! FRONT ROW SEATS TO OUR TRIUMPH!
DON'T BLINK, YOUR HIGHNESS, OR YOU MAY MISS IT!

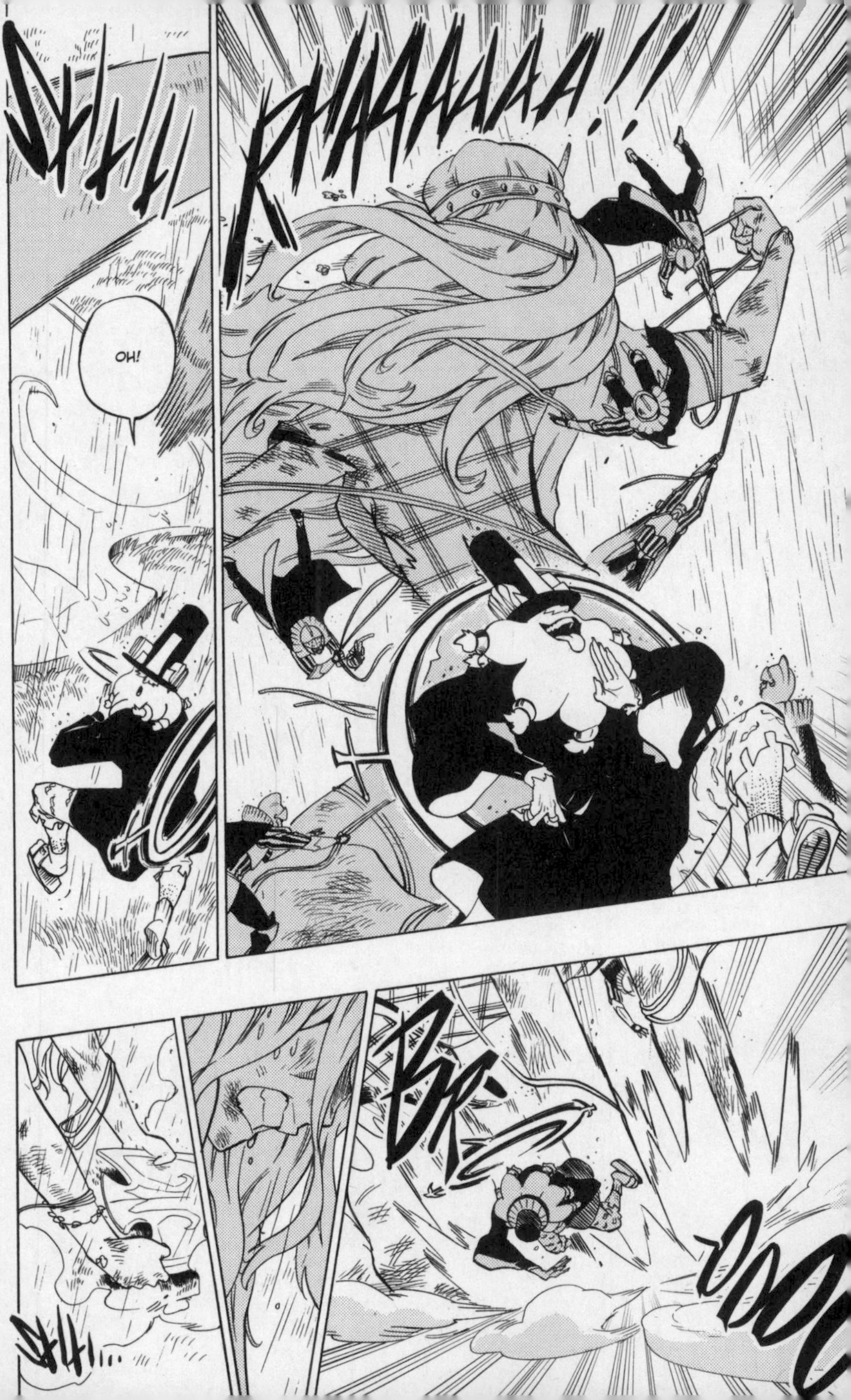
OH!

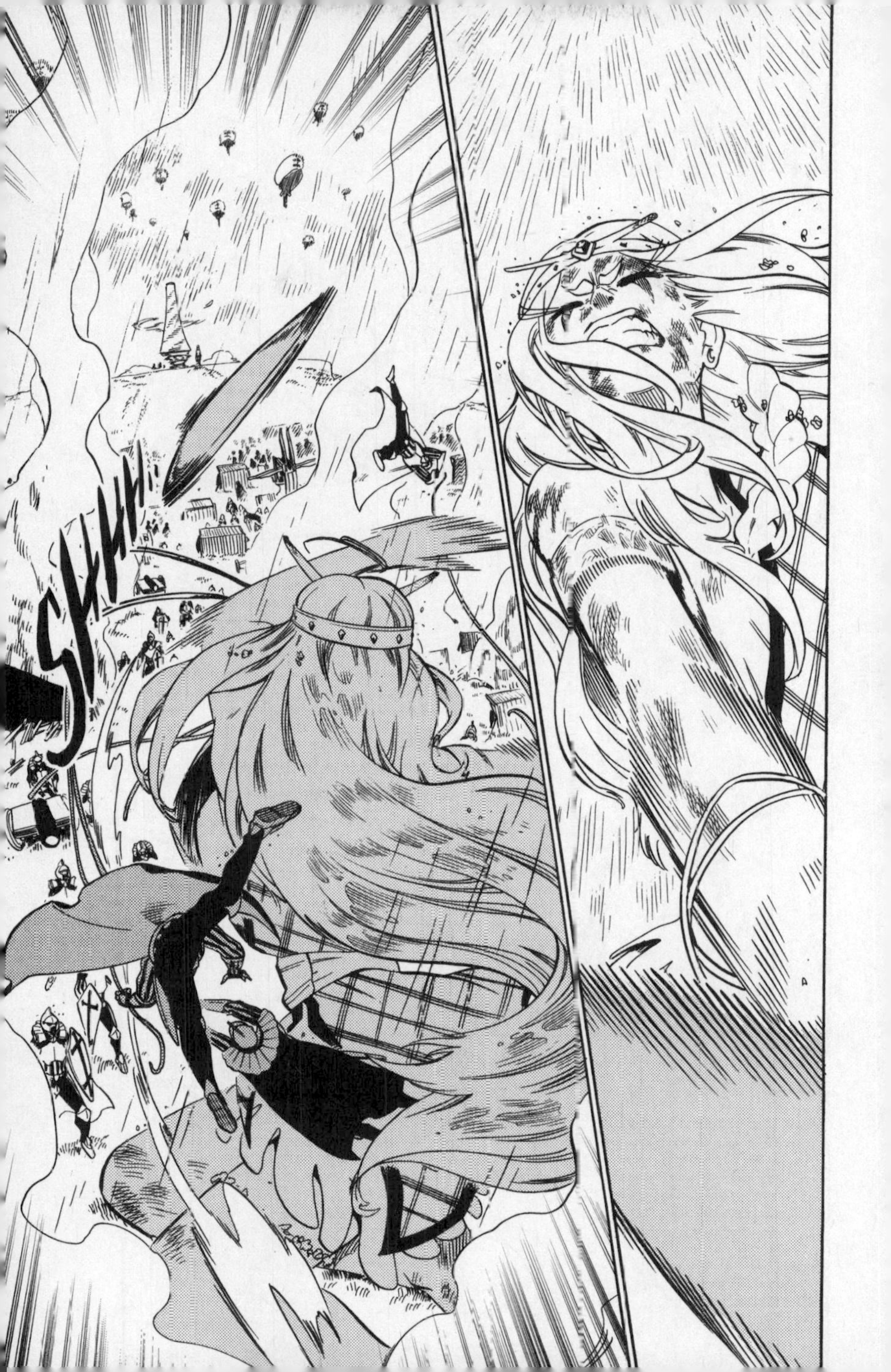
SHHH!

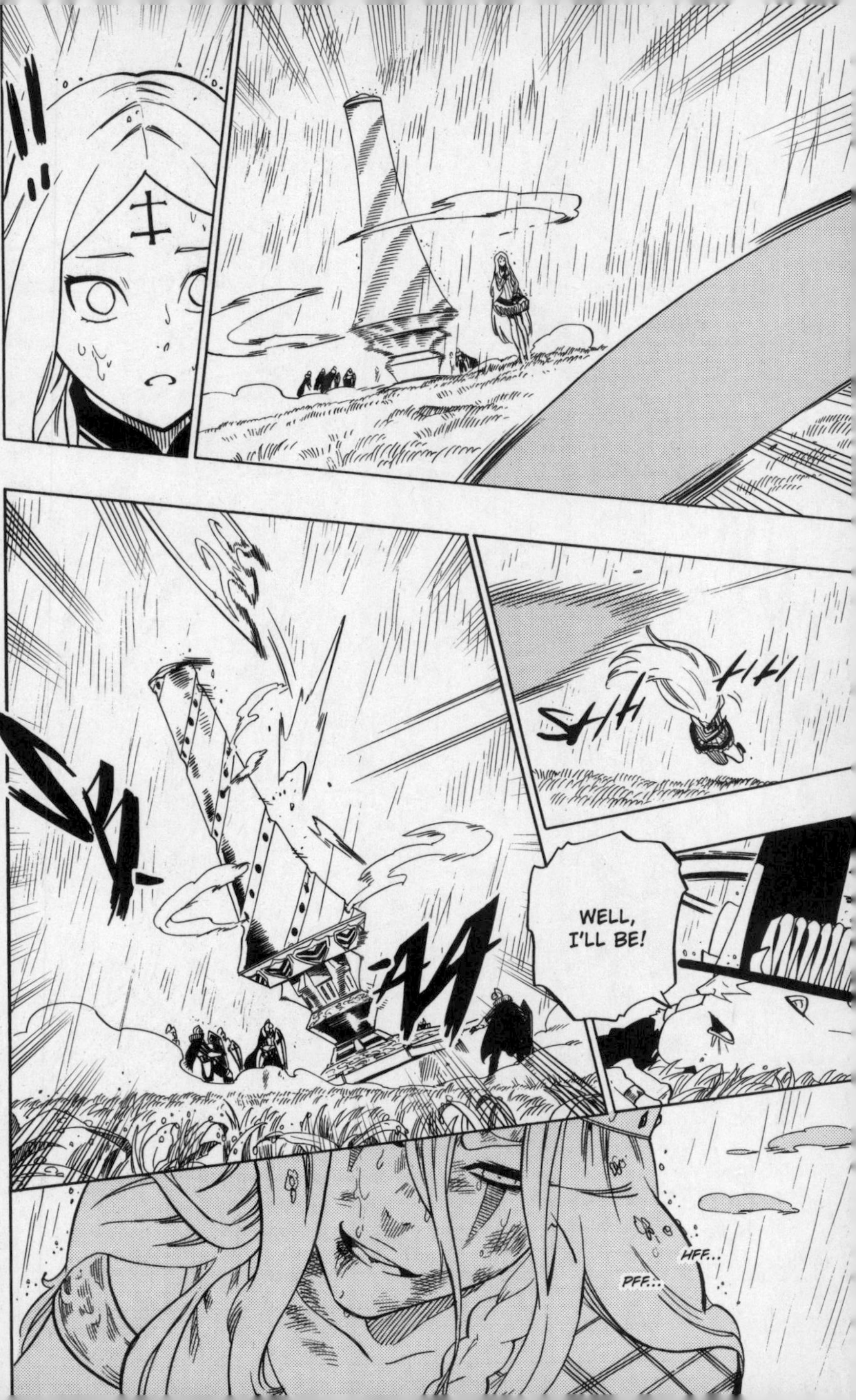
WELL, I'LL BE!
HFF...
PFF...

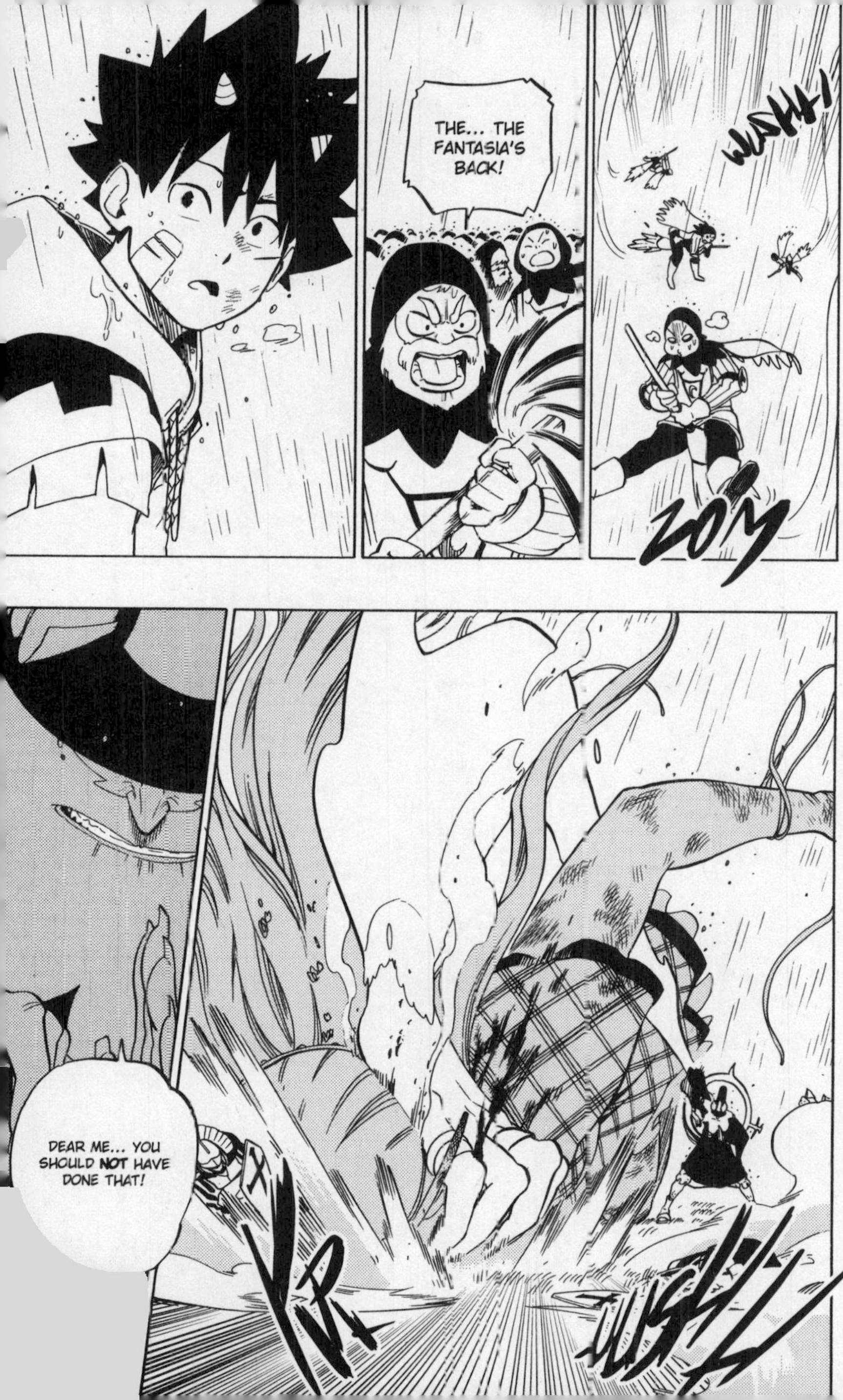
THE... THE FANTASIA'S BACK!
DEAR ME... YOU SHOULD **NOT** HAVE DONE THAT!

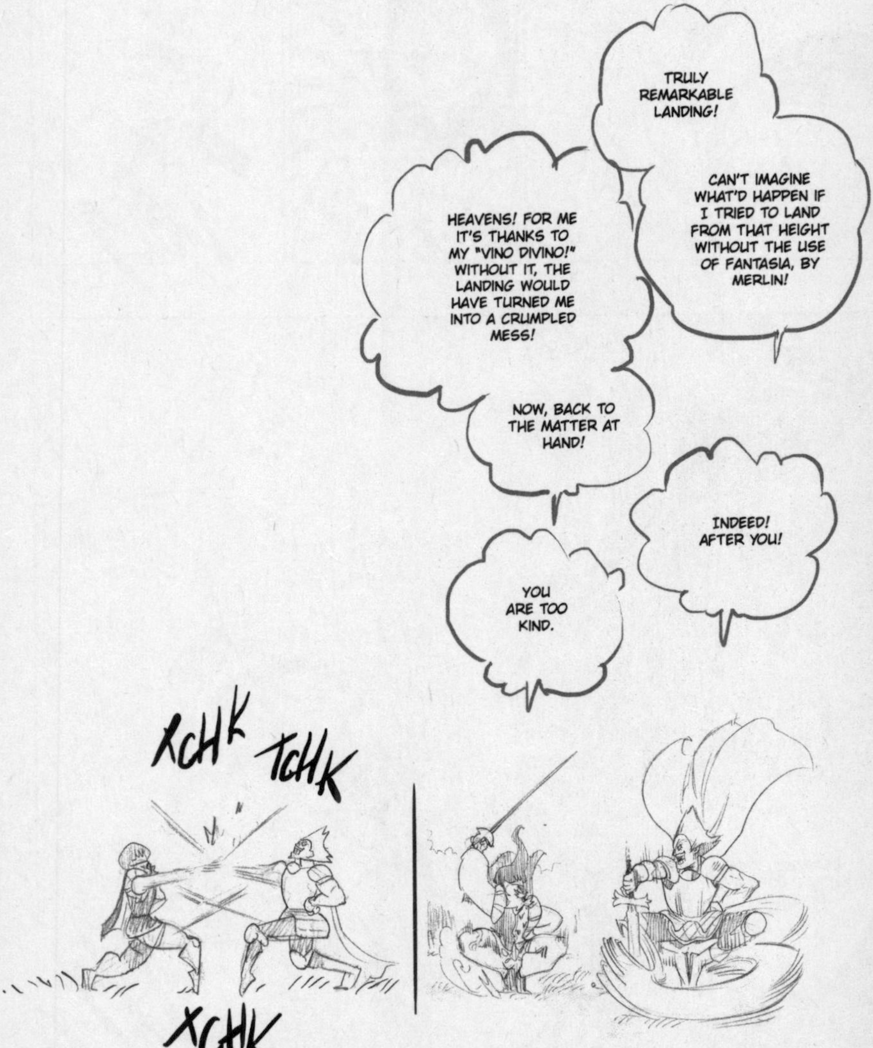
TRULY REMARKABLE LANDING!
CAN'T IMAGINE WHAT'D HAPPEN IF I TRIED TO LAND FROM THAT HEIGHT WITHOUT THE USE OF FANTASIA, BY MERLIN!
HEAVENS! FOR ME IT'S THANKS TO MY "VINO DIVINO!" WITHOUT IT, THE LANDING WOULD HAVE TURNED ME INTO A CRUMPLED MESS!
NOW, BACK TO THE MATTER AT HAND!
INDEED! AFTER YOU!
YOU ARE TOO KIND.
RCHK
TCHK
XCHK

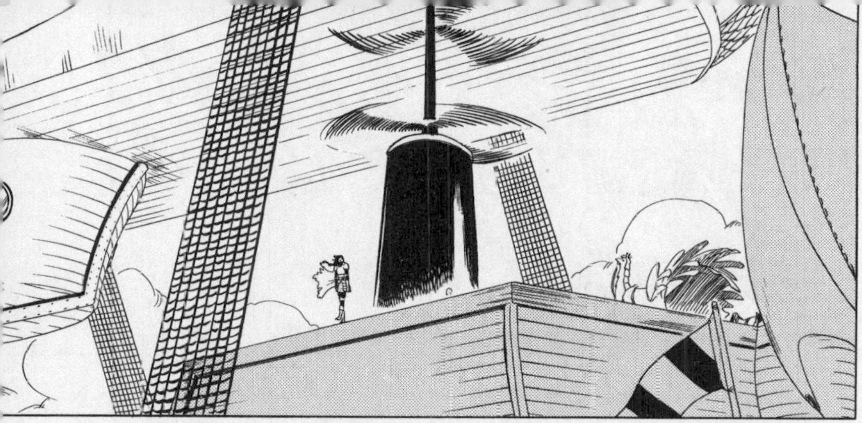

Chapter 63 Those Calling the Shots

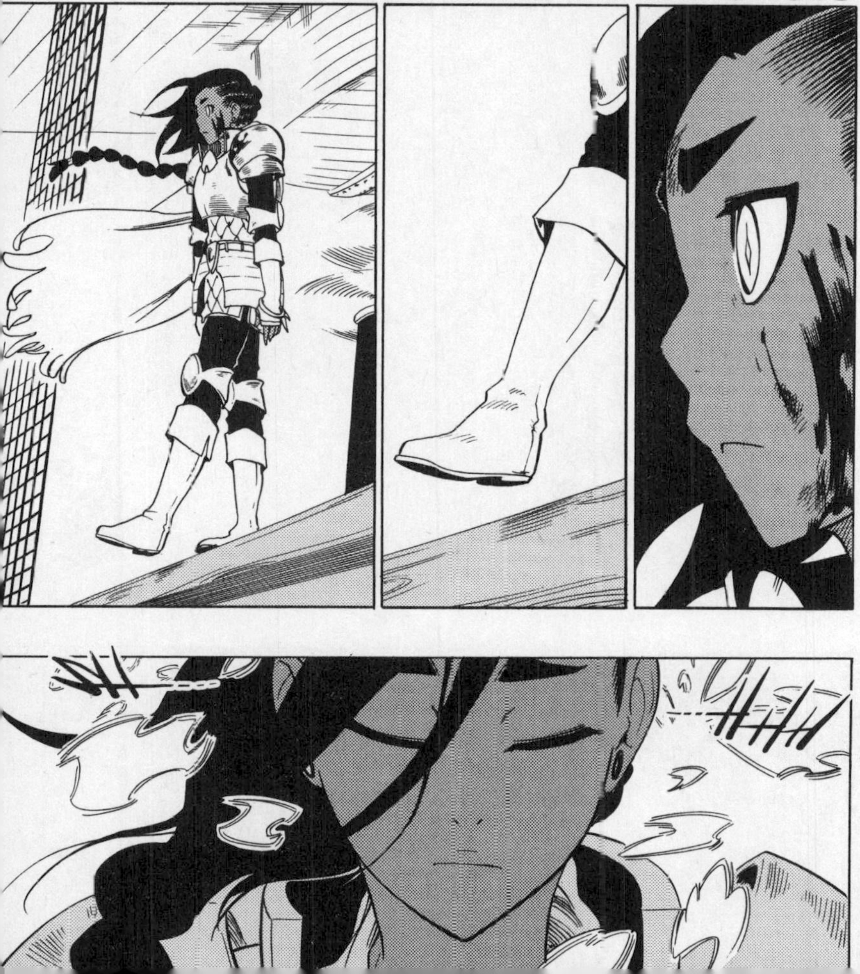

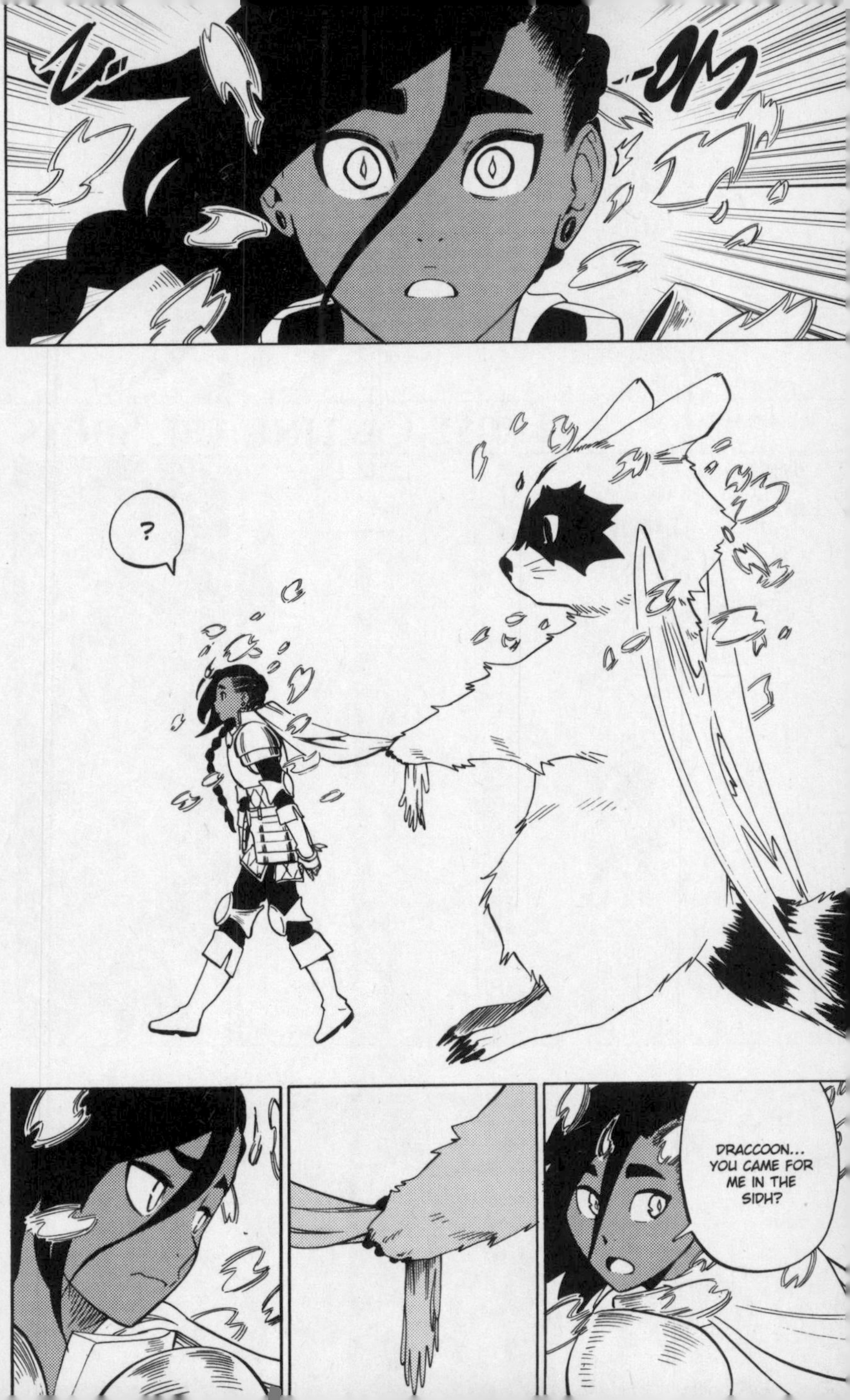
?
DRACCOON... YOU CAME FOR ME IN THE SIDH?

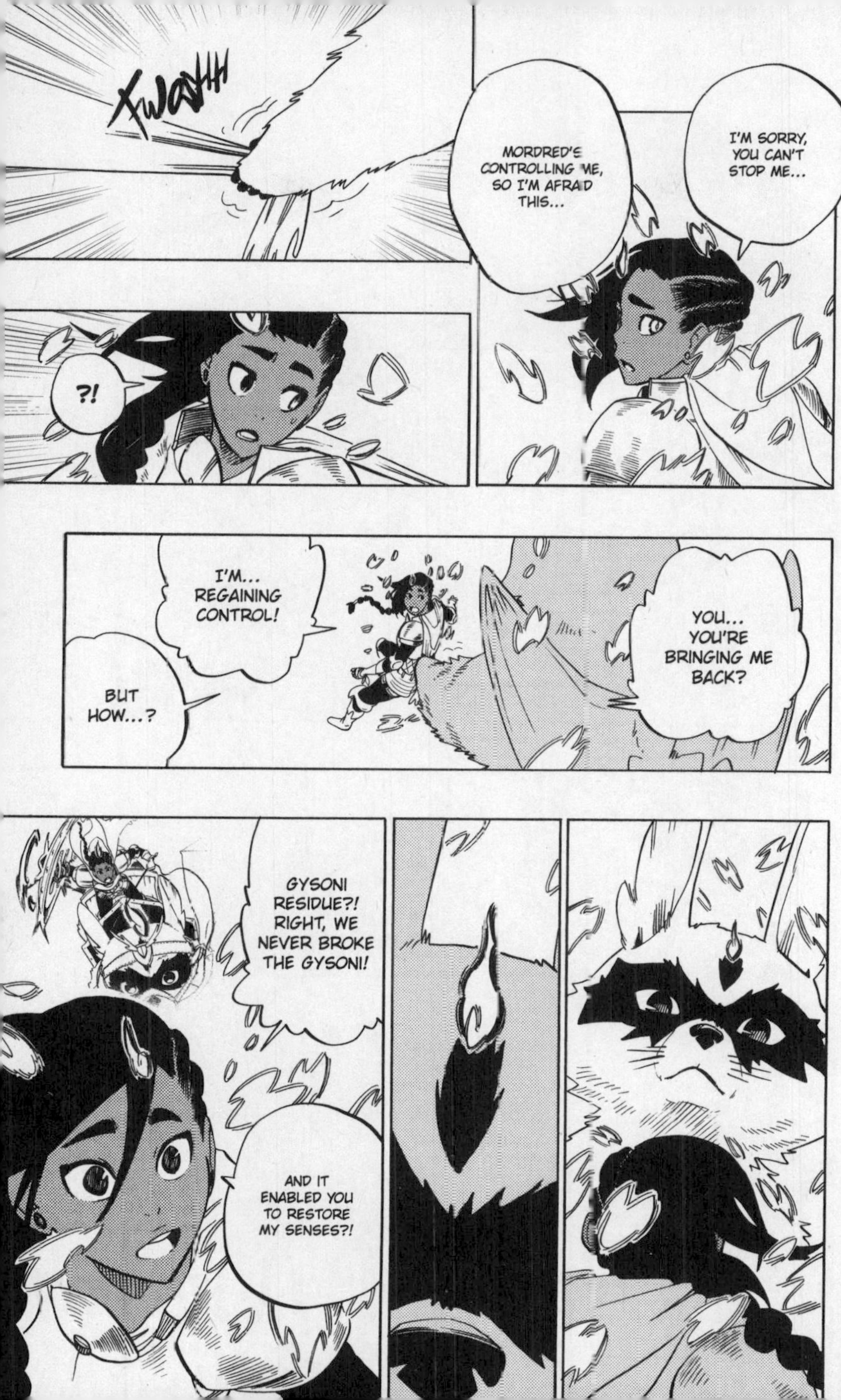
I'M SORRY, YOU CAN'T STOP ME...
MORDRED'S CONTROLLING ME, SO I'M AFRAID THIS...
FWASHH
?!
YOU... YOU'RE BRINGING ME BACK?
I'M... REGAINING CONTROL!
BUT HOW...?
GYSONI RESIDUE?! RIGHT, WE NEVER BROKE THE GYSONI!
AND IT ENABLED YOU TO RESTORE MY SENSES?!

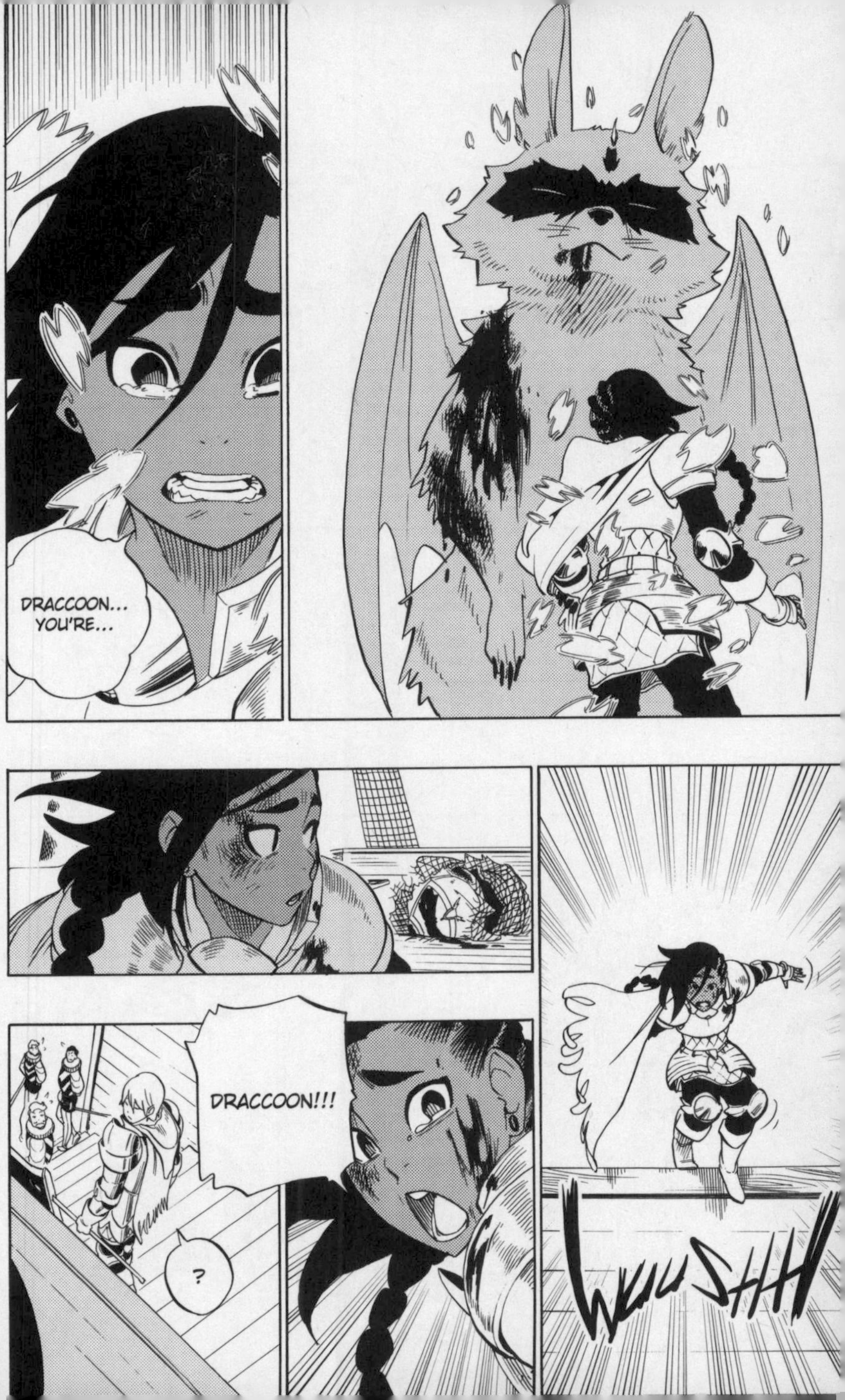
DRACCOON...
YOU'RE...
WHUSHH
DRACCOON!!!
?

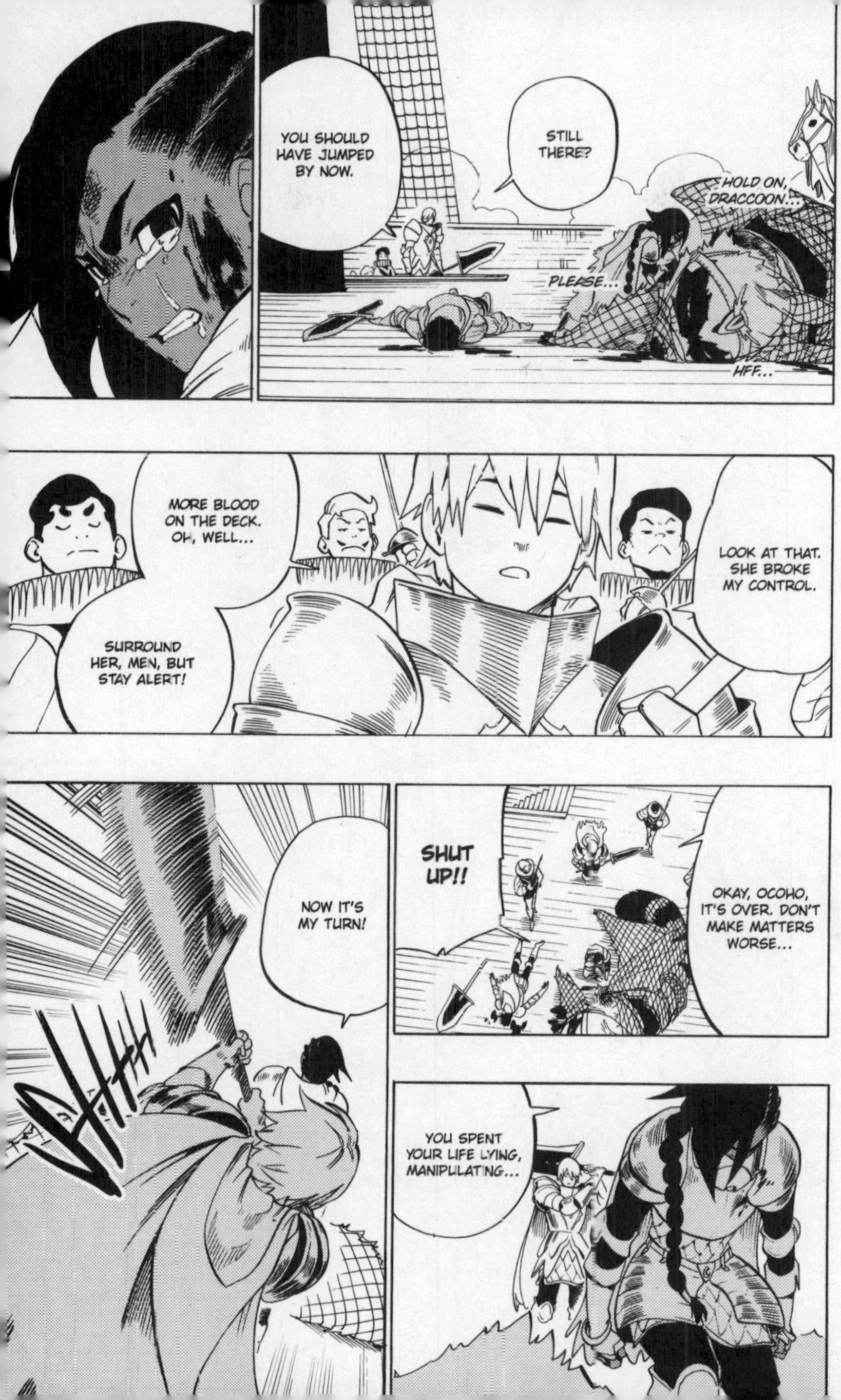
HOLD ON, DRACCOON...
STILL THERE?
YOU SHOULD HAVE JUMPED BY NOW.
PLEASE...
HFF...
LOOK AT THAT. SHE BROKE MY CONTROL.
MORE BLOOD ON THE DECK. OH, WELL...
SURROUND HER, MEN, BUT STAY ALERT!
OKAY, OCOHO, IT'S OVER. DON'T MAKE MATTERS WORSE...
SHUT UP!!
YOU SPENT YOUR LIFE LYING, MANIPULATING...
NOW IT'S MY TURN!

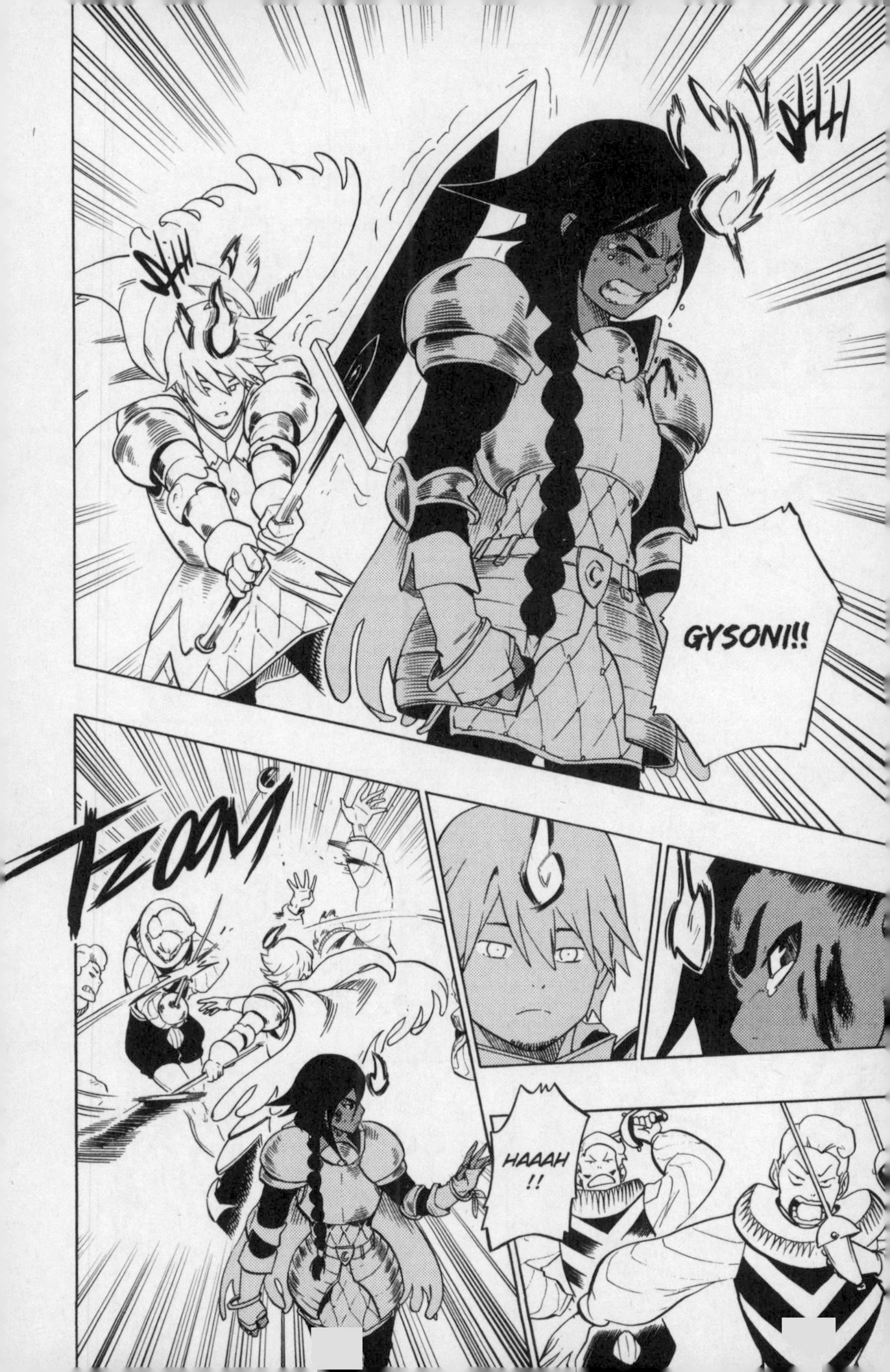
GYSONI!!
HAAAH !!
TZOOM

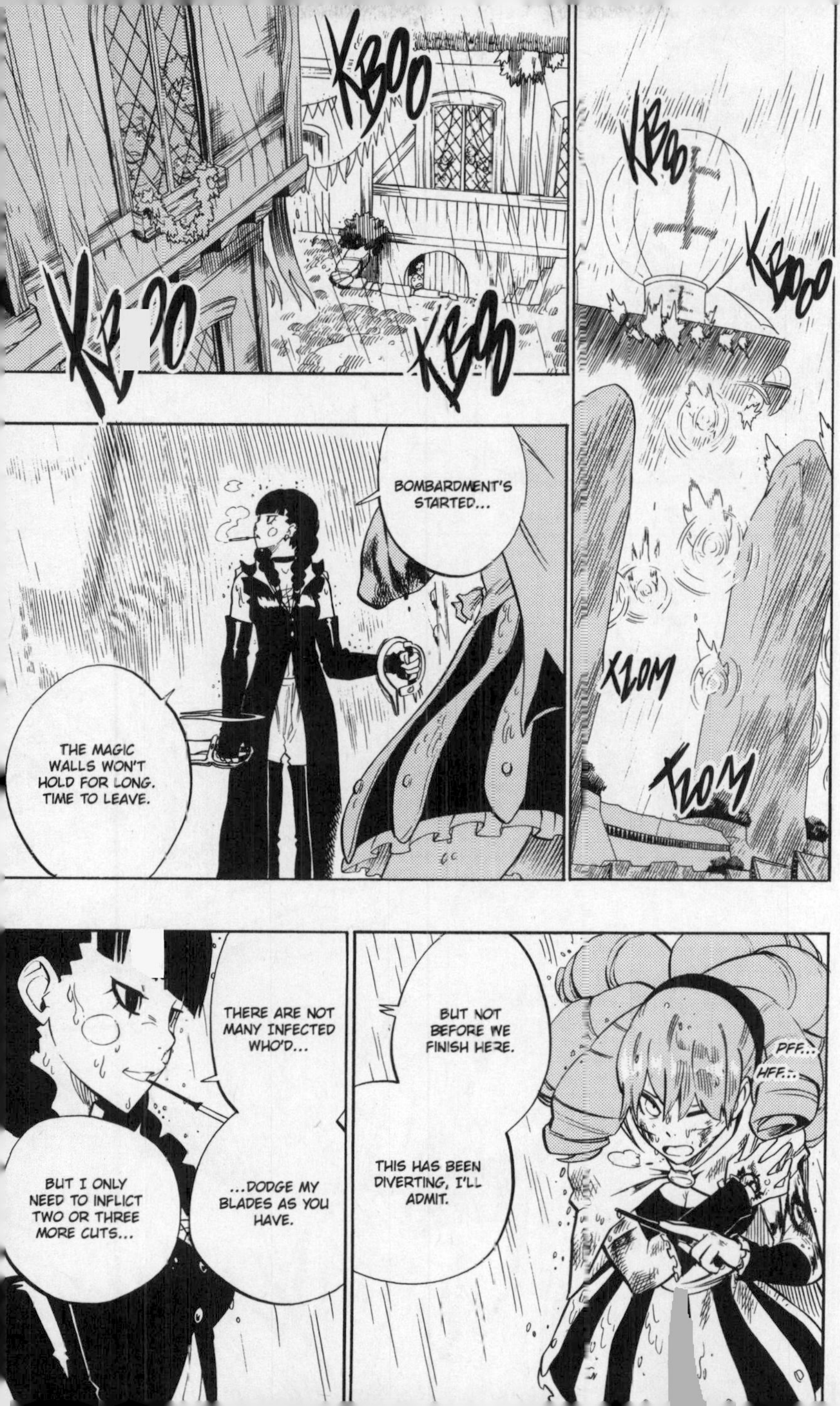

KBOO
KBOOO
KLOM
FZOM
KBOO
KBOO
BOMBARDMENT'S STARTED...
THE MAGIC WALLS WON'T HOLD FOR LONG. TIME TO LEAVE.
PFF...
HFF...
BUT NOT BEFORE WE FINISH HERE.
THIS HAS BEEN DIVERTING, I'LL ADMIT.
THERE ARE NOT MANY INFECTED WHO'D...
...DODGE MY BLADES AS YOU HAVE.
BUT I ONLY NEED TO INFLICT TWO OR THREE MORE CUTS...

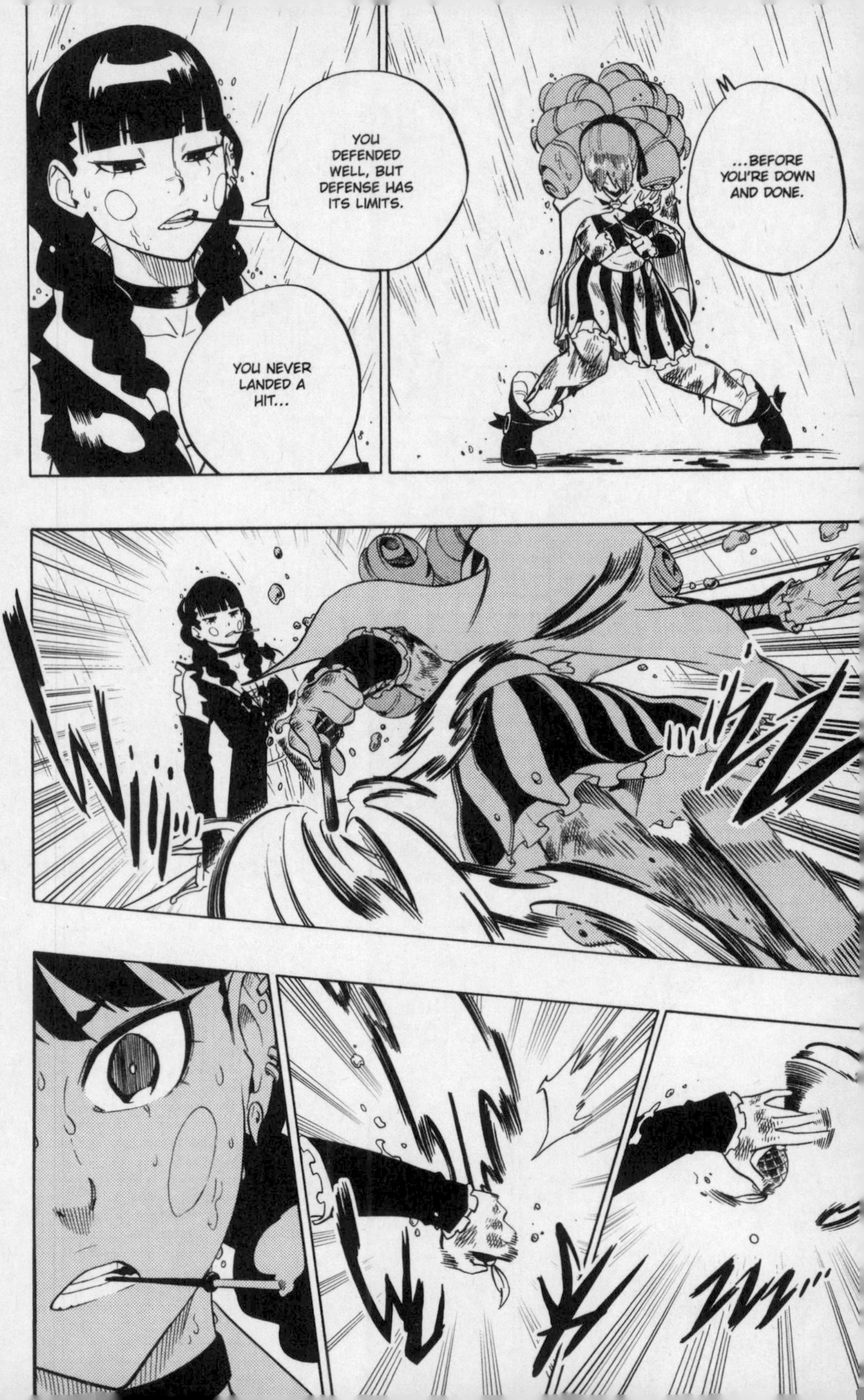
YOU DEFENDED WELL, BUT DEFENSE HAS ITS LIMITS.
YOU NEVER LANDED A HIT...
...BEFORE YOU'RE DOWN AND DONE.

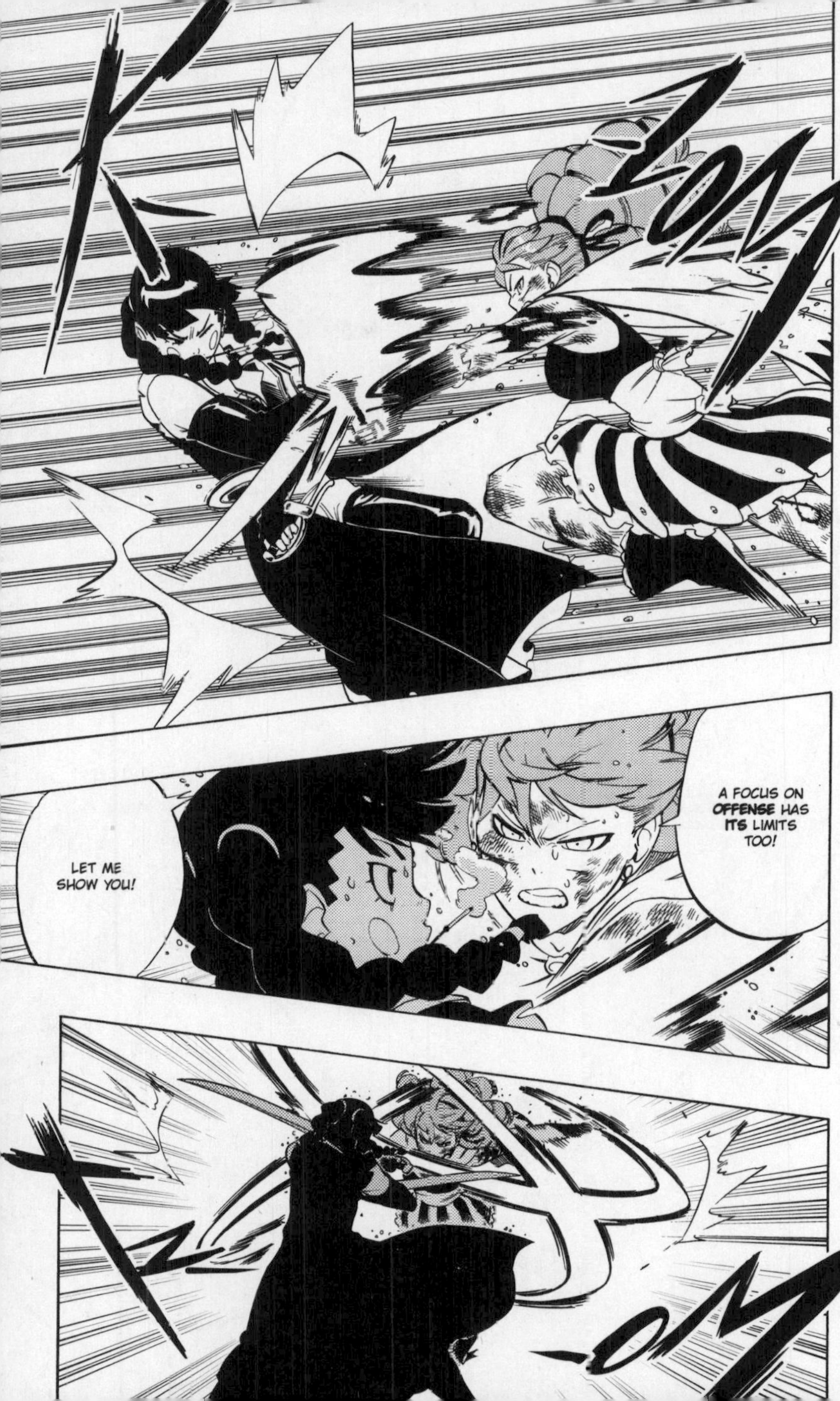
A FOCUS ON OFFENSE HAS ITS LIMITS TOO!
LET ME SHOW YOU!

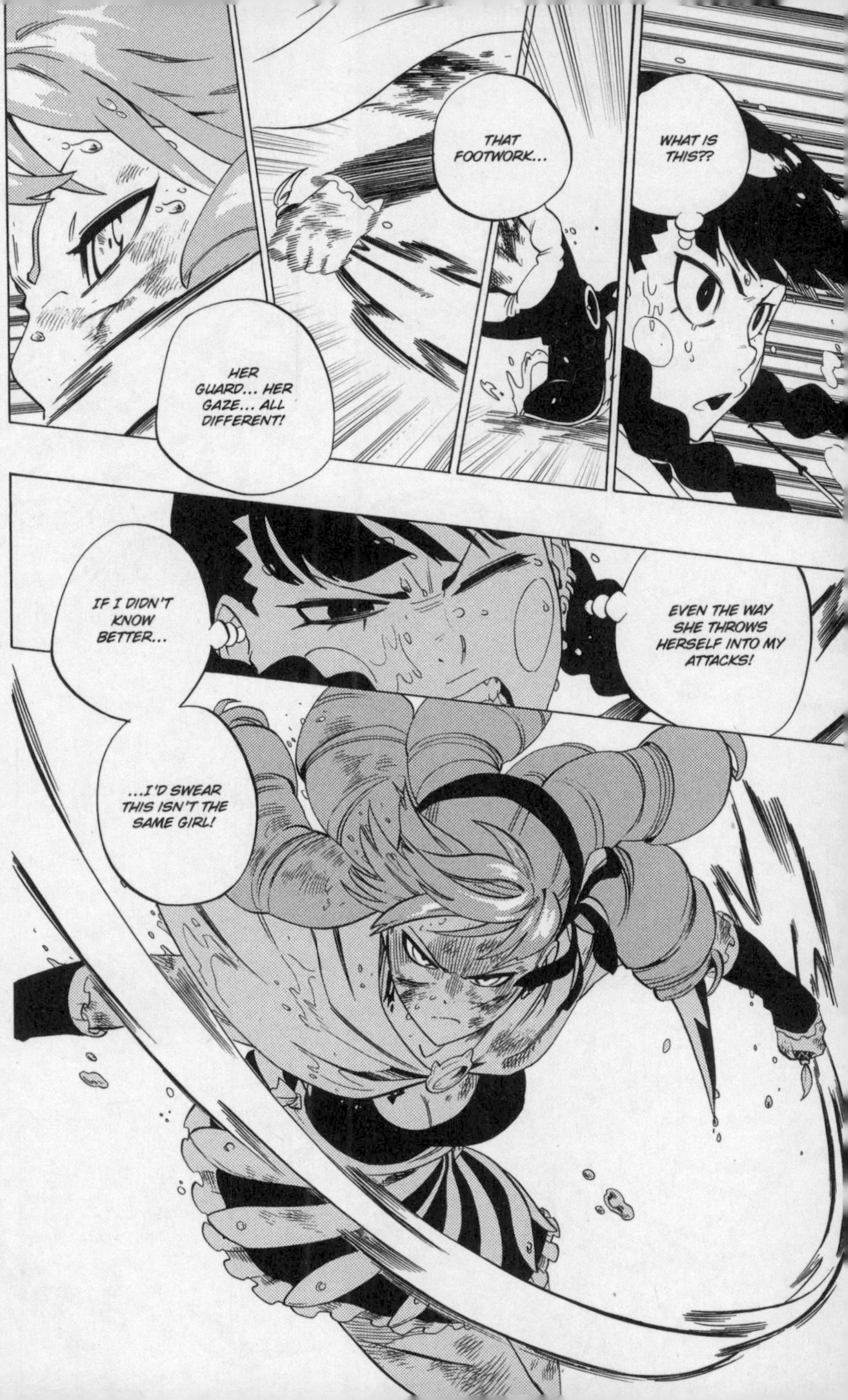
WHAT IS THIS??
THAT FOOTWORK...
HER GUARD... HER GAZE... ALL DIFFERENT!
EVEN THE WAY SHE THROWS HERSELF INTO MY ATTACKS!
IF I DIDN'T KNOW BETTER...
...I'D SWEAR THIS ISN'T THE SAME GIRL!

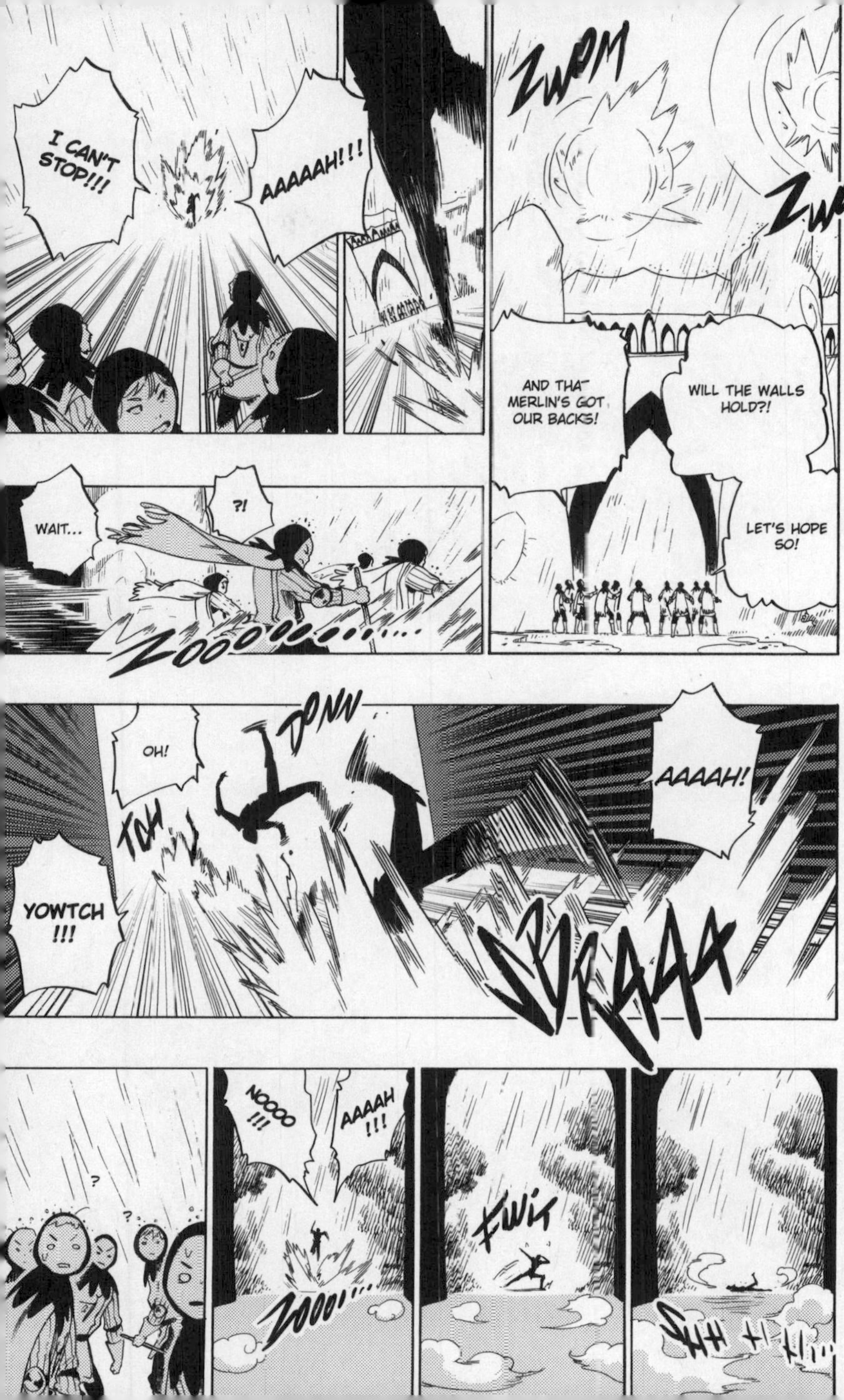
ZWOM
ZWOM
AAAAAH!!!
I CAN'T STOP!!!
WILL THE WALLS HOLD?!
AND THAT MERLIN'S GOT OUR BACKS!
LET'S HOPE SO!
?!
WAIT...
ZOOOOOOOO.......
AAAAH!
DONN
OH!
TCH
YOWTCH !!!
CRRAAA
FWIT
AAAAH !!!
NOOOO !!!
ZOOOI...
?
?

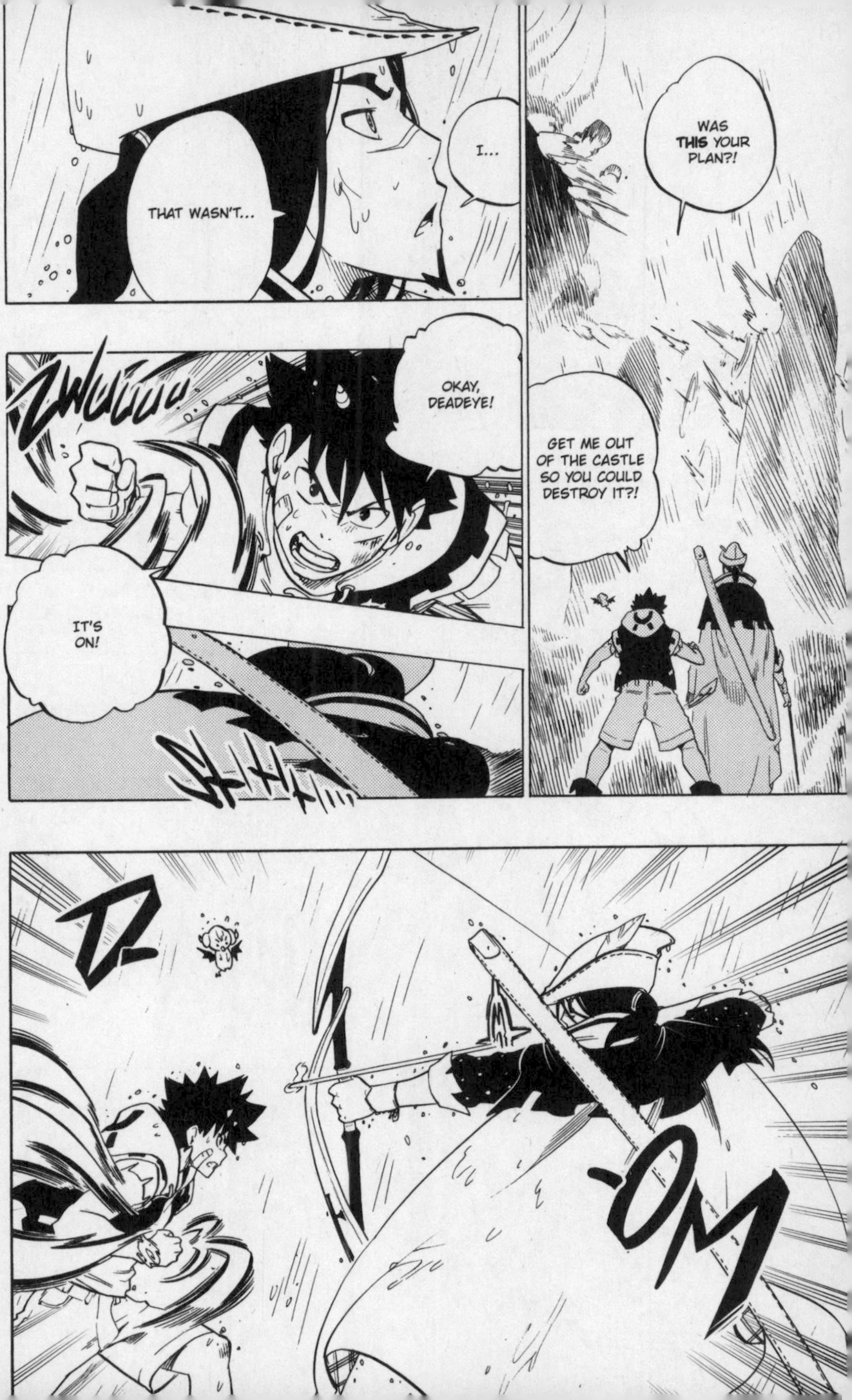
WAS THIS YOUR PLAN?!
GET ME OUT OF THE CASTLE SO YOU COULD DESTROY IT?!
I...
THAT WASN'T...
OKAY, DEADEYE!
IT'S ON!

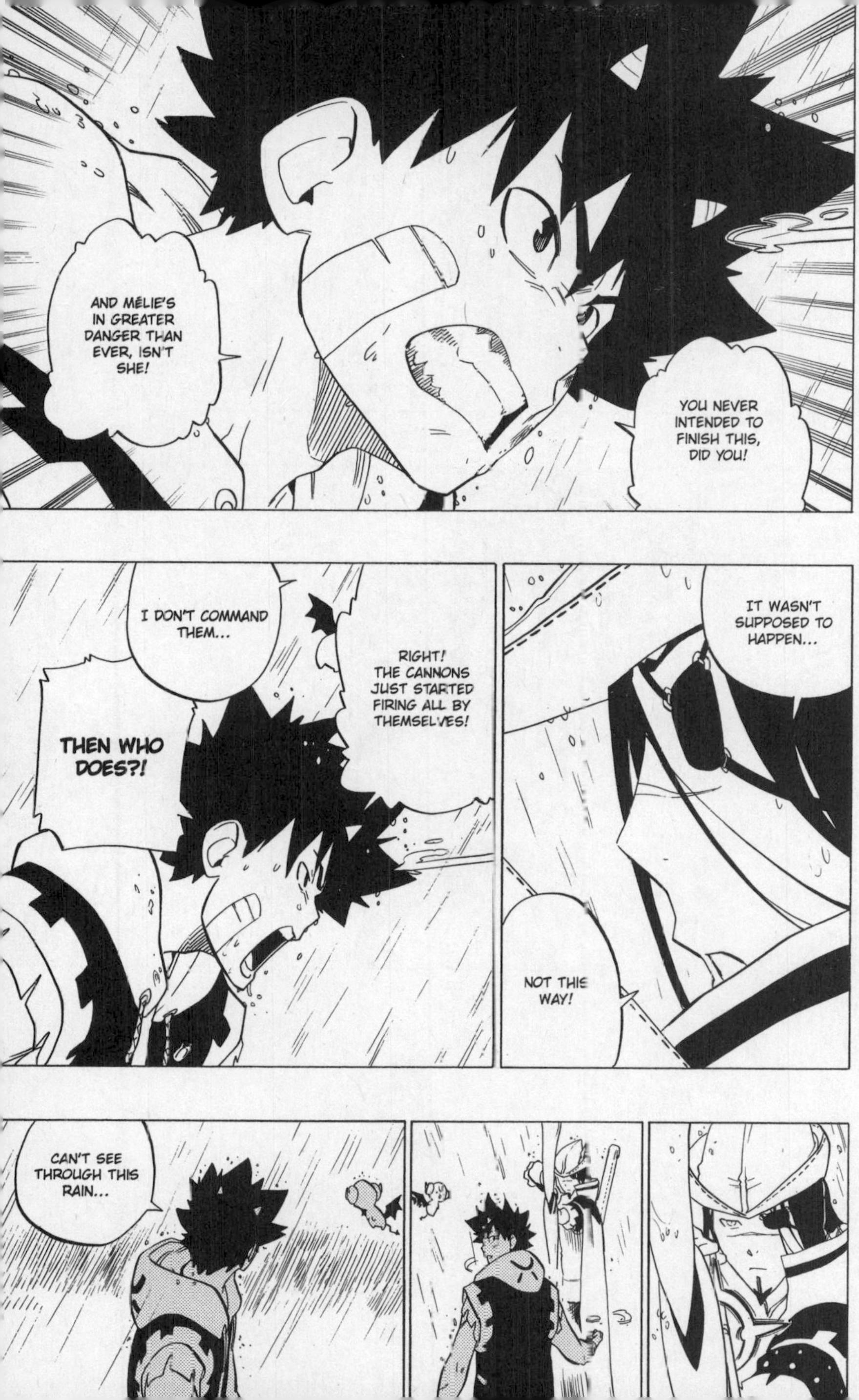
YOU NEVER INTENDED TO FINISH THIS, DID YOU!
AND MÉLIE'S IN GREATER DANGER THAN EVER, ISN'T SHE!
IT WASN'T SUPPOSED TO HAPPEN...
NOT THIS WAY!
I DON'T COMMAND THEM...
RIGHT! THE CANNONS JUST STARTED FIRING ALL BY THEMSELVES!
THEN WHO DOES?!
CAN'T SEE THROUGH THIS RAIN...

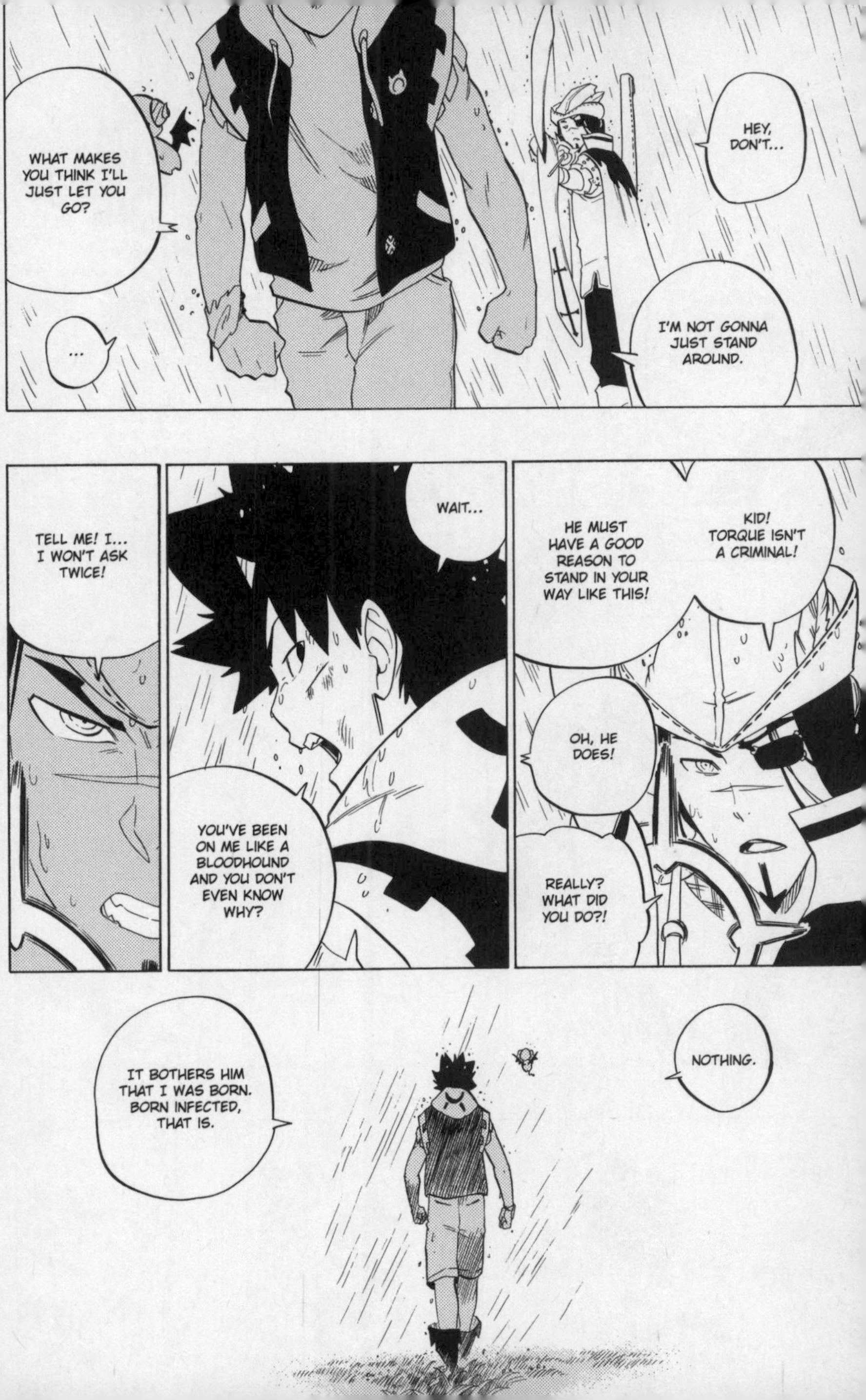
HEY, DON'T...
I'M NOT GONNA JUST STAND AROUND.
WHAT MAKES YOU THINK I'LL JUST LET YOU GO?
...
KID! TORQUE ISN'T A CRIMINAL!
HE MUST HAVE A GOOD REASON TO STAND IN YOUR WAY LIKE THIS!
OH, HE DOES!
REALLY? WHAT DID YOU DO?!
WAIT...
YOU'VE BEEN ON ME LIKE A BLOODHOUND AND YOU DON'T EVEN KNOW WHY?
TELL ME! I... I WON'T ASK TWICE!
NOTHING.
IT BOTHERS HIM THAT I WAS BORN. BORN INFECTED, THAT IS.

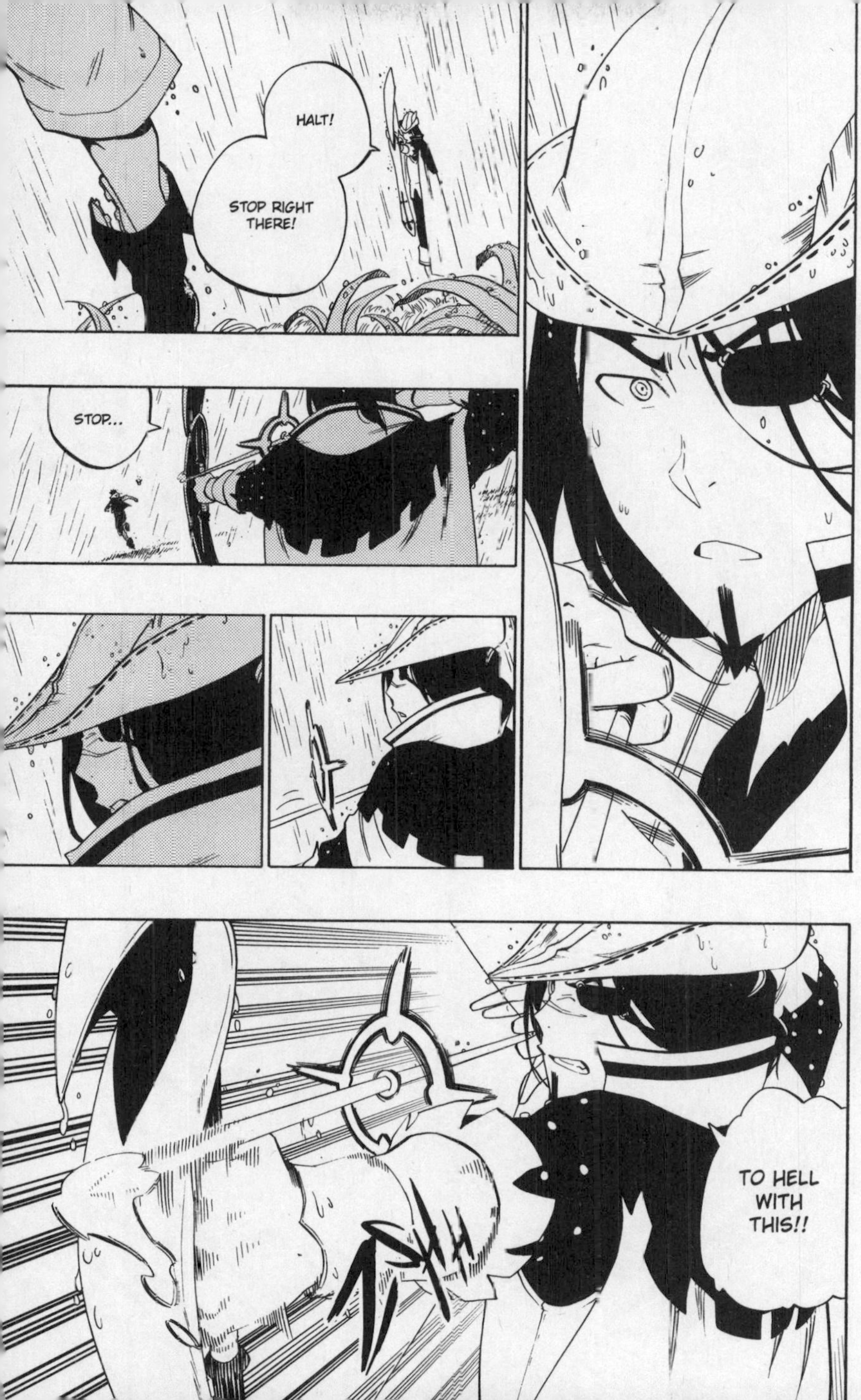
HALT!
STOP RIGHT THERE!
STOP...
TO HELL WITH THIS!!

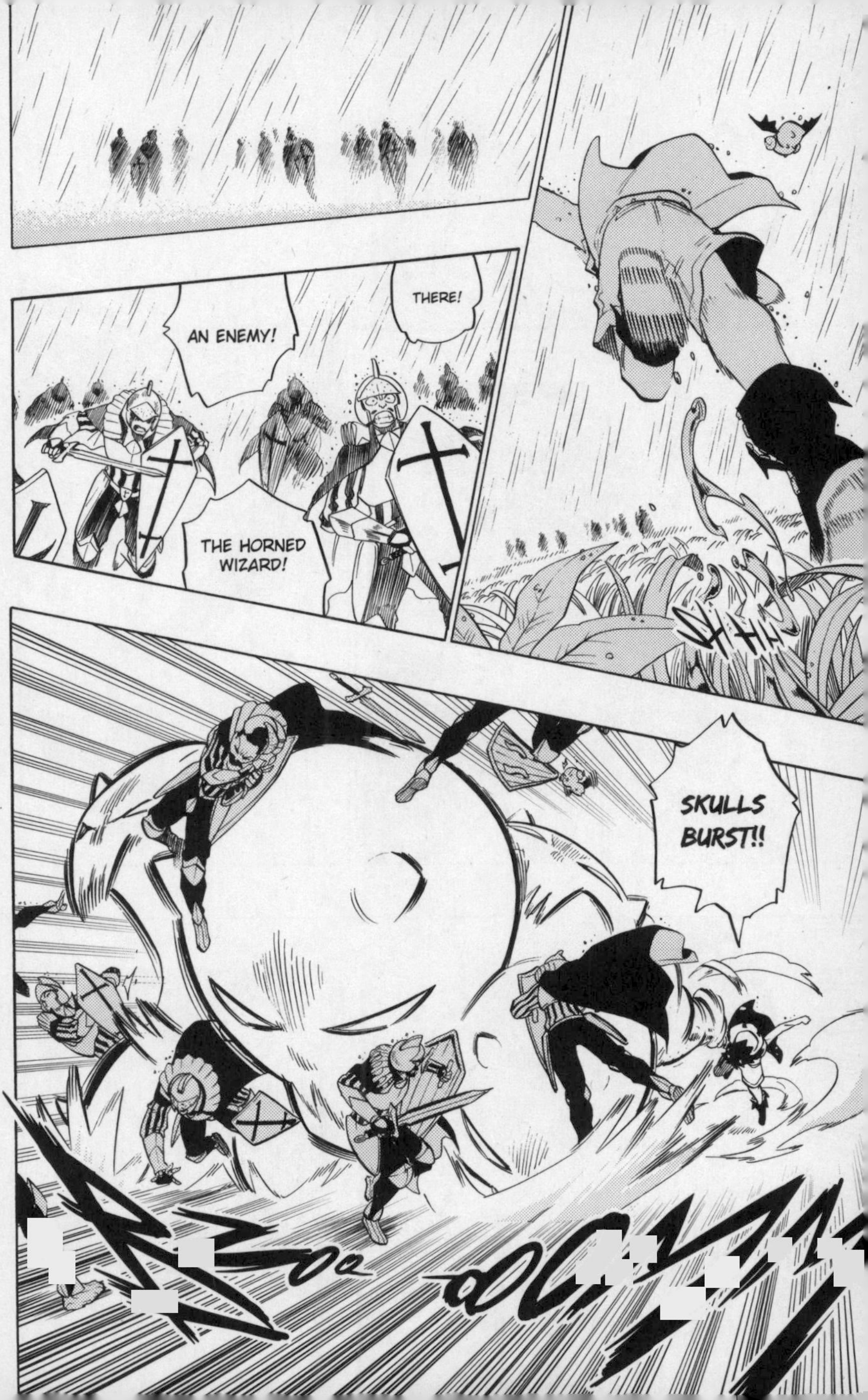
THERE!
AN ENEMY!
THE HORNED WIZARD!
SKULLS BURST!!

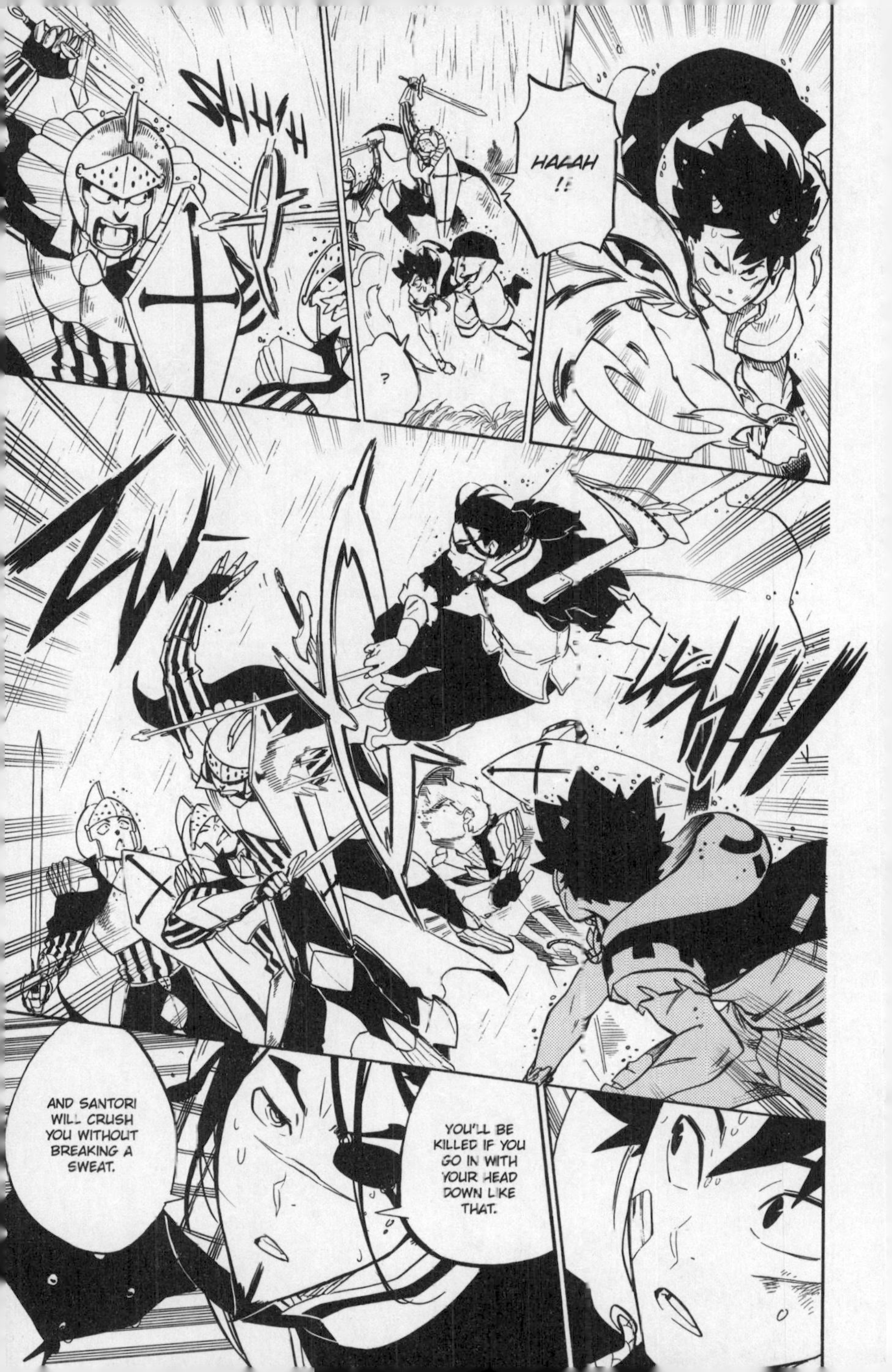
HAAAH !!
?
YOU'LL BE KILLED IF YOU GO IN WITH YOUR HEAD DOWN LIKE THAT.
AND SANTORI WILL CRUSH YOU WITHOUT BREAKING A SWEAT.

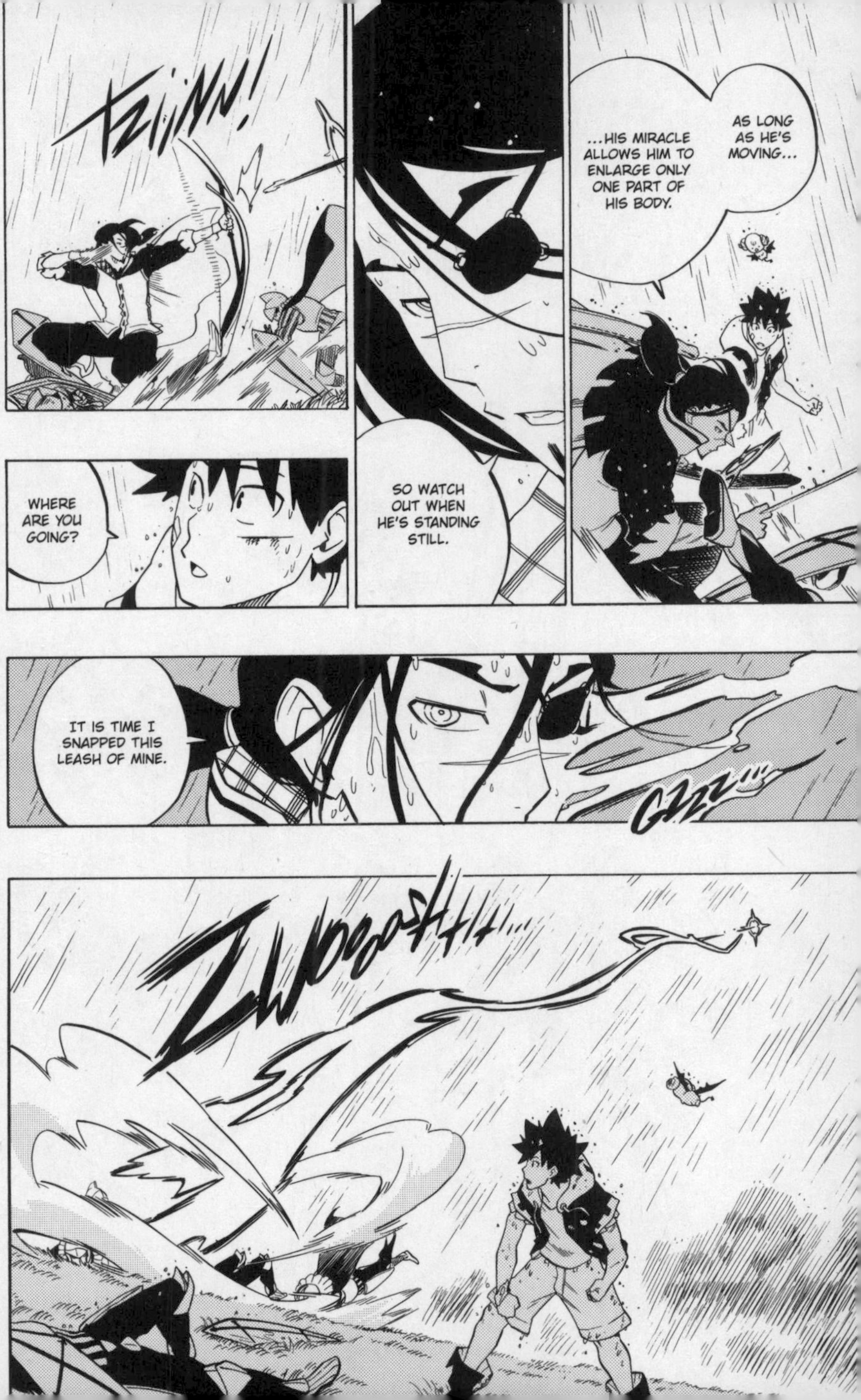
AS LONG AS HE'S MOVING...
...HIS MIRACLE ALLOWS HIM TO ENLARGE ONLY ONE PART OF HIS BODY.
SO WATCH OUT WHEN HE'S STANDING STILL.
TZIIINN!
WHERE ARE YOU GOING?
IT IS TIME I SNAPPED THIS LEASH OF MINE.
GZZZ!!
ZWOOOSHHH...

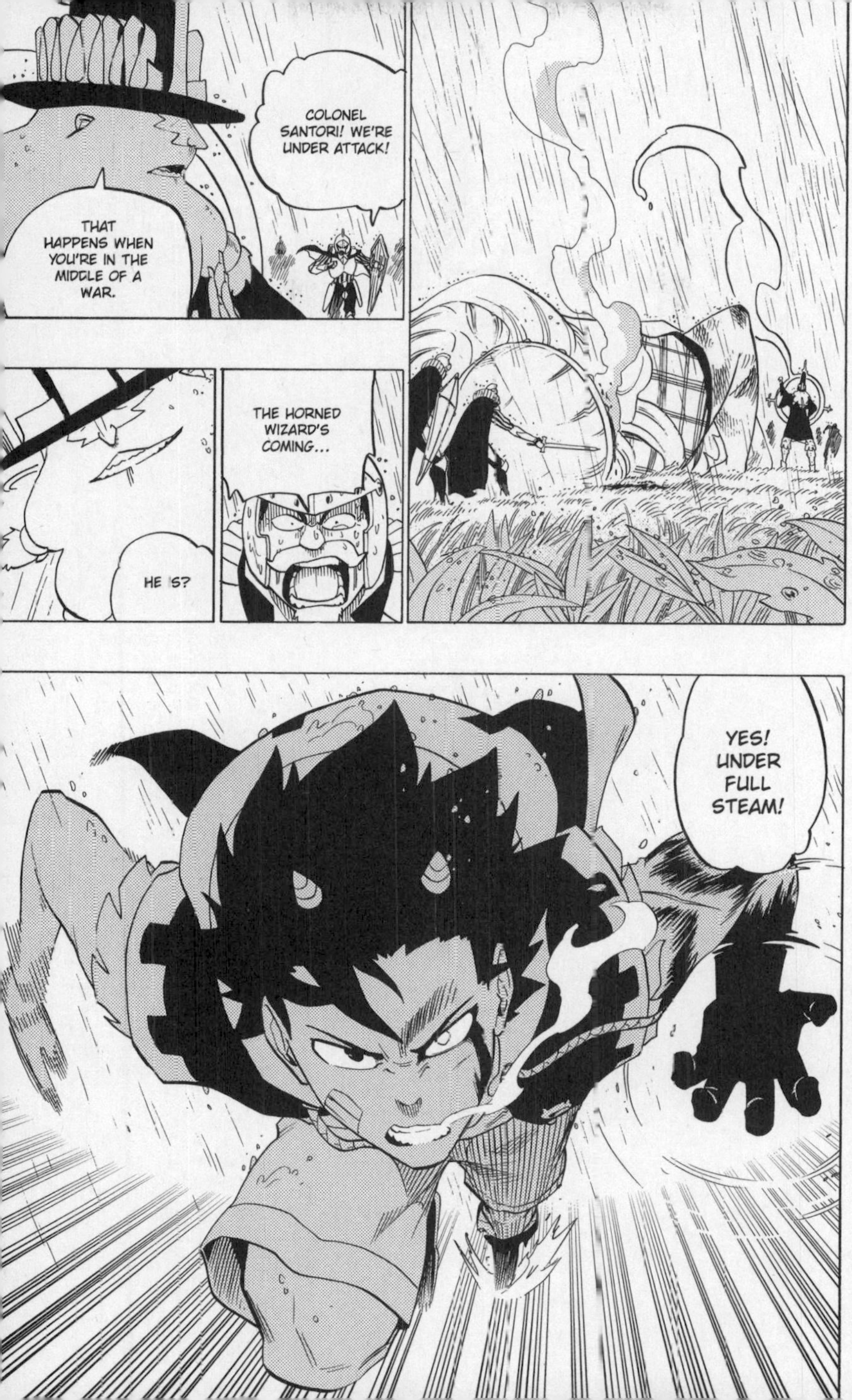
COLONEL SANTORI! WE'RE UNDER ATTACK!
THAT HAPPENS WHEN YOU'RE IN THE MIDDLE OF A WAR.
THE HORNED WIZARD'S COMING...
HE IS?
YES! UNDER FULL STEAM!

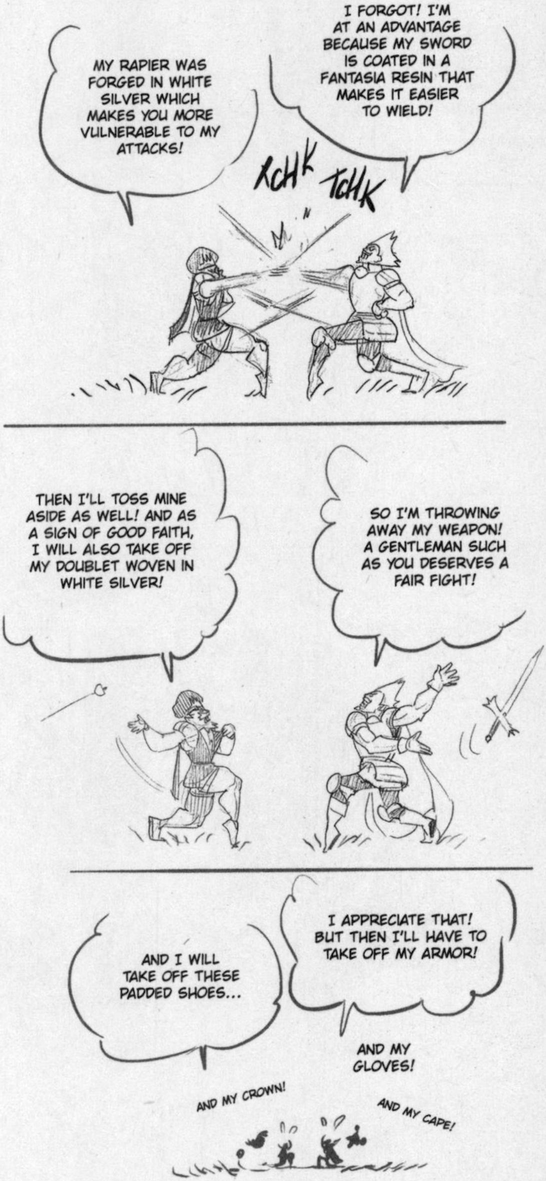
I FORGOT! I'M AT AN ADVANTAGE BECAUSE MY SWORD IS COATED IN A FANTASIA RESIN THAT MAKES IT EASIER TO WIELD!
MY RAPIER WAS FORGED IN WHITE SILVER WHICH MAKES YOU MORE VULNERABLE TO MY ATTACKS!
TCHK
TCHK
SO I'M THROWING AWAY MY WEAPON! A GENTLEMAN SUCH AS YOU DESERVES A FAIR FIGHT!
THEN I'LL TOSS MINE ASIDE AS WELL! AND AS A SIGN OF GOOD FAITH, I WILL ALSO TAKE OFF MY DOUBLET WOVEN IN WHITE SILVER!
I APPRECIATE THAT! BUT THEN I'LL HAVE TO TAKE OFF MY ARMOR!
AND MY GLOVES!
AND I WILL TAKE OFF THESE PADDED SHOES...
AND MY CAPE!
AND MY CROWN!

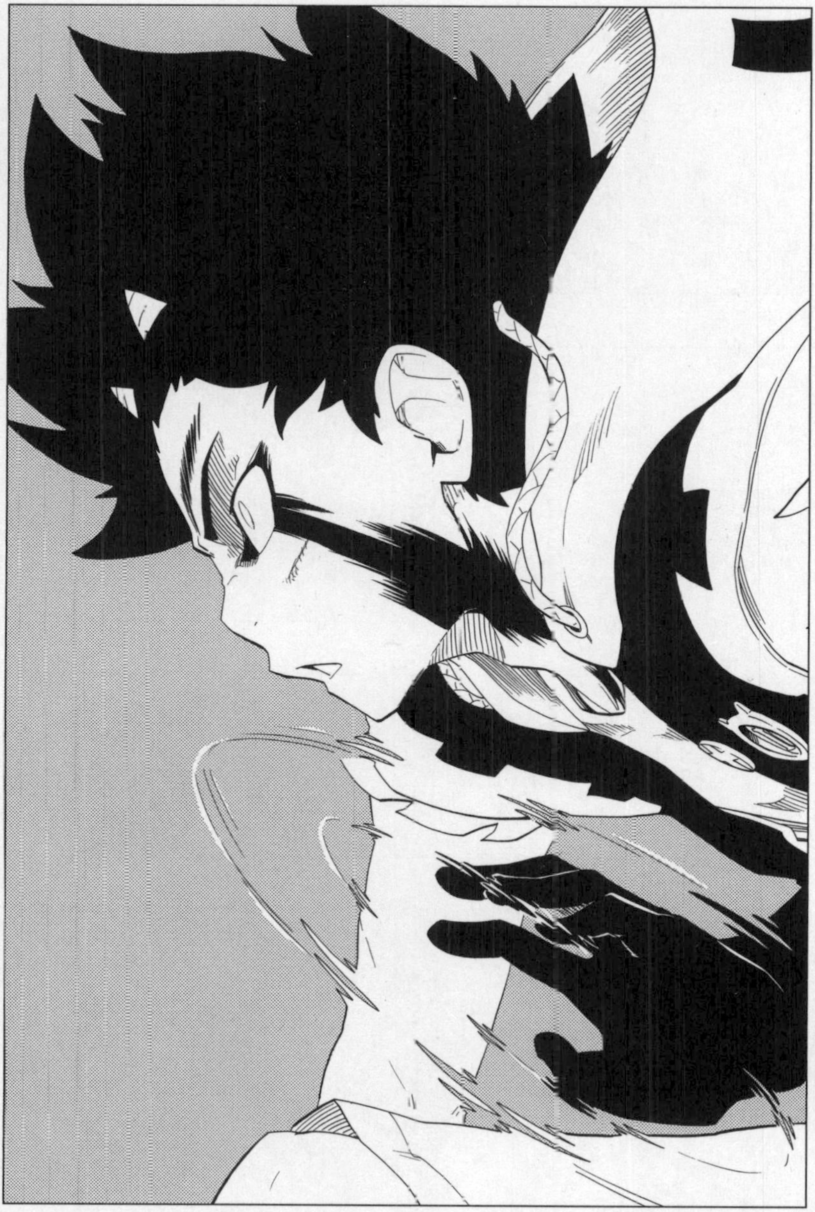

Chapter 64

The Queen's Head

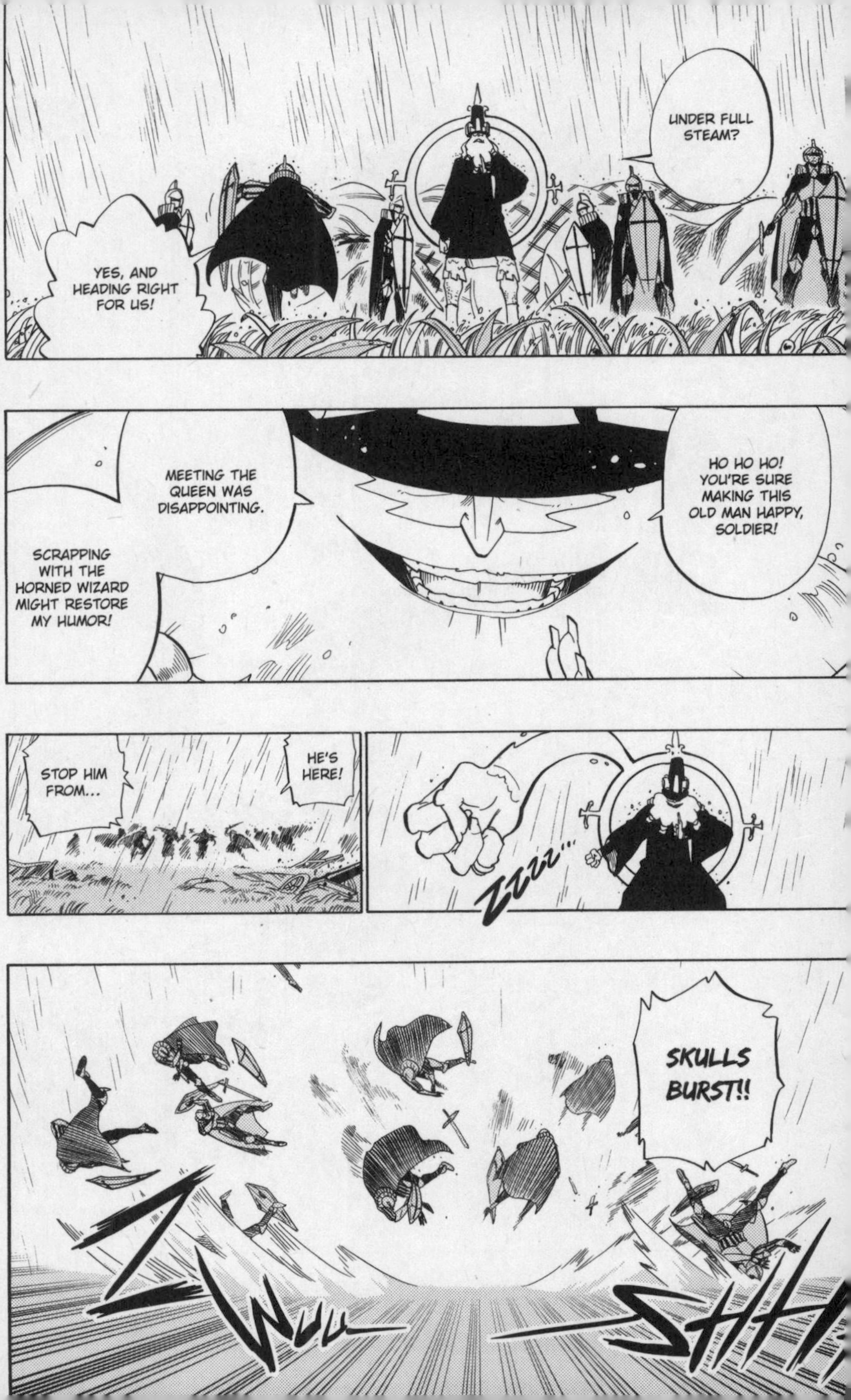
UNDER FULL STEAM?
YES, AND HEADING RIGHT FOR US!
HO HO HO! YOU'RE SURE MAKING THIS OLD MAN HAPPY, SOLDIER!
MEETING THE QUEEN WAS DISAPPOINTING.
SCRAPPING WITH THE HORNED WIZARD MIGHT RESTORE MY HUMOR!
ZZZZ...
HE'S HERE!
STOP HIM FROM...
SKULLS BURST!!
WUU
SHH

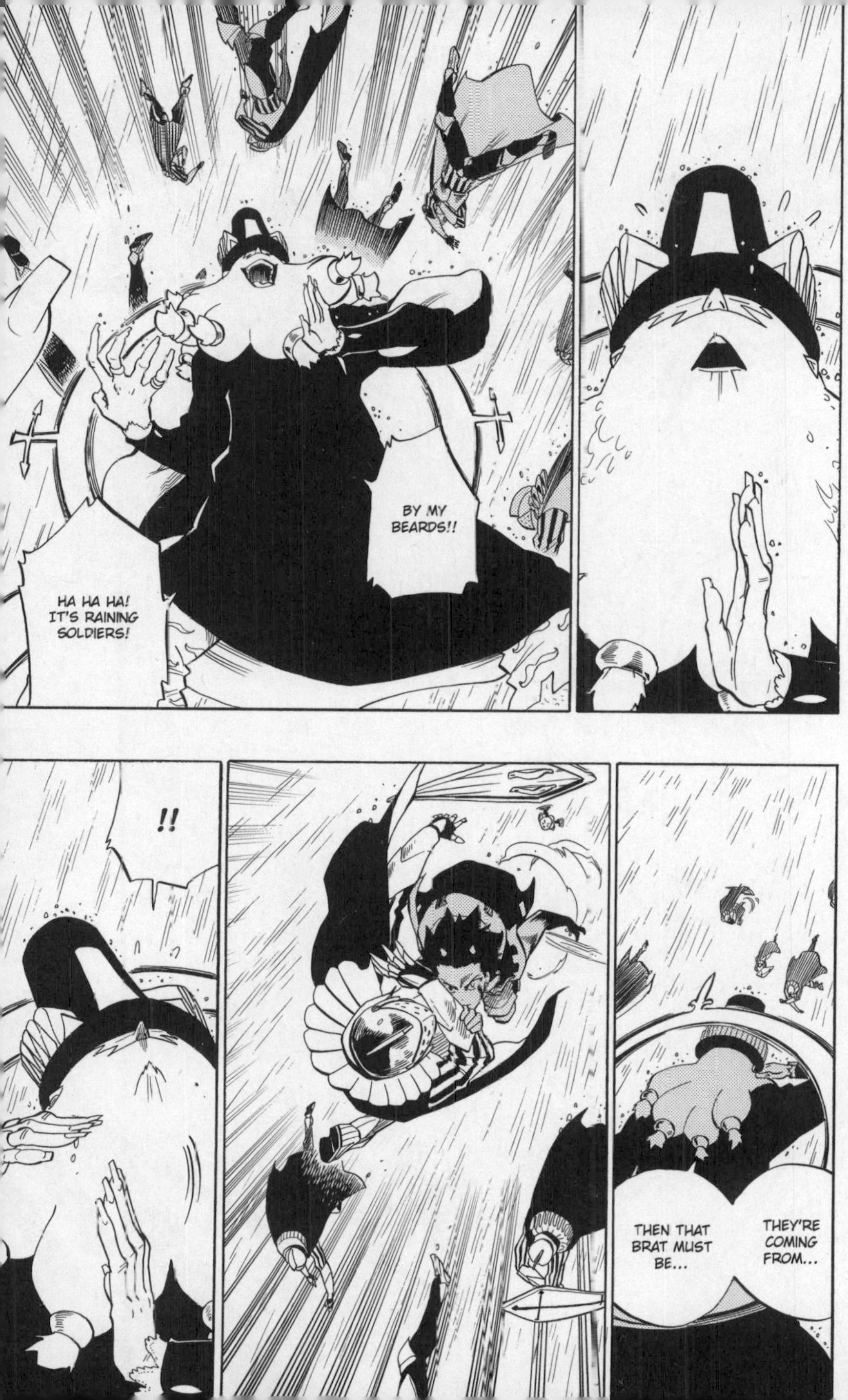
BY MY BEARDS!!
HA HA HA! IT'S RAINING SOLDIERS!
THEY'RE COMING FROM...
THEN THAT BRAT MUST BE...
!!

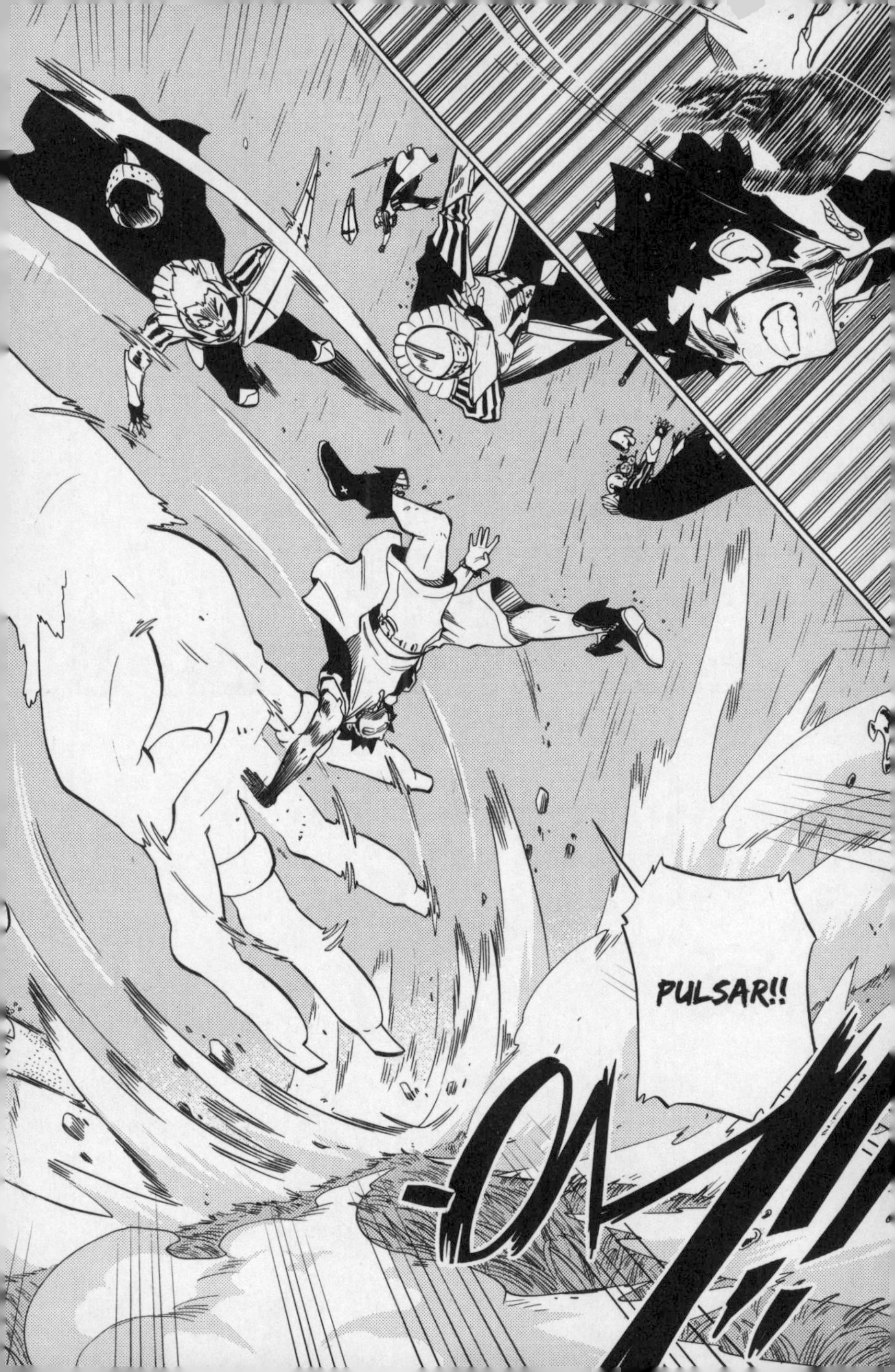
PULSAR!!

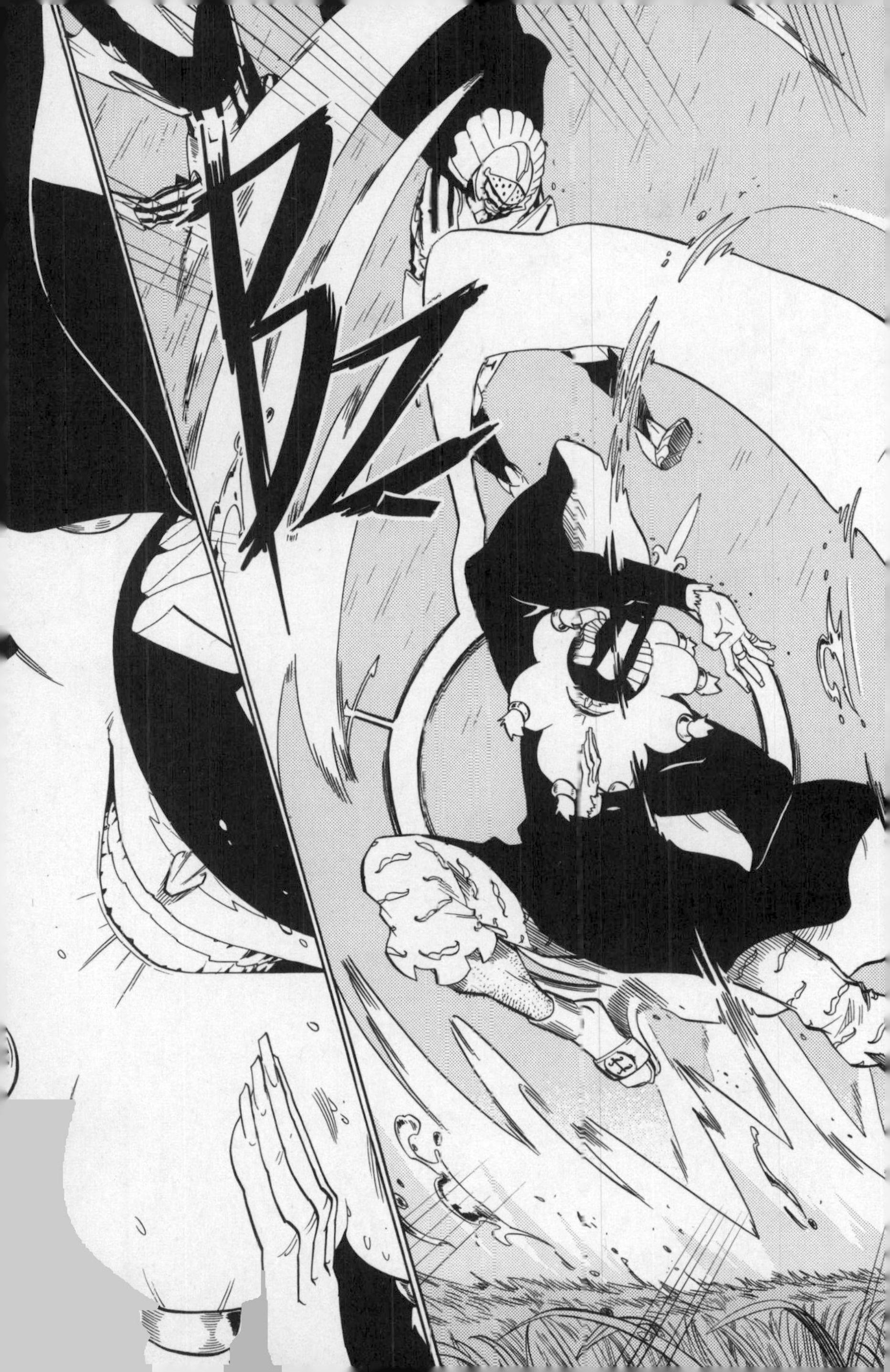

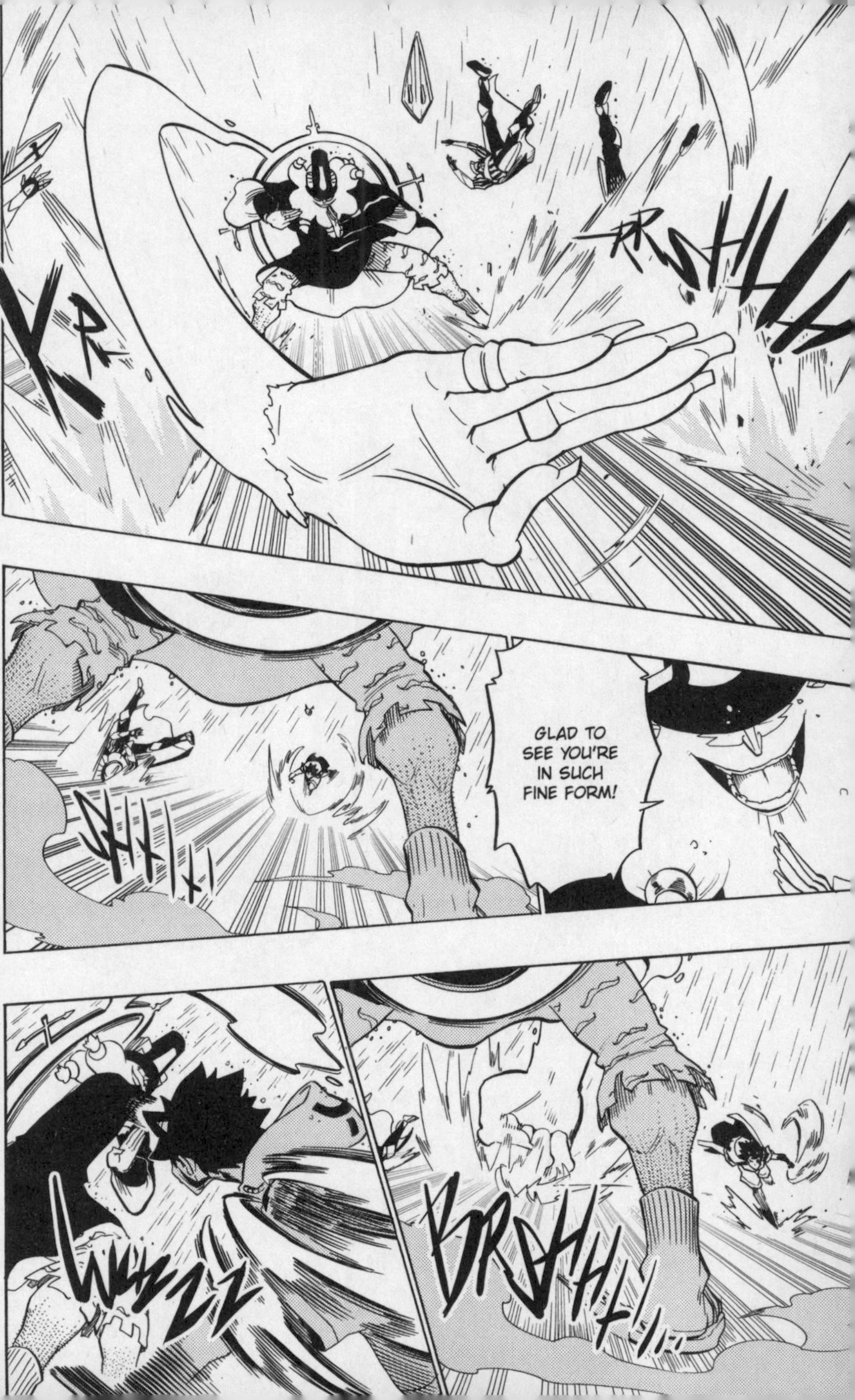
GLAD TO SEE YOU'RE IN SUCH FINE FORM!

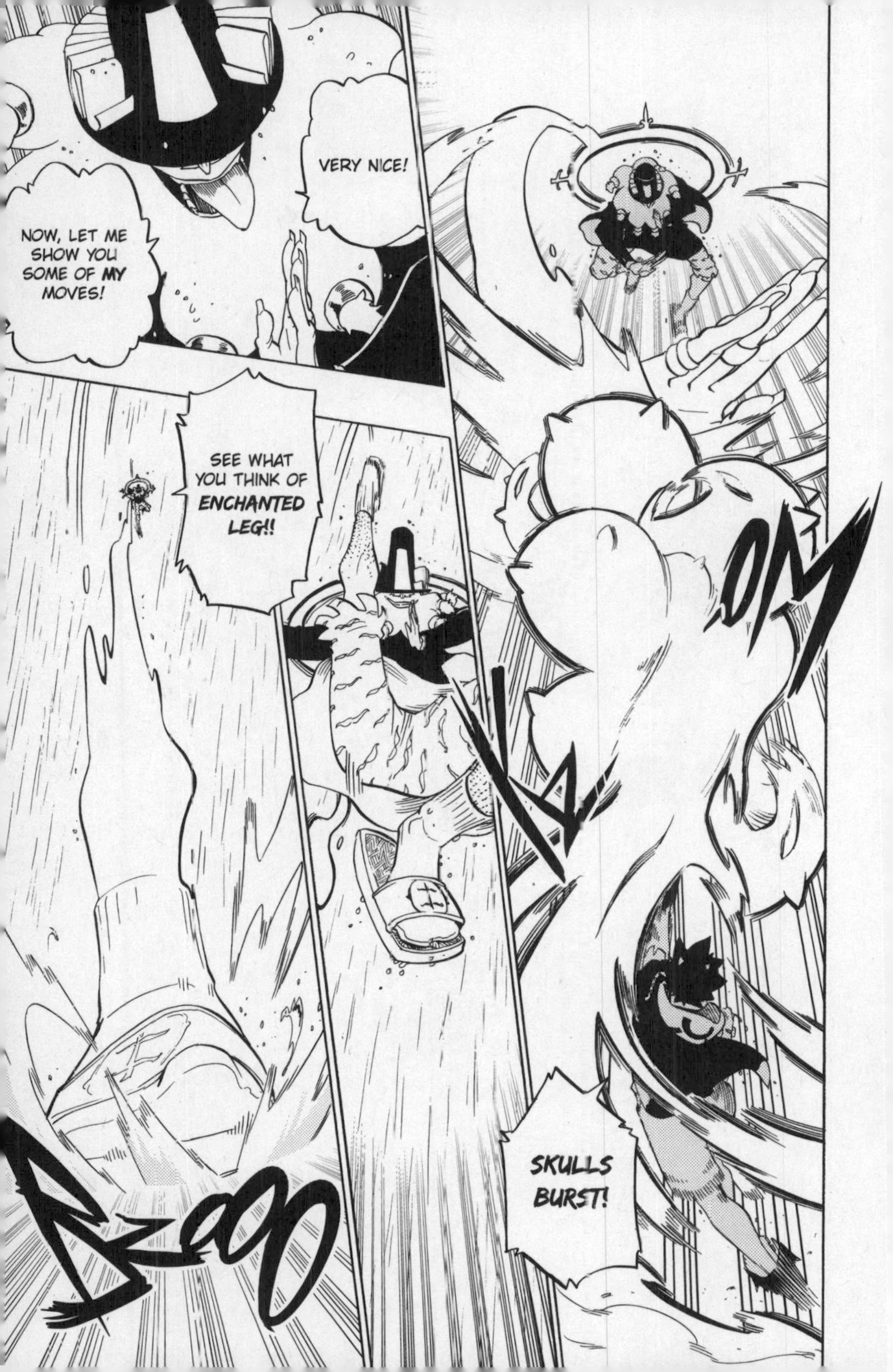
SKULLS BURST!
VERY NICE!
NOW, LET ME SHOW YOU SOME OF MY MOVES!
SEE WHAT YOU THINK OF ENCHANTED LEG!!

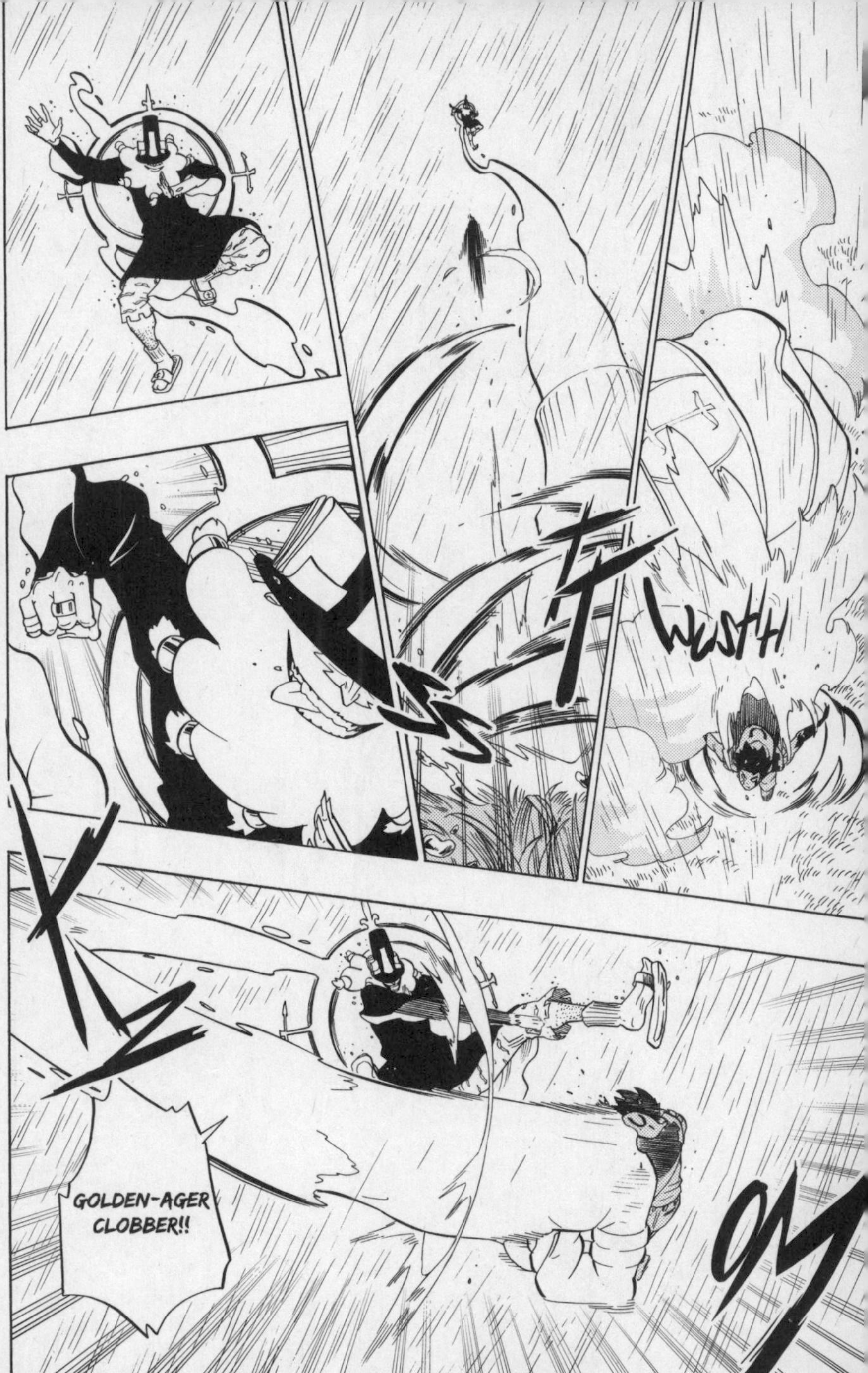
GOLDEN-AGER CLOBBER!!

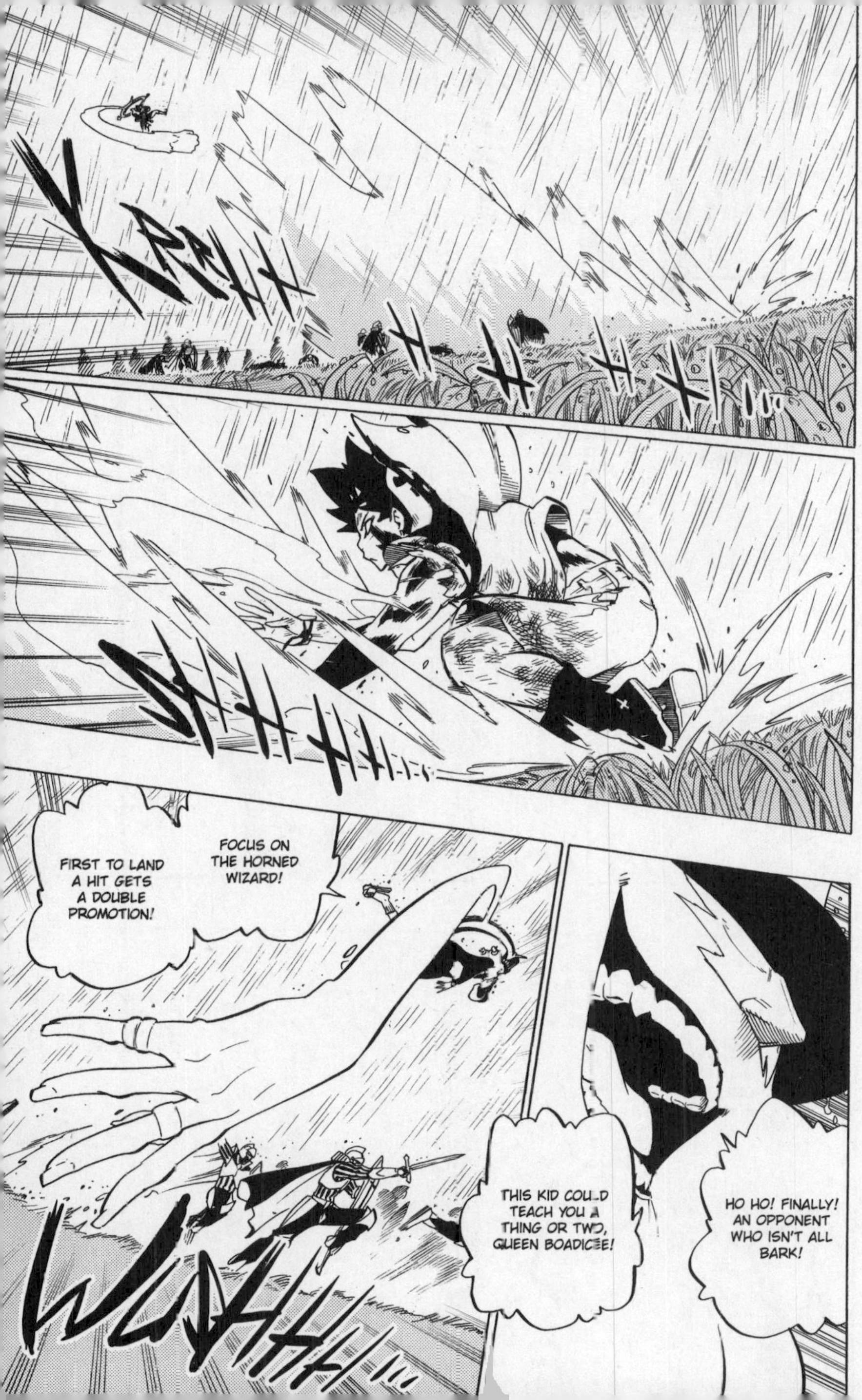
HO HO! FINALLY! AN OPPONENT WHO ISN'T ALL BARK!
THIS KID COULD TEACH YOU A THING OR TWO, QUEEN BOADICEE!
FOCUS ON THE HORNED WIZARD!
FIRST TO LAND A HIT GETS A DOUBLE PROMOTION!

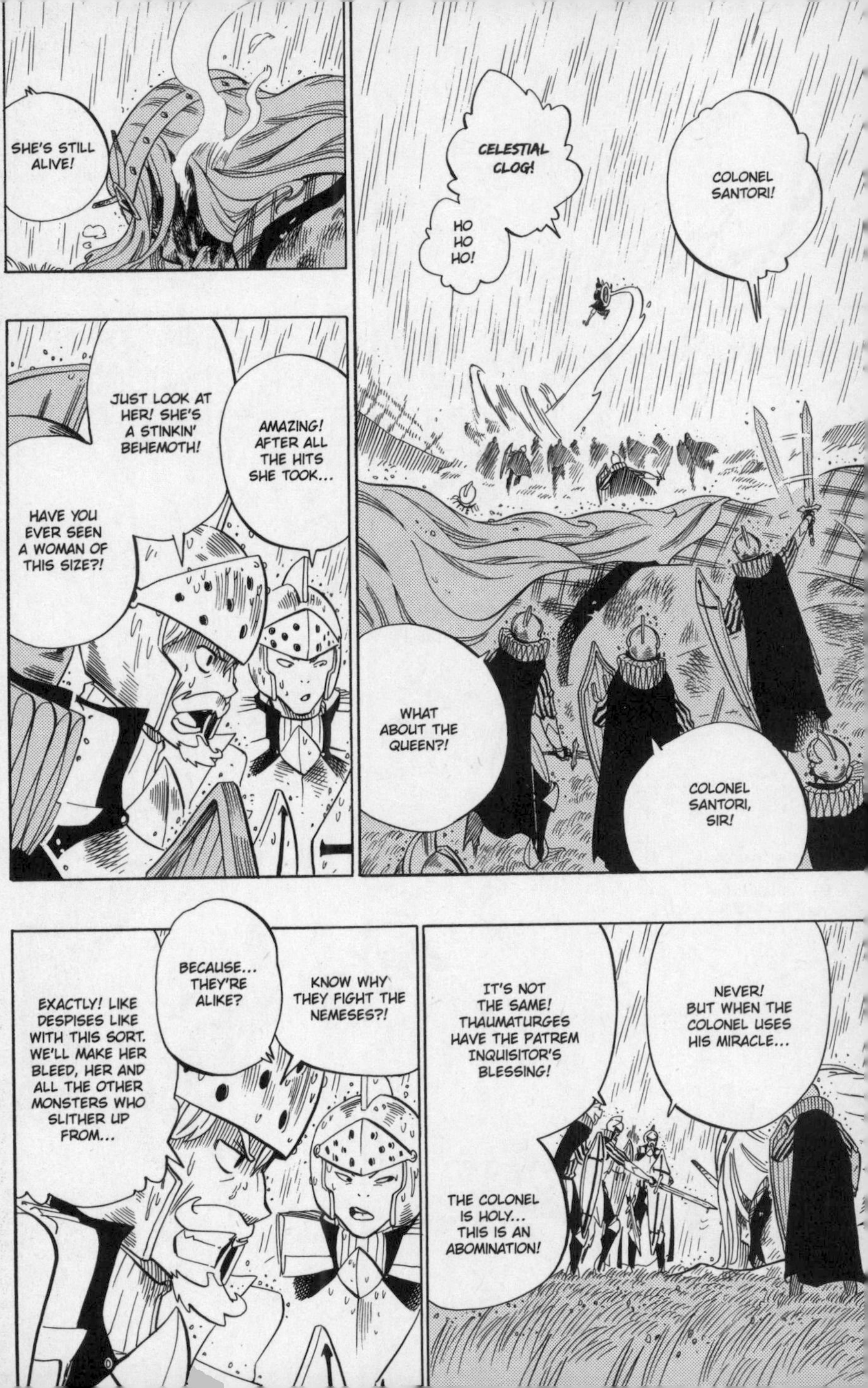
COLONEL SANTORI!
CELESTIAL CLOG!
HO HO HO!
COLONEL SANTORI, SIR!
WHAT ABOUT THE QUEEN?!
SHE'S STILL ALIVE!
AMAZING! AFTER ALL THE HITS SHE TOOK...
JUST LOOK AT HER! SHE'S A STINKIN' BEHEMOTH!
HAVE YOU EVER SEEN A WOMAN OF THIS SIZE?!
NEVER! BUT WHEN THE COLONEL USES HIS MIRACLE...
IT'S NOT THE SAME! THAUMATURGES HAVE THE PATREM INQUISITOR'S BLESSING!
THE COLONEL IS HOLY... THIS IS AN ABOMINATION!
KNOW WHY THEY FIGHT THE NEMESES?!
BECAUSE... THEY'RE ALIKE?
EXACTLY! LIKE DESPISES LIKE WITH THIS SORT. WE'LL MAKE HER BLEED, HER AND ALL THE OTHER MONSTERS WHO SLITHER UP FROM...

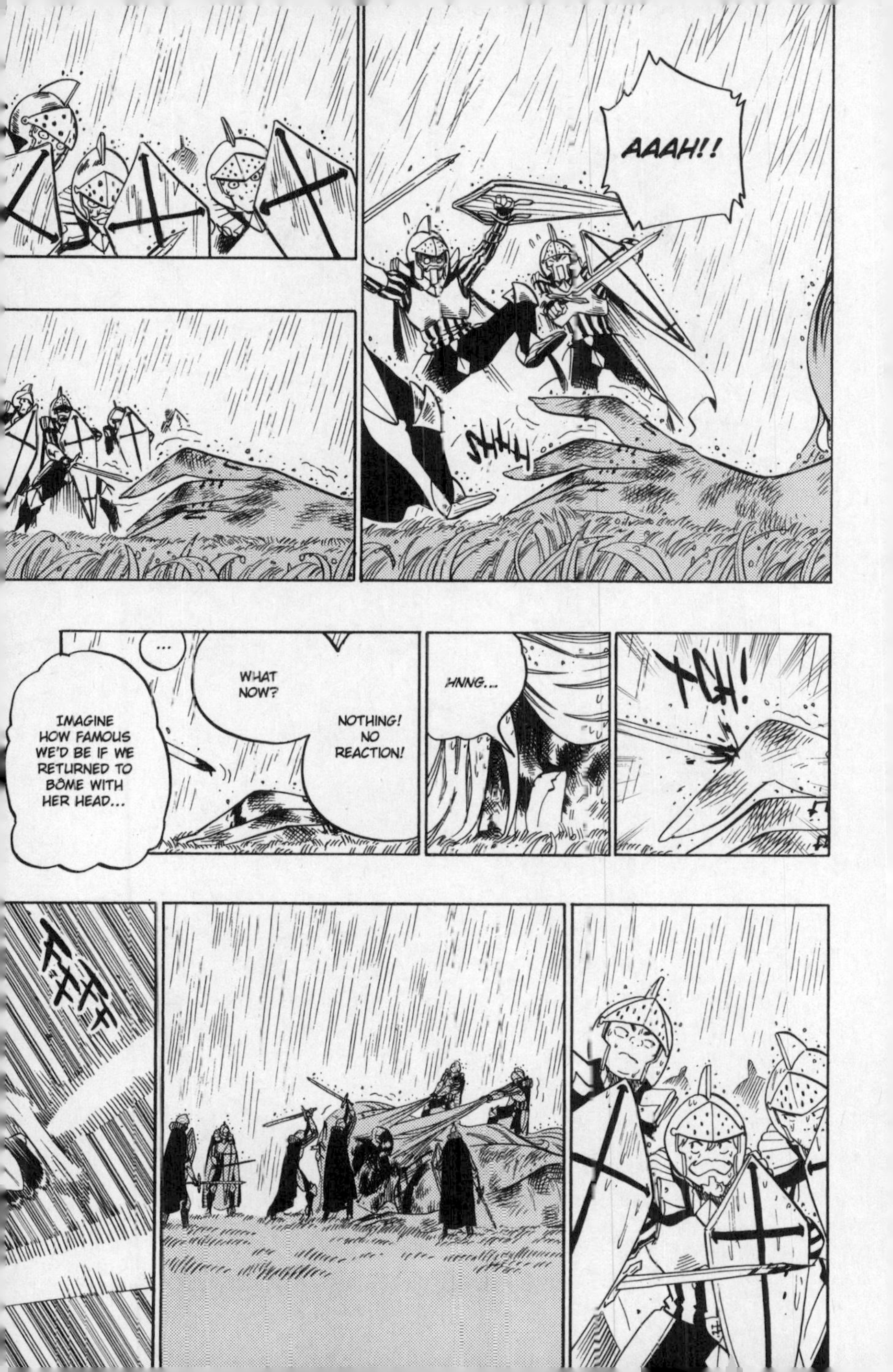
AAAH!!
TCH!
HNNG...
WHAT NOW?
NOTHING! NO REACTION!
...
IMAGINE HOW FAMOUS WE'D BE IF WE RETURNED TO BÔME WITH HER HEAD...

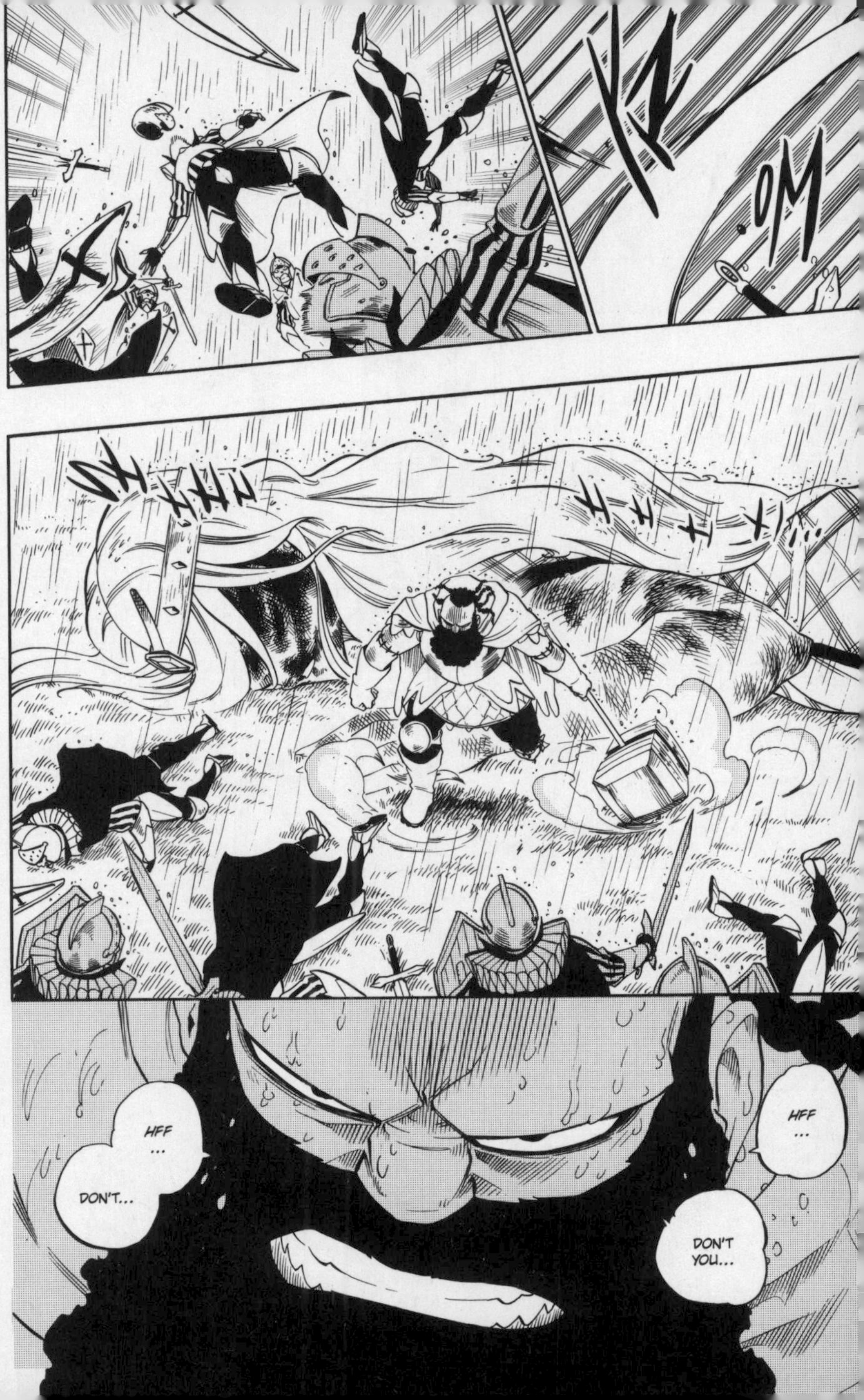
HFF ...
DON'T YOU...
HFF ...
DON'T...

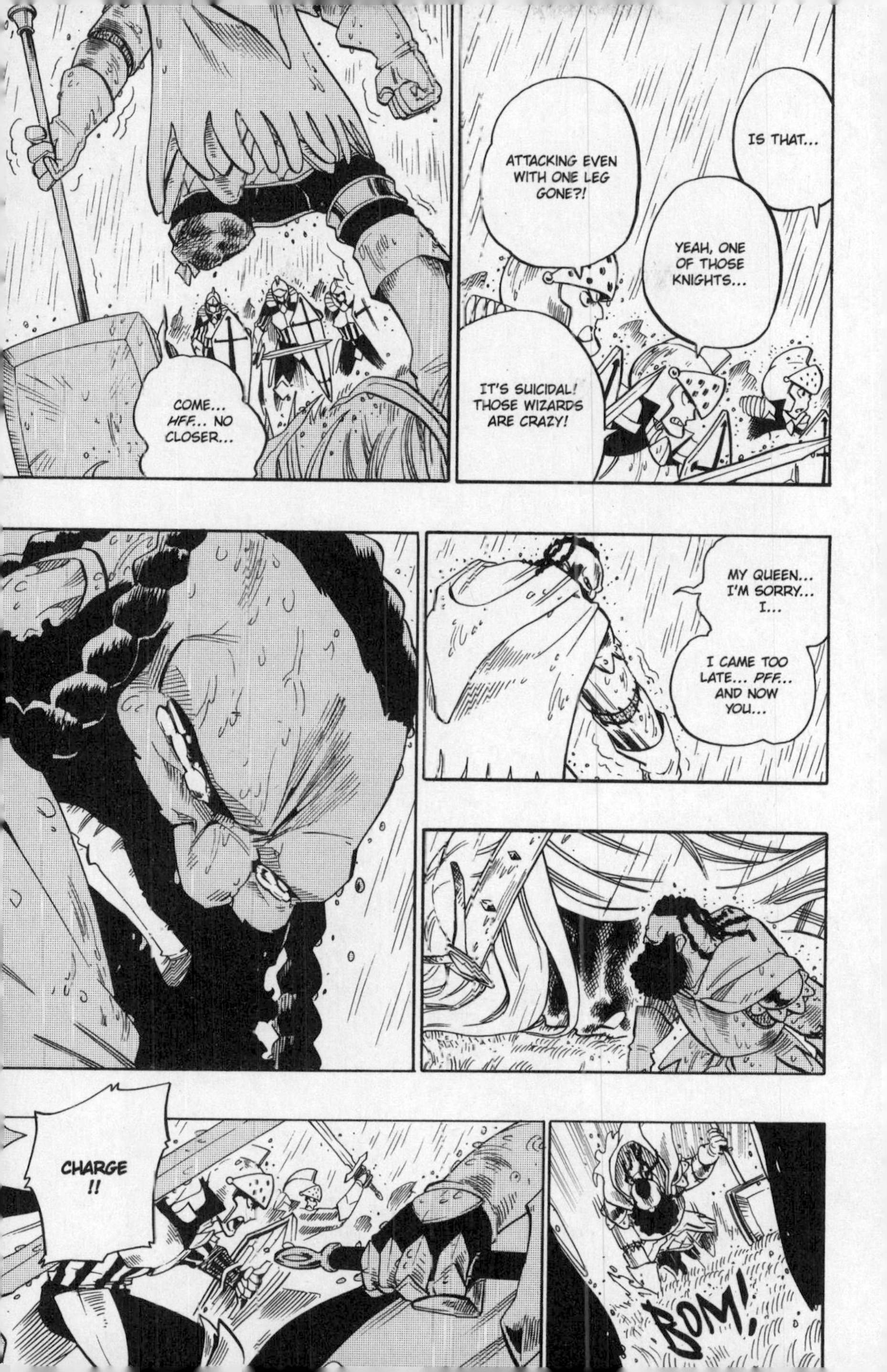
IS THAT...
ATTACKING EVEN WITH ONE LEG GONE?!
YEAH, ONE OF THOSE KNIGHTS...
IT'S SUICIDAL! THOSE WIZARDS ARE CRAZY!
COME... *HFF*... NO CLOSER...
MY QUEEN... I'M SORRY... I...
I CAME TOO LATE... *PFF*... AND NOW YOU...
BOM!
CHARGE !!

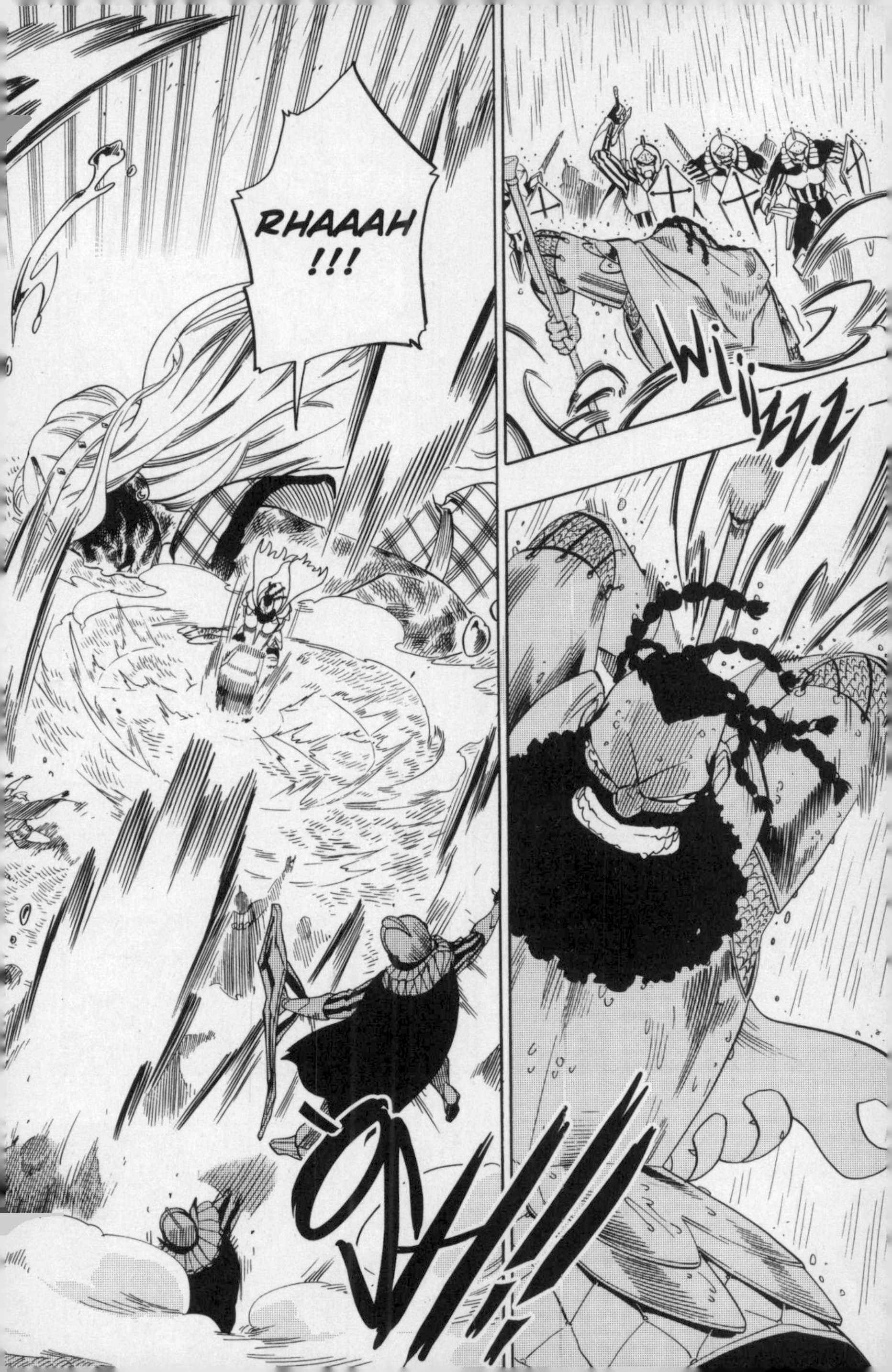
WIIZZZ
RHAAAH!!!

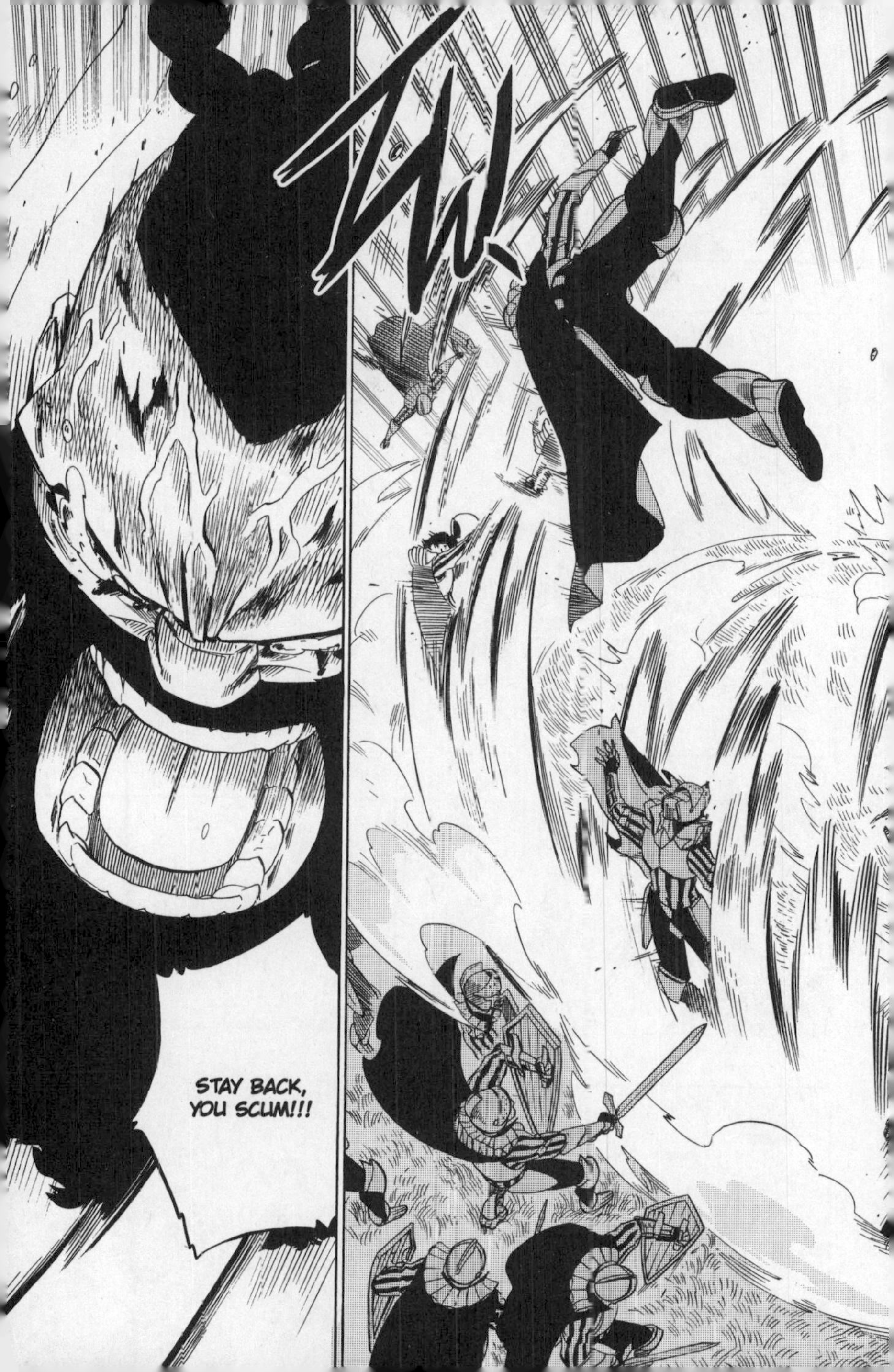
ZW!
STAY BACK, YOU SCUM!!!

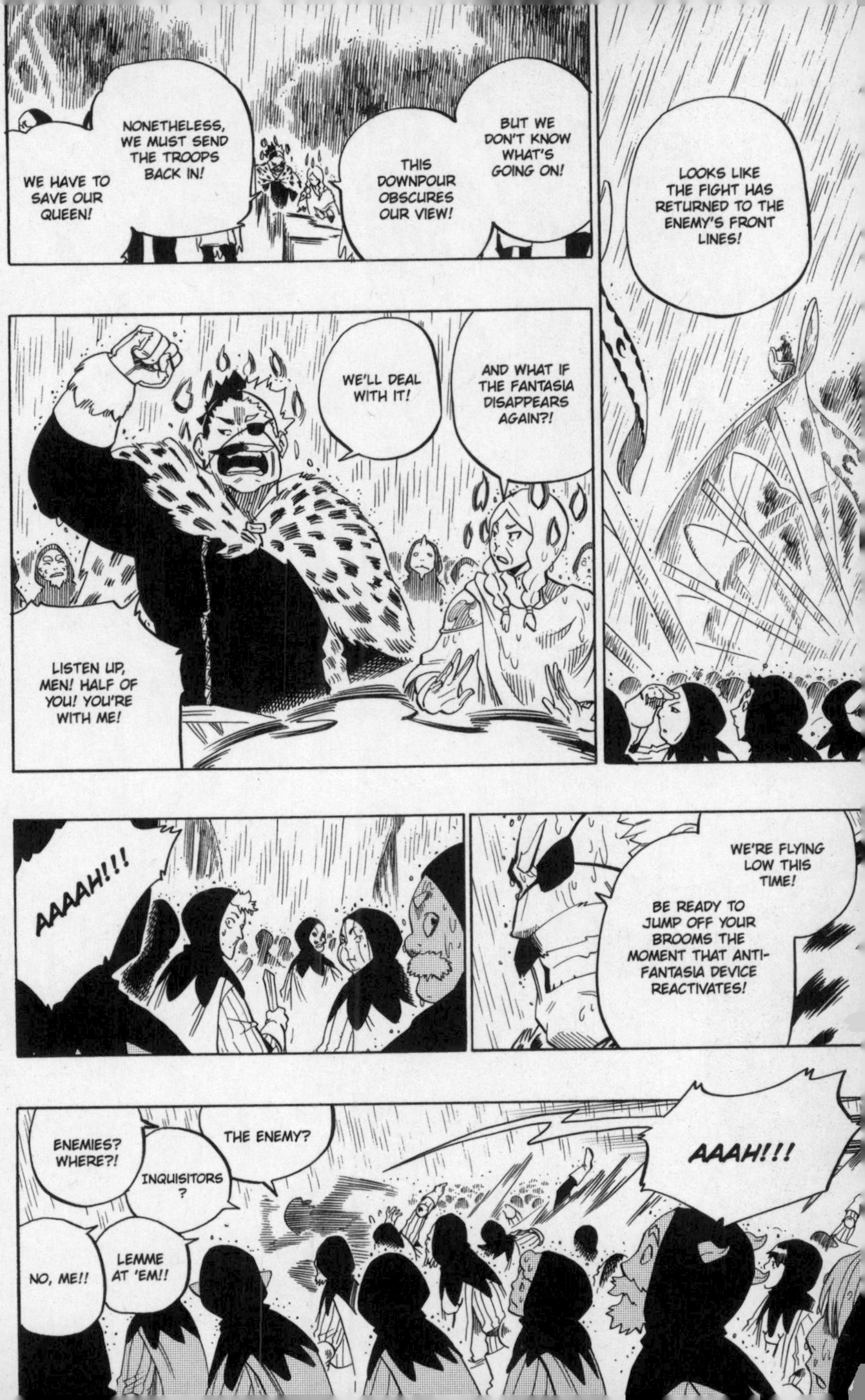
LOOKS LIKE THE FIGHT HAS RETURNED TO THE ENEMY'S FRONT LINES!
BUT WE DON'T KNOW WHAT'S GOING ON!
THIS DOWNPOUR OBSCURES OUR VIEW!
NONETHELESS, WE MUST SEND THE TROOPS BACK IN!
WE HAVE TO SAVE OUR QUEEN!
AND WHAT IF THE FANTASIA DISAPPEARS AGAIN?!
WE'LL DEAL WITH IT!
LISTEN UP, MEN! HALF OF YOU! YOU'RE WITH ME!
WE'RE FLYING LOW THIS TIME!
BE READY TO JUMP OFF YOUR BROOMS THE MOMENT THAT ANTI-FANTASIA DEVICE REACTIVATES!
AAAAH!!!
AAAH!!!
THE ENEMY?
ENEMIES? WHERE?!
INQUISITORS ?
LEMME AT 'EM!!
NO, ME!!

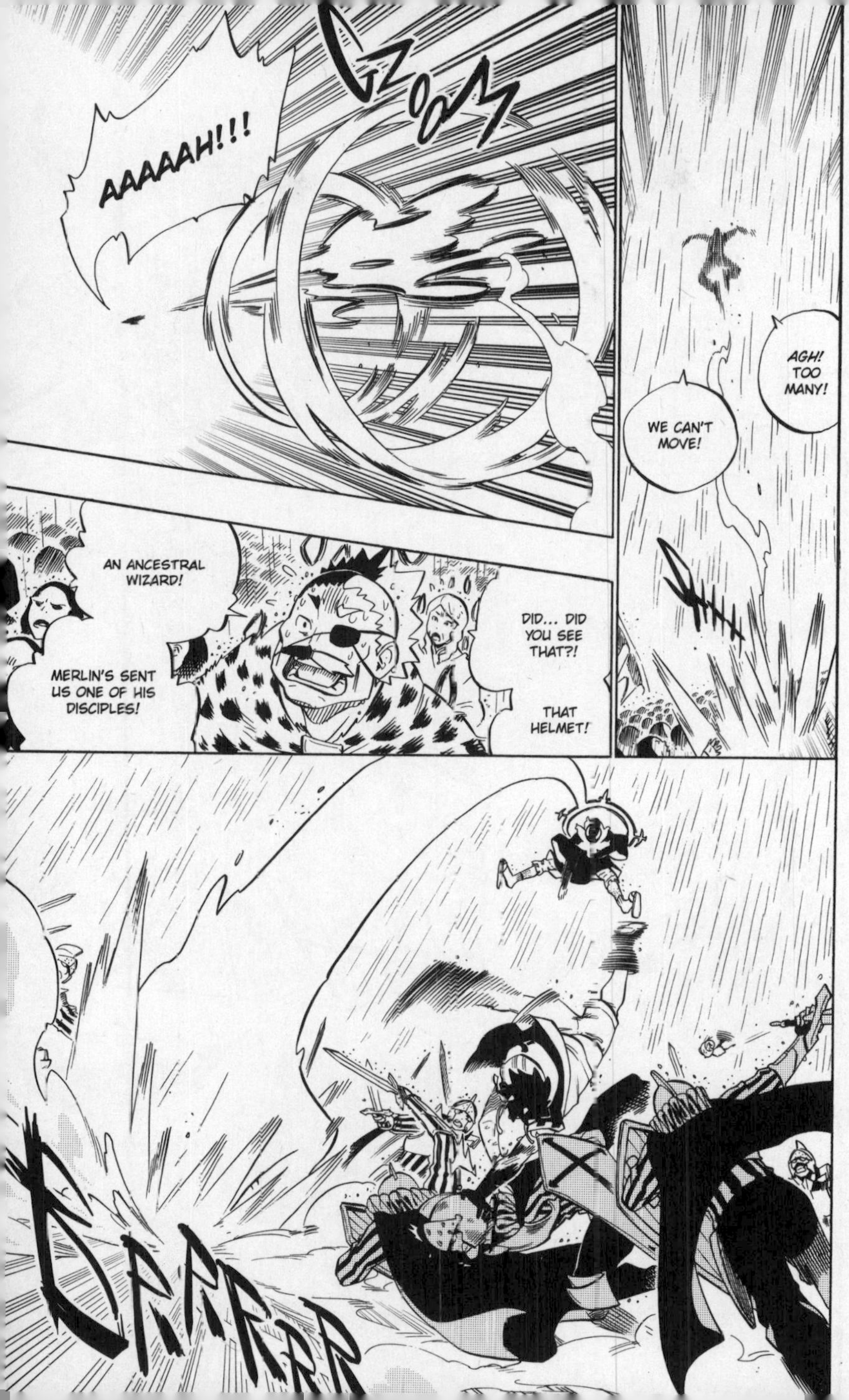
AGH! TOO MANY!
WE CAN'T MOVE!
GZOOM
AAAAAH!!!
DID... DID YOU SEE THAT?!
THAT HELMET!
AN ANCESTRAL WIZARD!
MERLIN'S SENT US ONE OF HIS DISCIPLES!

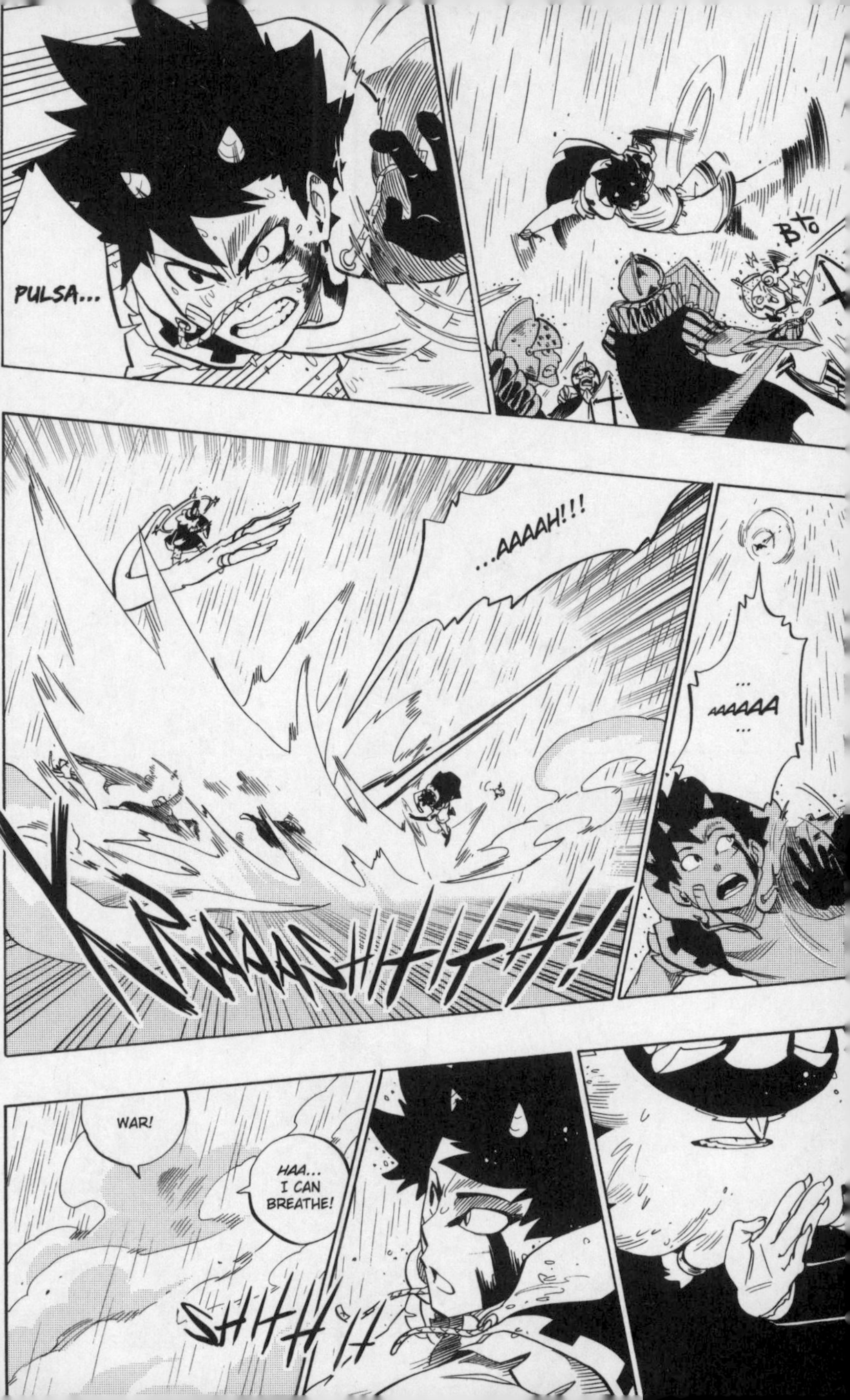
PULSA...
...AAAAAA...
...AAAAH!!!
KRAAASHHHHH!
HAA... I CAN BREATHE!
SHHH!!
WAR!

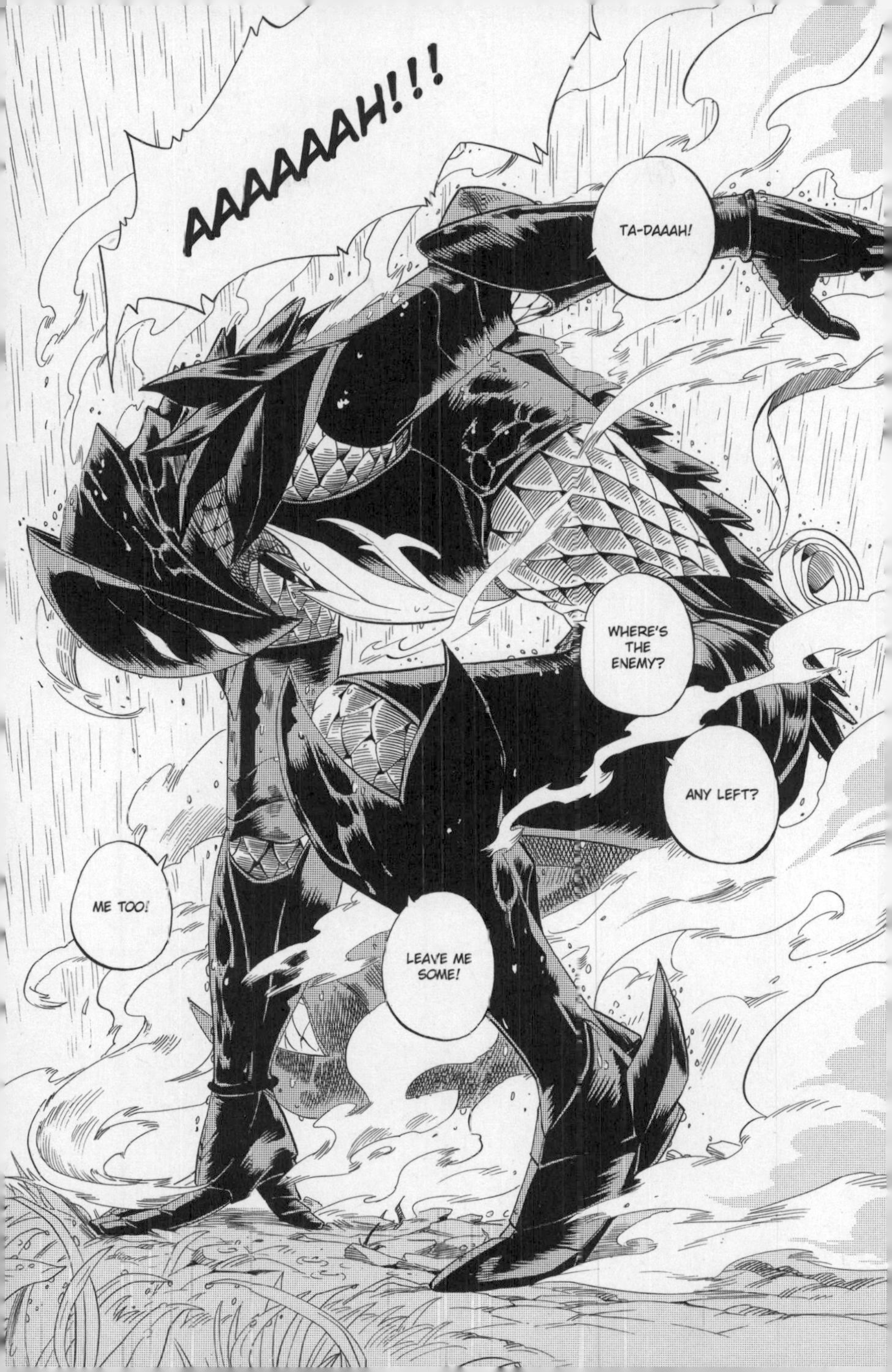
AAAAAAH!!!
TA-DAAAH!
WHERE'S THE ENEMY?
ANY LEFT?
LEAVE ME SOME!
ME TOO!

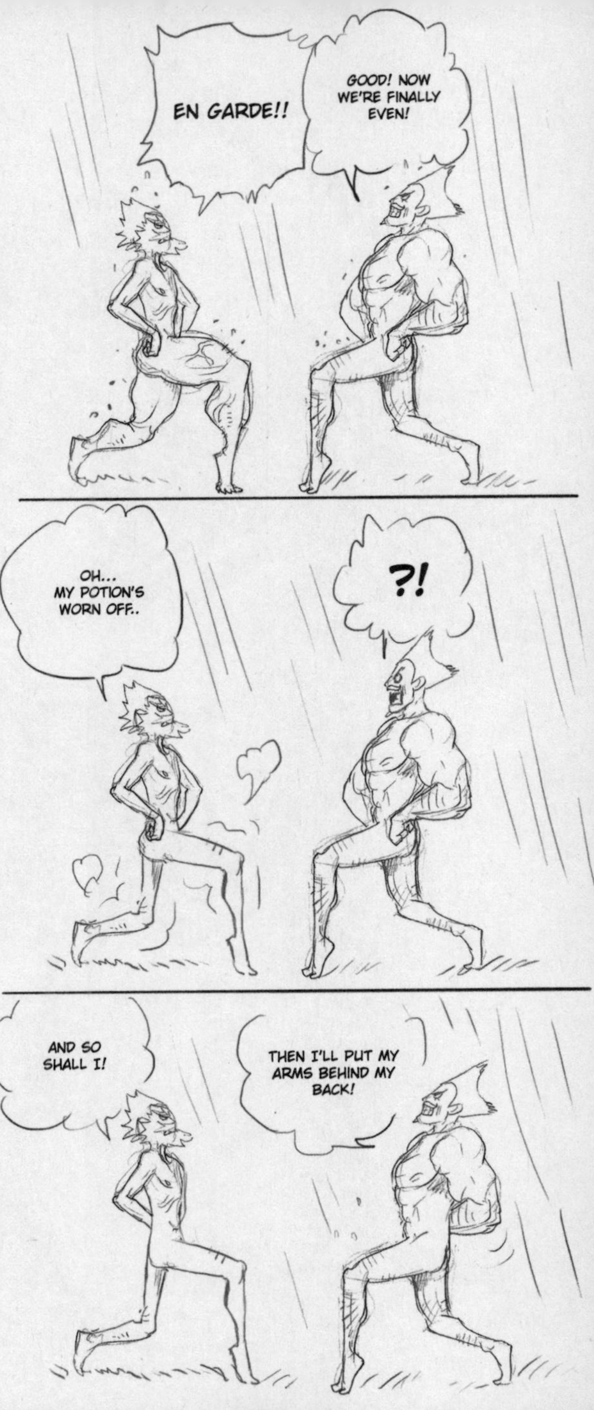
GOOD! NOW WE'RE FINALLY EVEN!
EN GARDE!!
?!
OH... MY POTION'S WORN OFF..
THEN I'LL PUT MY ARMS BEHIND MY BACK!
AND SO SHALL I!

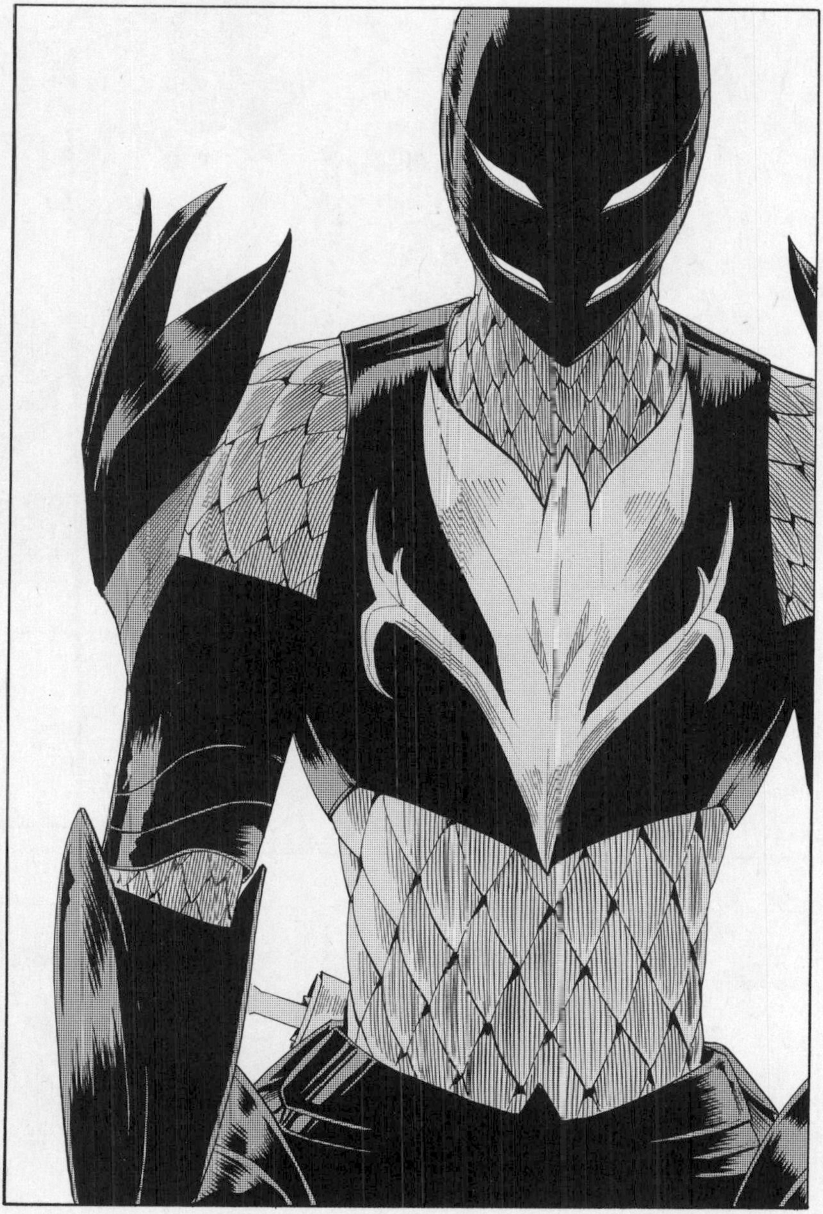

Chapter 65

Memory Stones

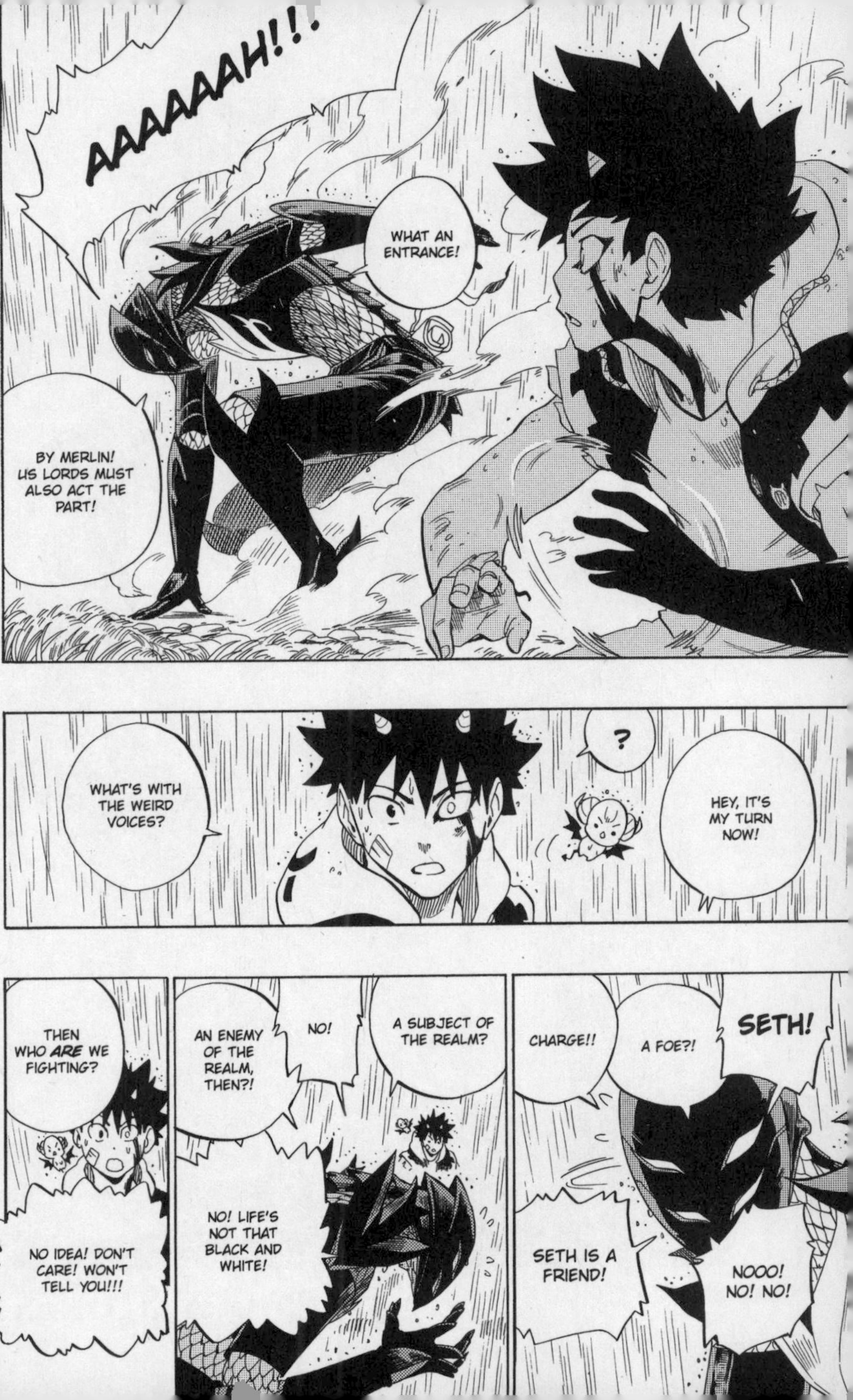
AAAAAAH!!!
WHAT AN ENTRANCE!
BY MERLIN! US LORDS MUST ALSO ACT THE PART!
HEY, IT'S MY TURN NOW!
?
WHAT'S WITH THE WEIRD VOICES?
SETH!
A FOE?!
CHARGE!!
NOOO! NO! NO!
SETH IS A FRIEND!
A SUBJECT OF THE REALM?
NO!
AN ENEMY OF THE REALM, THEN?!
NO! LIFE'S NOT THAT BLACK AND WHITE!
THEN WHO *ARE* WE FIGHTING?
NO IDEA! DON'T CARE! WON'T TELL YOU!!!

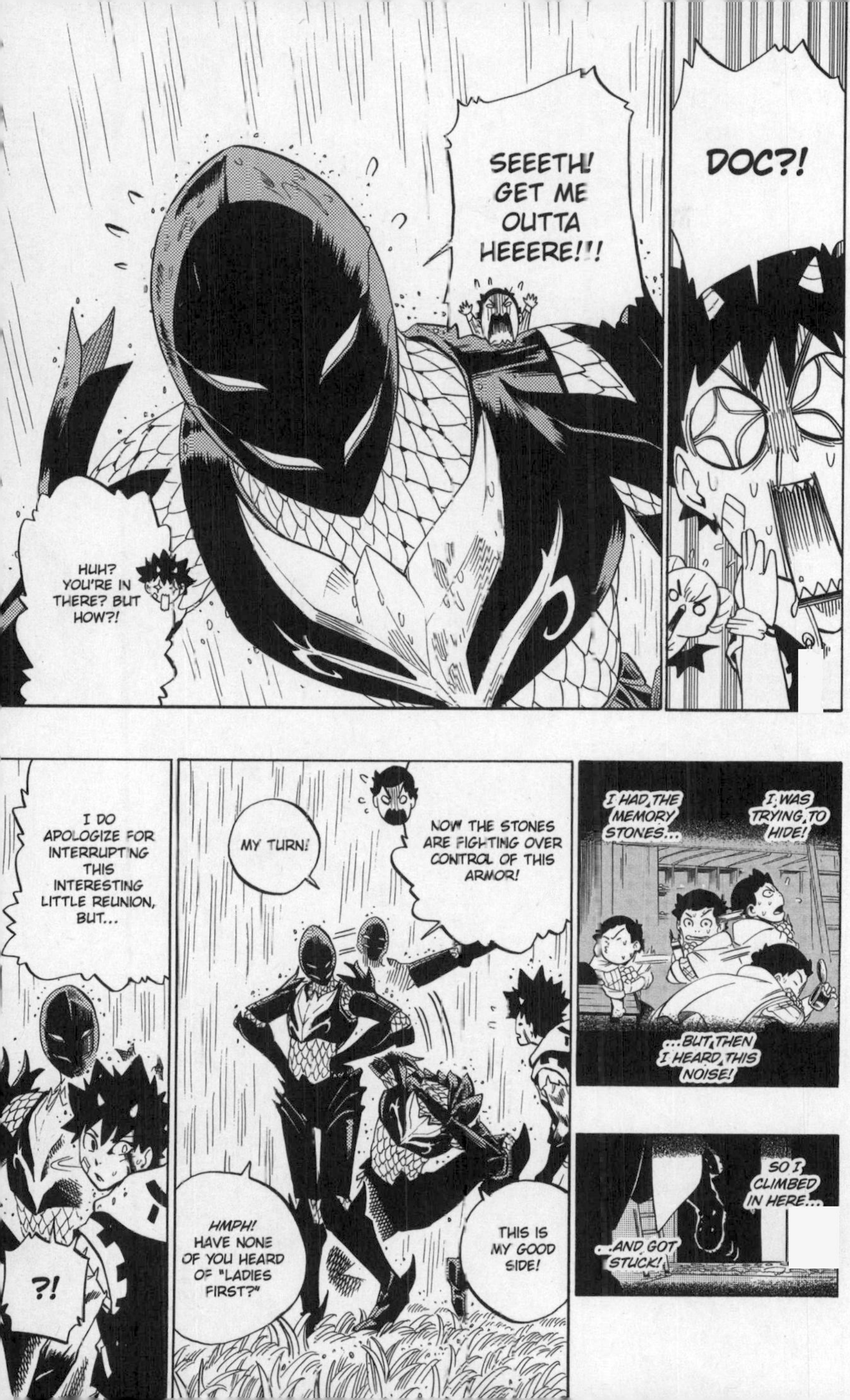
DOC?!
SEEETH! GET ME OUTTA HEEERE!!!
HUH? YOU'RE IN THERE? BUT HOW?!
I WAS TRYING TO HIDE!
I HAD THE MEMORY STONES...
...BUT THEN I HEARD THIS NOISE!
SO I CLIMBED IN HERE...
...AND GOT STUCK!
NOW THE STONES ARE FIGHTING OVER CONTROL OF THIS ARMOR!
MY TURN!
THIS IS MY GOOD SIDE!
HMPH! HAVE NONE OF YOU HEARD OF "LADIES FIRST?"
I DO APOLOGIZE FOR INTERRUPTING THIS INTERESTING LITTLE REUNION, BUT...
?!

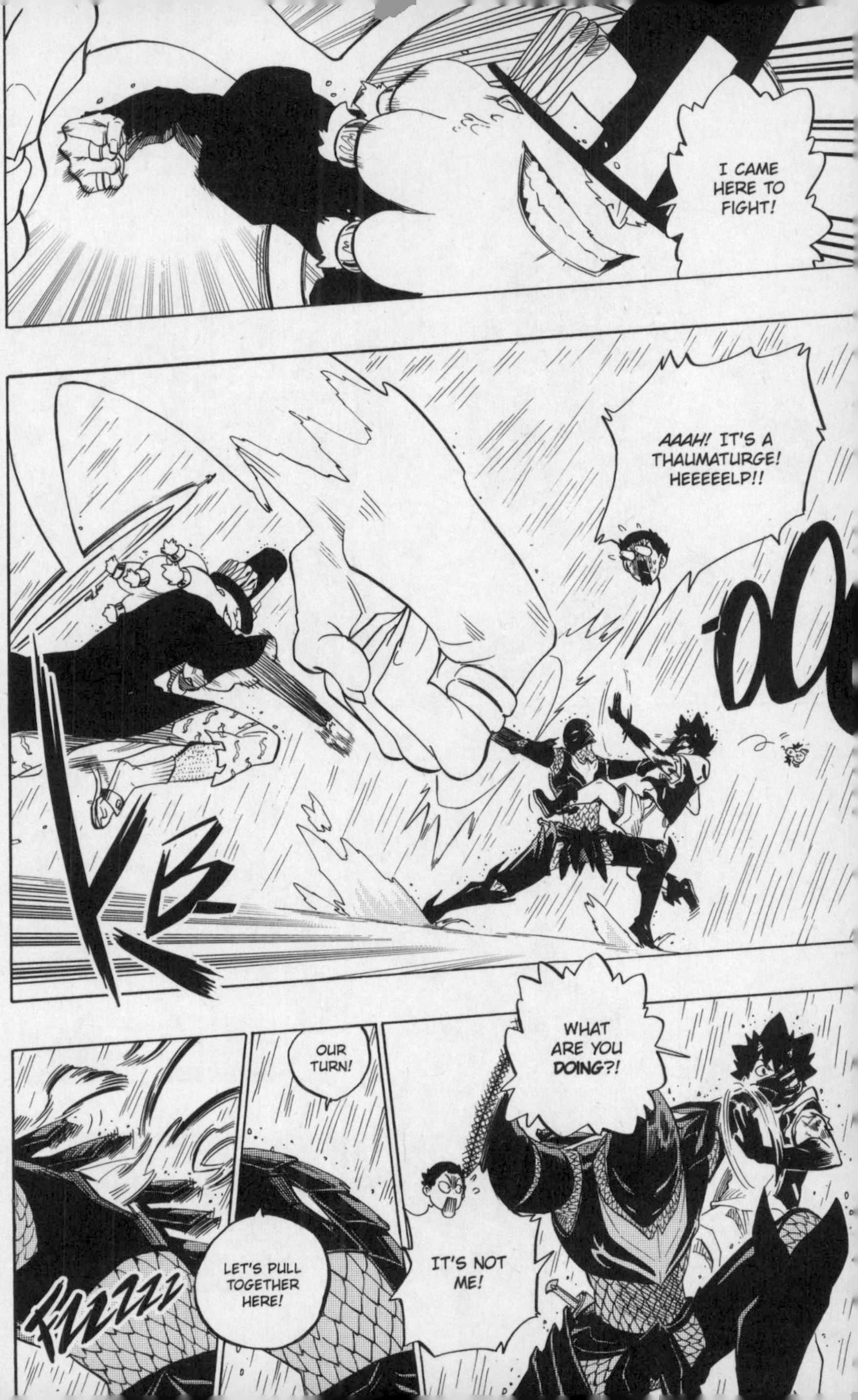
I CAME HERE TO FIGHT!
AAAH! IT'S A THAUMATURGE! HEEEEELP!!
WHAT ARE YOU **DOING**?!
IT'S NOT ME!
OUR TURN!
LET'S PULL TOGETHER HERE!

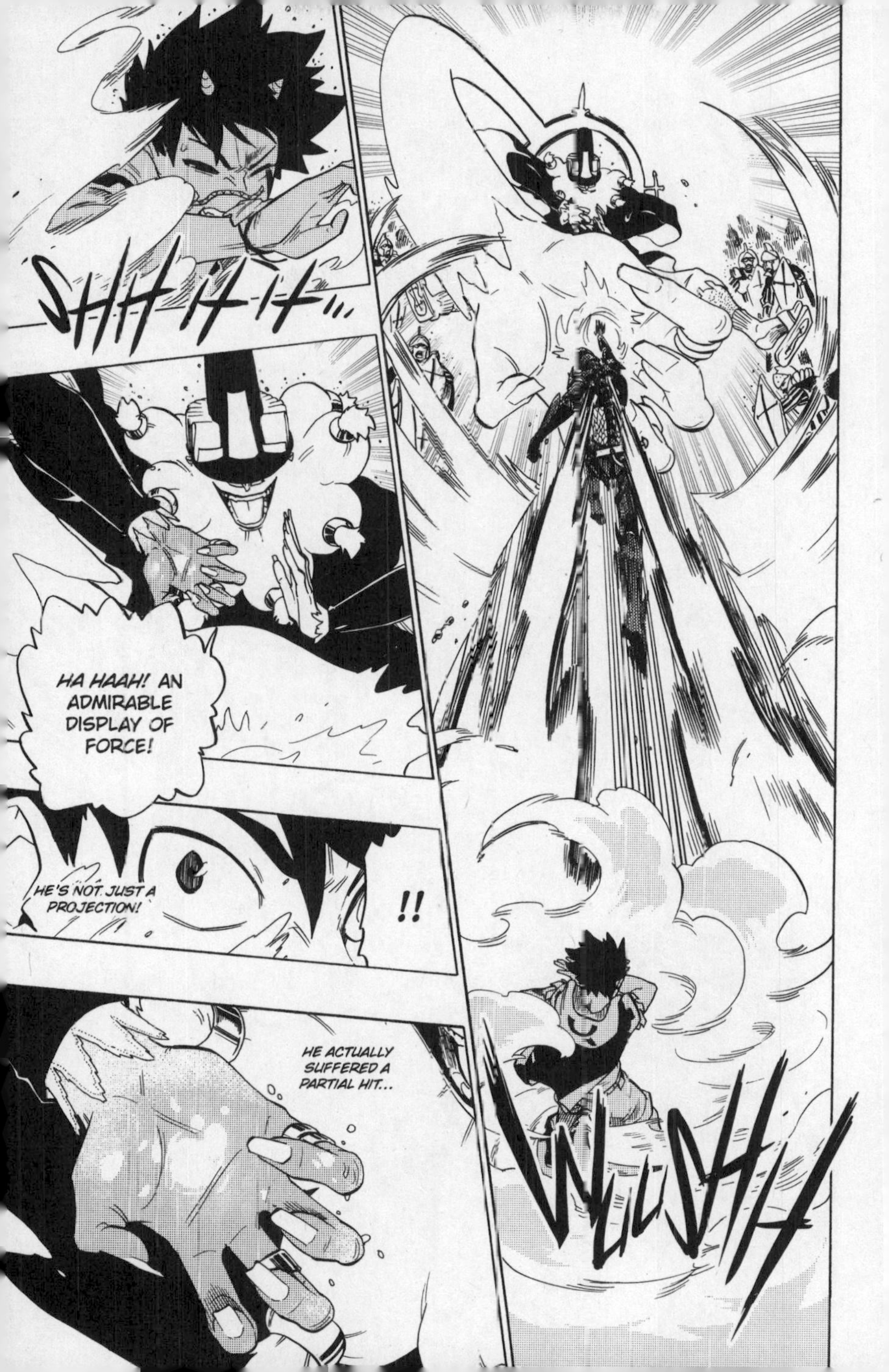
HA HAAH! AN ADMIRABLE DISPLAY OF FORCE!
HE'S NOT JUST A PROJECTION!
!!
HE ACTUALLY SUFFERED A PARTIAL HIT...

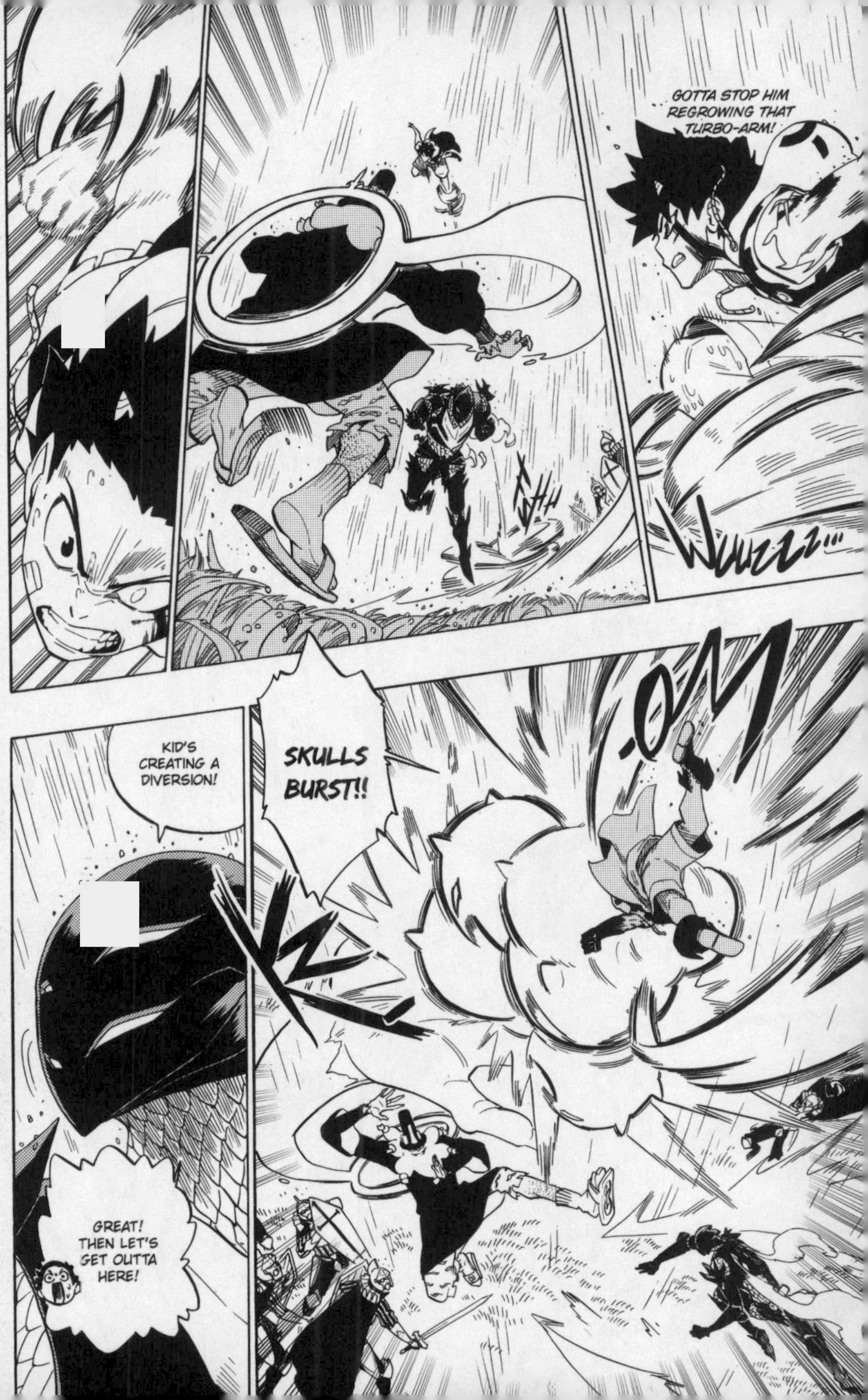
GOTTA STOP HIM REGROWING THAT TURBO-ARM!
WUUZZZ...
SKULLS BURST!!
KID'S CREATING A DIVERSION!
GREAT! THEN LET'S GET OUTTA HERE!

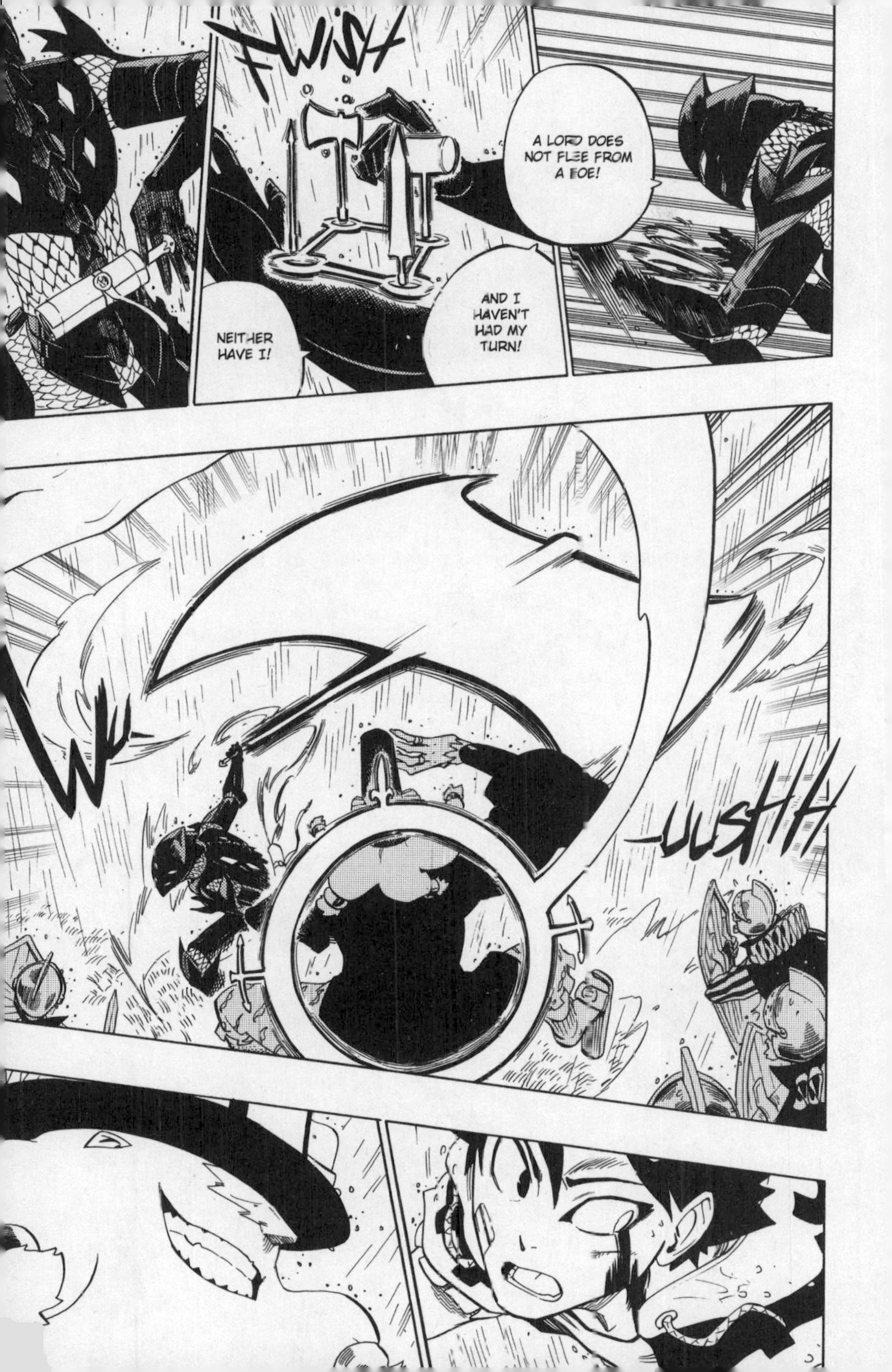
A LORD DOES NOT FLEE FROM A FOE!
FWISH
AND I HAVEN'T HAD MY TURN!
NEITHER HAVE I!
W
-UUSHH

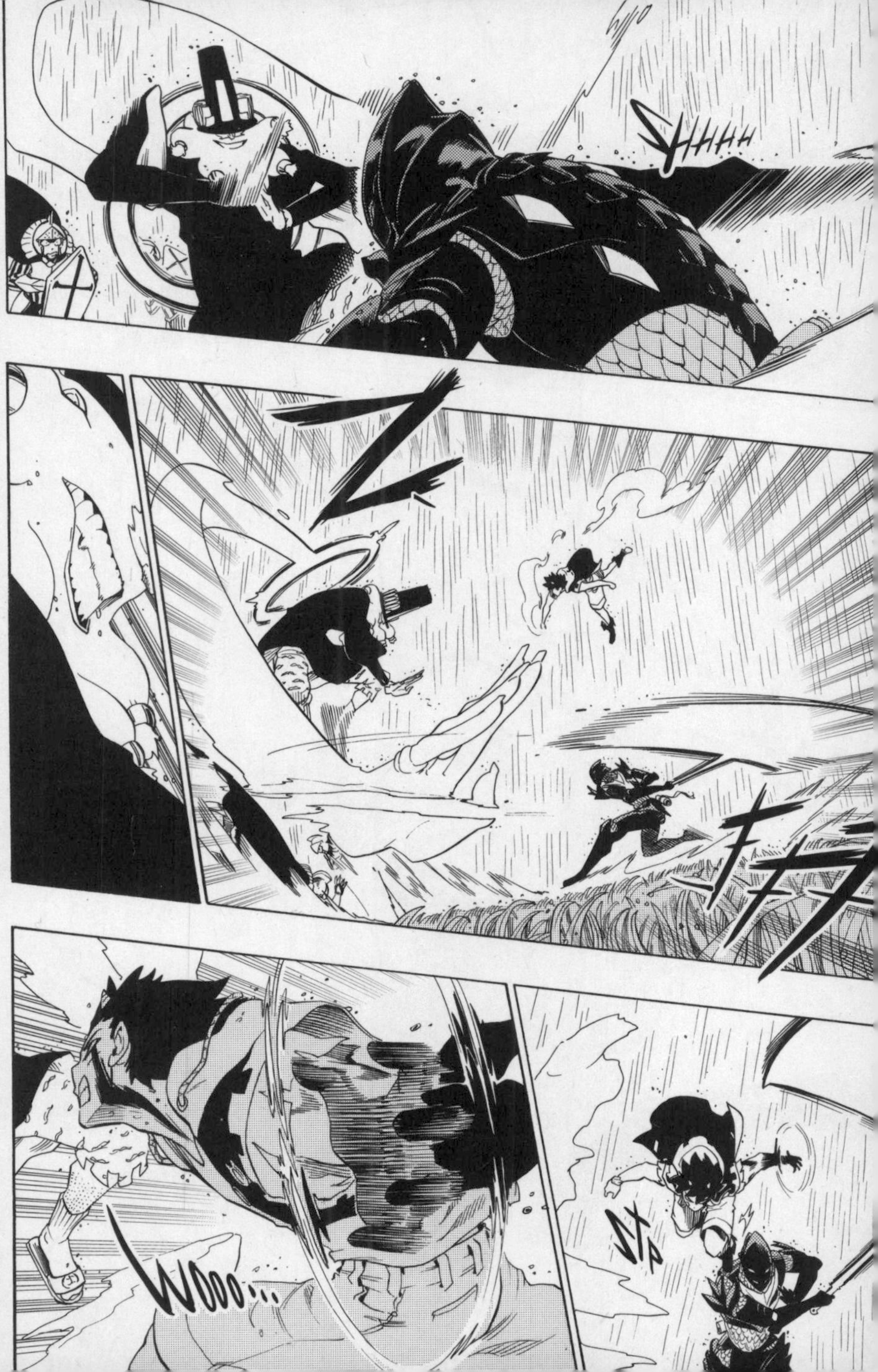
SHHHH
STP
WOOO...

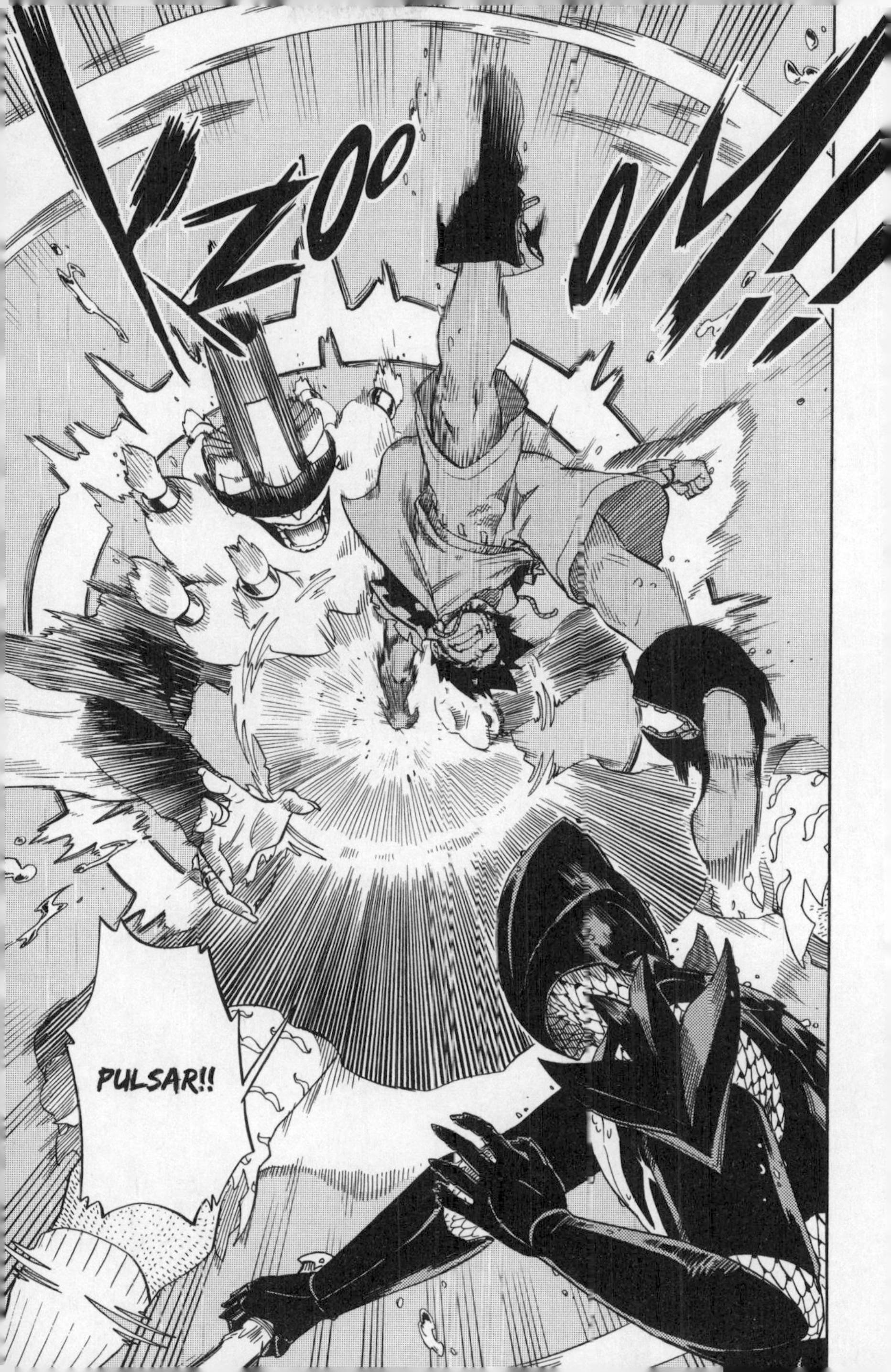
KZOOOOM!!
PULSAR!!

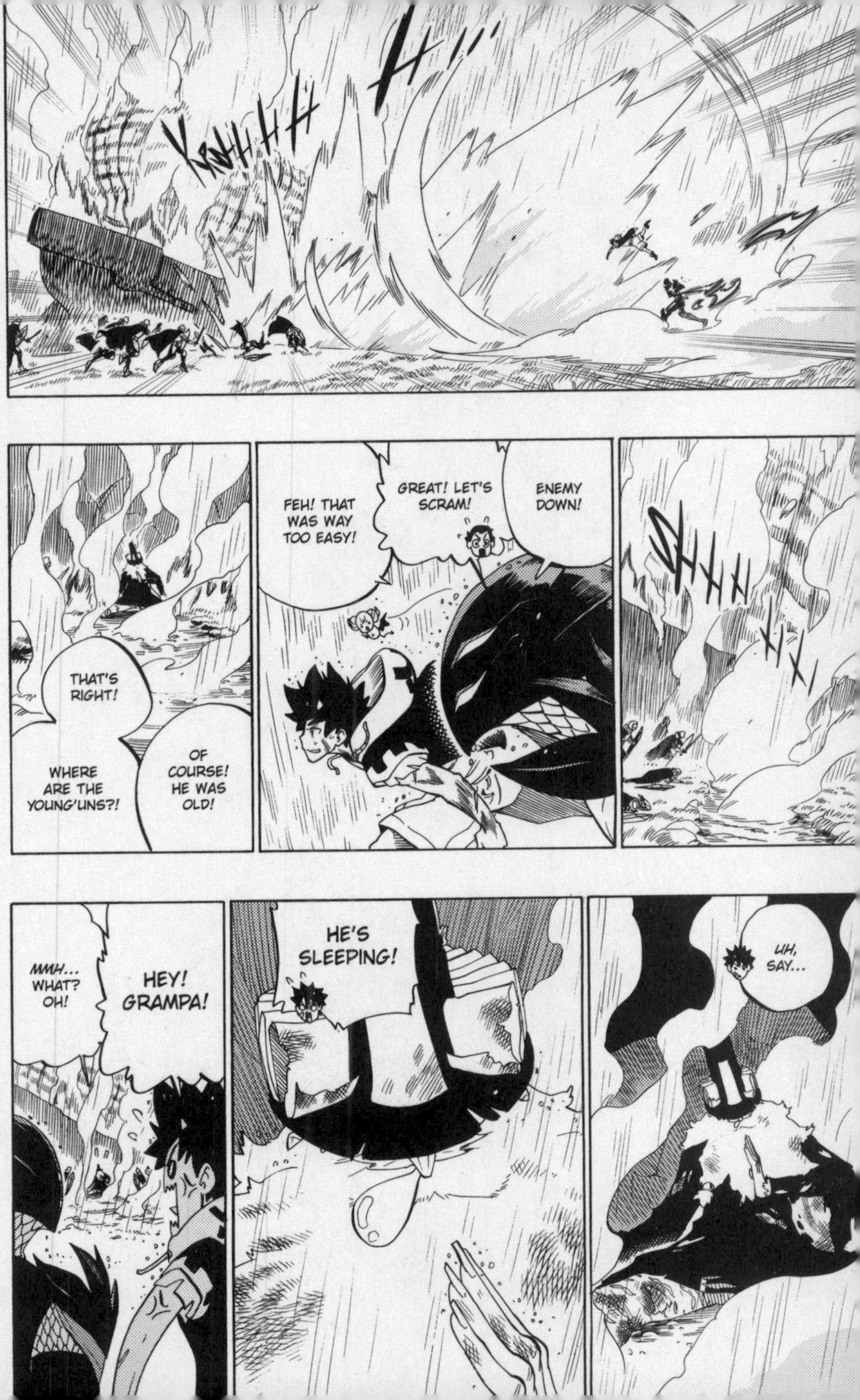
ENEMY DOWN!
GREAT! LET'S SCRAM!
FEH! THAT WAS WAY TOO EASY!
OF COURSE! HE WAS OLD!
THAT'S RIGHT!
WHERE ARE THE YOUNG'UNS?!
UH, SAY...
HE'S SLEEPING!
HEY! GRAMPA!
MMH... WHAT? OH!

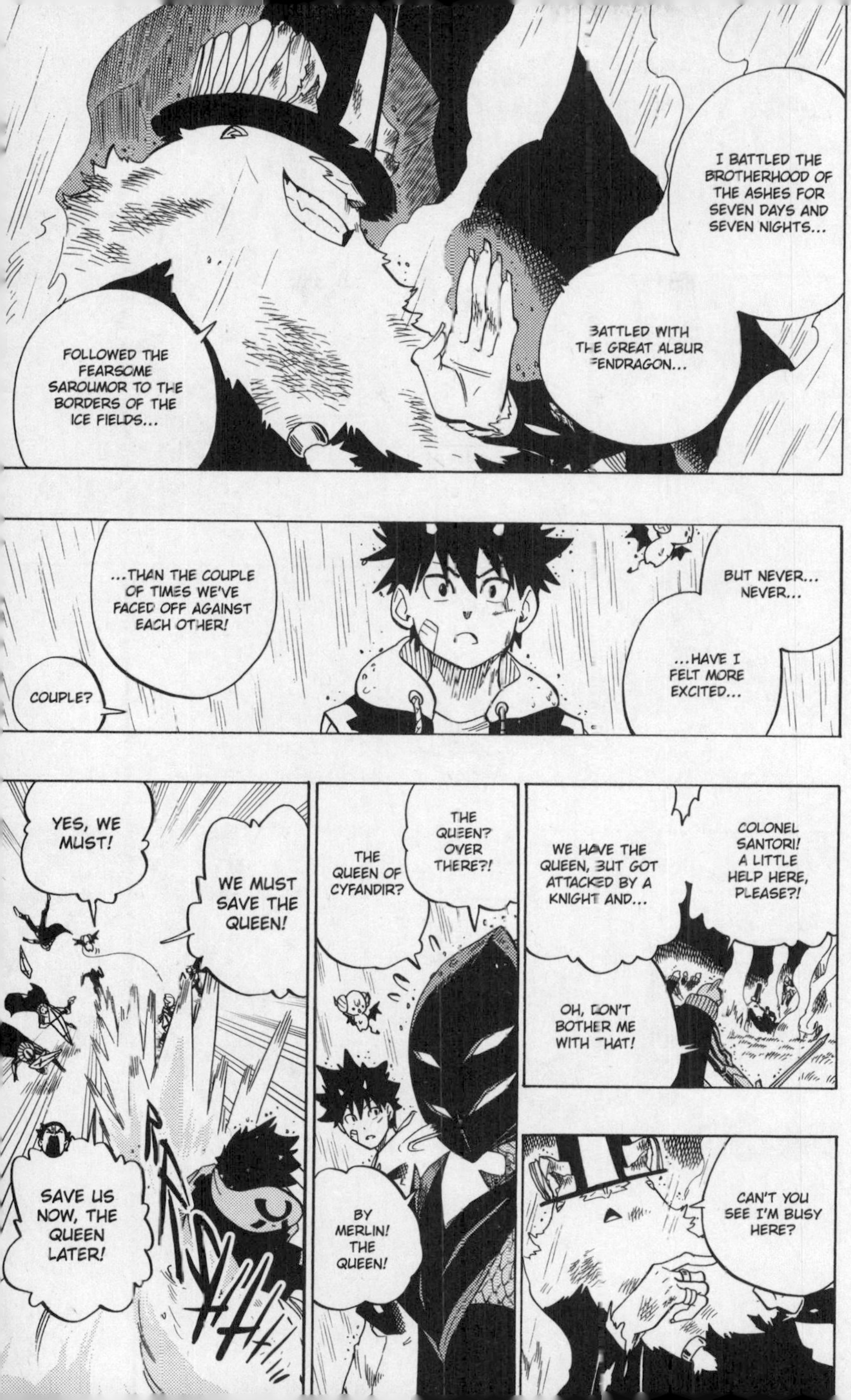
I BATTLED THE BROTHERHOOD OF THE ASHES FOR SEVEN DAYS AND SEVEN NIGHTS...
BATTLED WITH THE GREAT ALBUR PENDRAGON...
FOLLOWED THE FEARSOME SAROUMOR TO THE BORDERS OF THE ICE FIELDS...
BUT NEVER... NEVER...
...HAVE I FELT MORE EXCITED...
...THAN THE COUPLE OF TIMES WE'VE FACED OFF AGAINST EACH OTHER!
COUPLE?
COLONEL SANTORI! A LITTLE HELP HERE, PLEASE?!
WE HAVE THE QUEEN, BUT GOT ATTACKED BY A KNIGHT AND...
OH, DON'T BOTHER ME WITH THAT!
CAN'T YOU SEE I'M BUSY HERE?
THE QUEEN? OVER THERE?!
THE QUEEN OF CYFANDIR?
BY MERLIN! THE QUEEN!
WE MUST SAVE THE QUEEN!
YES, WE MUST!
SAVE US NOW, THE QUEEN LATER!

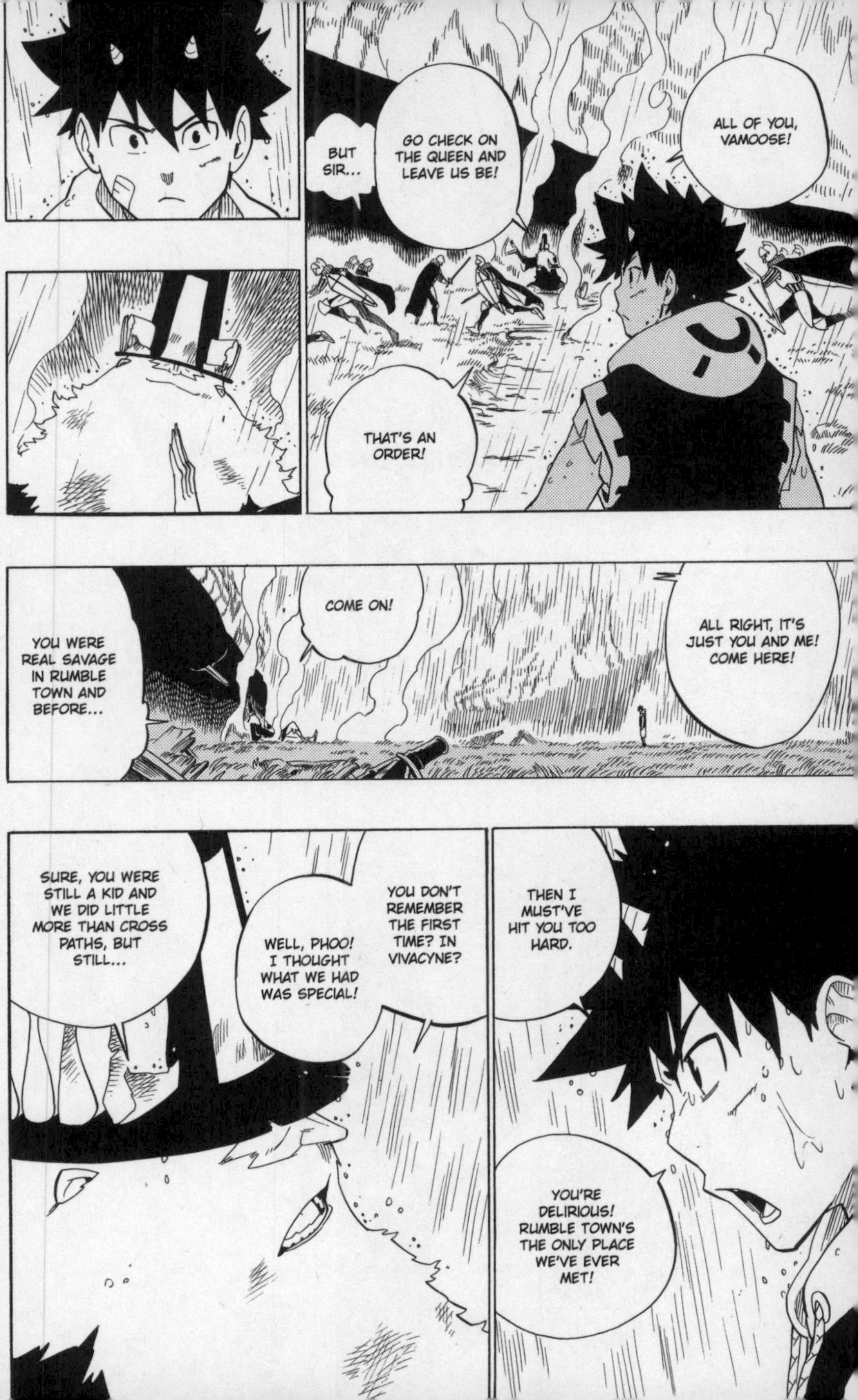
ALL OF YOU, VAMOOSE!
GO CHECK ON THE QUEEN AND LEAVE US BE!
BUT SIR...
THAT'S AN ORDER!
ALL RIGHT, IT'S JUST YOU AND ME! COME HERE!
COME ON!
YOU WERE REAL SAVAGE IN RUMBLE TOWN AND BEFORE...
THEN I MUST'VE HIT YOU TOO HARD.
YOU'RE DELIRIOUS! RUMBLE TOWN'S THE ONLY PLACE WE'VE EVER MET!
YOU DON'T REMEMBER THE FIRST TIME? IN VIVACYNE?
WELL, PHOO! I THOUGHT WHAT WE HAD WAS SPECIAL!
SURE, YOU WERE STILL A KID AND WE DID LITTLE MORE THAN CROSS PATHS, BUT STILL...

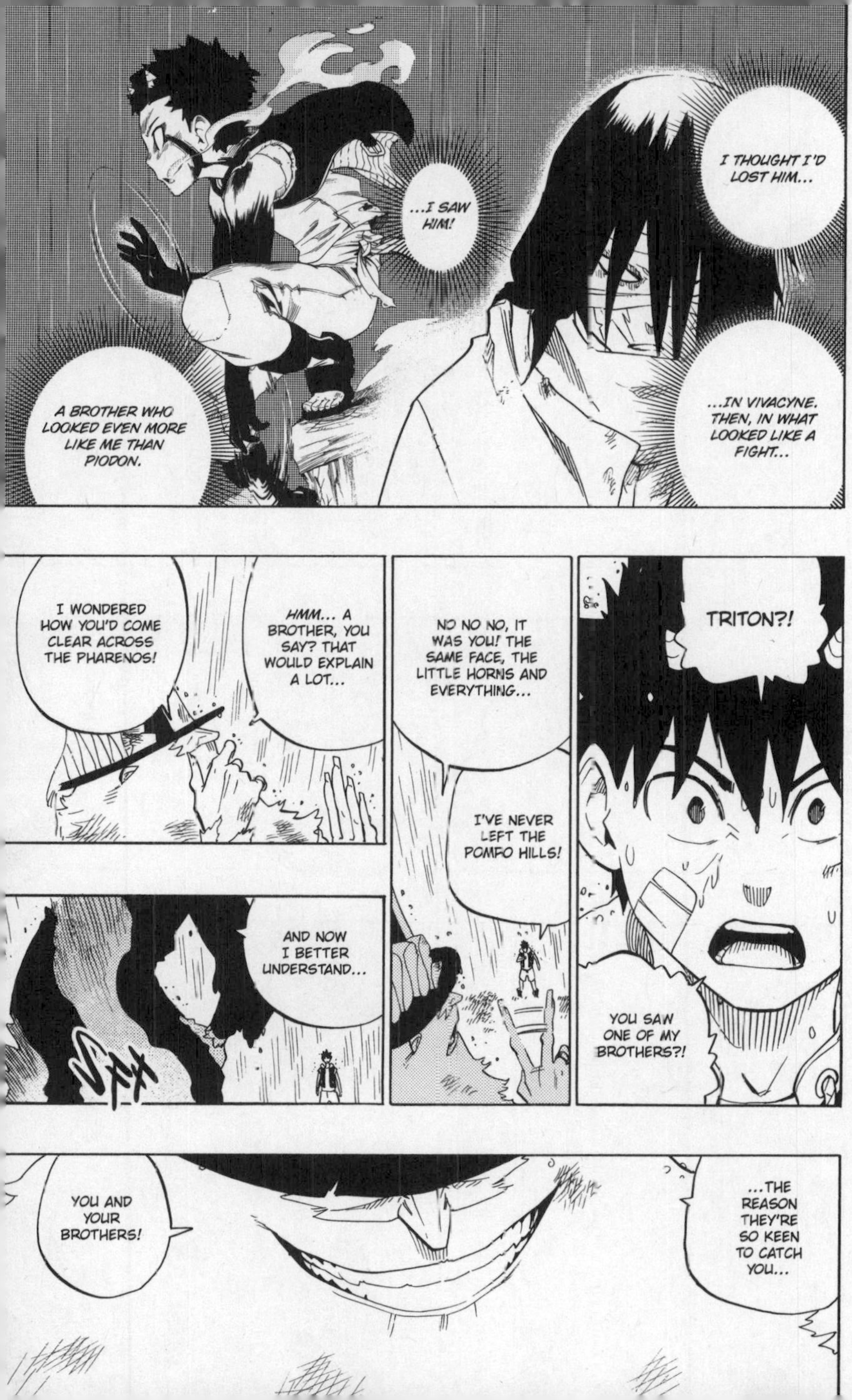
I THOUGHT I'D LOST HIM...
...IN VIVACYNE. THEN, IN WHAT LOOKED LIKE A FIGHT...
...I SAW HIM!
A BROTHER WHO LOOKED EVEN MORE LIKE ME THAN PIODON.
TRITON?!
YOU SAW ONE OF MY BROTHERS?!
NO NO NO, IT WAS YOU! THE SAME FACE, THE LITTLE HORNS AND EVERYTHING...
I'VE NEVER LEFT THE POMFO HILLS!
HMM... A BROTHER, YOU SAY? THAT WOULD EXPLAIN A LOT...
I WONDERED HOW YOU'D COME CLEAR ACROSS THE PHARENOS!
AND NOW I BETTER UNDERSTAND...
...THE REASON THEY'RE SO KEEN TO CATCH YOU...
YOU AND YOUR BROTHERS!

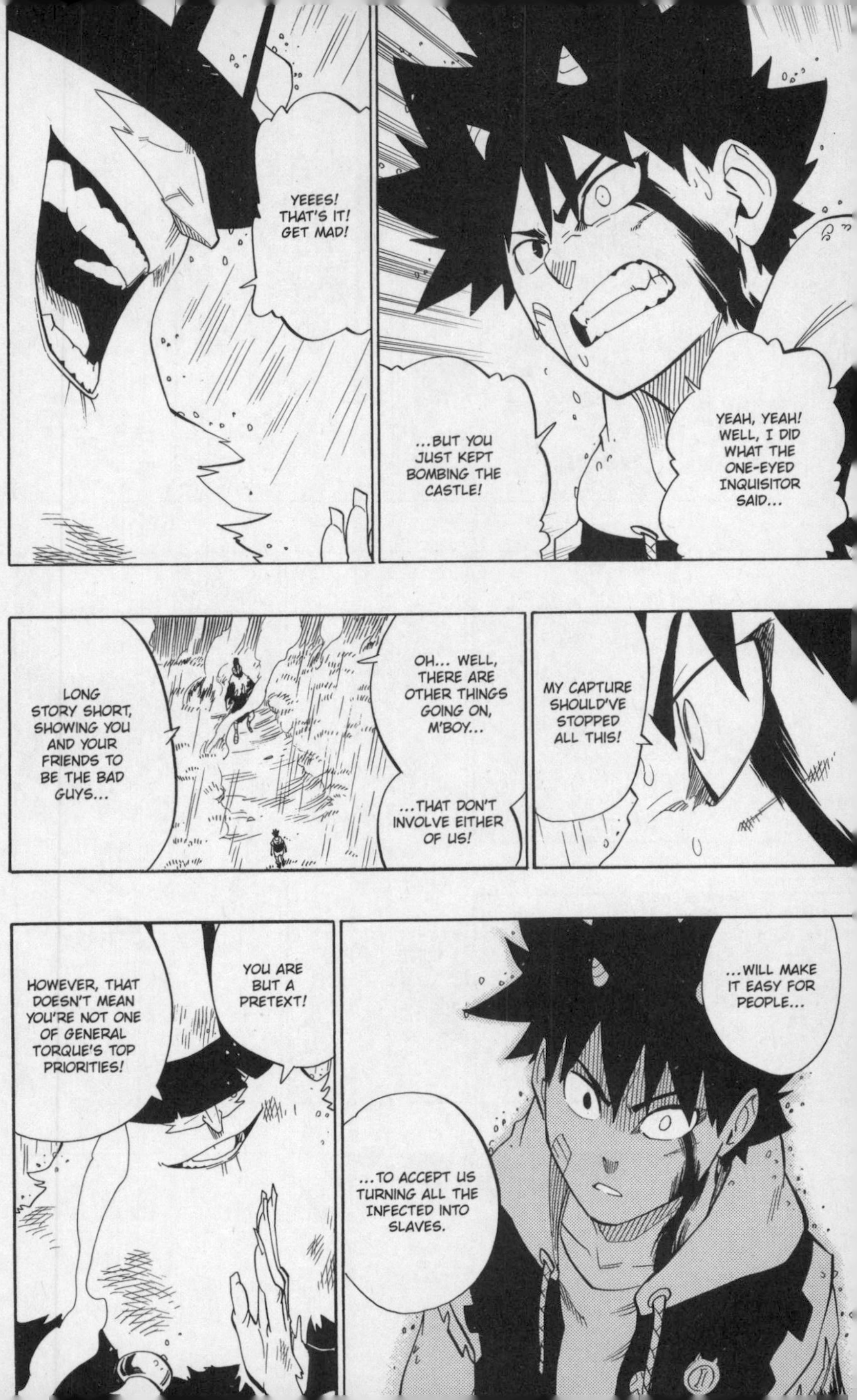
YEAH, YEAH! WELL, I DID WHAT THE ONE-EYED INQUISITOR SAID...
...BUT YOU JUST KEPT BOMBING THE CASTLE!
YEEES! THAT'S IT! GET MAD!
MY CAPTURE SHOULD'VE STOPPED ALL THIS!
OH... WELL, THERE ARE OTHER THINGS GOING ON, M'BOY...
...THAT DON'T INVOLVE EITHER OF US!
LONG STORY SHORT, SHOWING YOU AND YOUR FRIENDS TO BE THE BAD GUYS...
...WILL MAKE IT EASY FOR PEOPLE...
...TO ACCEPT US TURNING ALL THE INFECTED INTO SLAVES.
YOU ARE BUT A PRETEXT!
HOWEVER, THAT DOESN'T MEAN YOU'RE NOT ONE OF GENERAL TORQUE'S TOP PRIORITIES!

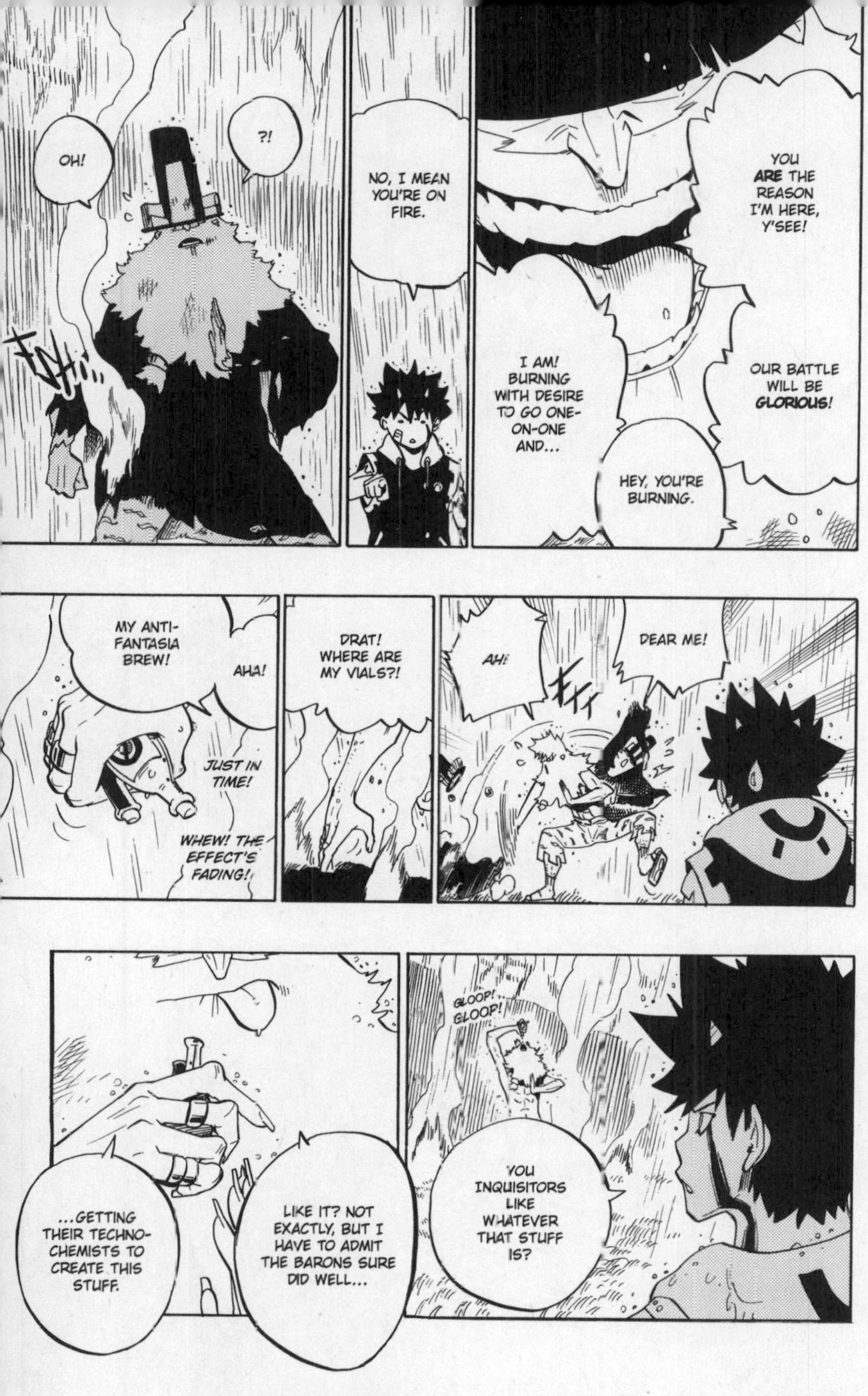
YOU ARE THE REASON I'M HERE, Y'SEE!
OUR BATTLE WILL BE GLORIOUS!
I AM! BURNING WITH DESIRE TO GO ONE-ON-ONE AND...
HEY, YOU'RE BURNING.
NO, I MEAN YOU'RE ON FIRE.
?!
OH!
DEAR ME!
AH!
DRAT! WHERE ARE MY VIALS?!
AHA!
MY ANTI-FANTASIA BREW!
JUST IN TIME!
WHEW! THE EFFECT'S FADING!
GLOOP! GLOOP!
YOU INQUISITORS LIKE WHATEVER THAT STUFF IS?
LIKE IT? NOT EXACTLY, BUT I HAVE TO ADMIT THE BARONS SURE DID WELL...
...GETTING THEIR TECHNO-CHEMISTS TO CREATE THIS STUFF.

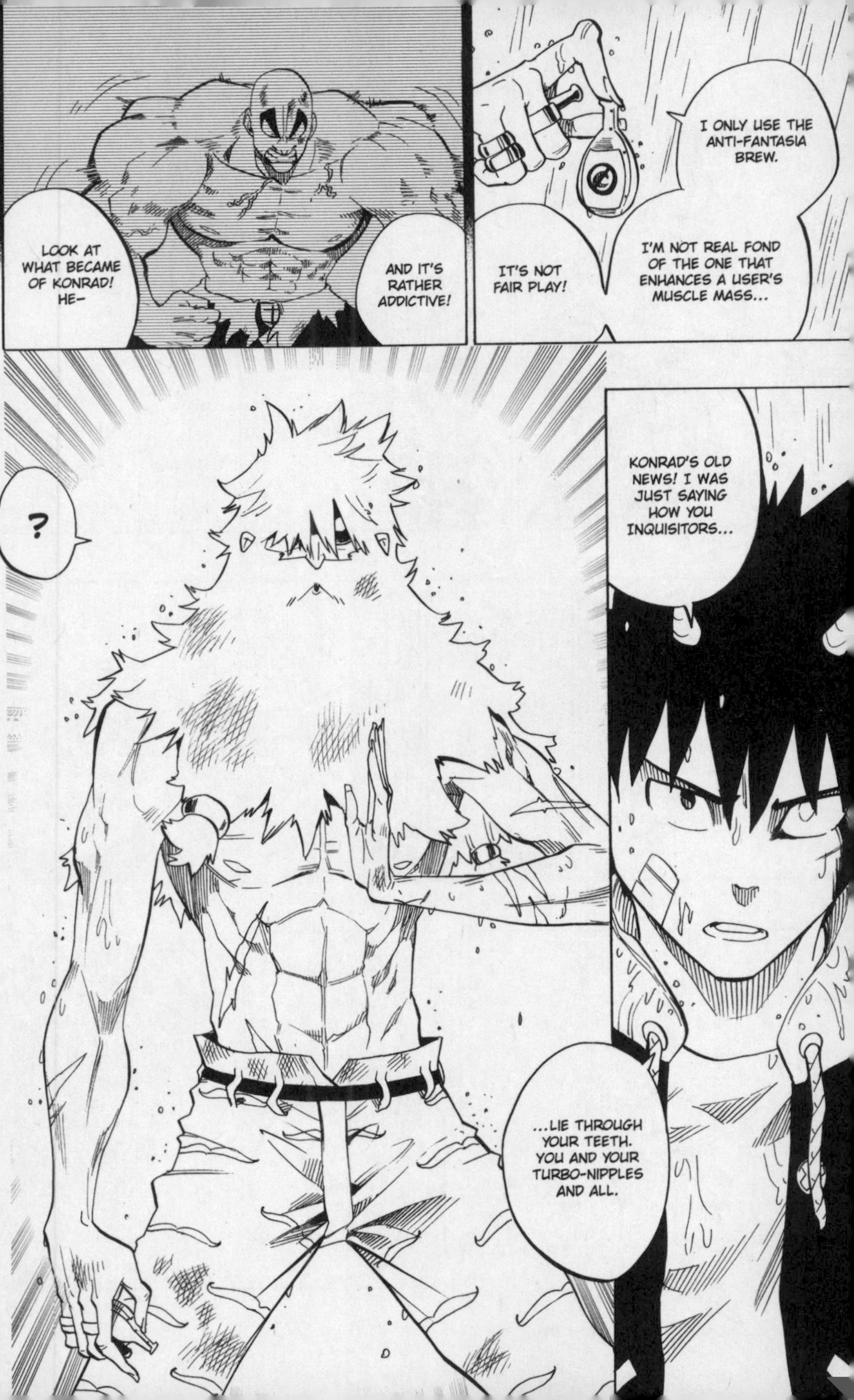
I ONLY USE THE ANTI-FANTASIA BREW.
I'M NOT REAL FOND OF THE ONE THAT ENHANCES A USER'S MUSCLE MASS...
IT'S NOT FAIR PLAY!
AND IT'S RATHER ADDICTIVE!
LOOK AT WHAT BECAME OF KONRAD! HE-
KONRAD'S OLD NEWS! I WAS JUST SAYING HOW YOU INQUISITORS...
...LIE THROUGH YOUR TEETH. YOU AND YOUR TURBO-NIPPLES AND ALL.
?

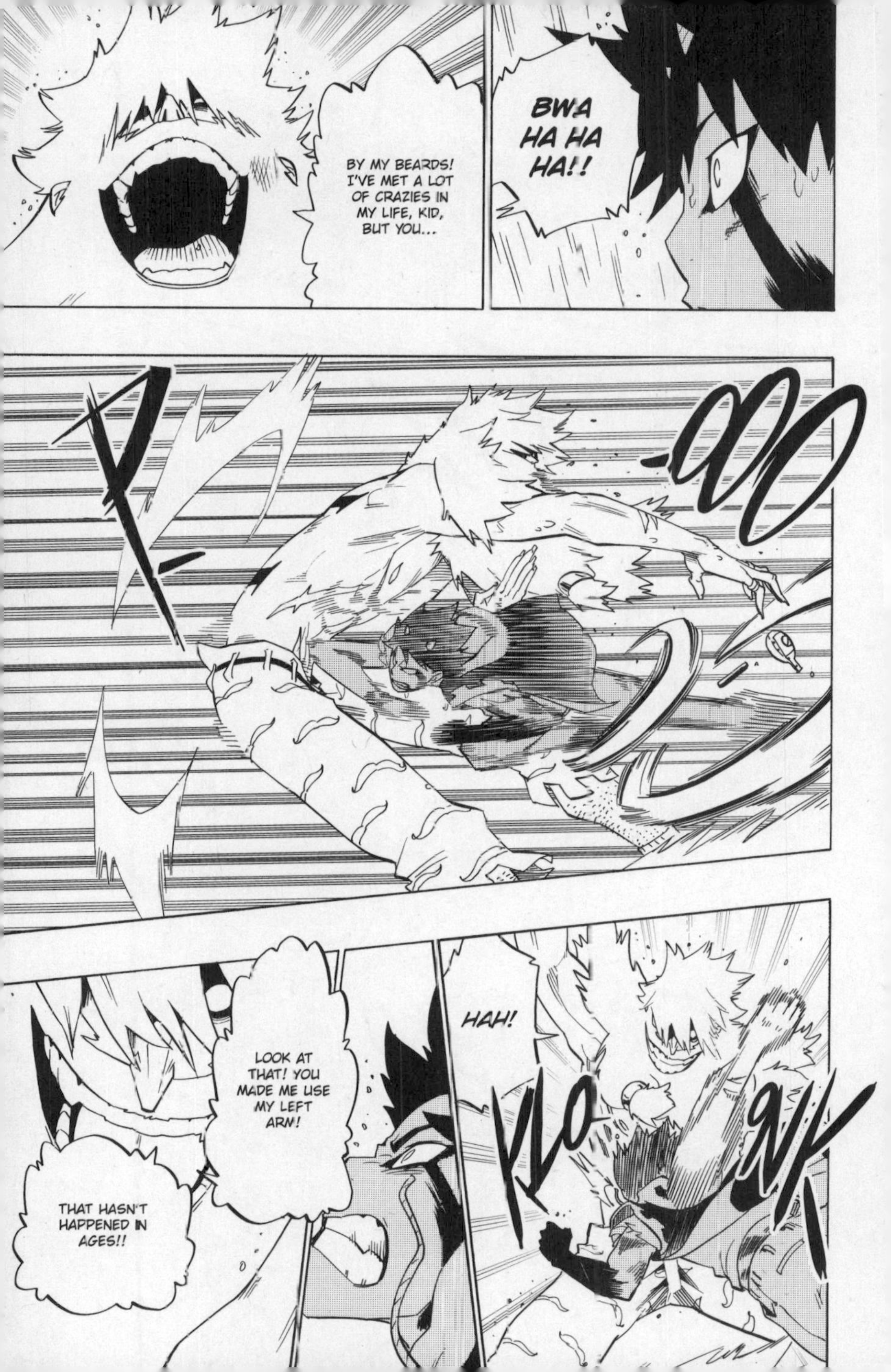
BWA HA HA HA!!
BY MY BEARDS! I'VE MET A LOT OF CRAZIES IN MY LIFE, KID, BUT YOU...
HAH!
LOOK AT THAT! YOU MADE ME USE MY LEFT ARM!
THAT HASN'T HAPPENED IN AGES!!

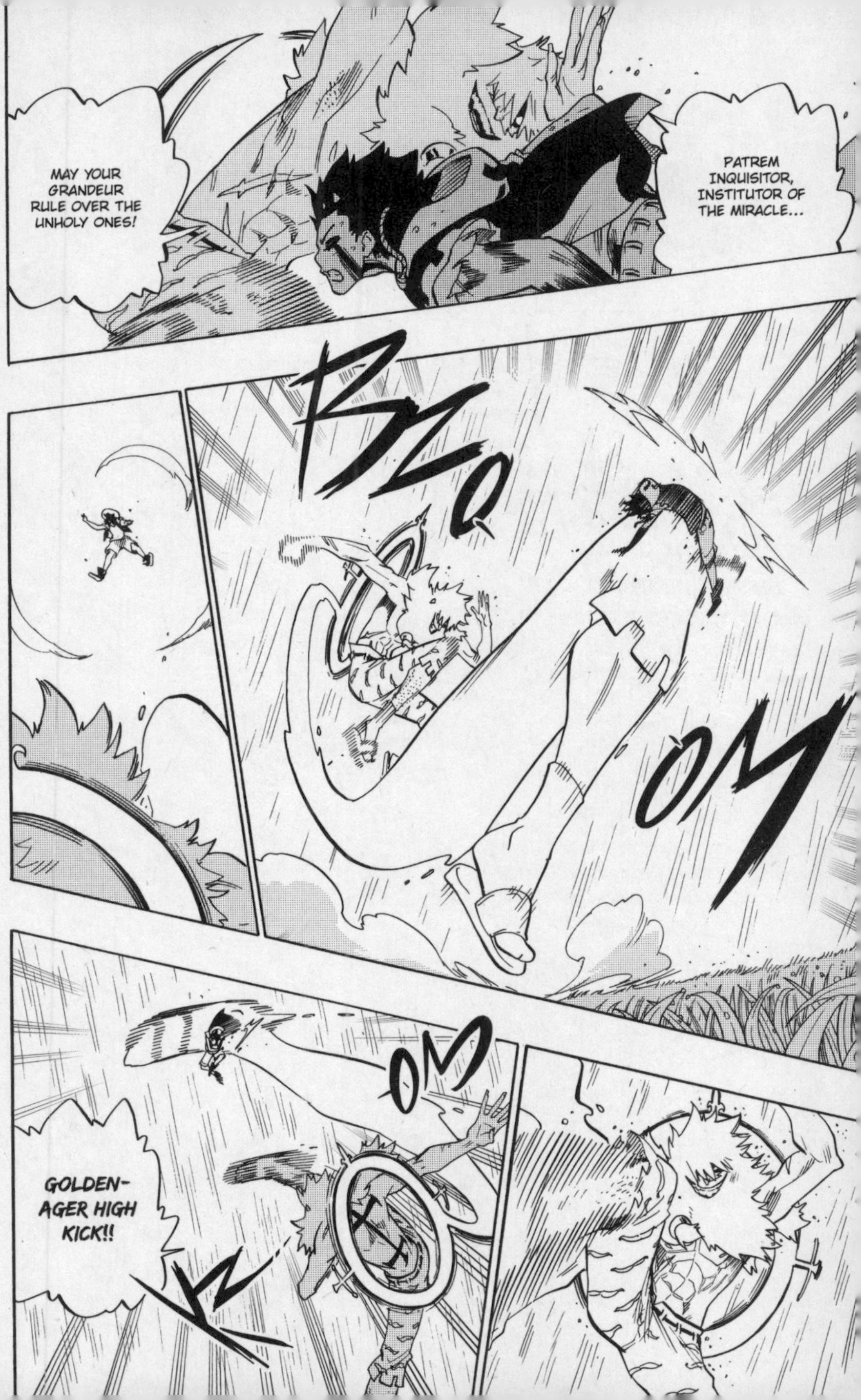
PATREM INQUISITOR, INSTITUTOR OF THE MIRACLE...
MAY YOUR GRANDEUR RULE OVER THE UNHOLY ONES!
GOLDEN-AGER HIGH KICK!!

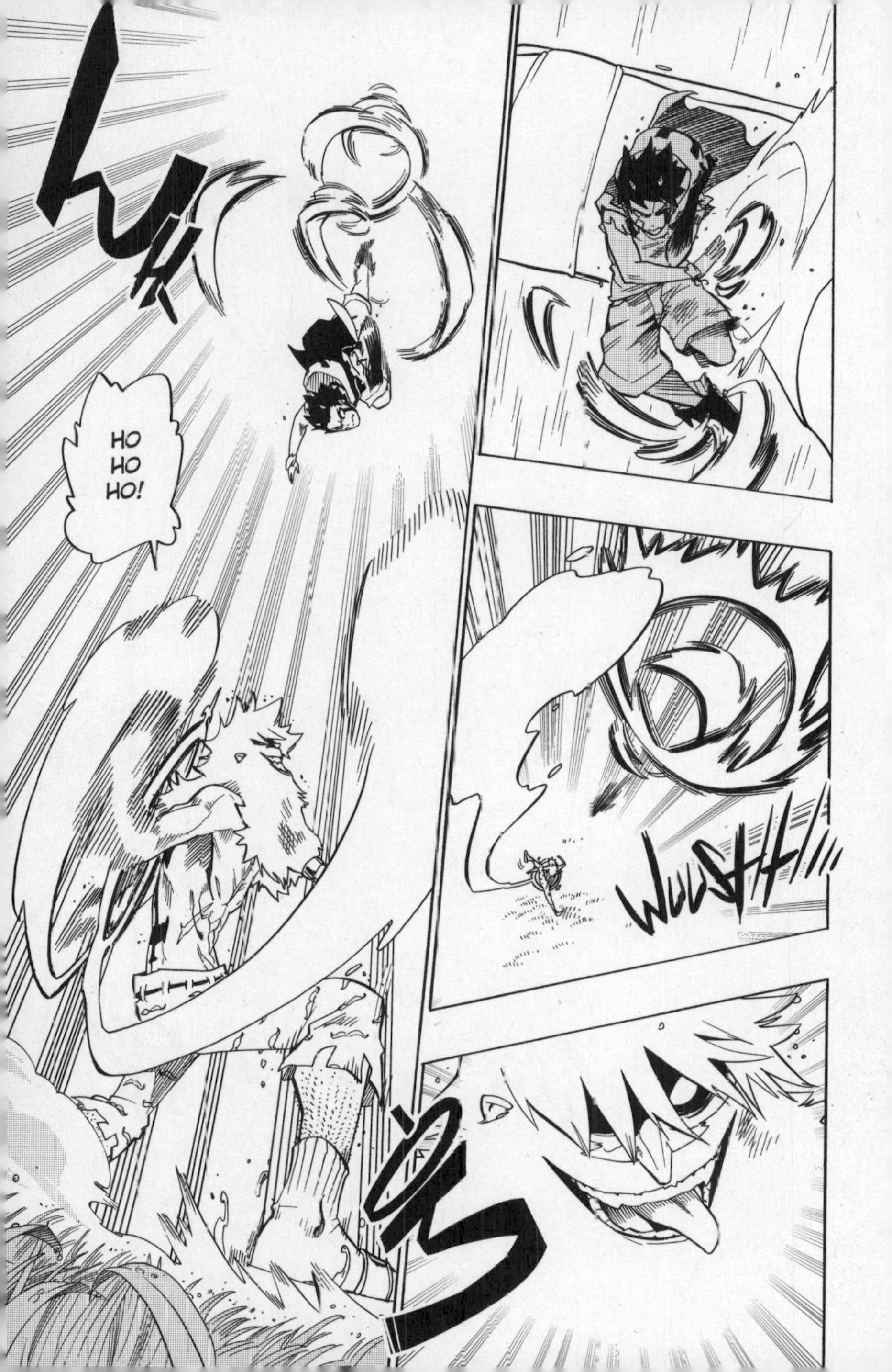
WUSHH!!
HO HO HO!

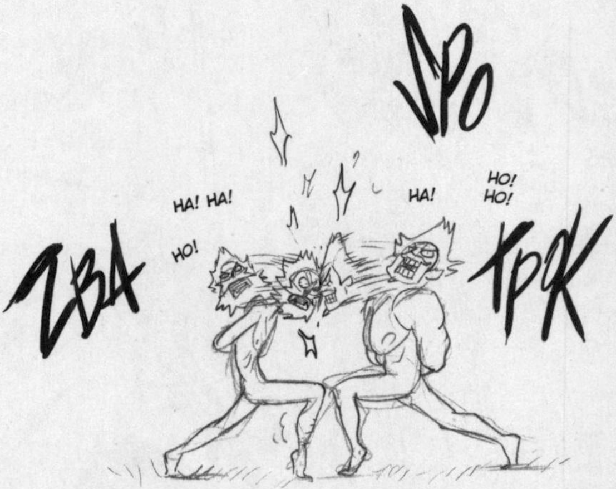
HO! HO!
HA!
HA! HA!
HO!
ZBA

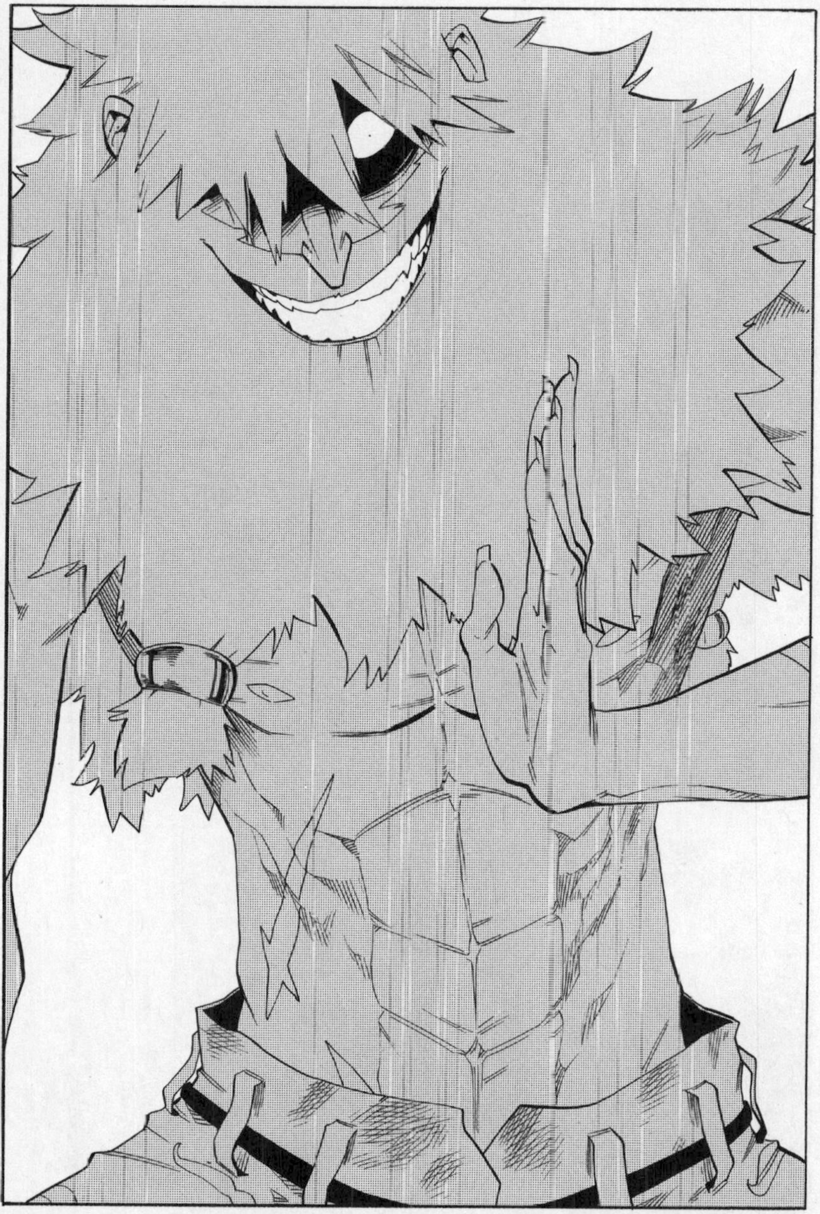

Chapter 66

The Armor of Pen Draig

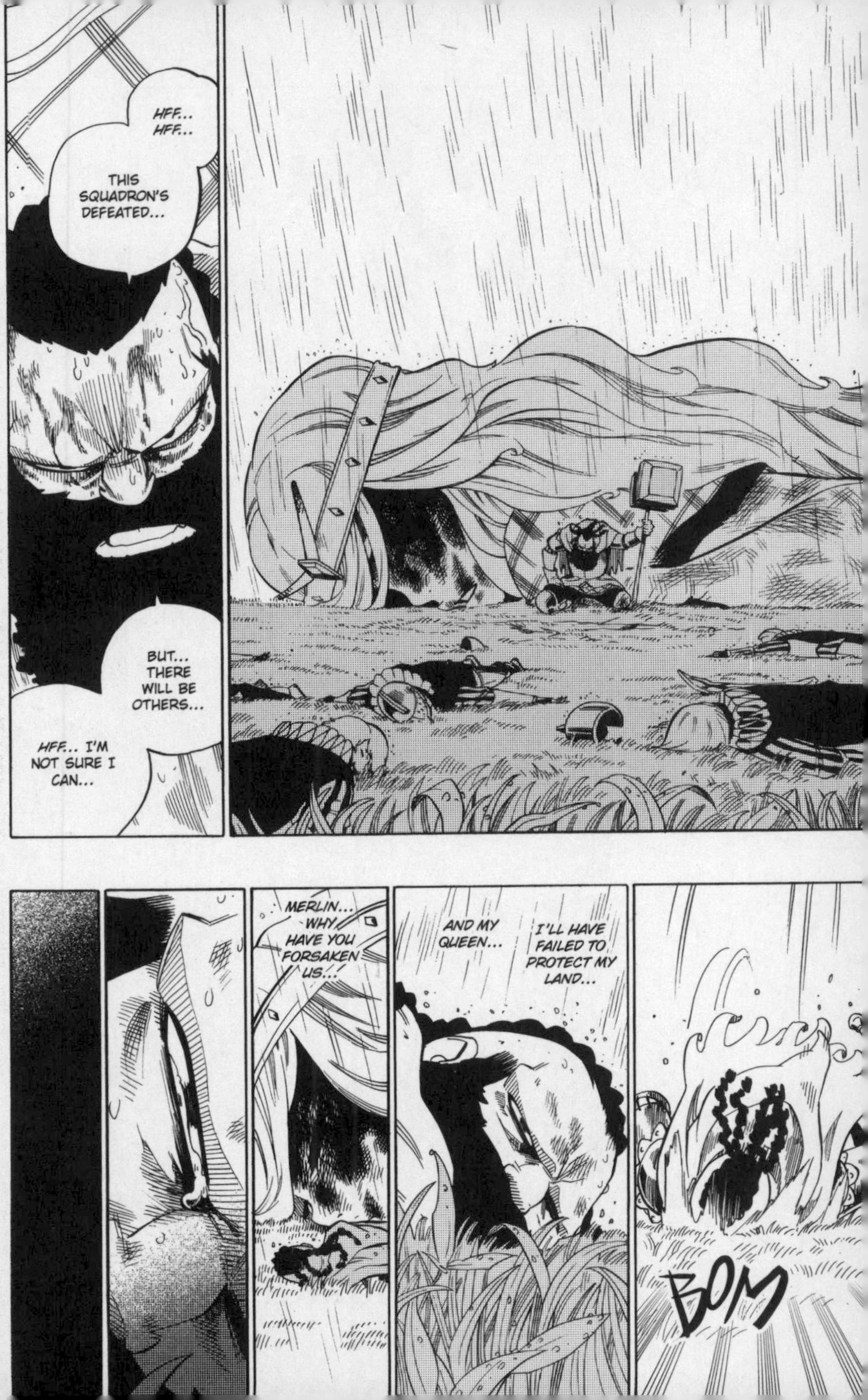
HFF... HFF...
THIS SQUADRON'S DEFEATED...
BUT... THERE WILL BE OTHERS...
HFF... I'M NOT SURE I CAN...
BOM
I'LL HAVE FAILED TO PROTECT MY LAND...
AND MY QUEEN...
MERLIN... WHY HAVE YOU FORSAKEN US...!

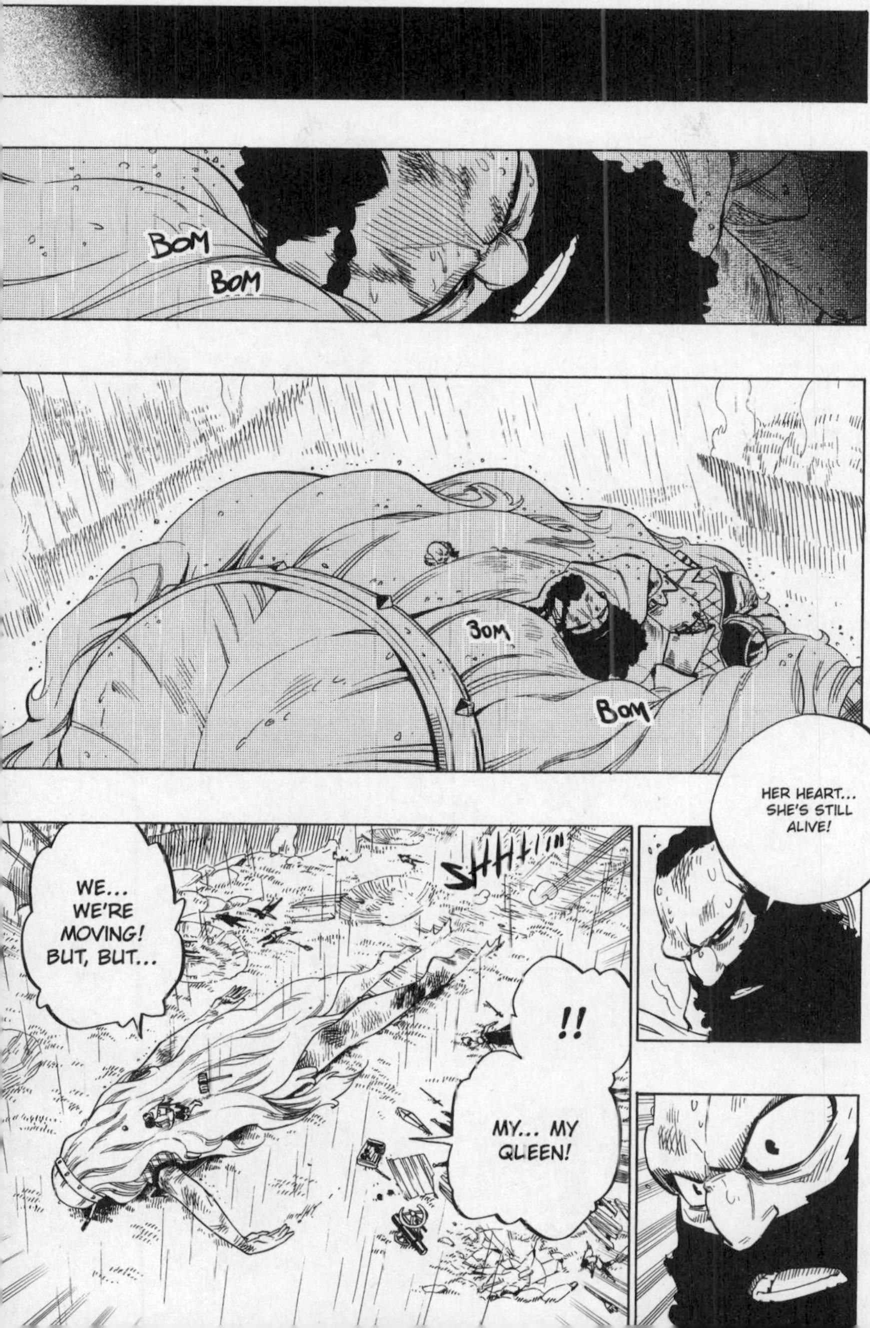
BOM
BOM
BOM
BOM
HER HEART... SHE'S STILL ALIVE!
!!
MY... MY QUEEN!
WE... WE'RE MOVING! BUT, BUT...

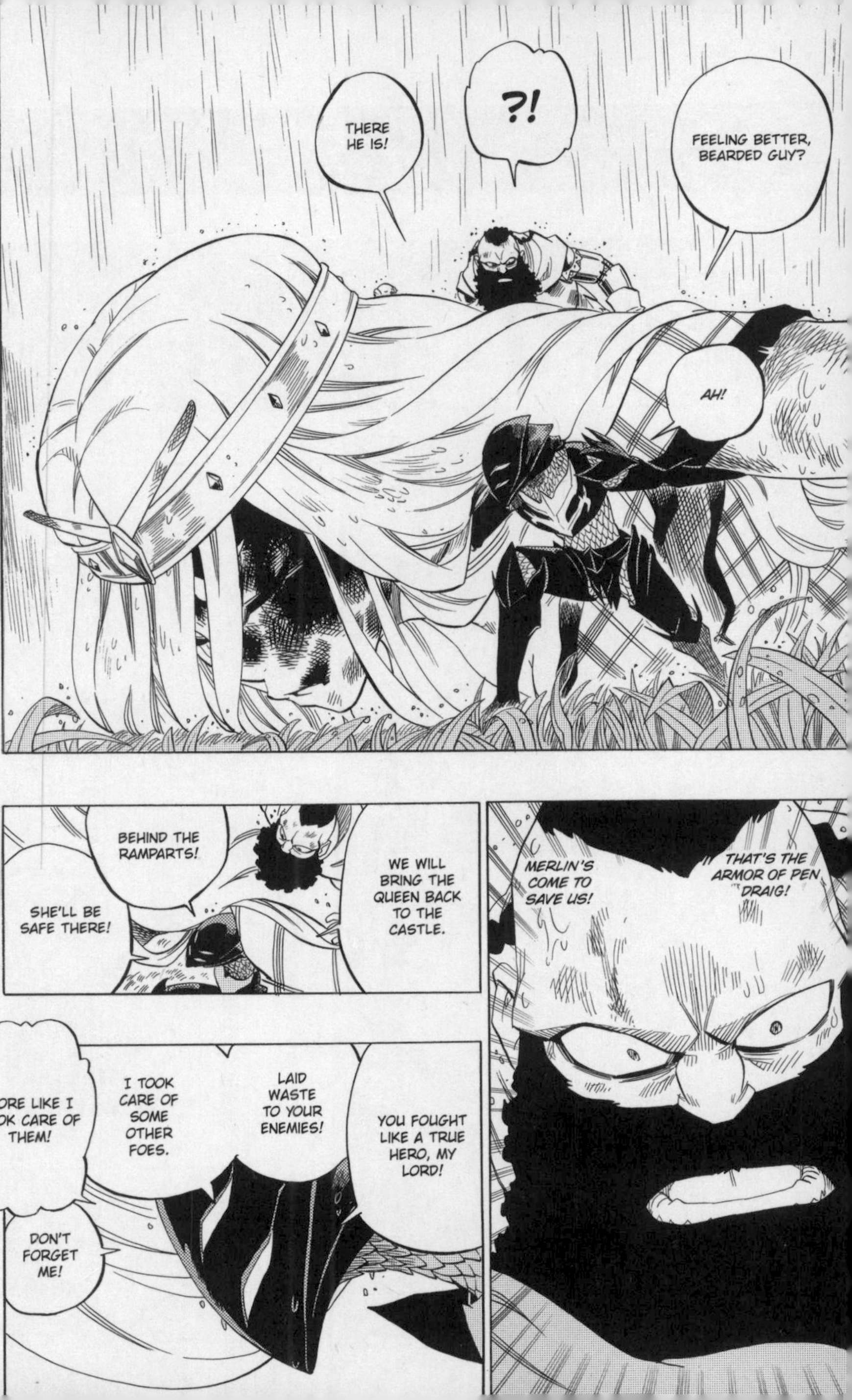
FEELING BETTER, BEARDED GUY?
?!
THERE HE IS!
AH!
THAT'S THE ARMOR OF PEN DRAIG!
MERLIN'S COME TO SAVE US!
WE WILL BRING THE QUEEN BACK TO THE CASTLE.
BEHIND THE RAMPARTS!
SHE'LL BE SAFE THERE!
YOU FOUGHT LIKE A TRUE HERO, MY LORD!
LAID WASTE TO YOUR ENEMIES!
I TOOK CARE OF SOME OTHER FOES.
MORE LIKE I TOOK CARE OF THEM!
DON'T FORGET ME!

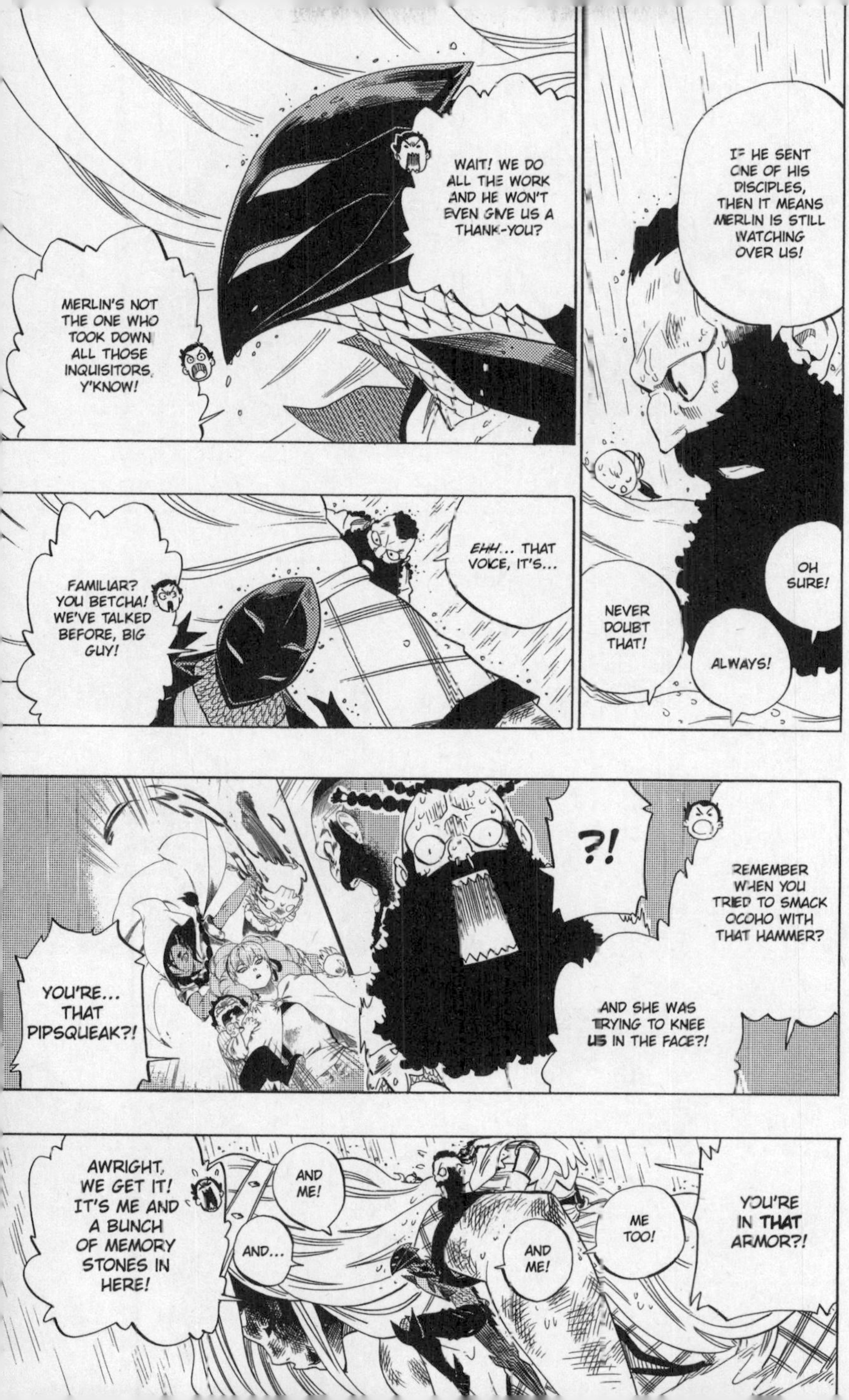
IF HE SENT ONE OF HIS DISCIPLES, THEN IT MEANS MERLIN IS STILL WATCHING OVER US!
OH SURE!
NEVER DOUBT THAT!
ALWAYS!
WAIT! WE DO ALL THE WORK AND HE WON'T EVEN GIVE US A THANK-YOU?
MERLIN'S NOT THE ONE WHO TOOK DOWN ALL THOSE INQUISITORS, Y'KNOW!
EHH... THAT VOICE, IT'S...
FAMILIAR? YOU BETCHA! WE'VE TALKED BEFORE, BIG GUY!
?!
REMEMBER WHEN YOU TRIED TO SMACK OCOHO WITH THAT HAMMER?
AND SHE WAS TRYING TO KNEE US IN THE FACE?!
YOU'RE... THAT PIPSQUEAK?!
YOU'RE IN THAT ARMOR?!
ME TOO!
AND ME!
AND ME!
AND...
AWRIGHT, WE GET IT! IT'S ME AND A BUNCH OF MEMORY STONES IN HERE!

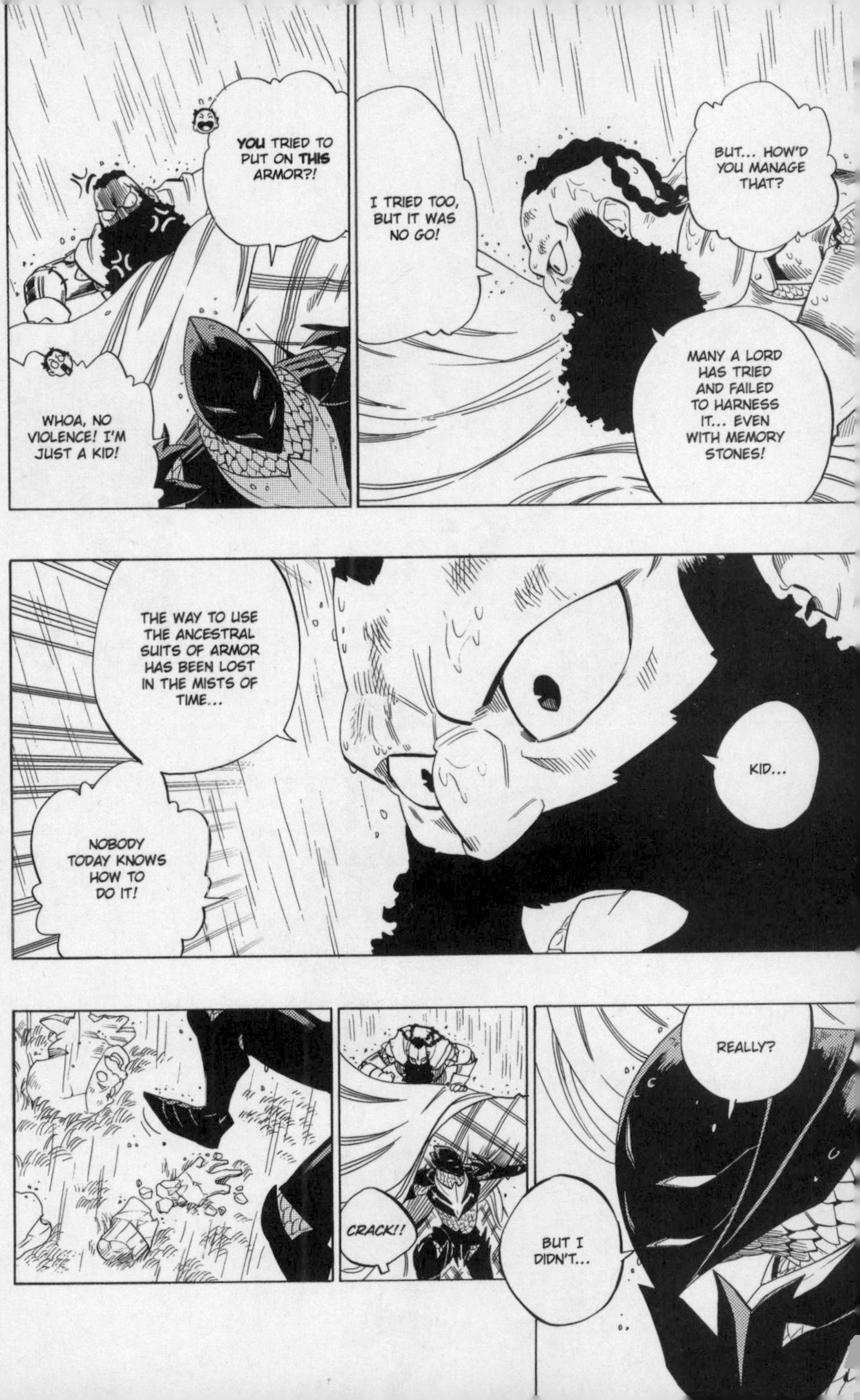
BUT... HOW'D YOU MANAGE THAT?
I TRIED TOO, BUT IT WAS NO GO!
MANY A LORD HAS TRIED AND FAILED TO HARNESS IT... EVEN WITH MEMORY STONES!
YOU TRIED TO PUT ON THIS ARMOR?!
WHOA, NO VIOLENCE! I'M JUST A KID!
KID...
THE WAY TO USE THE ANCESTRAL SUITS OF ARMOR HAS BEEN LOST IN THE MISTS OF TIME...
NOBODY TODAY KNOWS HOW TO DO IT!
REALLY?
BUT I DIDN'T...
CRACK!!

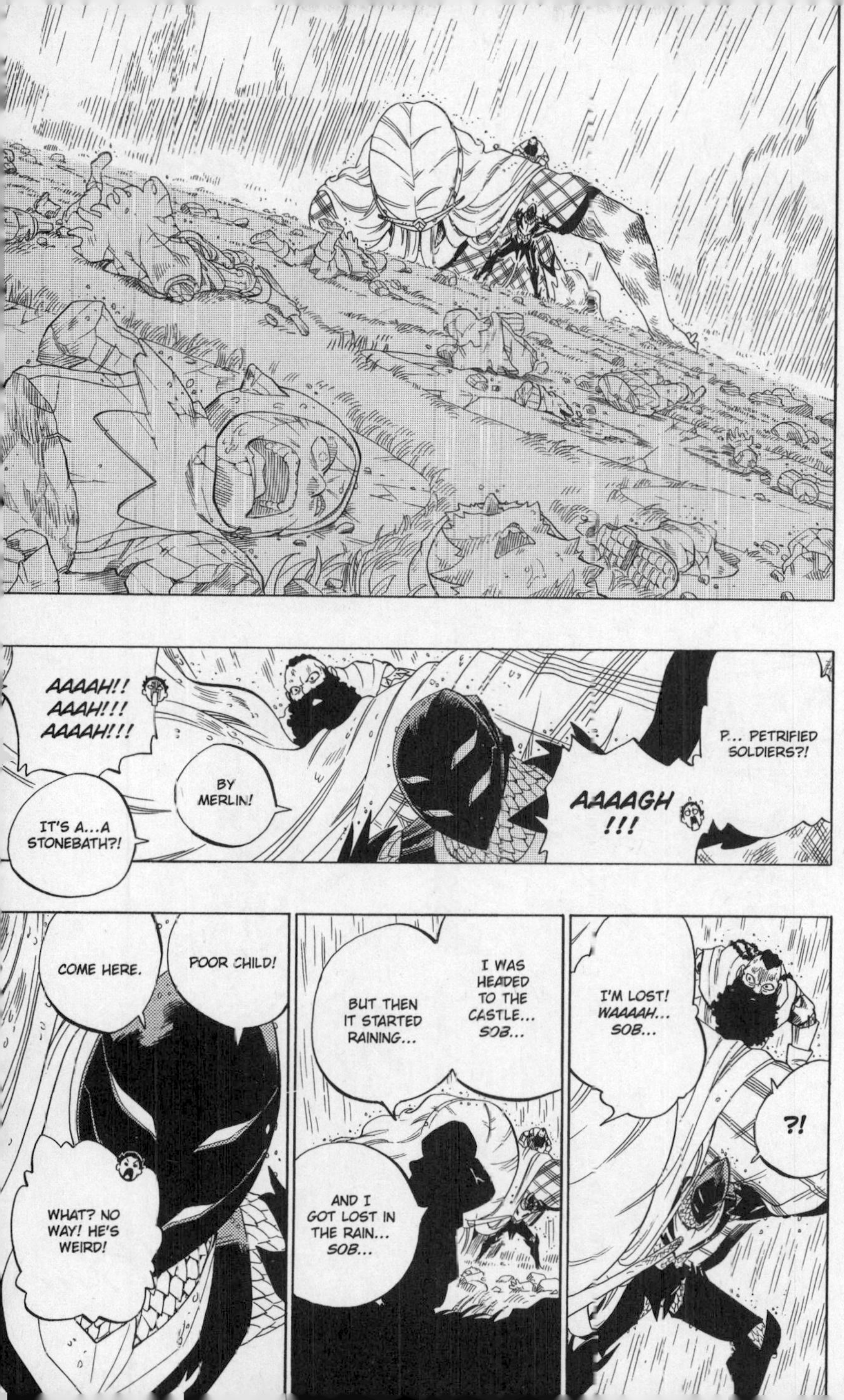
P... PETRIFIED SOLDIERS?!
AAAAGH!!!
BY MERLIN!
AAAAH!! AAAH!!! AAAAH!!!
IT'S A...A STONEBATH?!
I'M LOST! WAAAAH... SOB...
?!
I WAS HEADED TO THE CASTLE... SOB...
BUT THEN IT STARTED RAINING...
AND I GOT LOST IN THE RAIN... SOB...
POOR CHILD!
COME HERE.
WHAT? NO WAY! HE'S WEIRD!

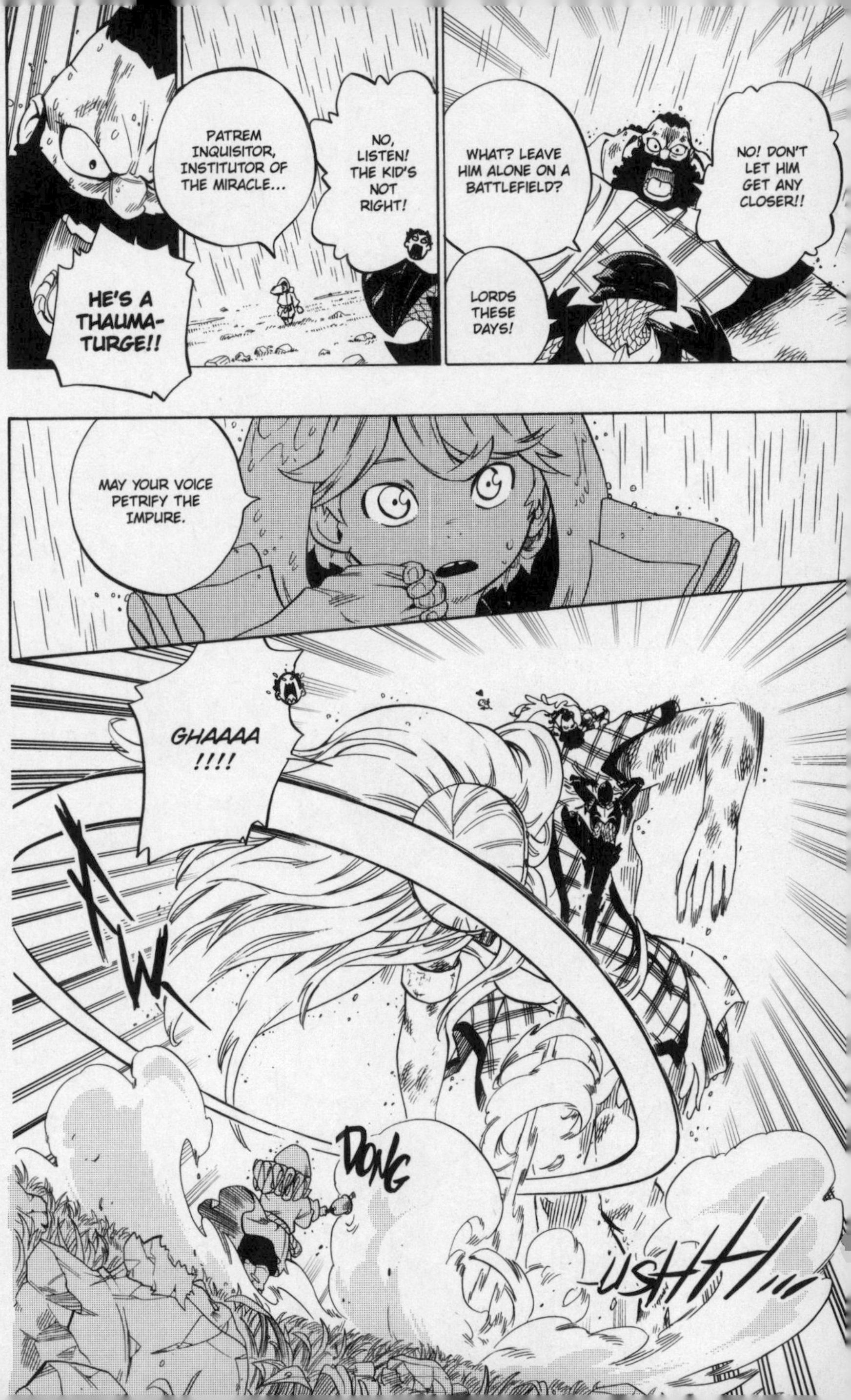
NO! DON'T LET HIM GET ANY CLOSER!!
WHAT? LEAVE HIM ALONE ON A BATTLEFIELD?
LORDS THESE DAYS!
NO, LISTEN! THE KID'S NOT RIGHT!
PATREM INQUISITOR, INSTITUTOR OF THE MIRACLE...
HE'S A THAUMA-TURGE!!
MAY YOUR VOICE PETRIFY THE IMPURE.
GHAAAA !!!!
DONG

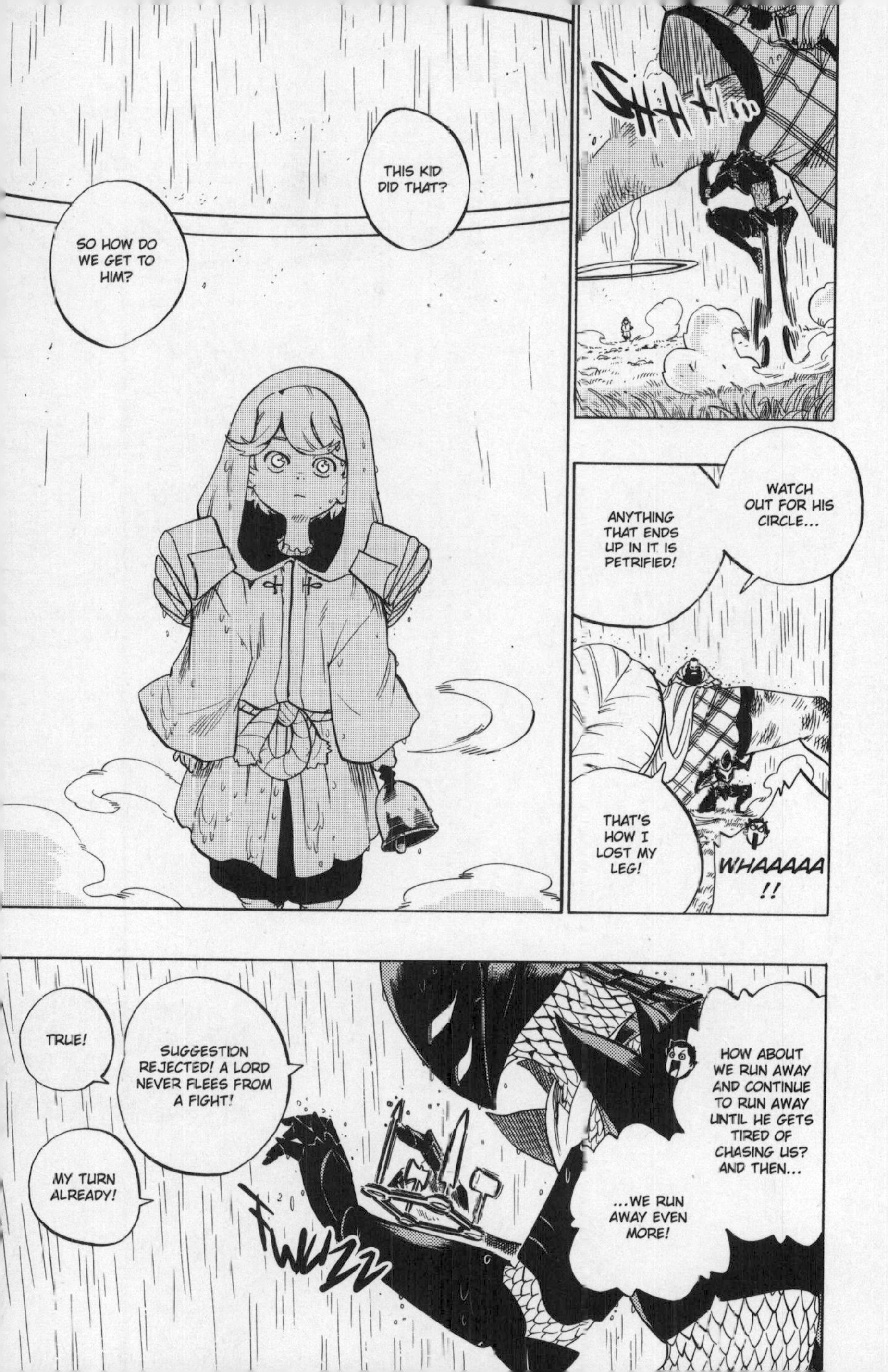
SHH...
WATCH OUT FOR HIS CIRCLE...
ANYTHING THAT ENDS UP IN IT IS PETRIFIED!
THAT'S HOW I LOST MY LEG!
WHAAAAA!!
THIS KID DID THAT?
SO HOW DO WE GET TO HIM?
HOW ABOUT WE RUN AWAY AND CONTINUE TO RUN AWAY UNTIL HE GETS TIRED OF CHASING US? AND THEN...
...WE RUN AWAY EVEN MORE!
SUGGESTION REJECTED! A LORD NEVER FLEES FROM A FIGHT!
TRUE!
MY TURN ALREADY!
FWUZZ

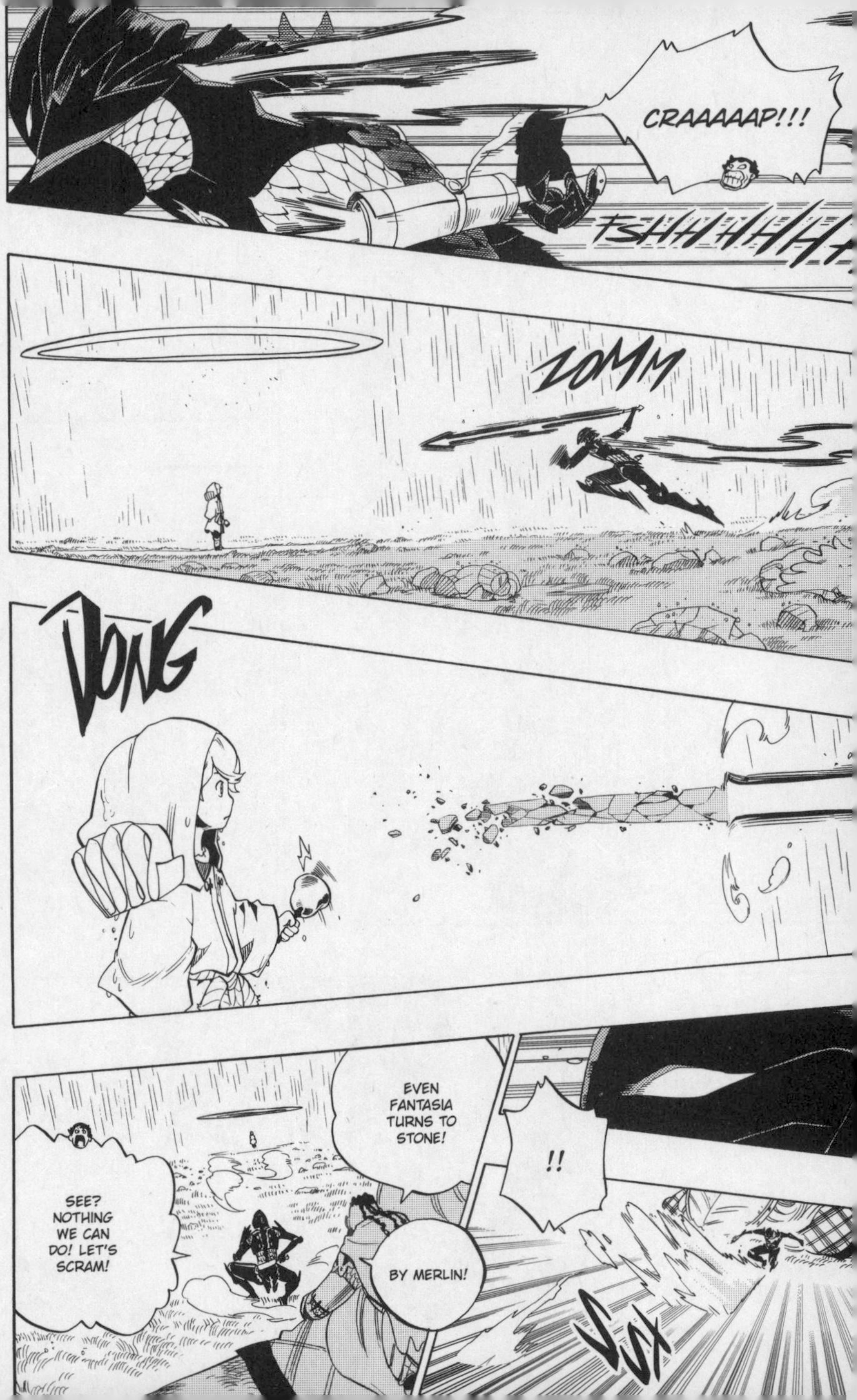
CRAAAAAP!!!
FSHHHHHH
ZOMM
DONG
!!
EVEN FANTASIA TURNS TO STONE!
BY MERLIN!
SEE? NOTHING WE CAN DO! LET'S SCRAM!

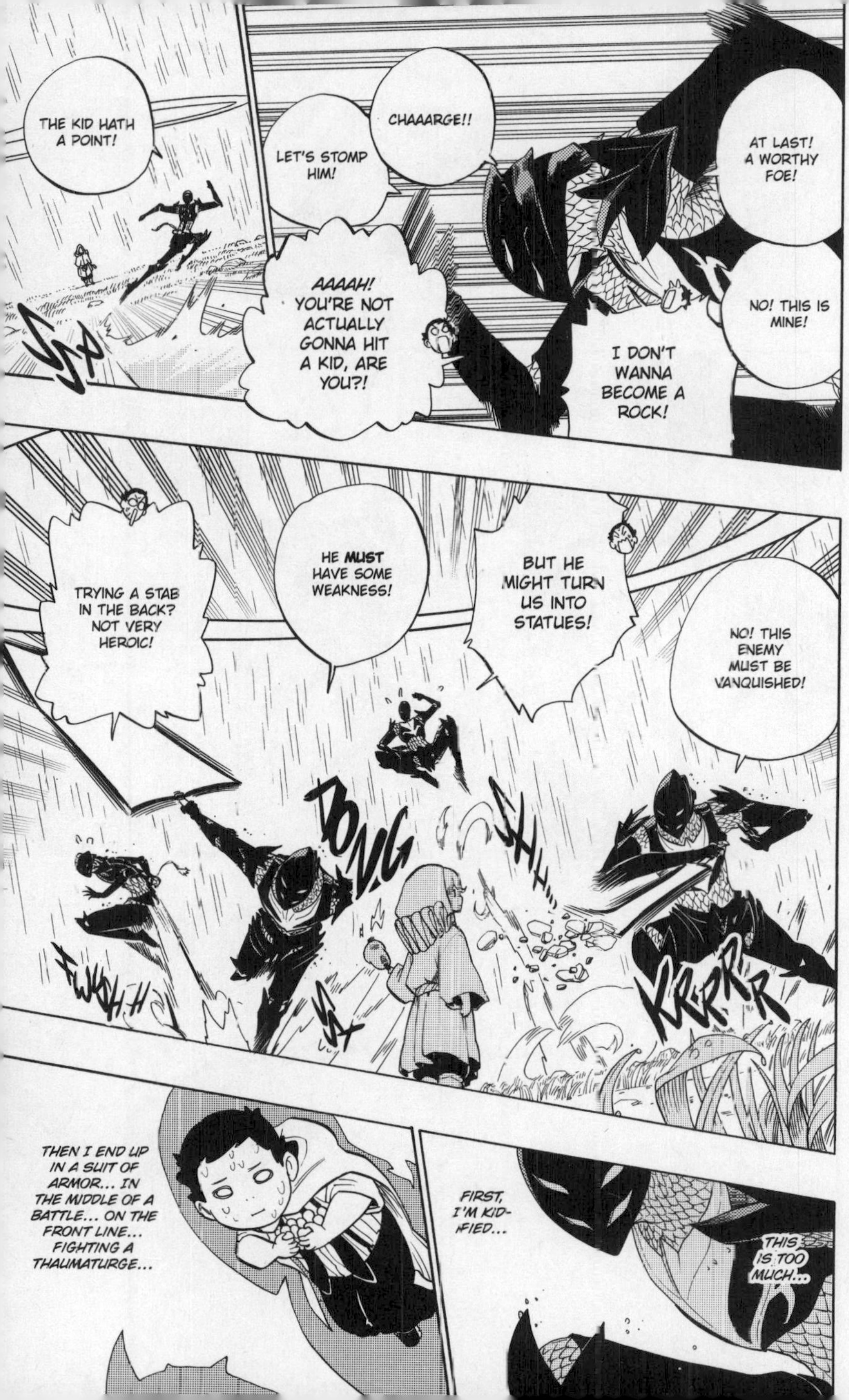
AT LAST! A WORTHY FOE!
NO! THIS IS MINE!
CHAAARGE!!
LET'S STOMP HIM!
I DON'T WANNA BECOME A ROCK!
AAAAH! YOU'RE NOT ACTUALLY GONNA HIT A KID, ARE YOU?!
THE KID HATH A POINT!
NO! THIS ENEMY MUST BE VANQUISHED!
BUT HE MIGHT TURN US INTO STATUES!
HE **MUST** HAVE SOME WEAKNESS!
TRYING A STAB IN THE BACK? NOT VERY HEROIC!
DONG
FIRST, I'M KID-FIED...
THIS IS TOO MUCH...
THEN I END UP IN A SUIT OF ARMOR... IN THE MIDDLE OF A BATTLE... ON THE FRONT LINE... FIGHTING A THAUMATURGE...

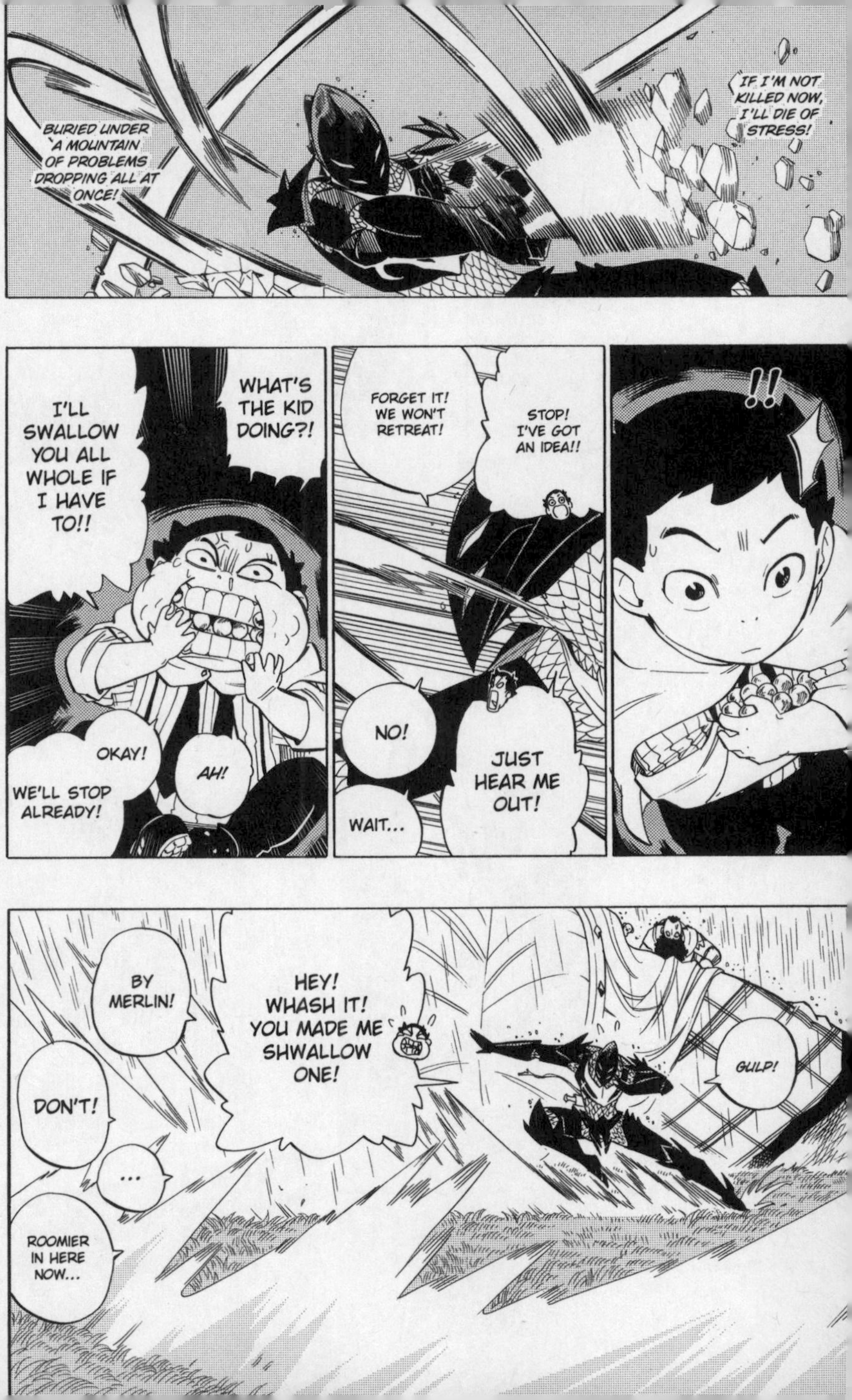
IF I'M NOT KILLED NOW, I'LL DIE OF STRESS!
BURIED UNDER A MOUNTAIN OF PROBLEMS DROPPING ALL AT ONCE!
!!
STOP! I'VE GOT AN IDEA!!
FORGET IT! WE WON'T RETREAT!
JUST HEAR ME OUT!
NO!
WAIT...
WHAT'S THE KID DOING?!
I'LL SWALLOW YOU ALL WHOLE IF I HAVE TO!!
AH!
OKAY!
WE'LL STOP ALREADY!
GULP!
HEY! WHASH IT! YOU MADE ME SHWALLOW ONE!
BY MERLIN!
DON'T!
...
ROOMIER IN HERE NOW...

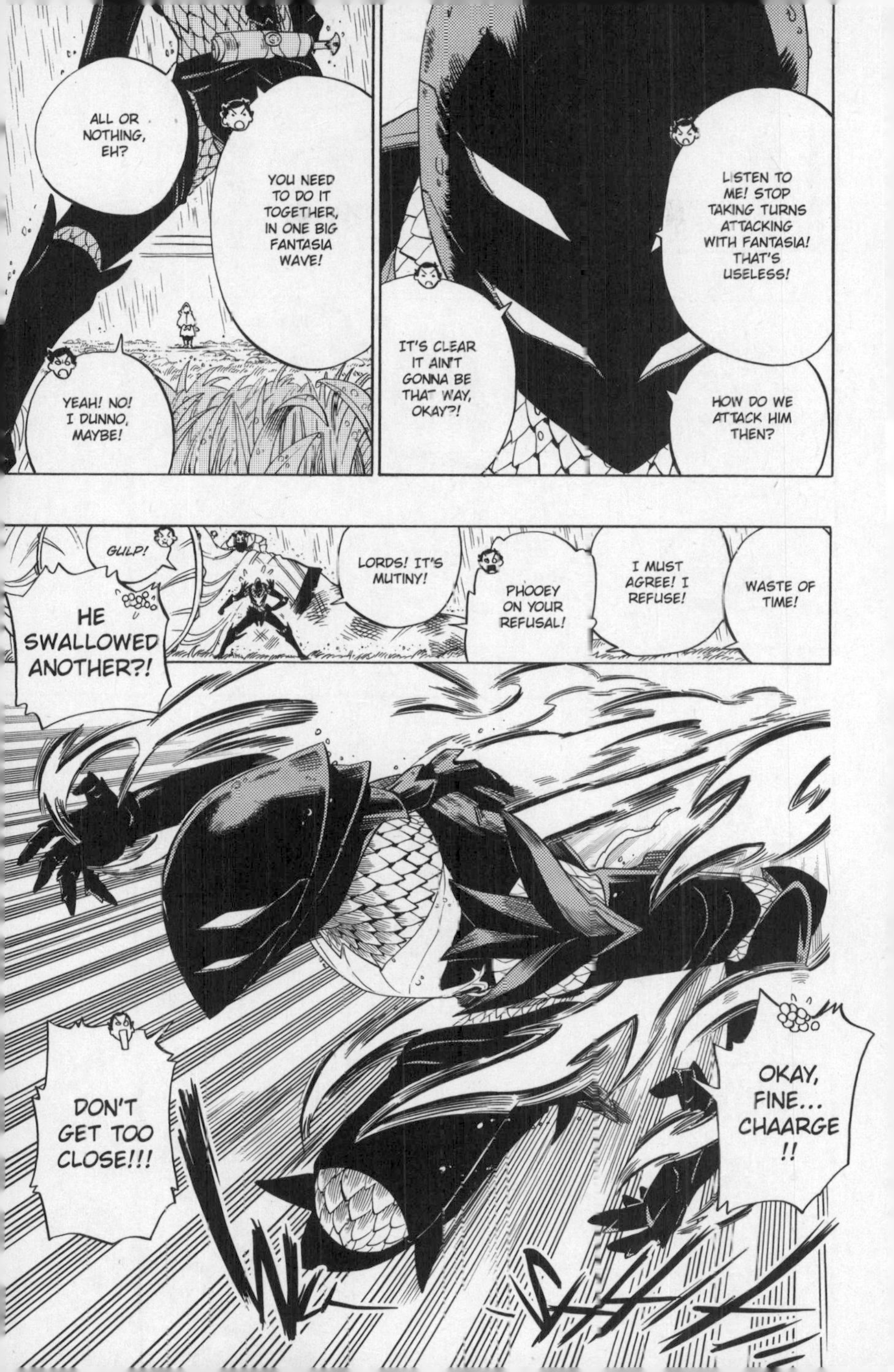
LISTEN TO ME! STOP TAKING TURNS ATTACKING WITH FANTASIA! THAT'S USELESS!
IT'S CLEAR IT AIN'T GONNA BE THAT WAY, OKAY?!
HOW DO WE ATTACK HIM THEN?
YOU NEED TO DO IT TOGETHER, IN ONE BIG FANTASIA WAVE!
ALL OR NOTHING, EH?
YEAH! NO! I DUNNO, MAYBE!
WASTE OF TIME!
I MUST AGREE! I REFUSE!
PHOOEY ON YOUR REFUSAL!
LORDS! IT'S MUTINY!
GULP!
HE SWALLOWED ANOTHER?!
OKAY, FINE... CHAARGE !!
DON'T GET TOO CLOSE!!!

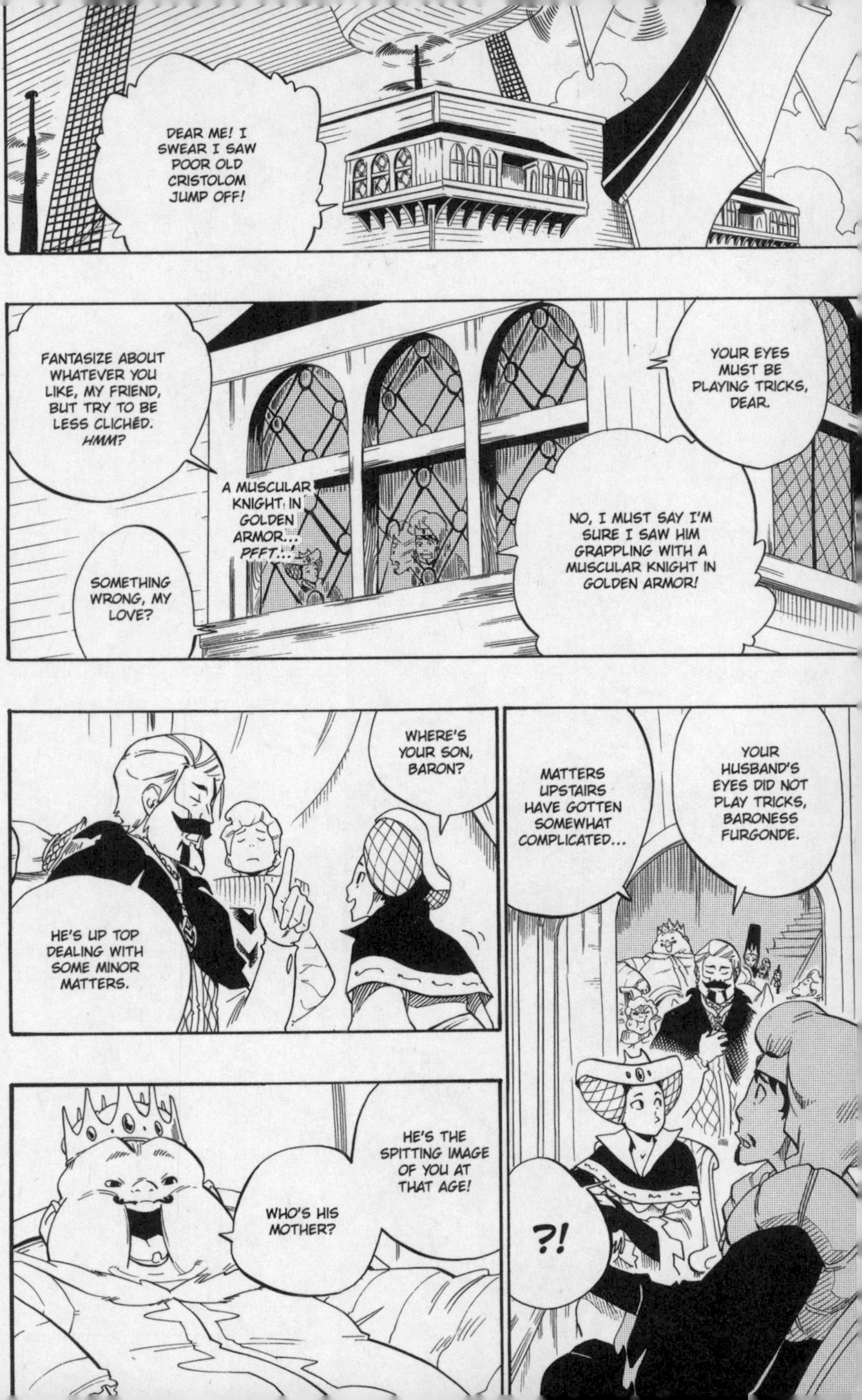
DEAR ME! I SWEAR I SAW POOR OLD CRISTOLOM JUMP OFF!
YOUR EYES MUST BE PLAYING TRICKS, DEAR.
NO, I MUST SAY I'M SURE I SAW HIM GRAPPLING WITH A MUSCULAR KNIGHT IN GOLDEN ARMOR!
FANTASIZE ABOUT WHATEVER YOU LIKE, MY FRIEND, BUT TRY TO BE LESS CLICHÉD. *HMM?*
A MUSCULAR KNIGHT IN GOLDEN ARMOR... *PFFT...*
SOMETHING WRONG, MY LOVE?
YOUR HUSBAND'S EYES DID NOT PLAY TRICKS, BARONESS FURGONDE.
MATTERS UPSTAIRS HAVE GOTTEN SOMEWHAT COMPLICATED...
?!
WHERE'S YOUR SON, BARON?
HE'S UP TOP DEALING WITH SOME MINOR MATTERS.
HE'S THE SPITTING IMAGE OF YOU AT THAT AGE!
WHO'S HIS MOTHER?

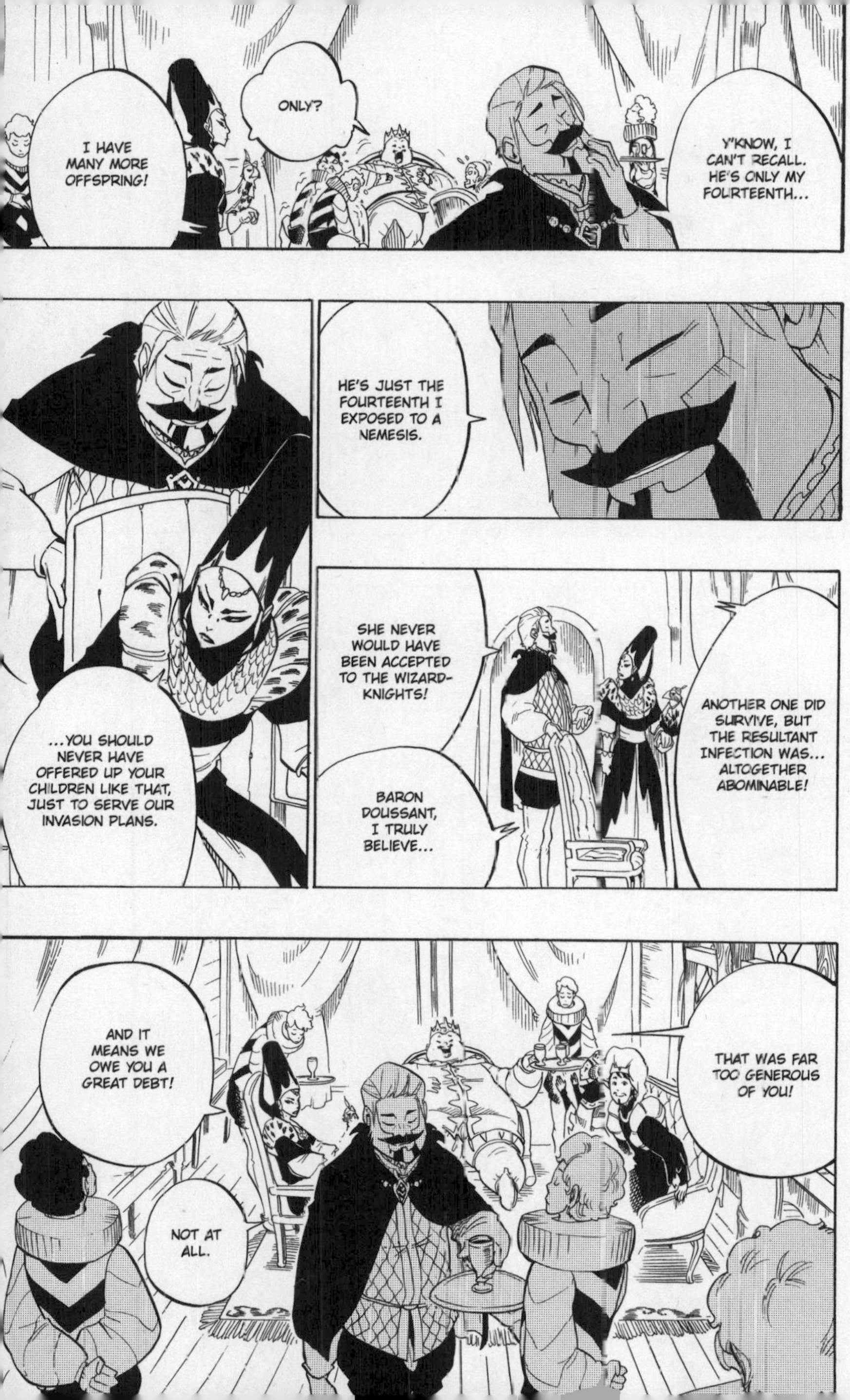
Y'KNOW, I CAN'T RECALL. HE'S ONLY MY FOURTEENTH...
ONLY?
I HAVE MANY MORE OFFSPRING!
HE'S JUST THE FOURTEENTH I EXPOSED TO A NEMESIS.
ANOTHER ONE DID SURVIVE, BUT THE RESULTANT INFECTION WAS... ALTOGETHER ABOMINABLE!
SHE NEVER WOULD HAVE BEEN ACCEPTED TO THE WIZARD-KNIGHTS!
BARON DOUSSANT, I TRULY BELIEVE...
...YOU SHOULD NEVER HAVE OFFERED UP YOUR CHILDREN LIKE THAT, JUST TO SERVE OUR INVASION PLANS.
THAT WAS FAR TOO GENEROUS OF YOU!
AND IT MEANS WE OWE YOU A GREAT DEBT!
NOT AT ALL.

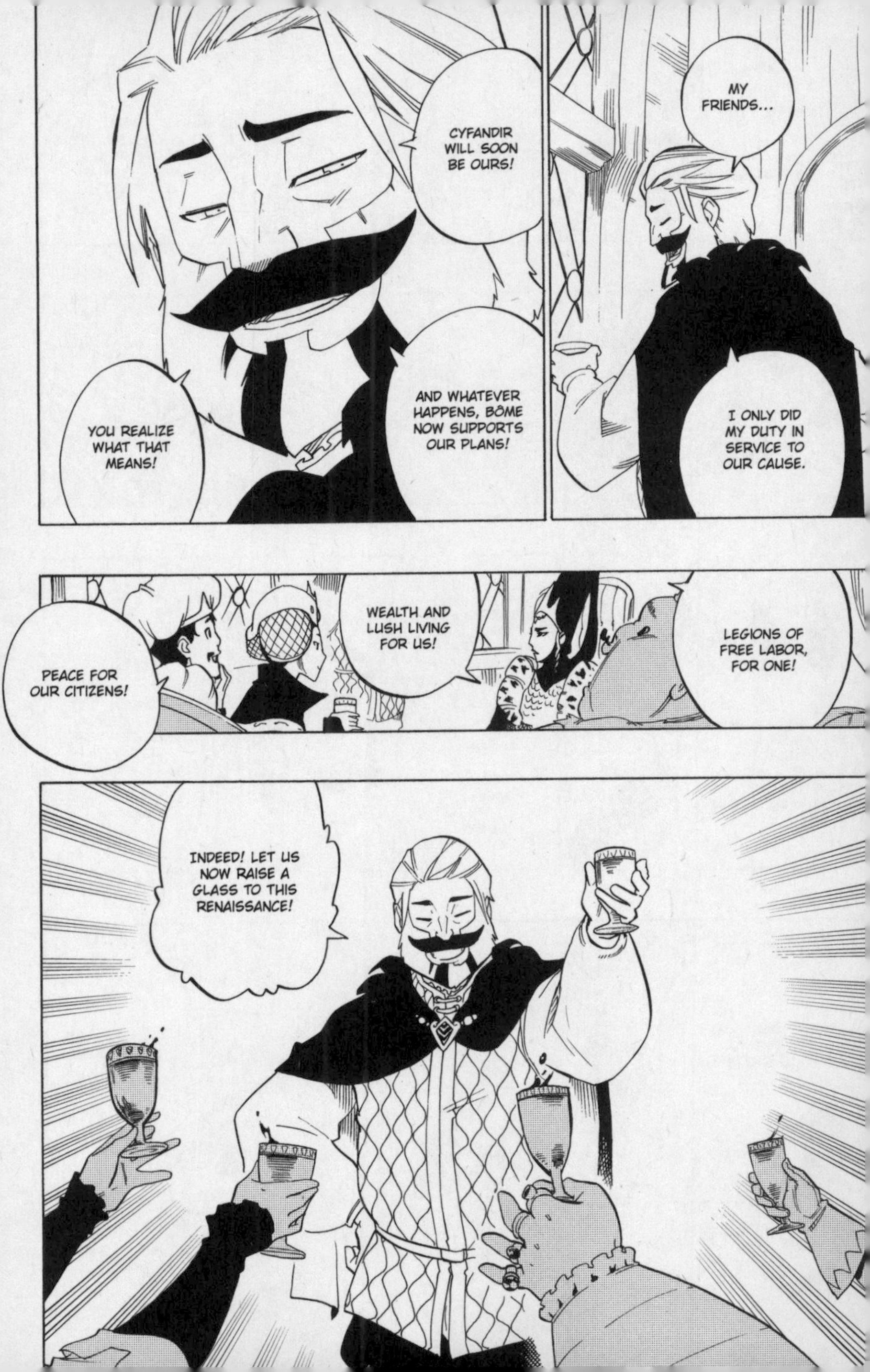
MY FRIENDS...
I ONLY DID MY DUTY IN SERVICE TO OUR CAUSE.
CYFANDIR WILL SOON BE OURS!
AND WHATEVER HAPPENS, BÔME NOW SUPPORTS OUR PLANS!
YOU REALIZE WHAT THAT MEANS!
LEGIONS OF FREE LABOR, FOR ONE!
WEALTH AND LUSH LIVING FOR US!
PEACE FOR OUR CITIZENS!
INDEED! LET US NOW RAISE A GLASS TO THIS RENAISSANCE!

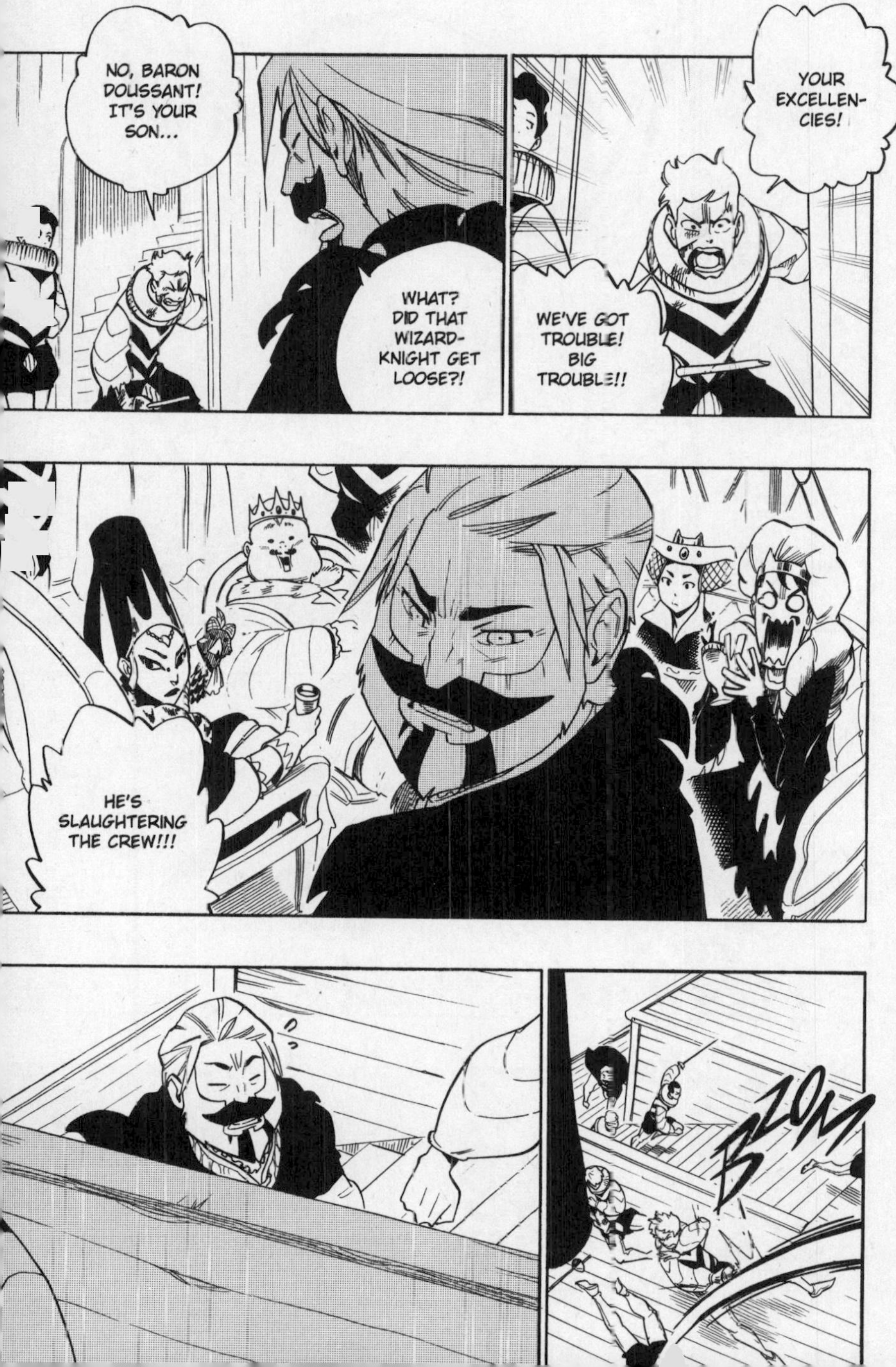
YOUR EXCELLEN-CIES!
WE'VE GOT TROUBLE! BIG TROUBLE!!
WHAT? DID THAT WIZARD-KNIGHT GET LOOSE?!
NO, BARON DOUSSANT! IT'S YOUR SON...
HE'S SLAUGHTERING THE CREW!!!
BZOM

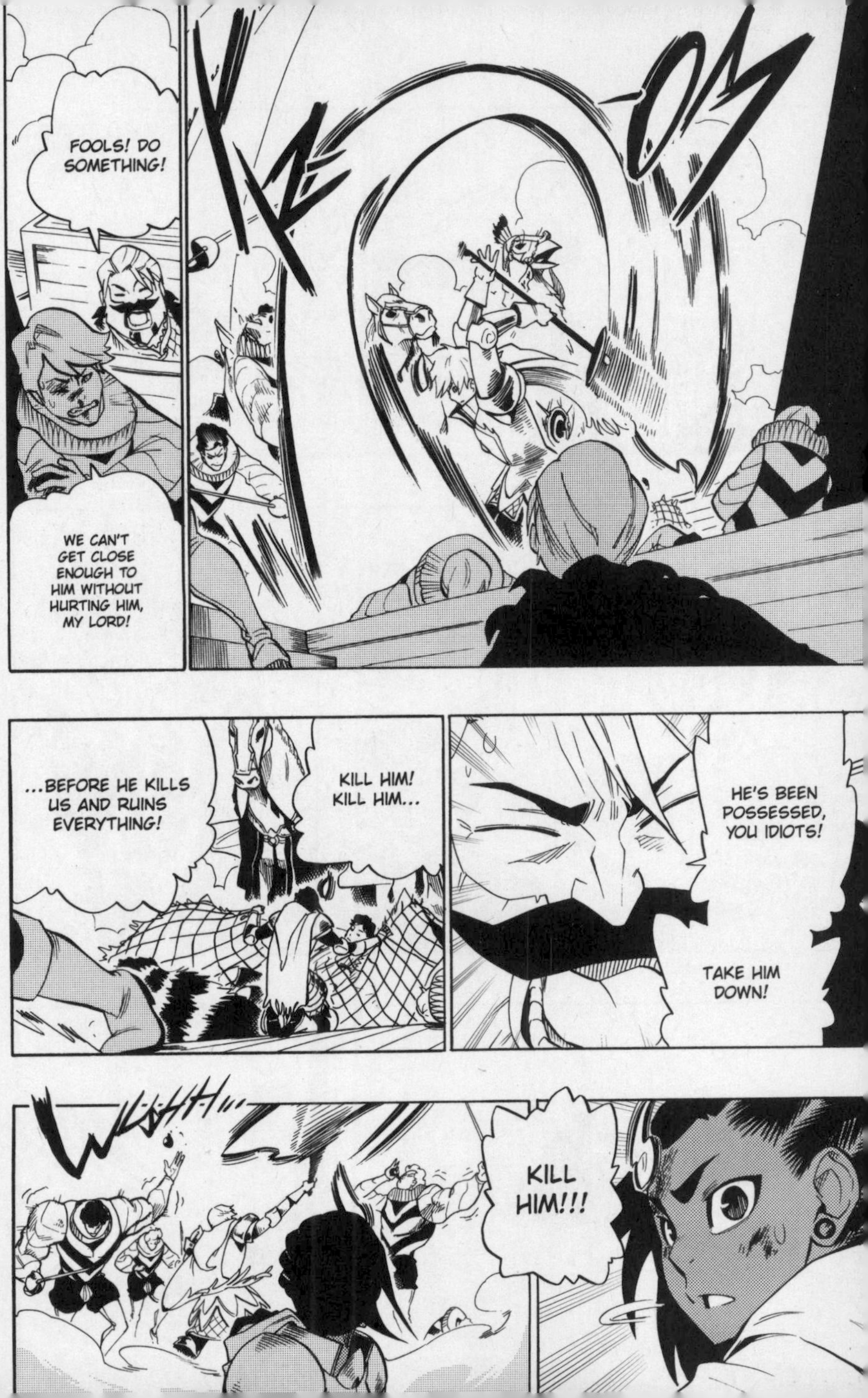
FOOLS! DO SOMETHING!
WE CAN'T GET CLOSE ENOUGH TO HIM WITHOUT HURTING HIM, MY LORD!
HE'S BEEN POSSESSED, YOU IDIOTS!
TAKE HIM DOWN!
KILL HIM! KILL HIM...
...BEFORE HE KILLS US AND RUINS EVERYTHING!
KILL HIM!!!

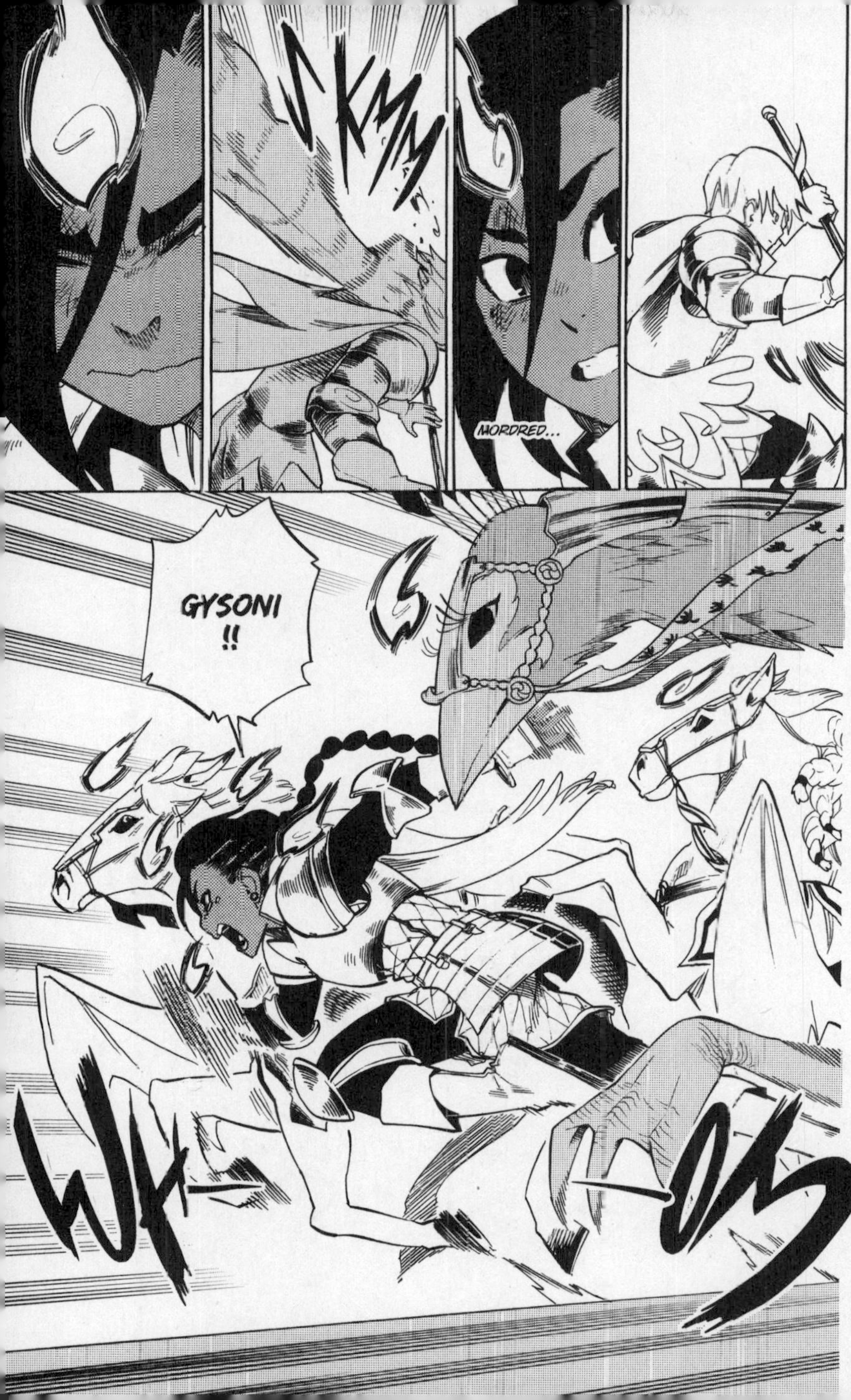
MORDRED...
GYSONI !!

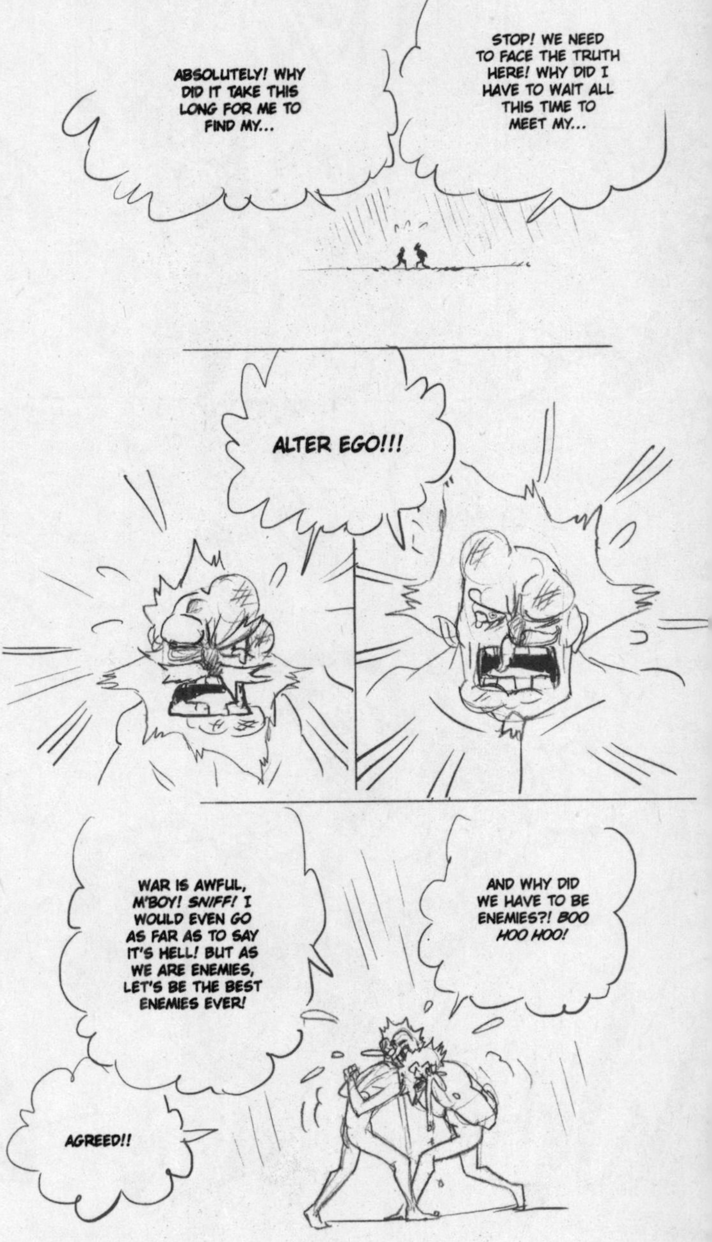
STOP! WE NEED TO FACE THE TRUTH HERE! WHY DID I HAVE TO WAIT ALL THIS TIME TO MEET MY...
ABSOLUTELY! WHY DID IT TAKE THIS LONG FOR ME TO FIND MY...
ALTER EGO!!!
AND WHY DID WE HAVE TO BE ENEMIES?! *BOO HOO HOO!*
WAR IS AWFUL, M'BOY! *SNIFF!* I WOULD EVEN GO AS FAR AS TO SAY IT'S HELL! BUT AS WE ARE ENEMIES, LET'S BE THE BEST ENEMIES EVER!
AGREED!!

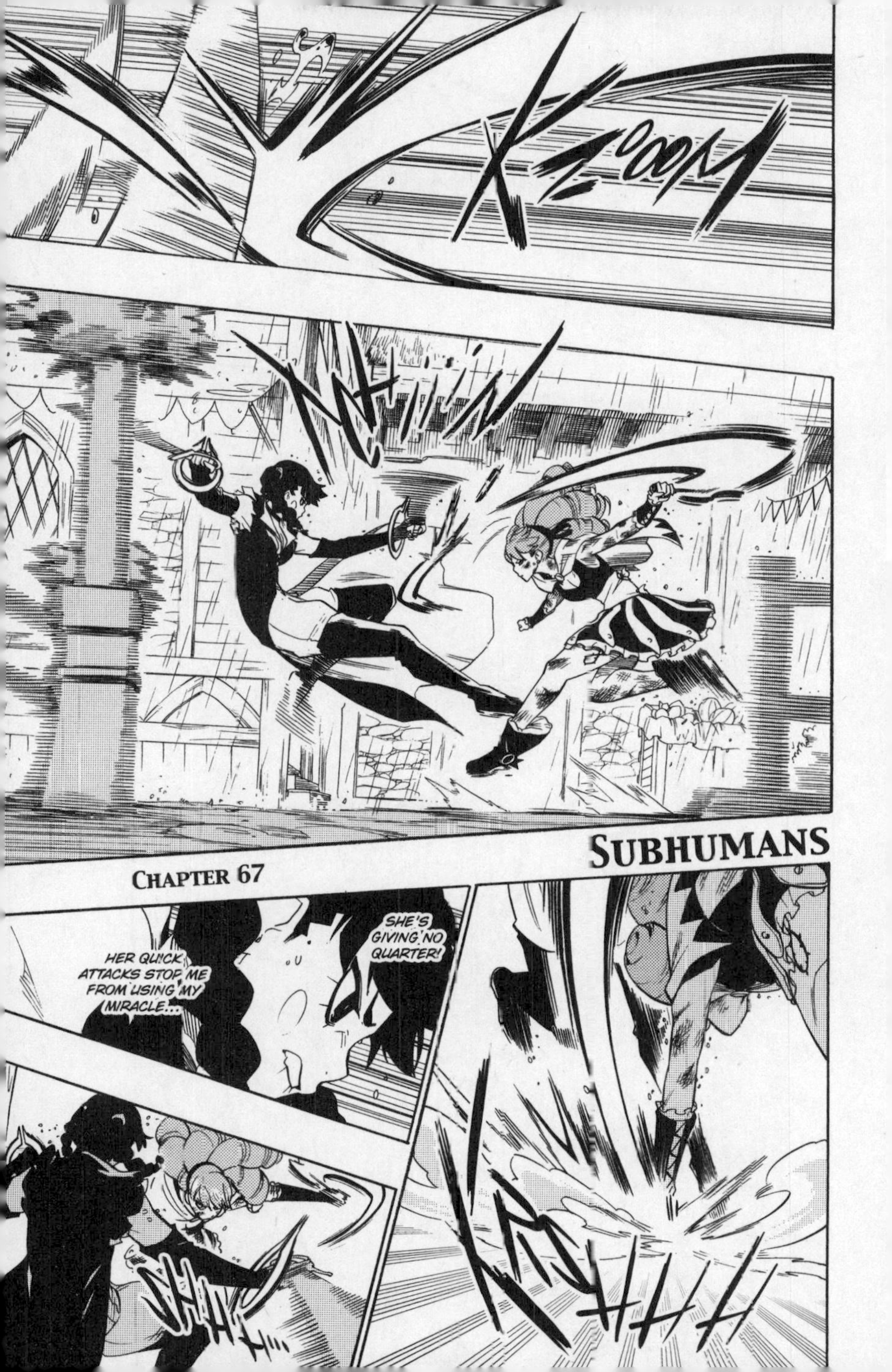
SUBHUMANS
CHAPTER 67
SHE'S GIVING NO QUARTER!
HER QUICK ATTACKS STOP ME FROM USING MY MIRACLE...

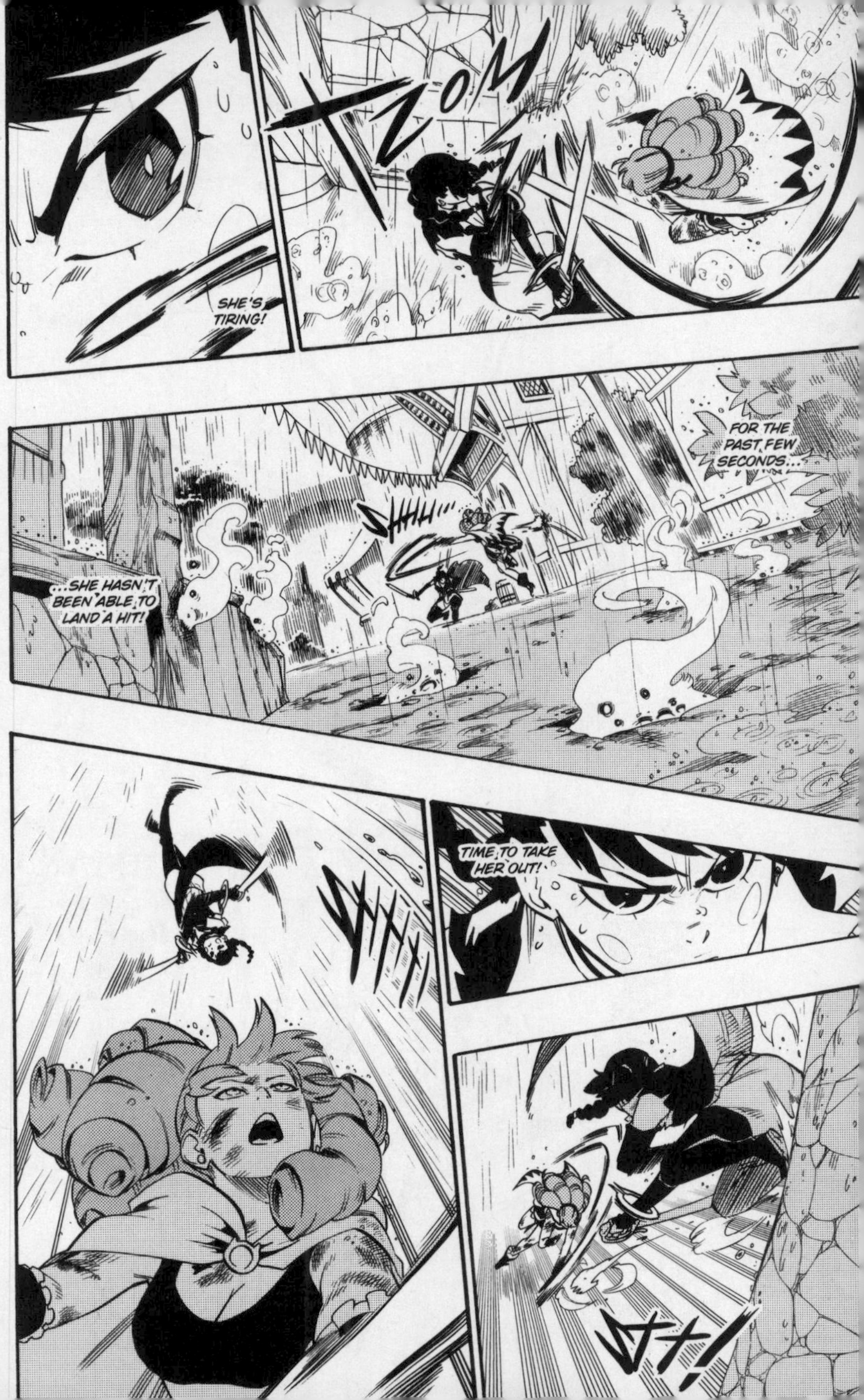
ZOM
SHE'S TIRING!
FOR THE PAST FEW SECONDS...
...SHE HASN'T BEEN ABLE TO LAND A HIT!
TIME TO TAKE HER OUT!

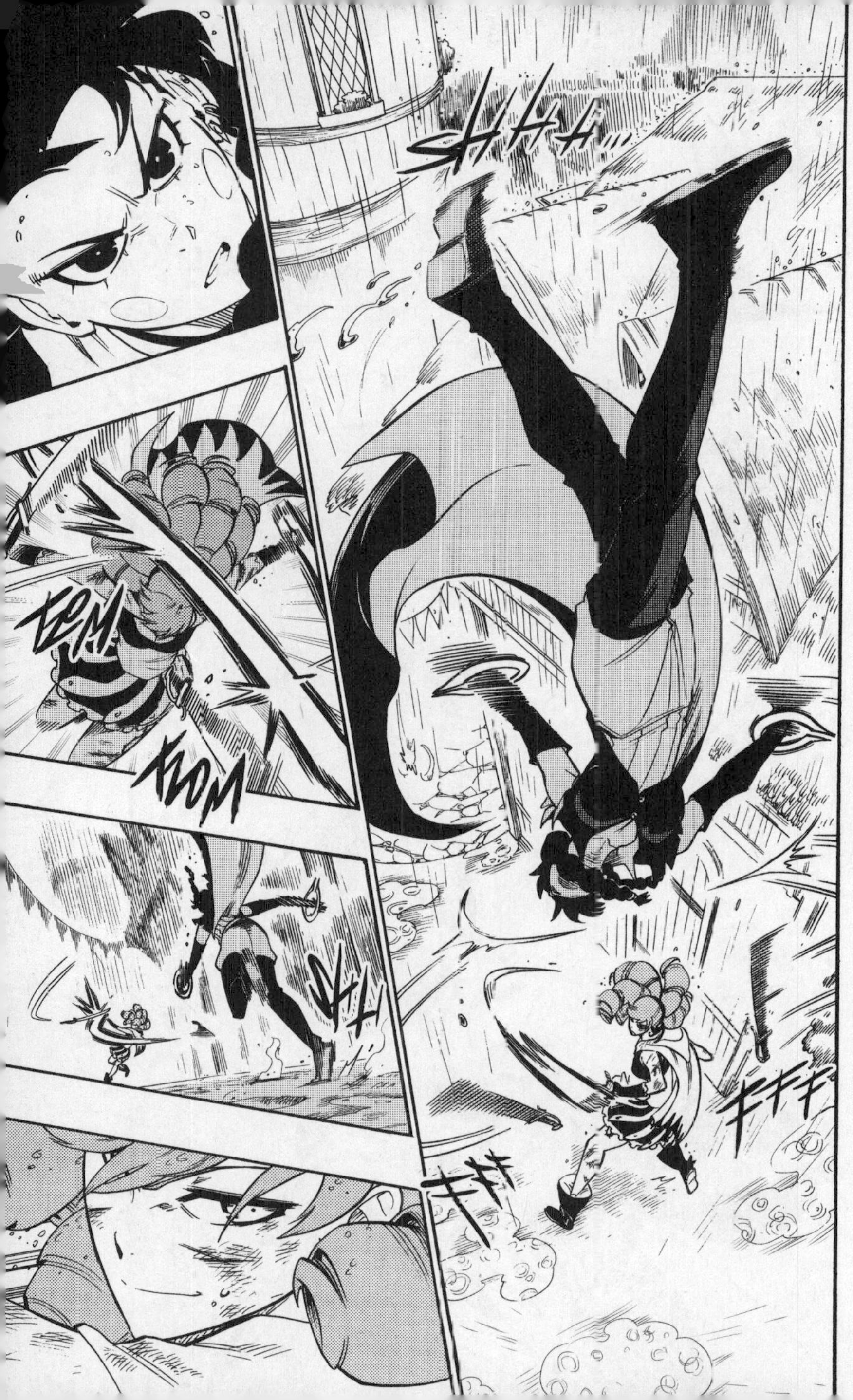
SHHH...
FFF
FFF
KLOM

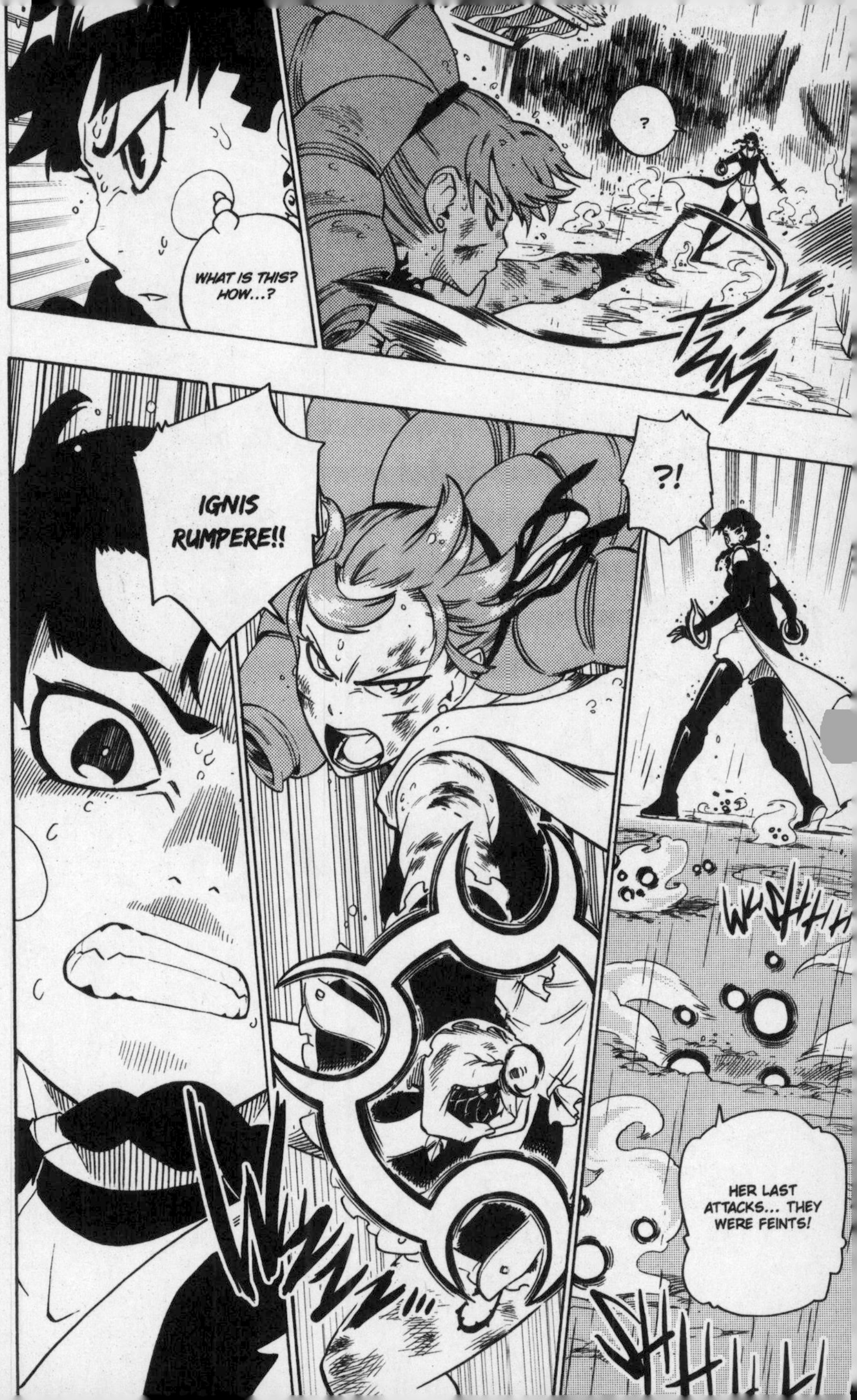
?
WHAT IS THIS? HOW...?
?!
HER LAST ATTACKS... THEY WERE FEINTS!
IGNIS RUMPERE!!

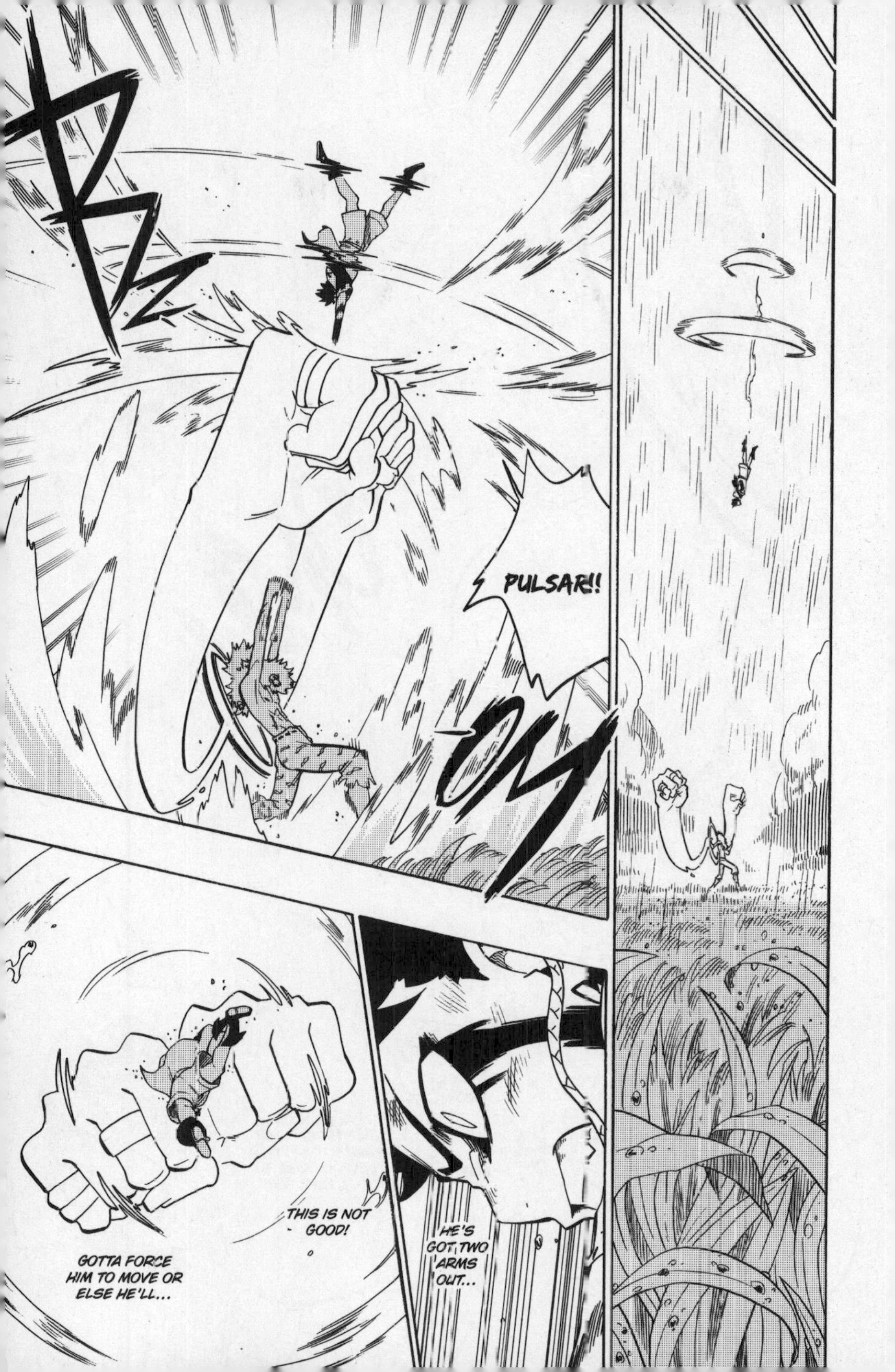
PULSAR!!
HE'S GOT TWO ARMS OUT...
THIS IS NOT GOOD!
GOTTA FORCE HIM TO MOVE OR ELSE HE'LL...

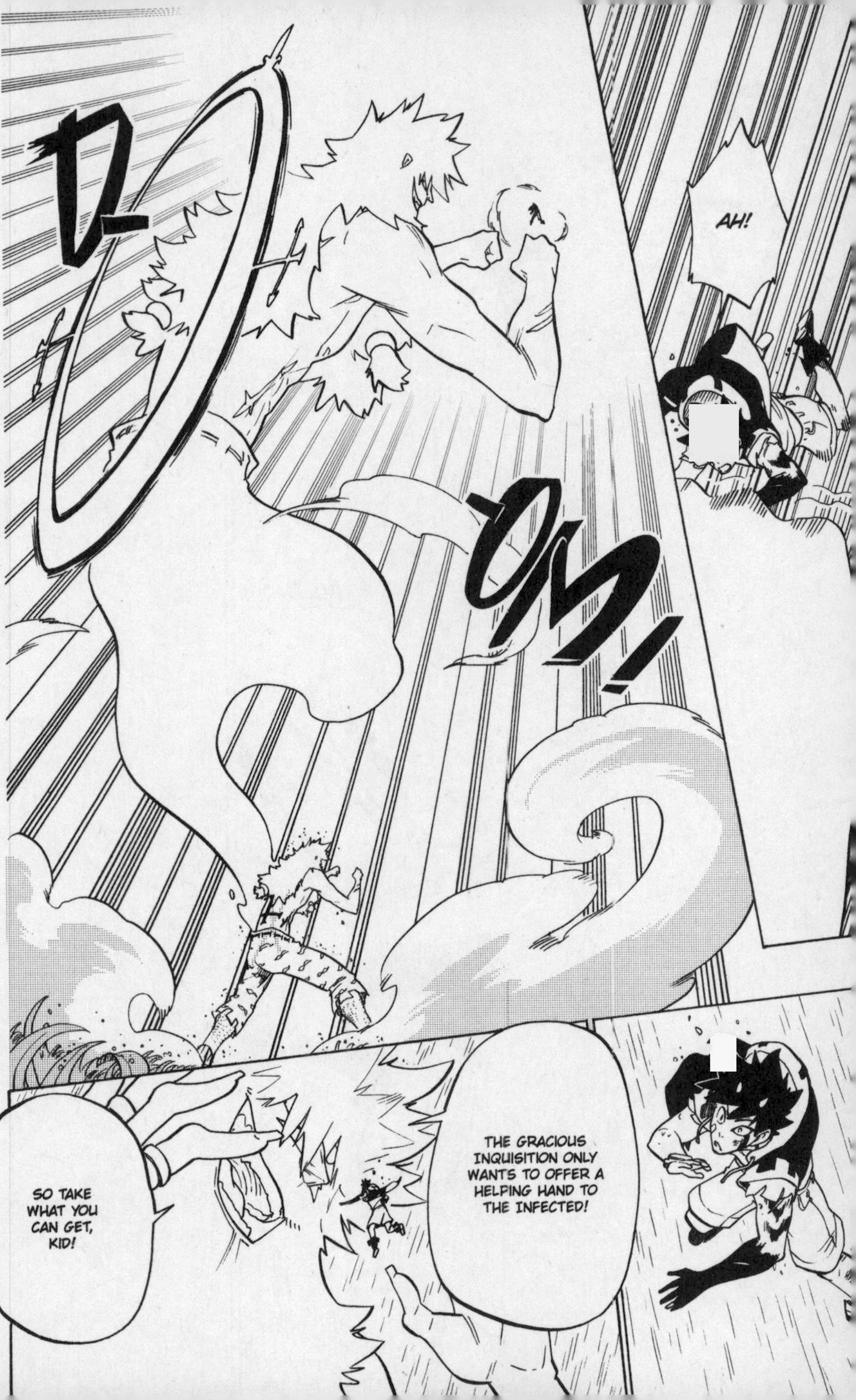
AH!
D-
OM!
THE GRACIOUS INQUISITION ONLY WANTS TO OFFER A HELPING HAND TO THE INFECTED!
SO TAKE WHAT YOU CAN GET, KID!

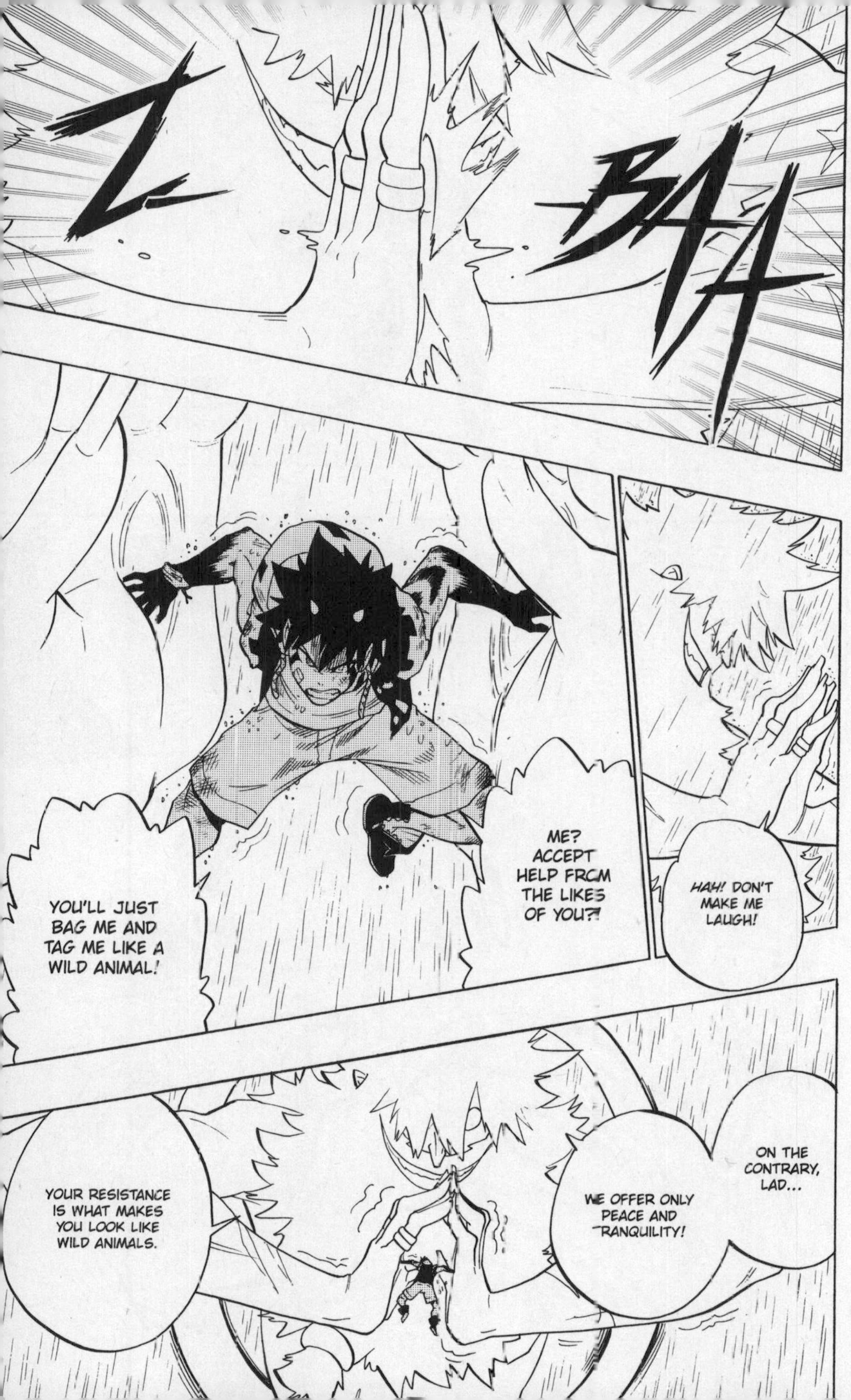
ZBAA
HAH! DON'T MAKE ME LAUGH!
ME? ACCEPT HELP FROM THE LIKES OF YOU?!
YOU'LL JUST BAG ME AND TAG ME LIKE A WILD ANIMAL!
ON THE CONTRARY, LAD...
WE OFFER ONLY PEACE AND TRANQUILITY!
YOUR RESISTANCE IS WHAT MAKES YOU LOOK LIKE WILD ANIMALS.

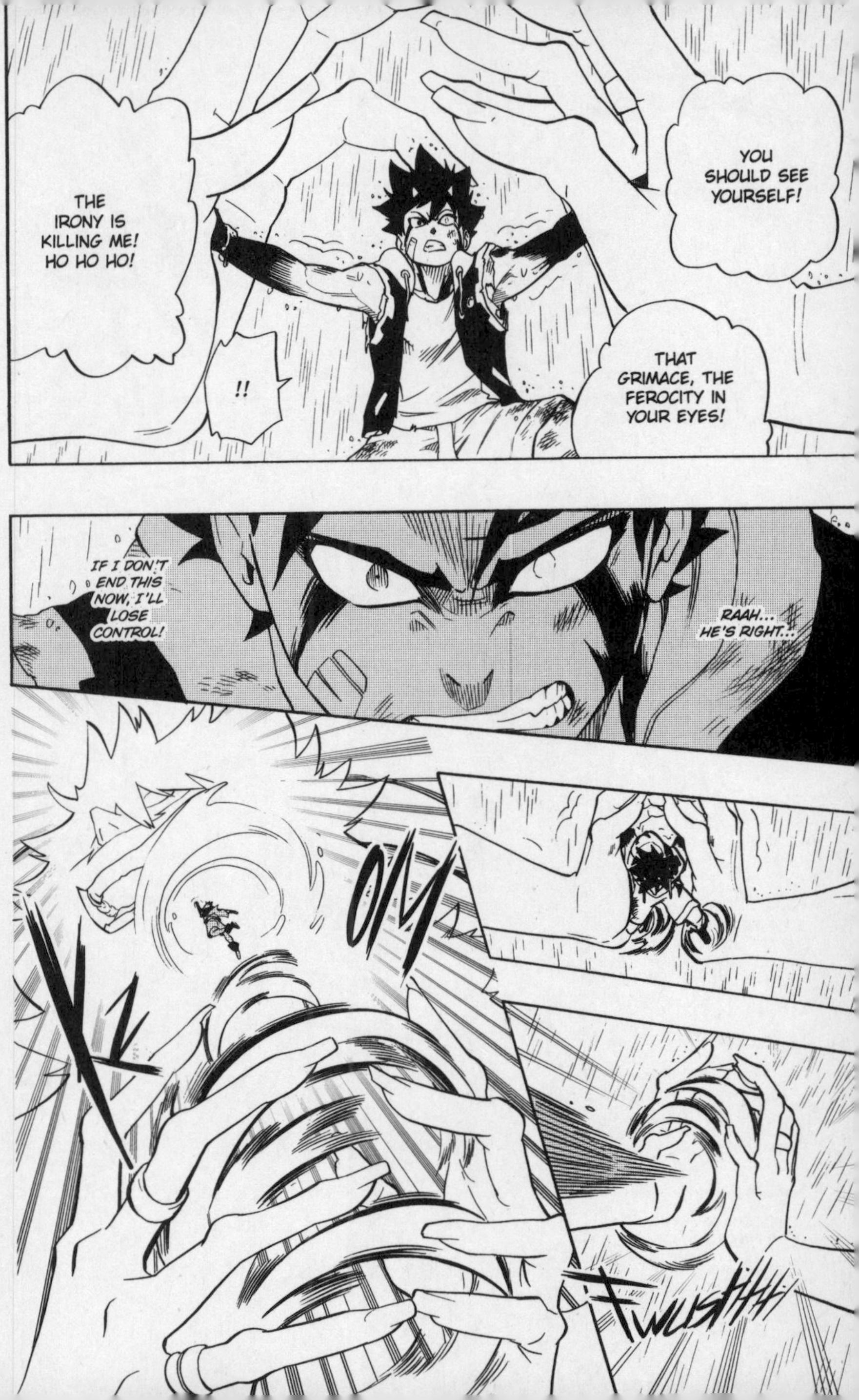
YOU SHOULD SEE YOURSELF!
THAT GRIMACE, THE FEROCITY IN YOUR EYES!
THE IRONY IS KILLING ME! HO HO HO!
!!
RAAH... HE'S RIGHT...
IF I DON'T END THIS NOW, I'LL LOSE CONTROL!
FWUSHH

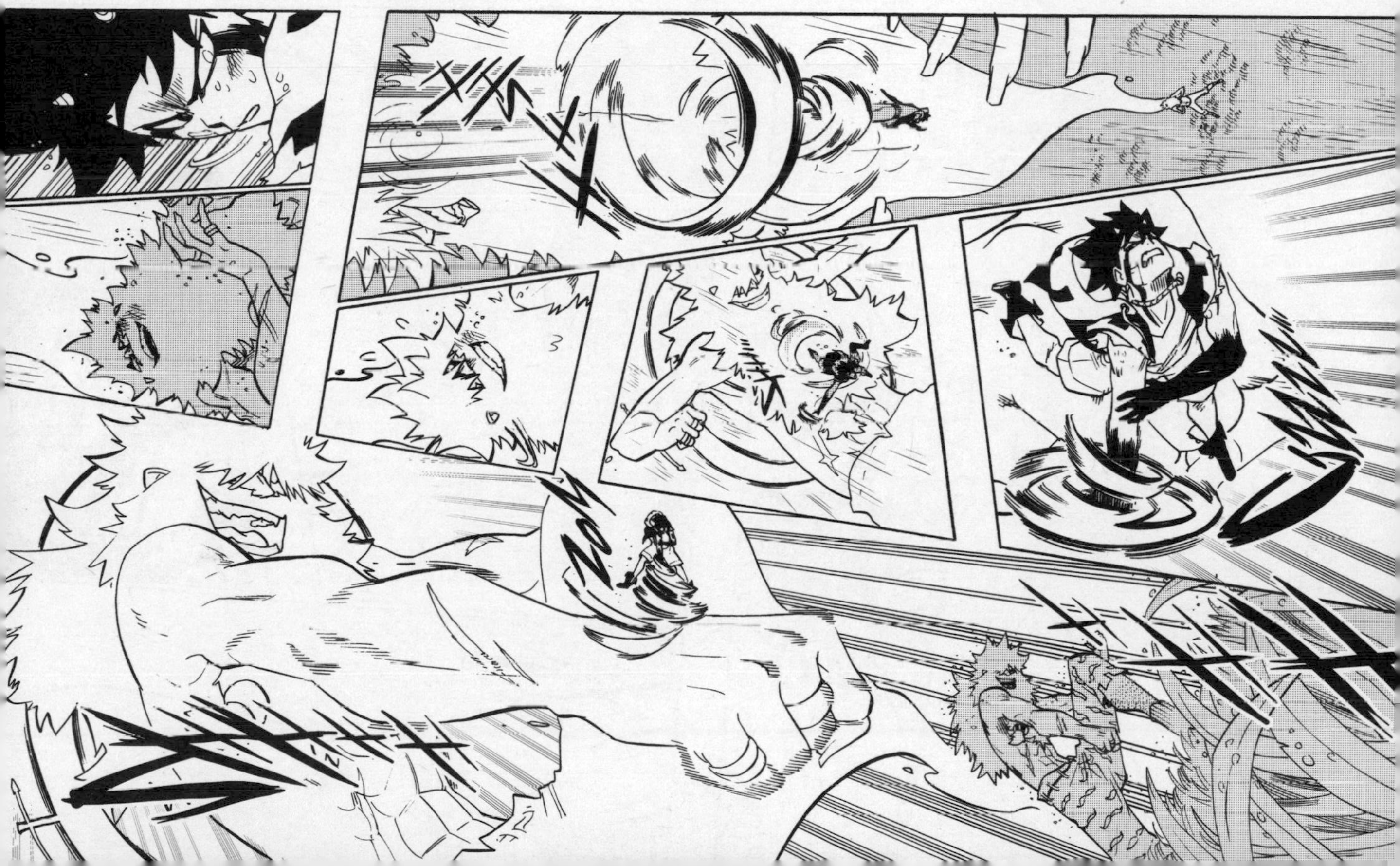

ZOM

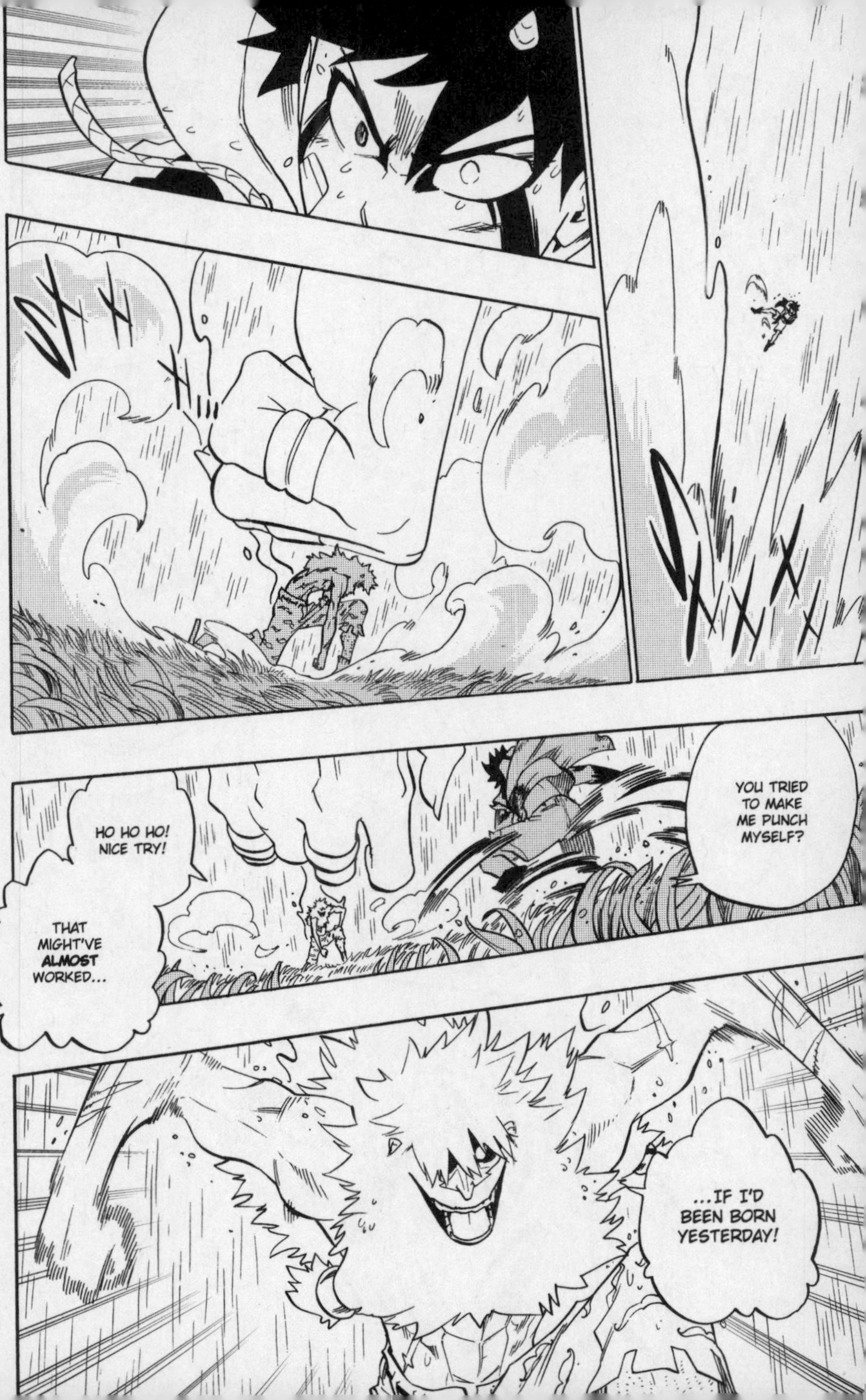
YOU TRIED TO MAKE ME PUNCH MYSELF?
HO HO HO! NICE TRY!
THAT MIGHT'VE **ALMOST** WORKED...
...IF I'D BEEN BORN YESTERDAY!

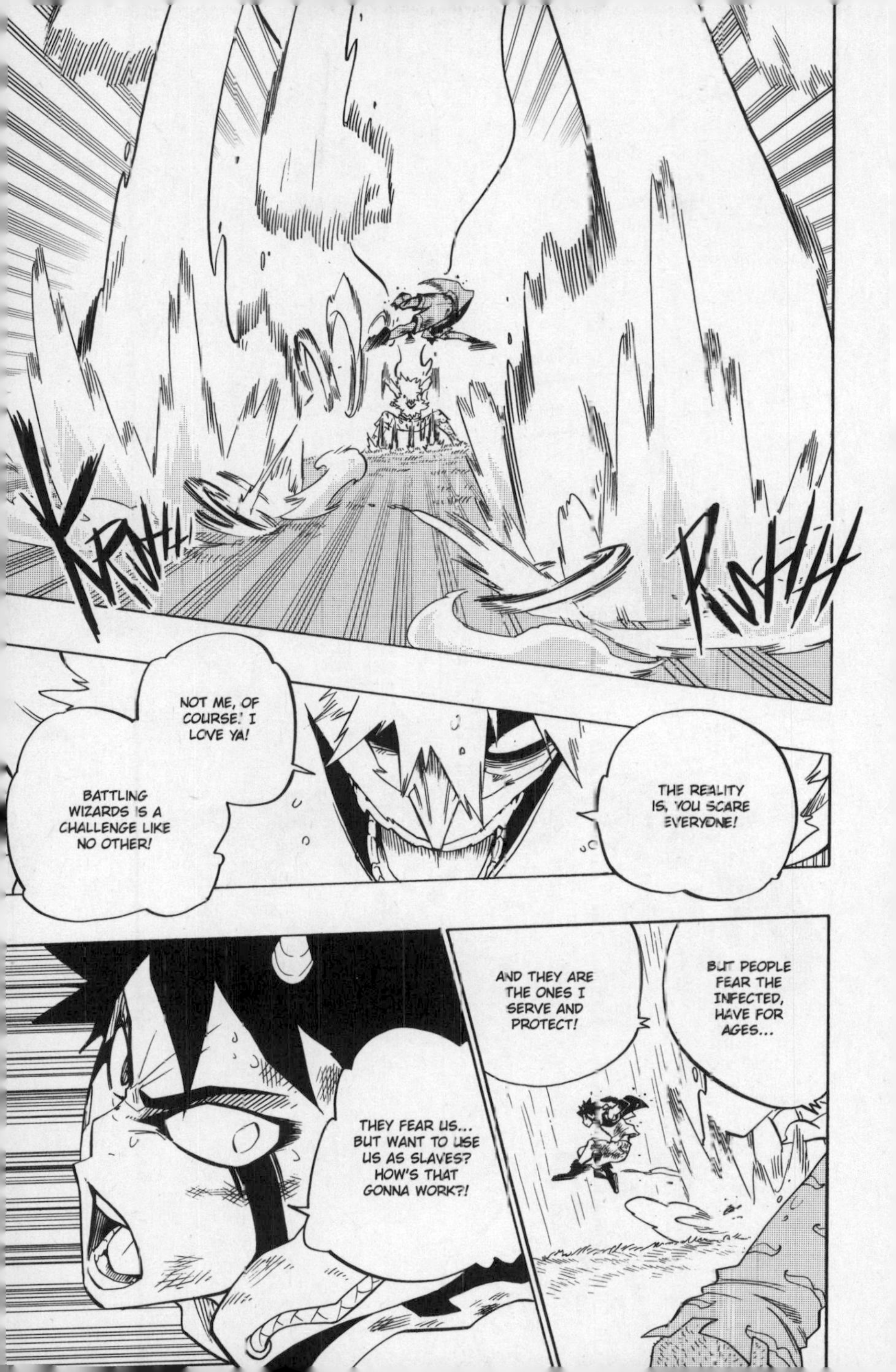

RSHH
KRSHH
THE REALITY IS, YOU SCARE EVERYONE!
NOT ME, OF COURSE. I LOVE YA!
BATTLING WIZARDS IS A CHALLENGE LIKE NO OTHER!
BUT PEOPLE FEAR THE INFECTED, HAVE FOR AGES...
AND THEY ARE THE ONES I SERVE AND PROTECT!
THEY FEAR US... BUT WANT TO USE US AS SLAVES? HOW'S THAT GONNA WORK?!

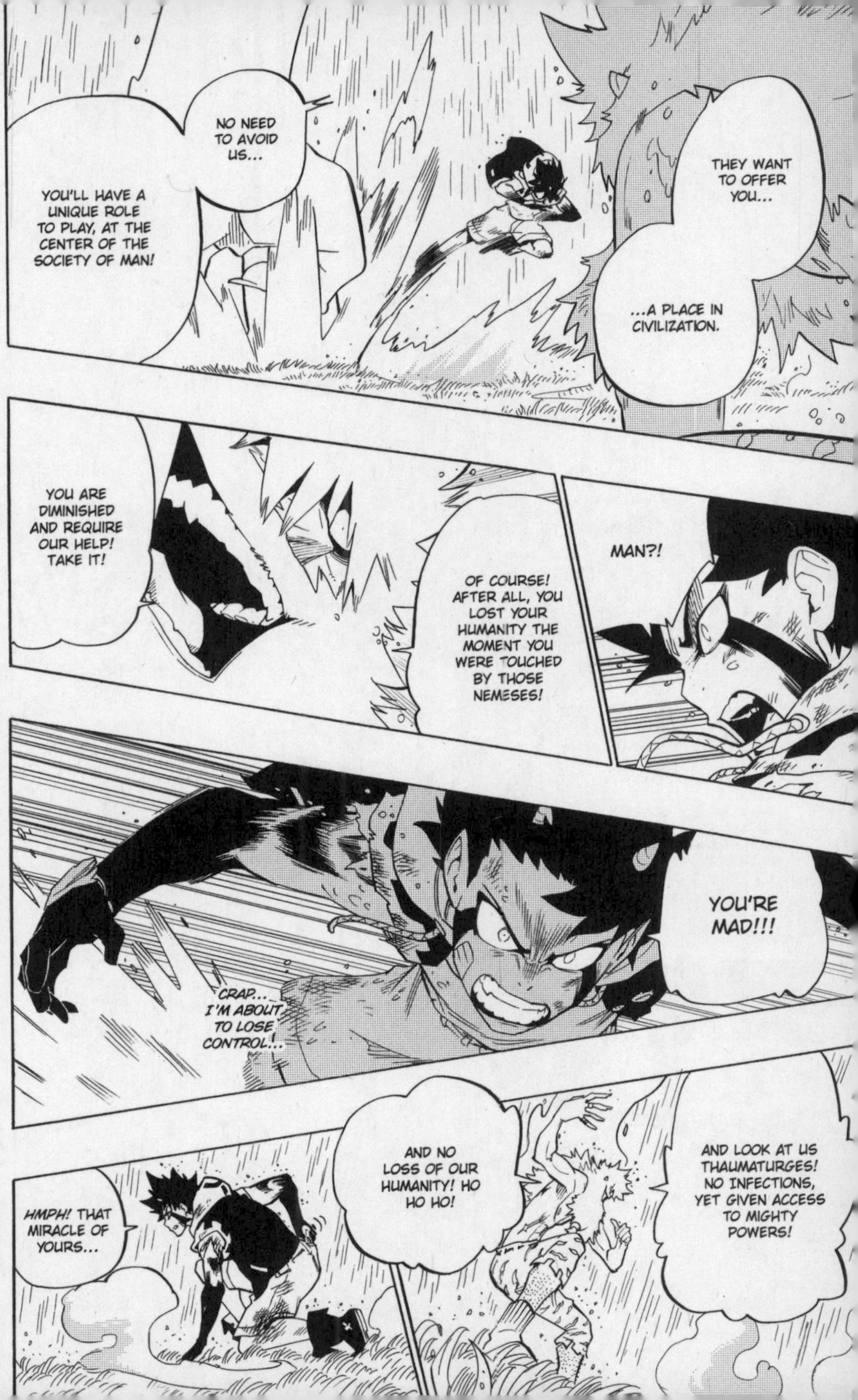

THEY WANT TO OFFER YOU...
...A PLACE IN CIVILIZATION.
NO NEED TO AVOID US...
YOU'LL HAVE A UNIQUE ROLE TO PLAY, AT THE CENTER OF THE SOCIETY OF MAN!
MAN?!
OF COURSE! AFTER ALL, YOU LOST YOUR HUMANITY THE MOMENT YOU WERE TOUCHED BY THOSE NEMESES!
YOU ARE DIMINISHED AND REQUIRE OUR HELP! TAKE IT!
YOU'RE MAD!!!
CRAP... I'M ABOUT TO LOSE CONTROL...
AND LOOK AT US THAUMATURGES! NO INFECTIONS, YET GIVEN ACCESS TO MIGHTY POWERS!
AND NO LOSS OF OUR HUMANITY! HO HO HO!
HMPH! THAT MIRACLE OF YOURS...

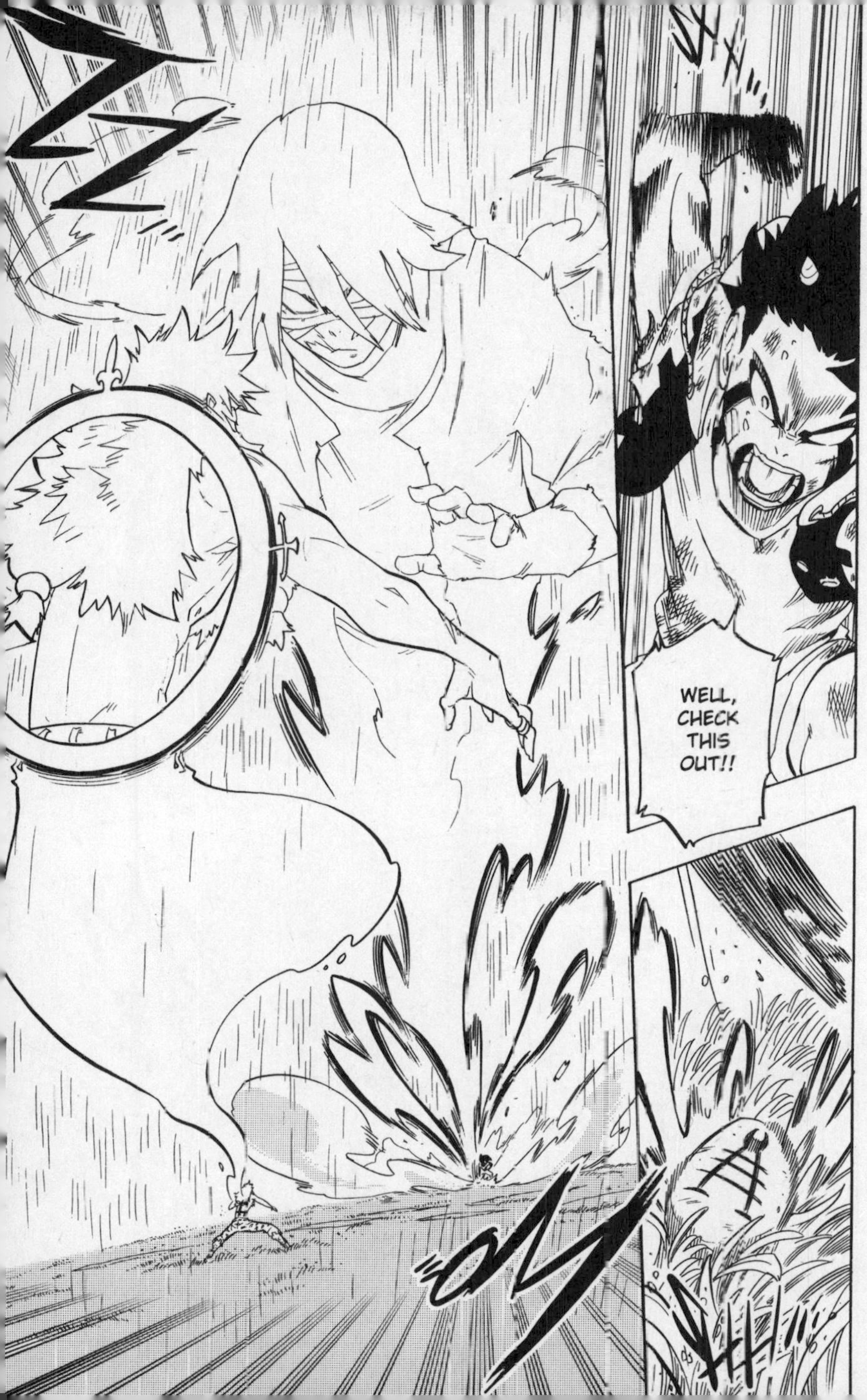
WELL, CHECK THIS OUT!!

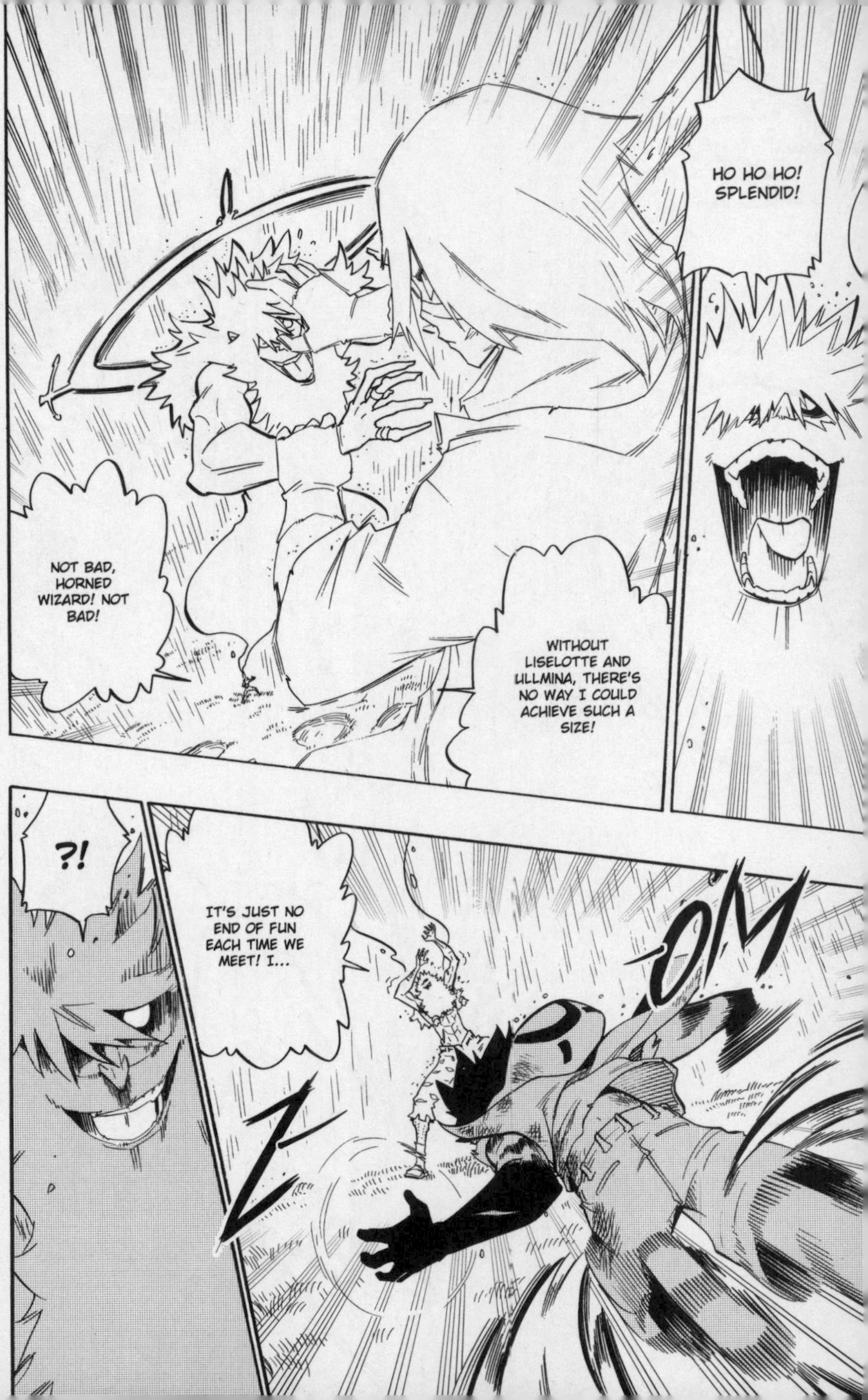
HO HO HO! SPLENDID!
NOT BAD, HORNED WIZARD! NOT BAD!
WITHOUT LISELOTTE AND ULLMINA, THERE'S NO WAY I COULD ACHIEVE SUCH A SIZE!
IT'S JUST NO END OF FUN EACH TIME WE MEET! I...
ZOM
?!

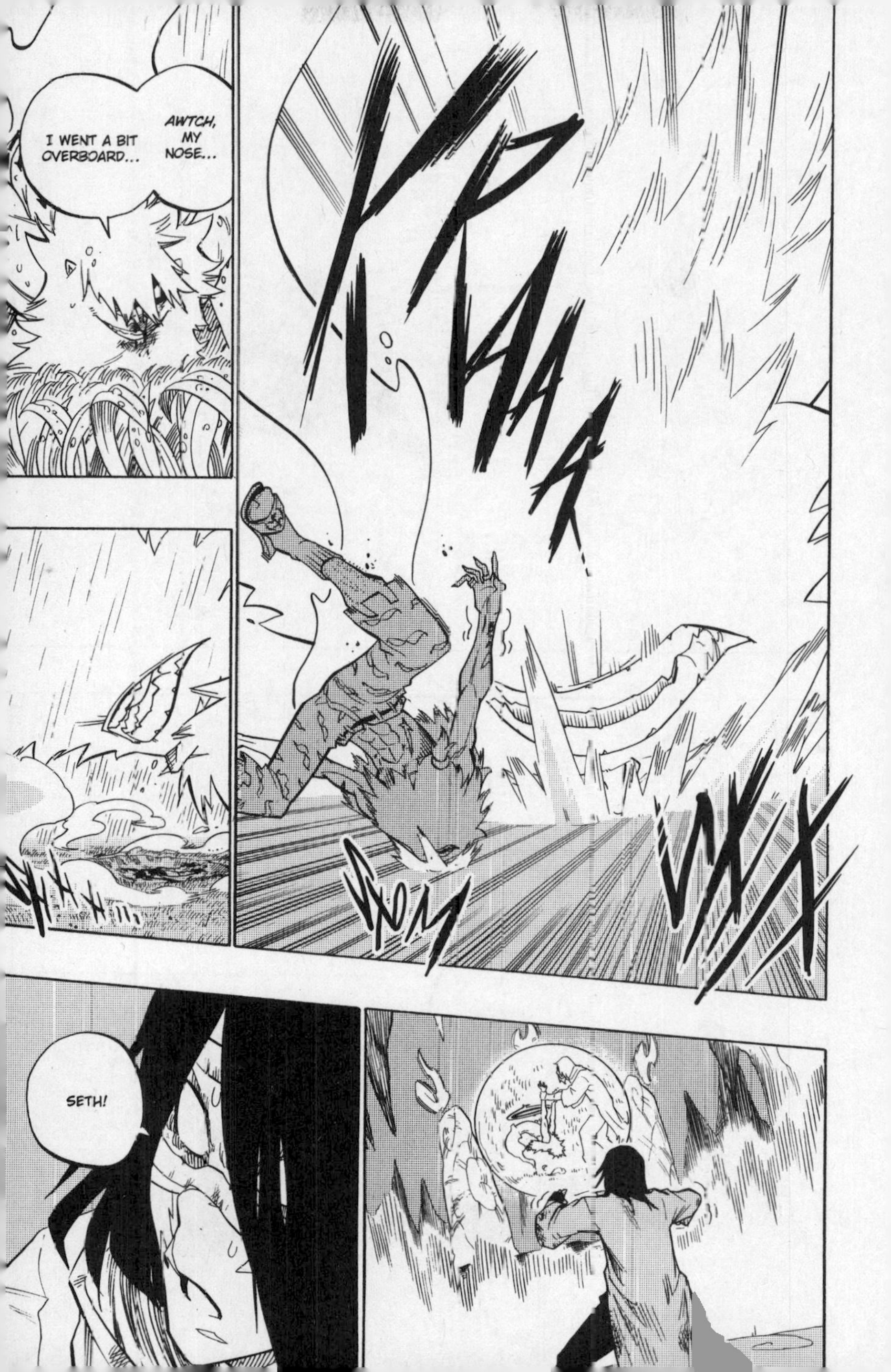
AWTCH, MY NOSE...
I WENT A BIT OVERBOARD...
SETH!

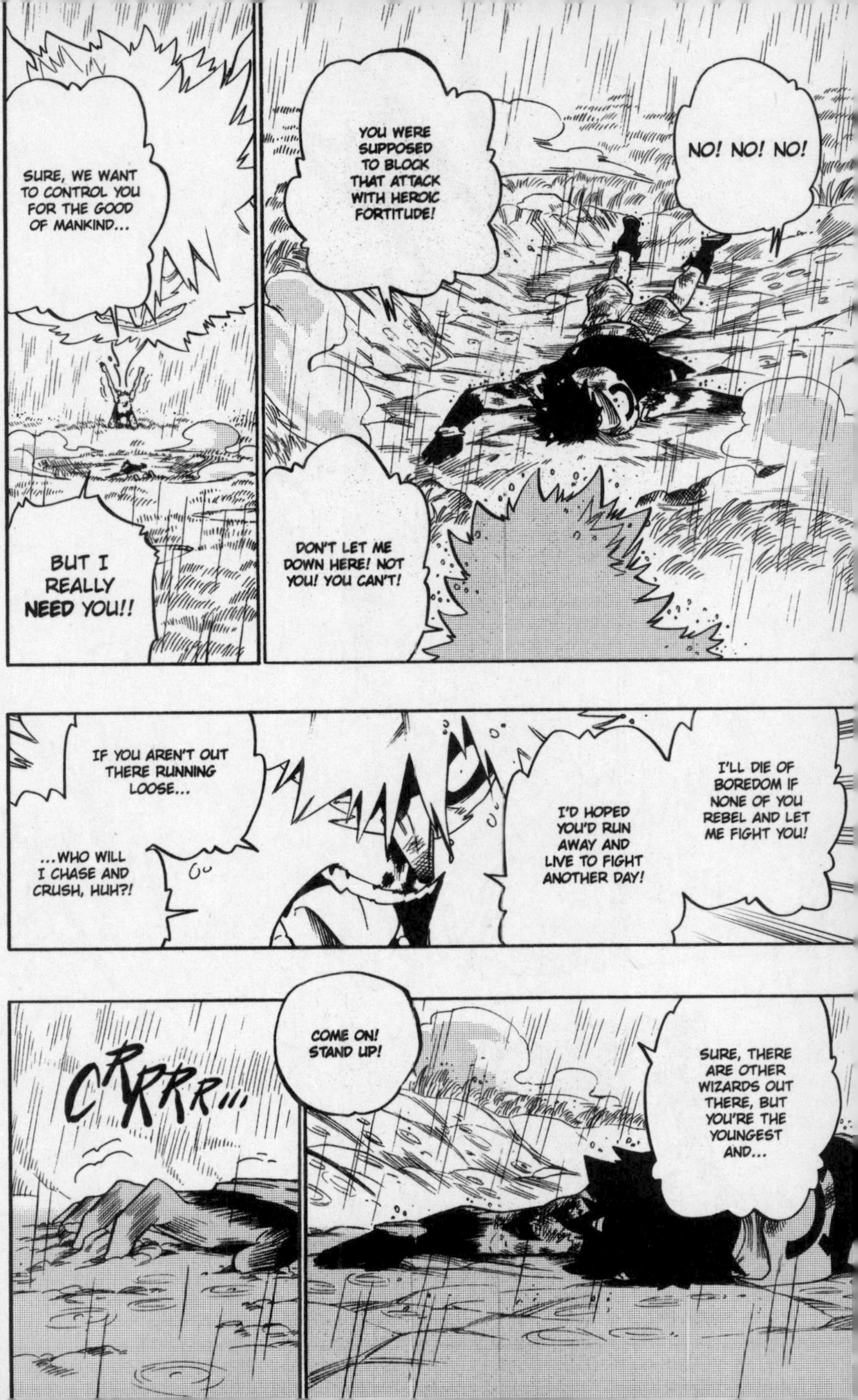
NO! NO! NO!
YOU WERE SUPPOSED TO BLOCK THAT ATTACK WITH HEROIC FORTITUDE!
DON'T LET ME DOWN HERE! NOT YOU! YOU CAN'T!
SURE, WE WANT TO CONTROL YOU FOR THE GOOD OF MANKIND...
BUT I REALLY NEED YOU!!
I'LL DIE OF BOREDOM IF NONE OF YOU REBEL AND LET ME FIGHT YOU!
I'D HOPED YOU'D RUN AWAY AND LIVE TO FIGHT ANOTHER DAY!
IF YOU AREN'T OUT THERE RUNNING LOOSE...
...WHO WILL I CHASE AND CRUSH, HUH?!
SURE, THERE ARE OTHER WIZARDS OUT THERE, BUT YOU'RE THE YOUNGEST AND...
COME ON! STAND UP!
CRRRRR

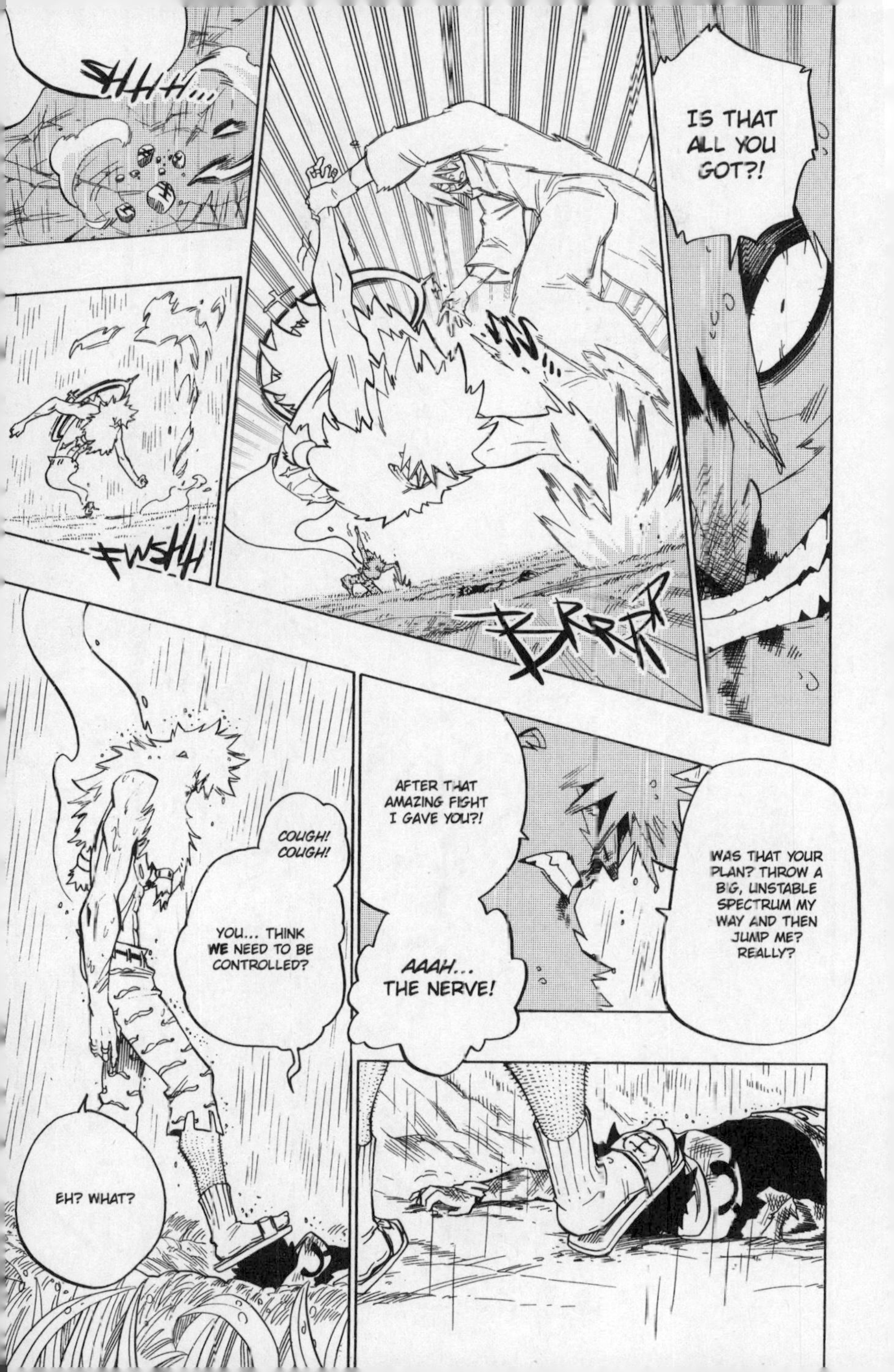
IS THAT ALL YOU GOT?!
SHHH...
FWSHH
WAS THAT YOUR PLAN? THROW A BIG, UNSTABLE SPECTRUM MY WAY AND THEN JUMP ME? REALLY?
AFTER THAT AMAZING FIGHT I GAVE YOU?!
AAAH... THE NERVE!
COUGH! COUGH!
YOU... THINK WE NEED TO BE CONTROLLED?
EH? WHAT?

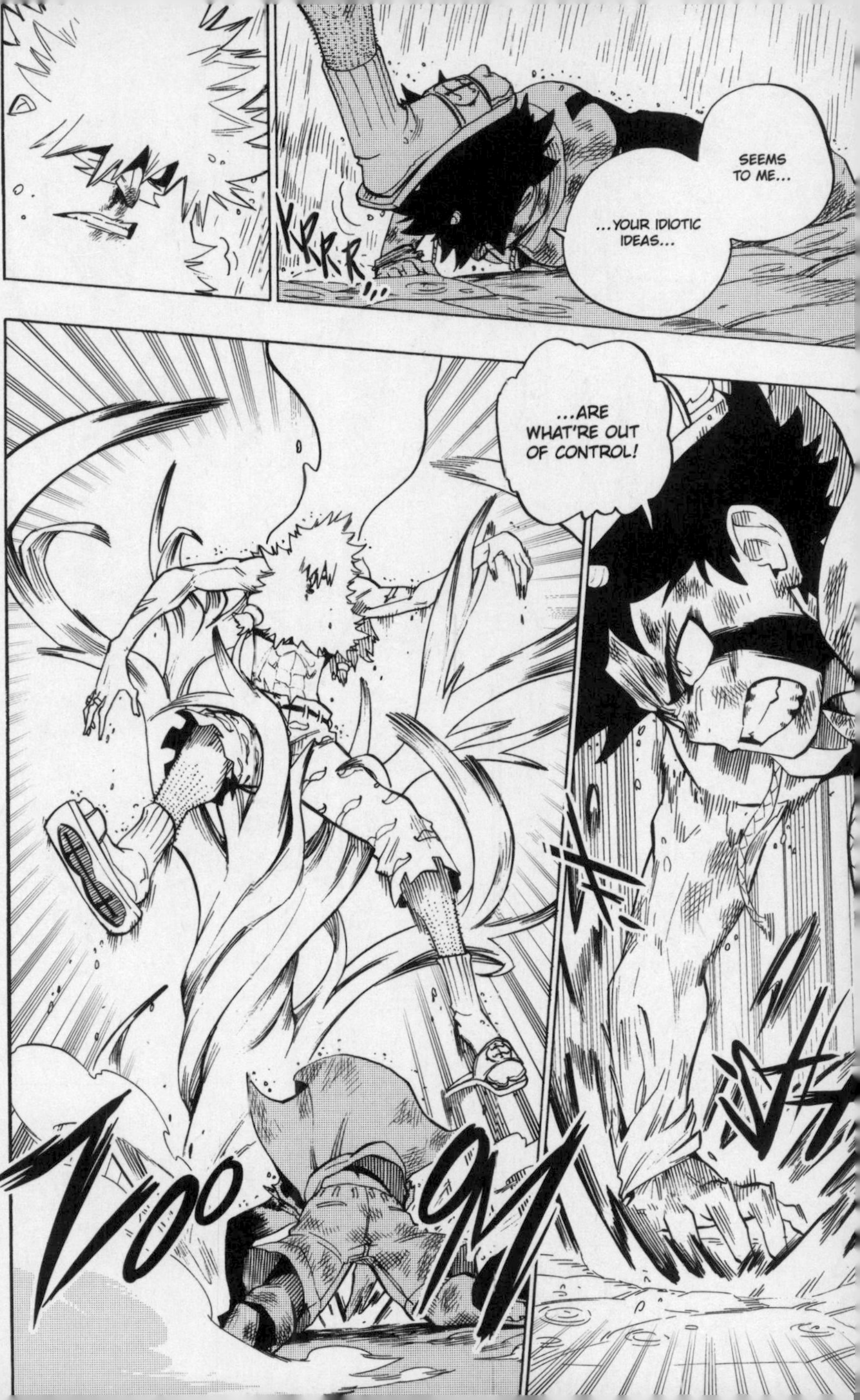
SEEMS TO ME...
...YOUR IDIOTIC IDEAS...
...ARE WHAT'RE OUT OF CONTROL!

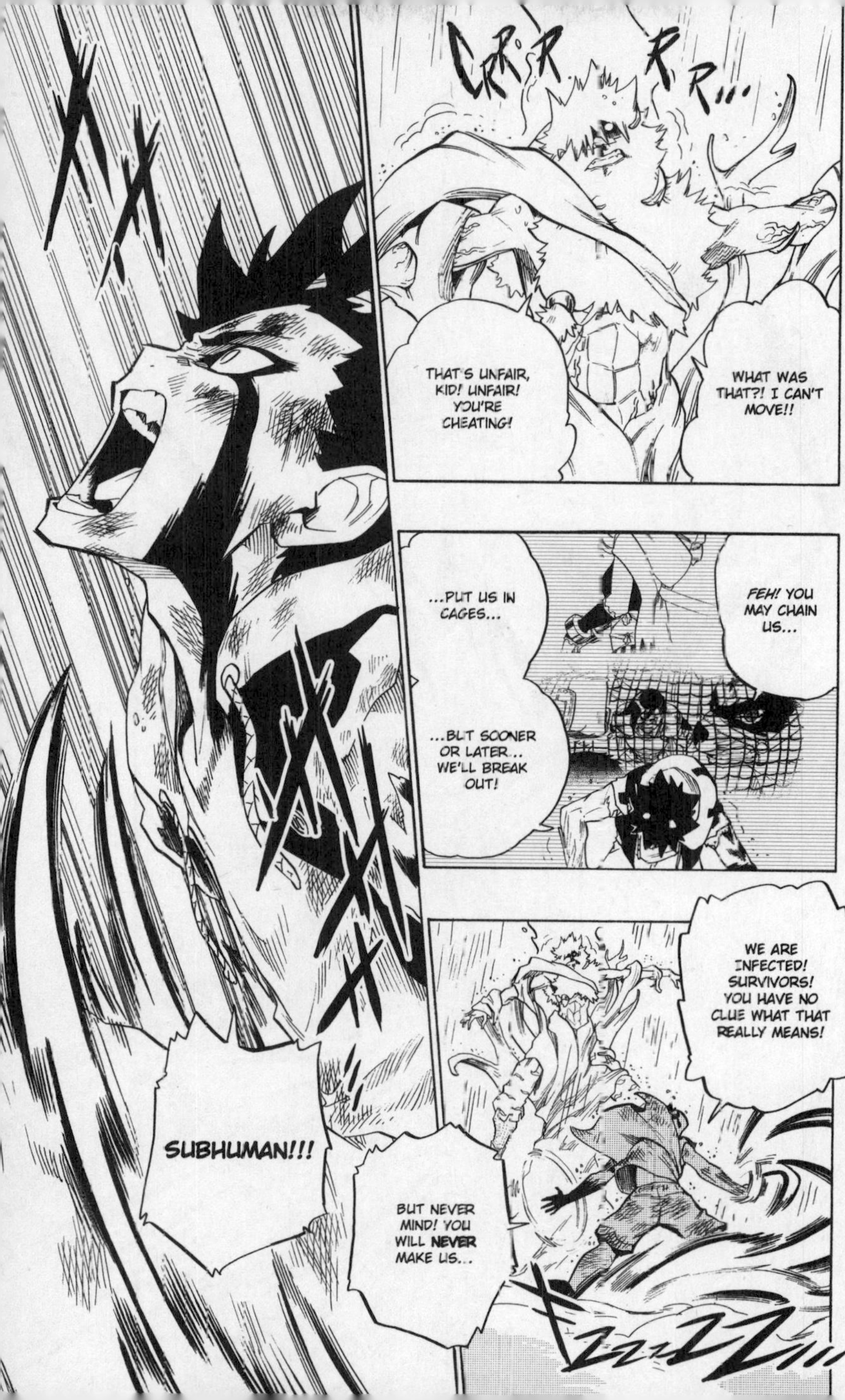
WHAT WAS THAT?! I CAN'T MOVE!!
THAT'S UNFAIR, KID! UNFAIR! YOU'RE CHEATING!
FEH! YOU MAY CHAIN US...
...PUT US IN CAGES...
...BUT SOONER OR LATER... WE'LL BREAK OUT!
WE ARE INFECTED! SURVIVORS! YOU HAVE NO CLUE WHAT THAT REALLY MEANS!
BUT NEVER MIND! YOU WILL NEVER MAKE US...
SUBHUMAN!!!

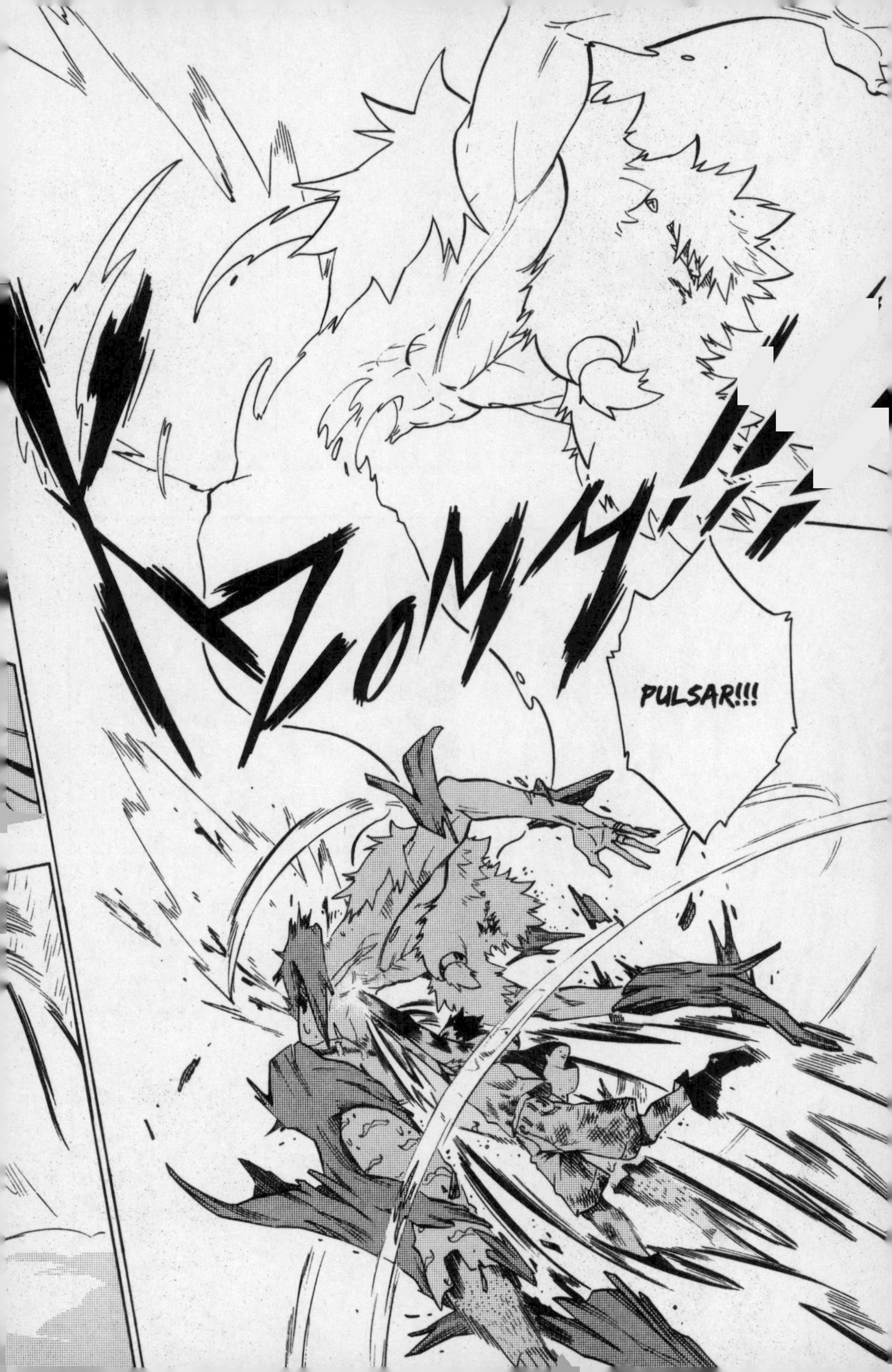
PULSAR!!!

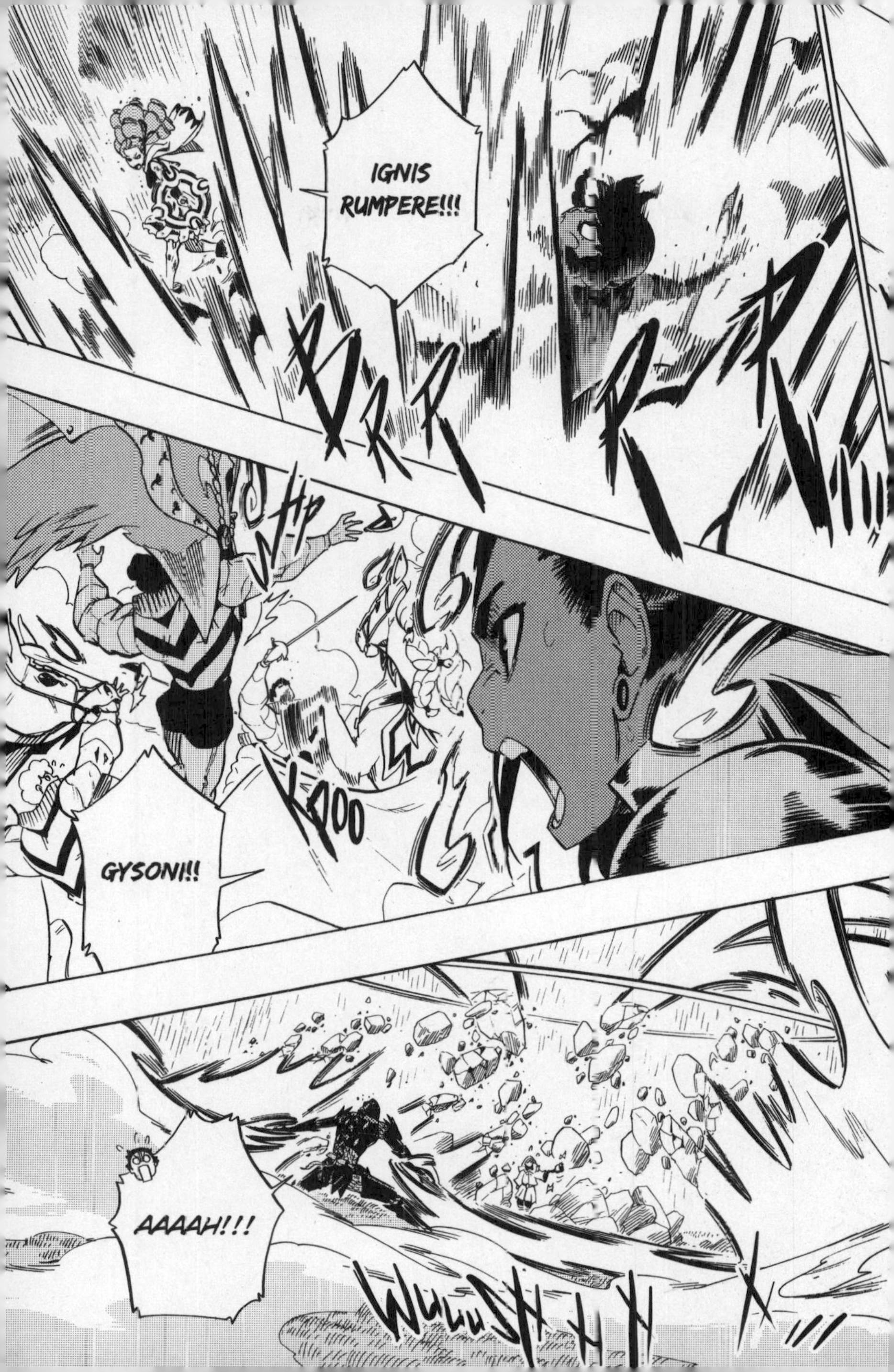
IGNIS RUMPERE!!!
KOOO
GYSONI!!!
AAAAH!!!

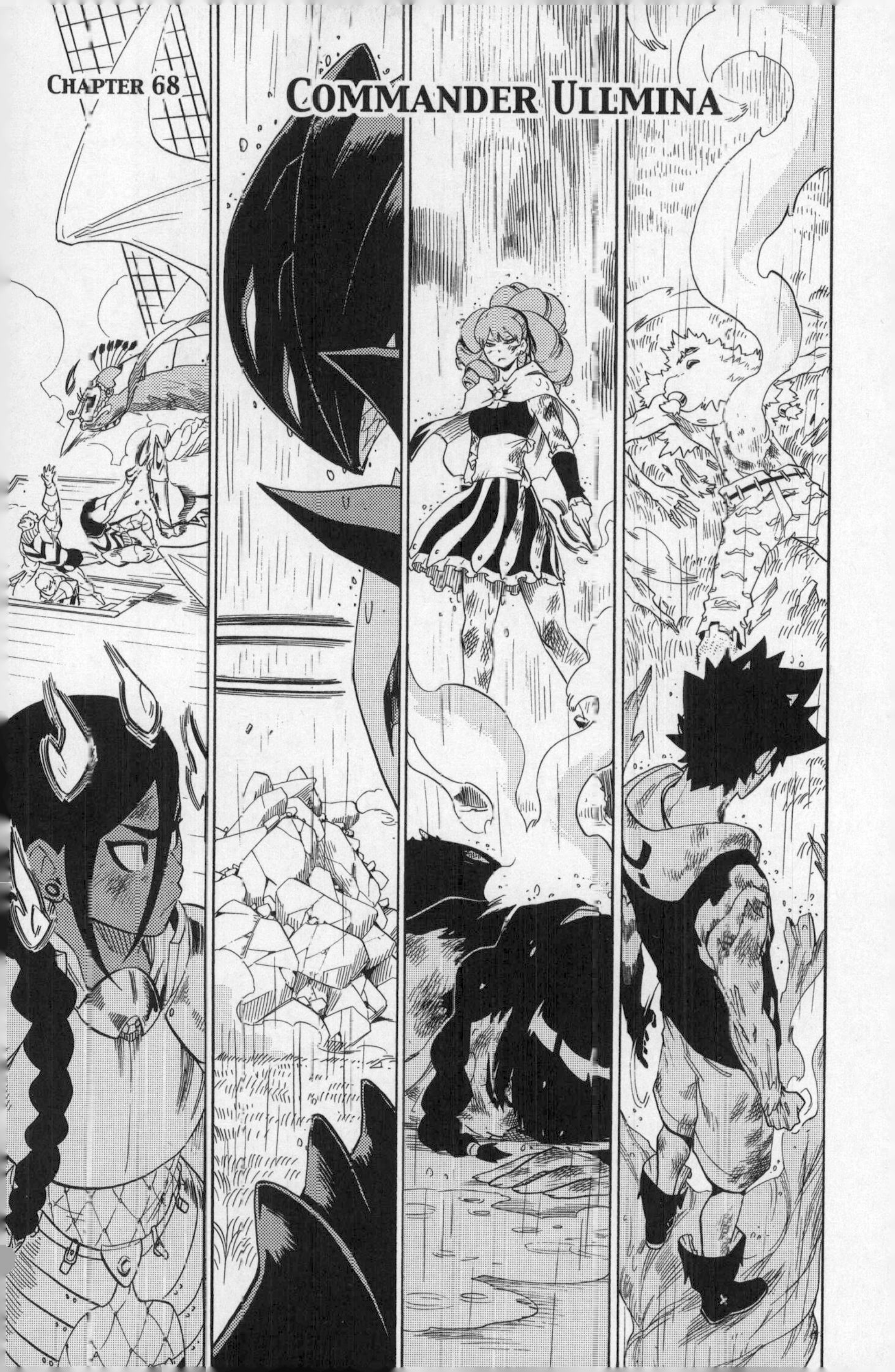
Chapter 68
Commander Ullmina

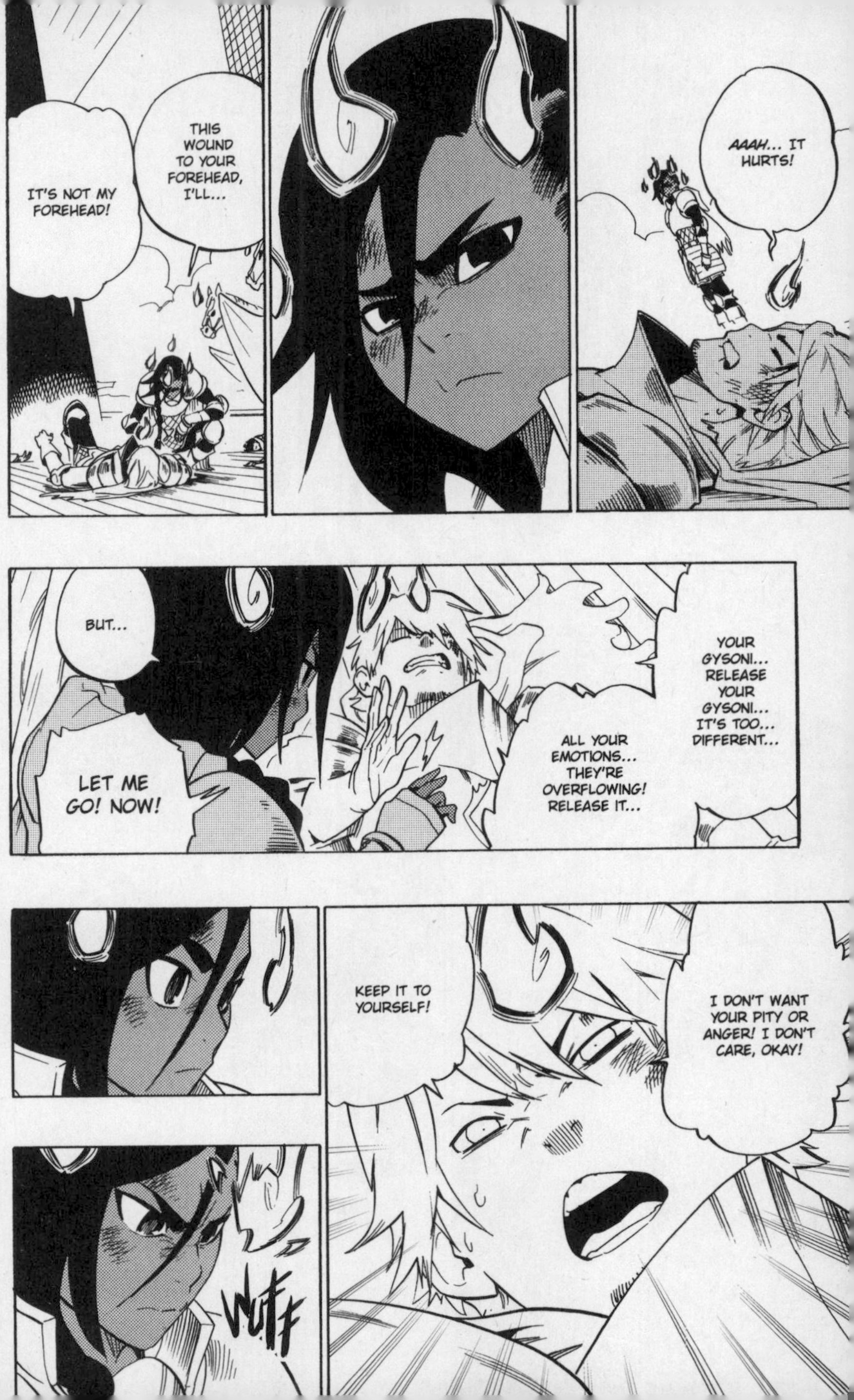
AAAH... IT HURTS!
THIS WOUND TO YOUR FOREHEAD, I'LL...
IT'S NOT MY FOREHEAD!
YOUR GYSONI... RELEASE YOUR GYSONI... IT'S TOO... DIFFERENT...
ALL YOUR EMOTIONS... THEY'RE OVERFLOWING! RELEASE IT...
BUT...
LET ME GO! NOW!
I DON'T WANT YOUR PITY OR ANGER! I DON'T CARE, OKAY!
KEEP IT TO YOURSELF!
WUFF

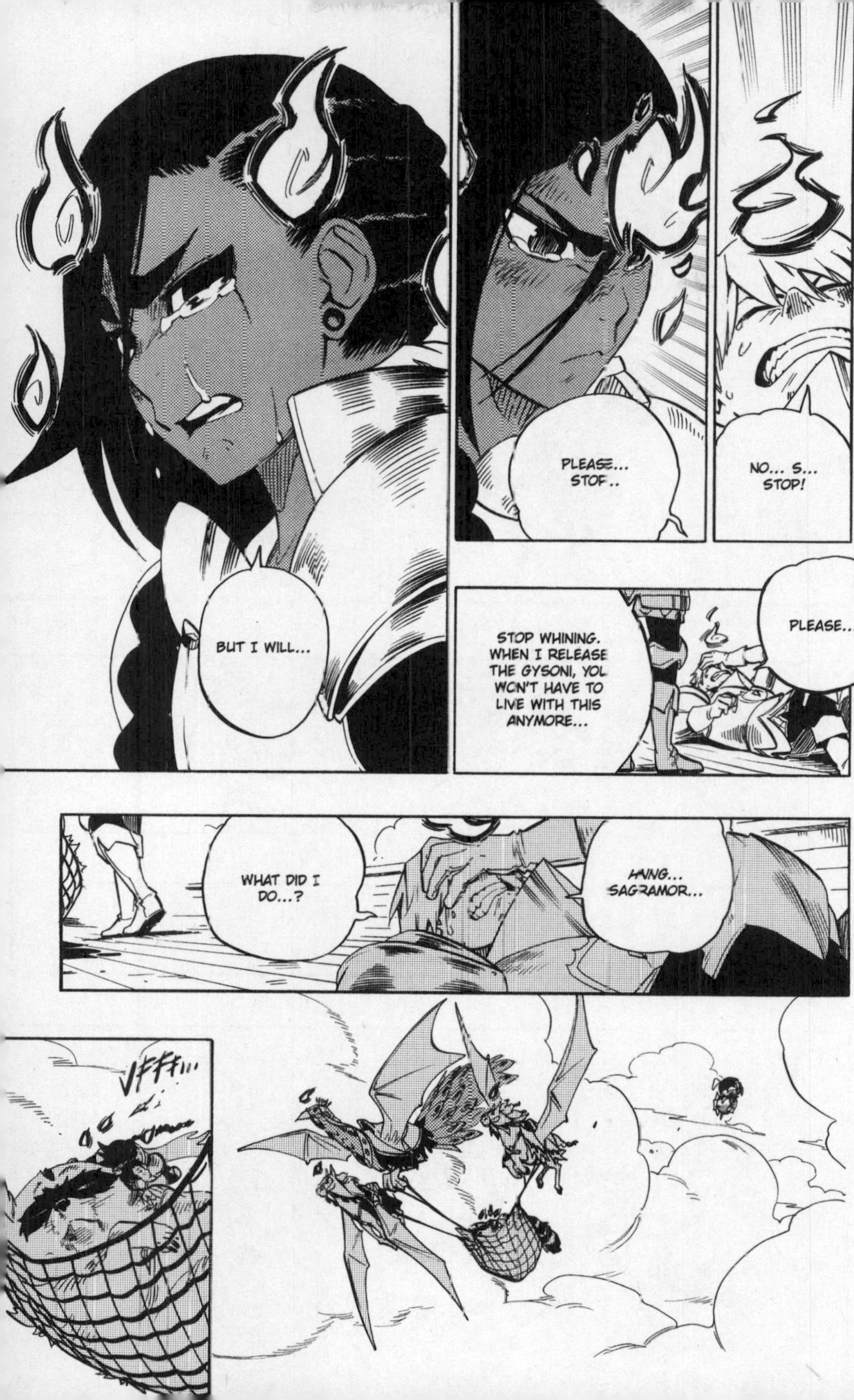
NO... S... STOP!
PLEASE... STOP..
PLEASE...
STOP WHINING. WHEN I RELEASE THE GYSONI, YOU WON'T HAVE TO LIVE WITH THIS ANYMORE...
BUT I WILL...
HNNG... SAGRAMOR...
WHAT DID I DO...?
VFFF...

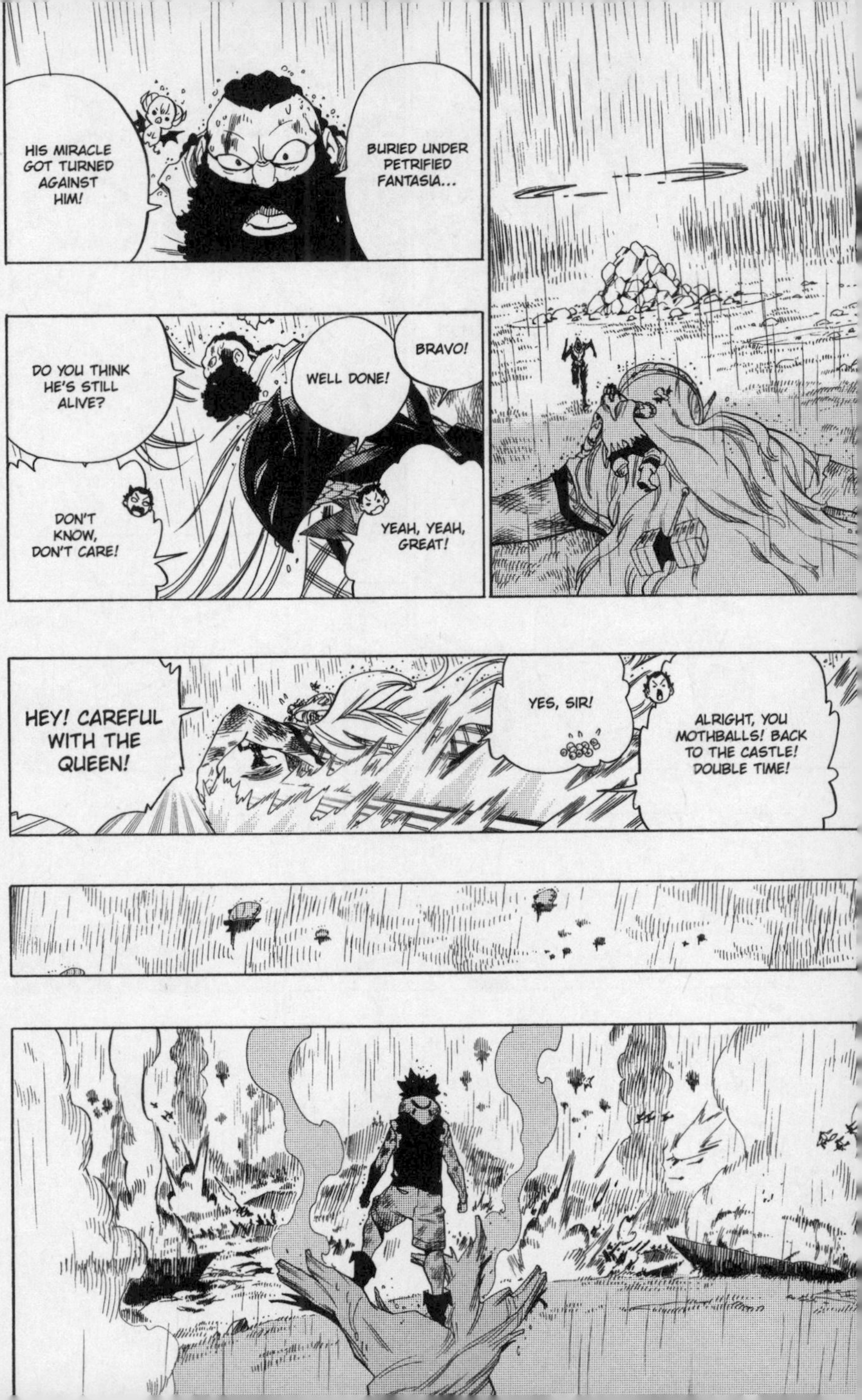
BURIED UNDER PETRIFIED FANTASIA...
HIS MIRACLE GOT TURNED AGAINST HIM!
BRAVO!
WELL DONE!
DO YOU THINK HE'S STILL ALIVE?
YEAH, YEAH, GREAT!
DON'T KNOW, DON'T CARE!
ALRIGHT, YOU MOTHBALLS! BACK TO THE CASTLE! DOUBLE TIME!
YES, SIR!
HEY! CAREFUL WITH THE QUEEN!

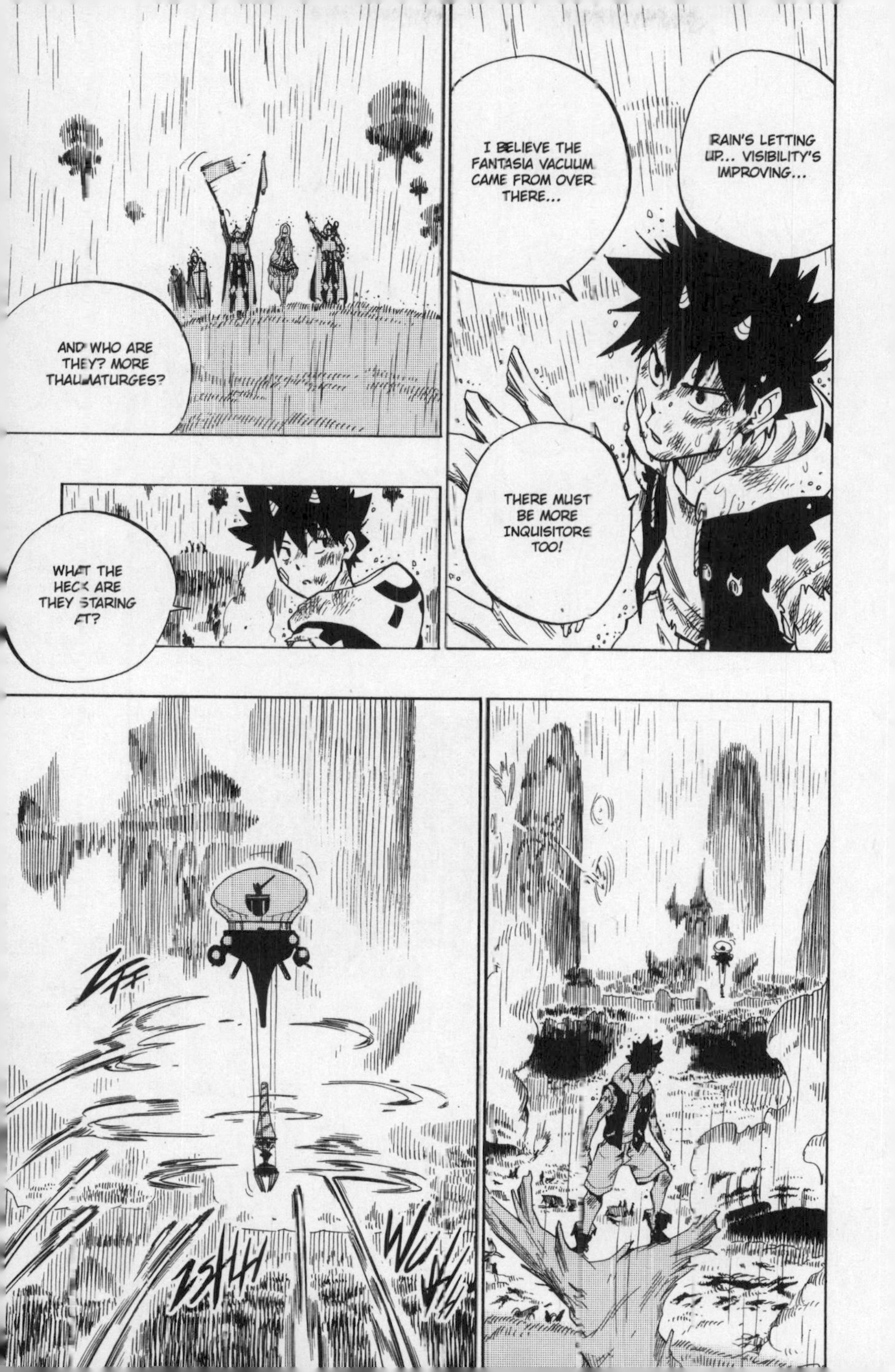
RAIN'S LETTING UP... VISIBILITY'S IMPROVING...
I BELIEVE THE FANTASIA VACUUM CAME FROM OVER THERE...
THERE MUST BE MORE INQUISITORS TOO!
AND WHO ARE THEY? MORE THAUMATURGES?
WHAT THE HECK ARE THEY STARING AT?

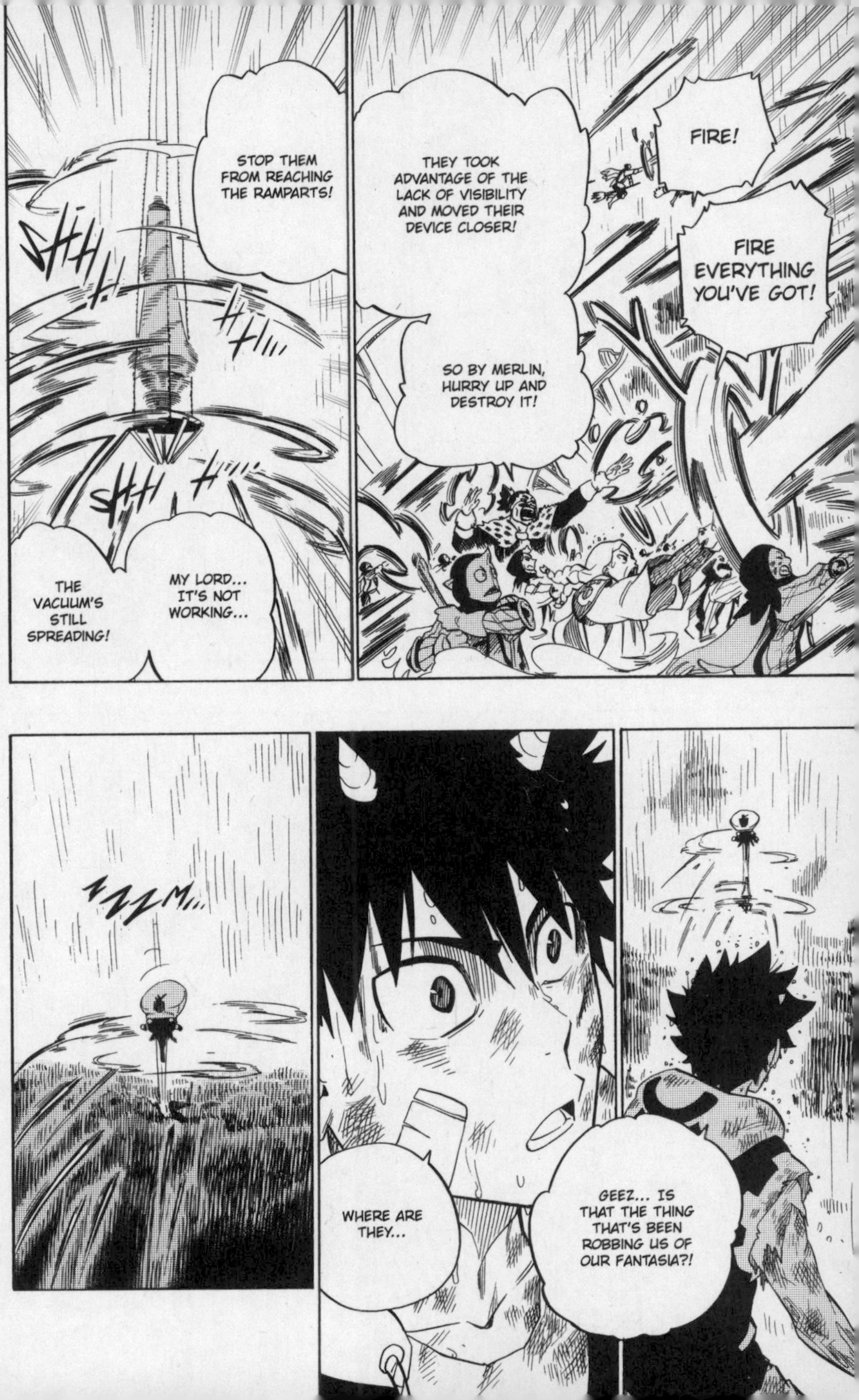
FIRE!
FIRE EVERYTHING YOU'VE GOT!
THEY TOOK ADVANTAGE OF THE LACK OF VISIBILITY AND MOVED THEIR DEVICE CLOSER!
SO BY MERLIN, HURRY UP AND DESTROY IT!
STOP THEM FROM REACHING THE RAMPARTS!
MY LORD... IT'S NOT WORKING...
THE VACUUM'S STILL SPREADING!
GEEZ... IS THAT THE THING THAT'S BEEN ROBBING US OF OUR FANTASIA?!
WHERE ARE THEY...
ZZZM...

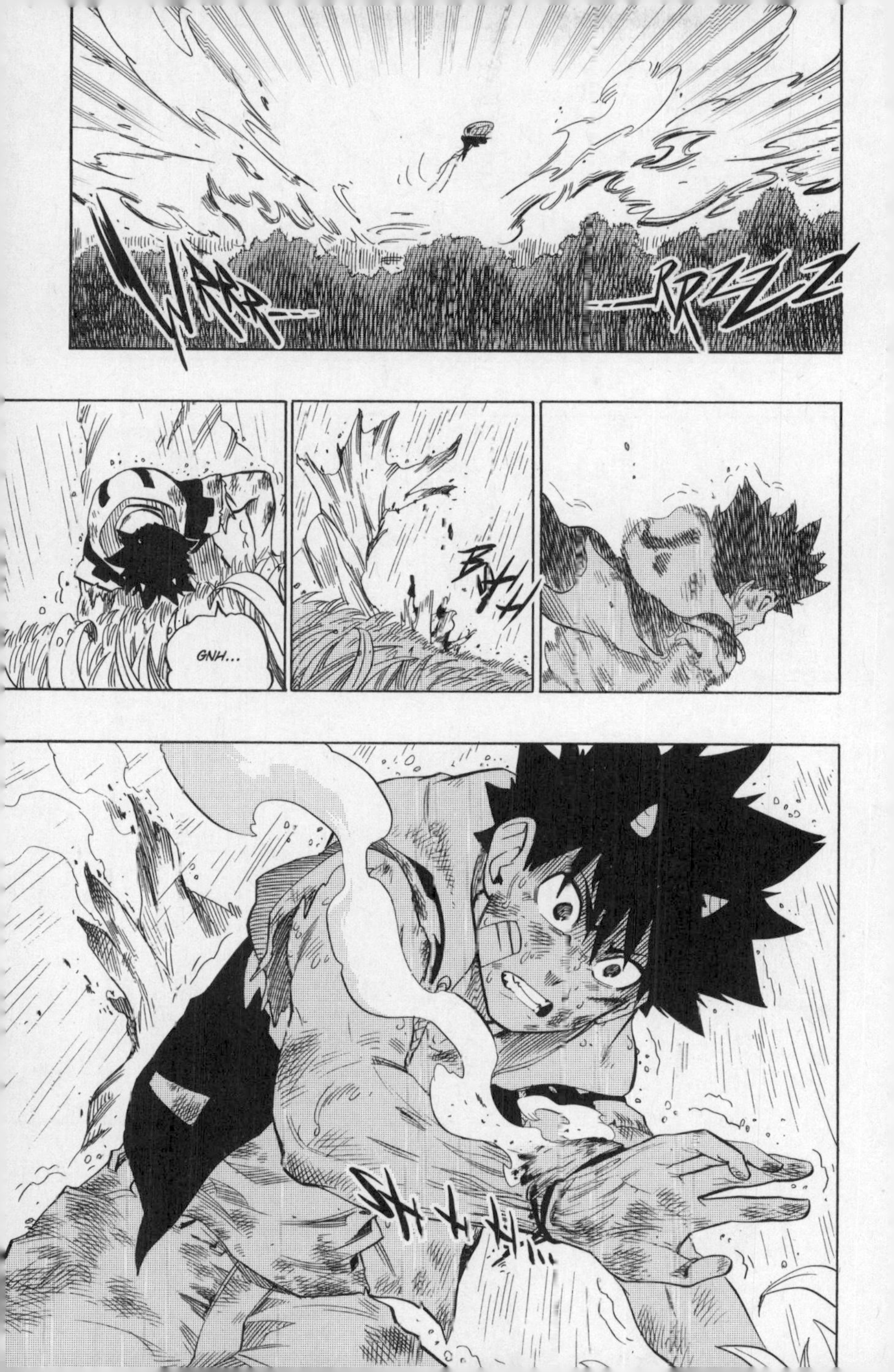
WRRR—
—RRZZZ
GNH...

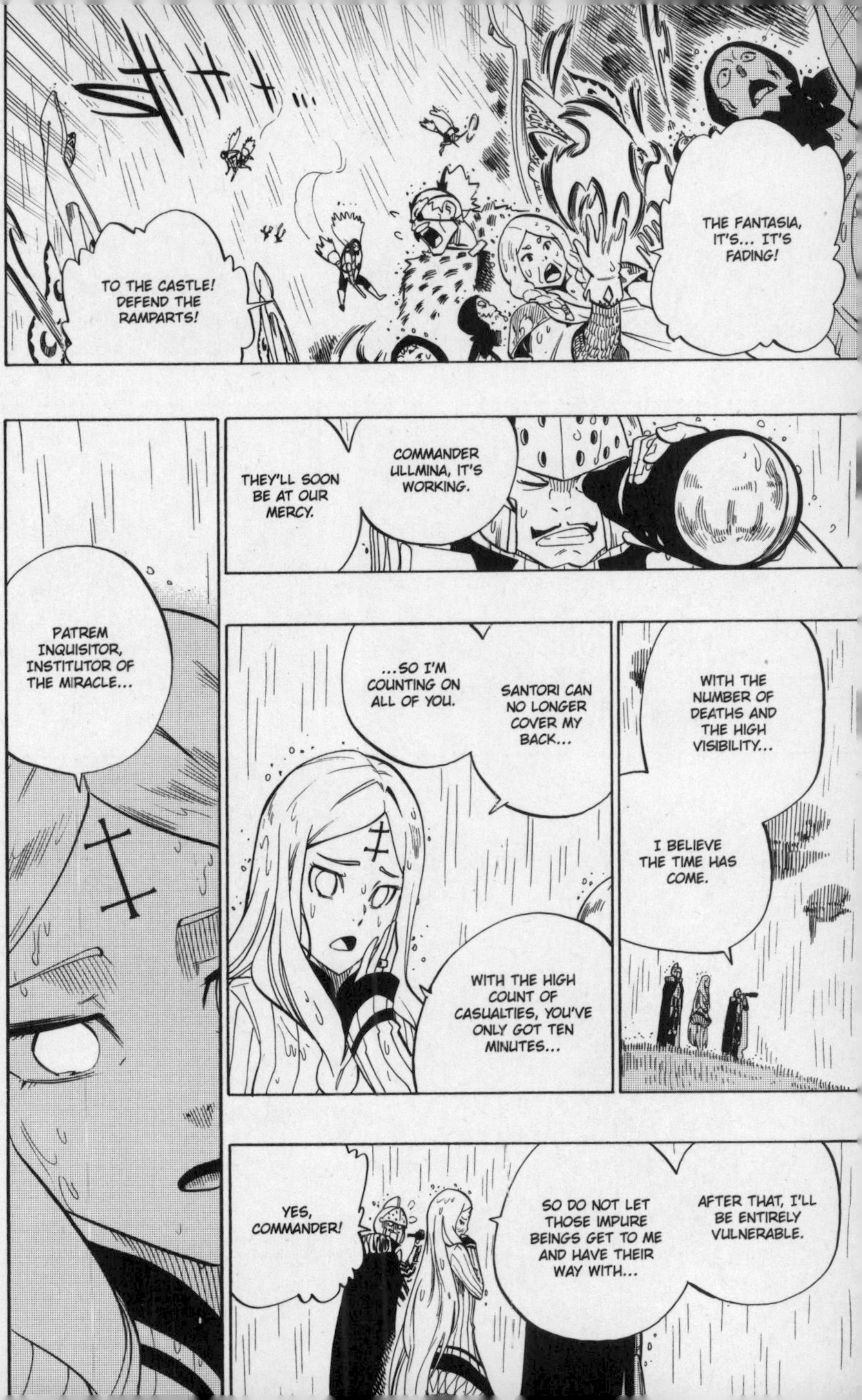
THE FANTASIA, IT'S... IT'S FADING!
TO THE CASTLE! DEFEND THE RAMPARTS!
COMMANDER ULLMINA, IT'S WORKING.
THEY'LL SOON BE AT OUR MERCY.
WITH THE NUMBER OF DEATHS AND THE HIGH VISIBILITY...
I BELIEVE THE TIME HAS COME.
SANTORI CAN NO LONGER COVER MY BACK...
...SO I'M COUNTING ON ALL OF YOU.
WITH THE HIGH COUNT OF CASUALTIES, YOU'VE ONLY GOT TEN MINUTES...
AFTER THAT, I'LL BE ENTIRELY VULNERABLE.
SO DO NOT LET THOSE IMPURE BEINGS GET TO ME AND HAVE THEIR WAY WITH...
YES, COMMANDER!
PATREM INQUISITOR, INSTITUTOR OF THE MIRACLE...

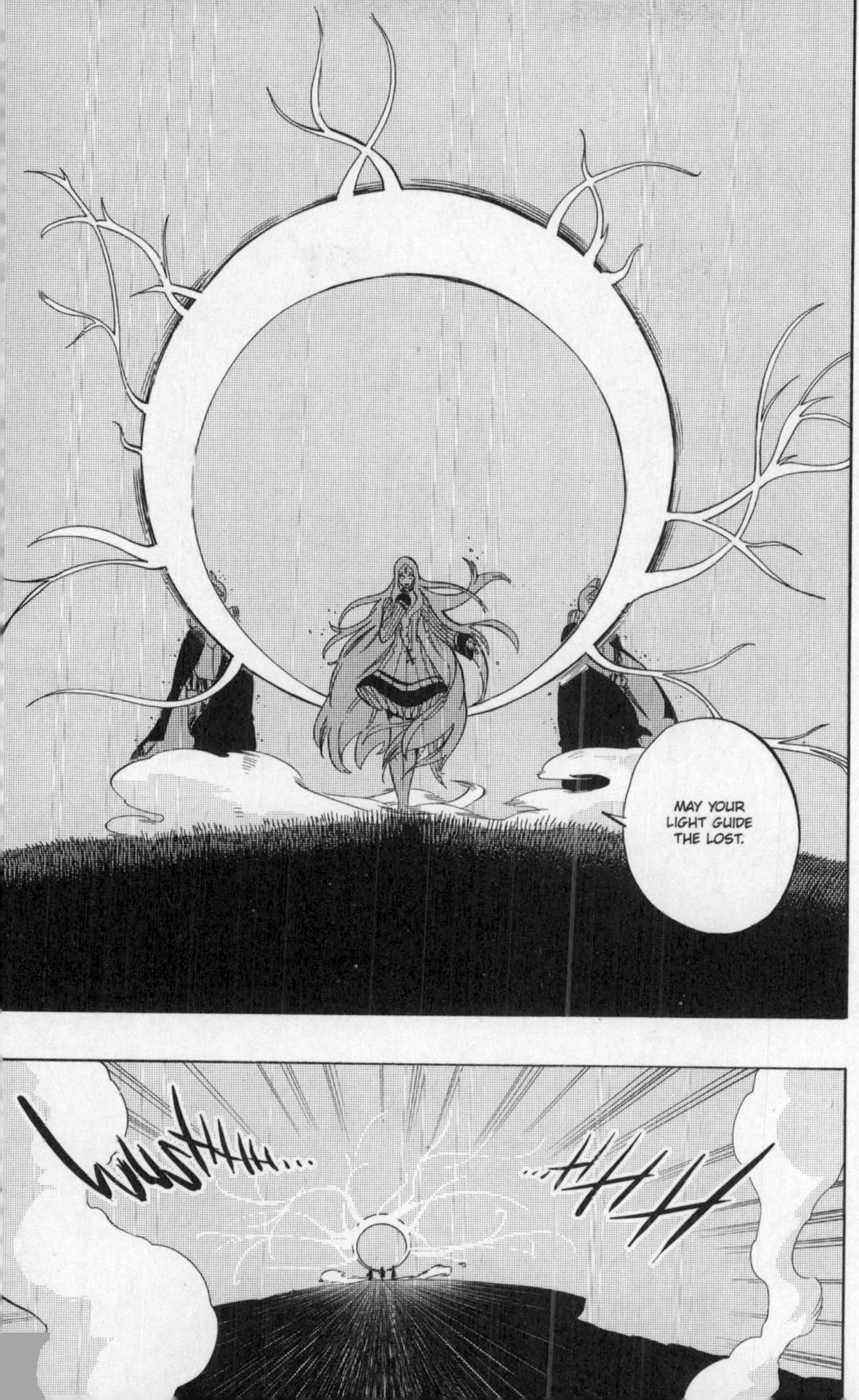
MAY YOUR LIGHT GUIDE THE LOST.
WUSHHHH...
...HHHH

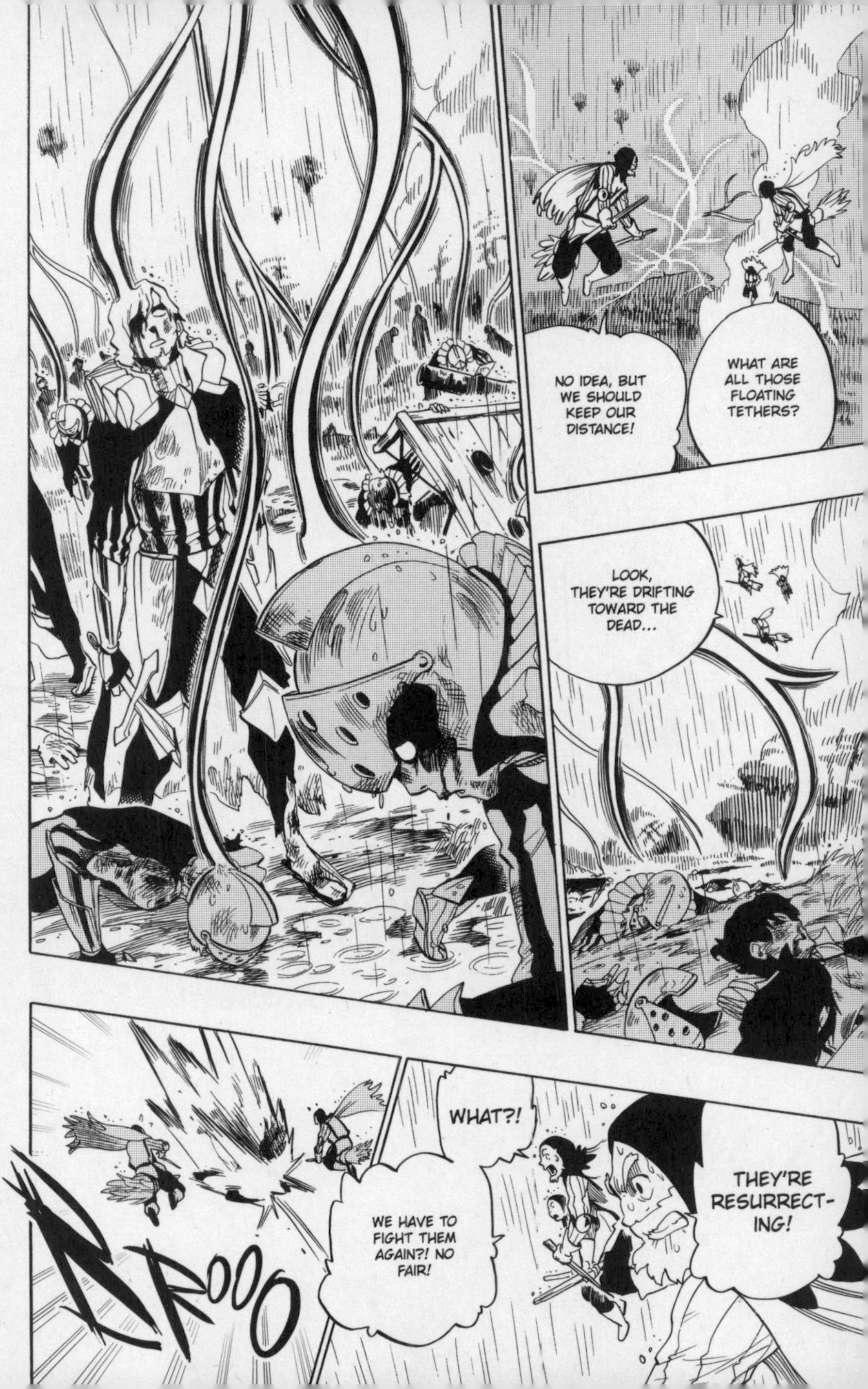
WHAT ARE ALL THOSE FLOATING TETHERS?
NO IDEA, BUT WE SHOULD KEEP OUR DISTANCE!
LOOK, THEY'RE DRIFTING TOWARD THE DEAD...
THEY'RE RESURRECT-ING!
WHAT?!
WE HAVE TO FIGHT THEM AGAIN?! NO FAIR!
ZROOO

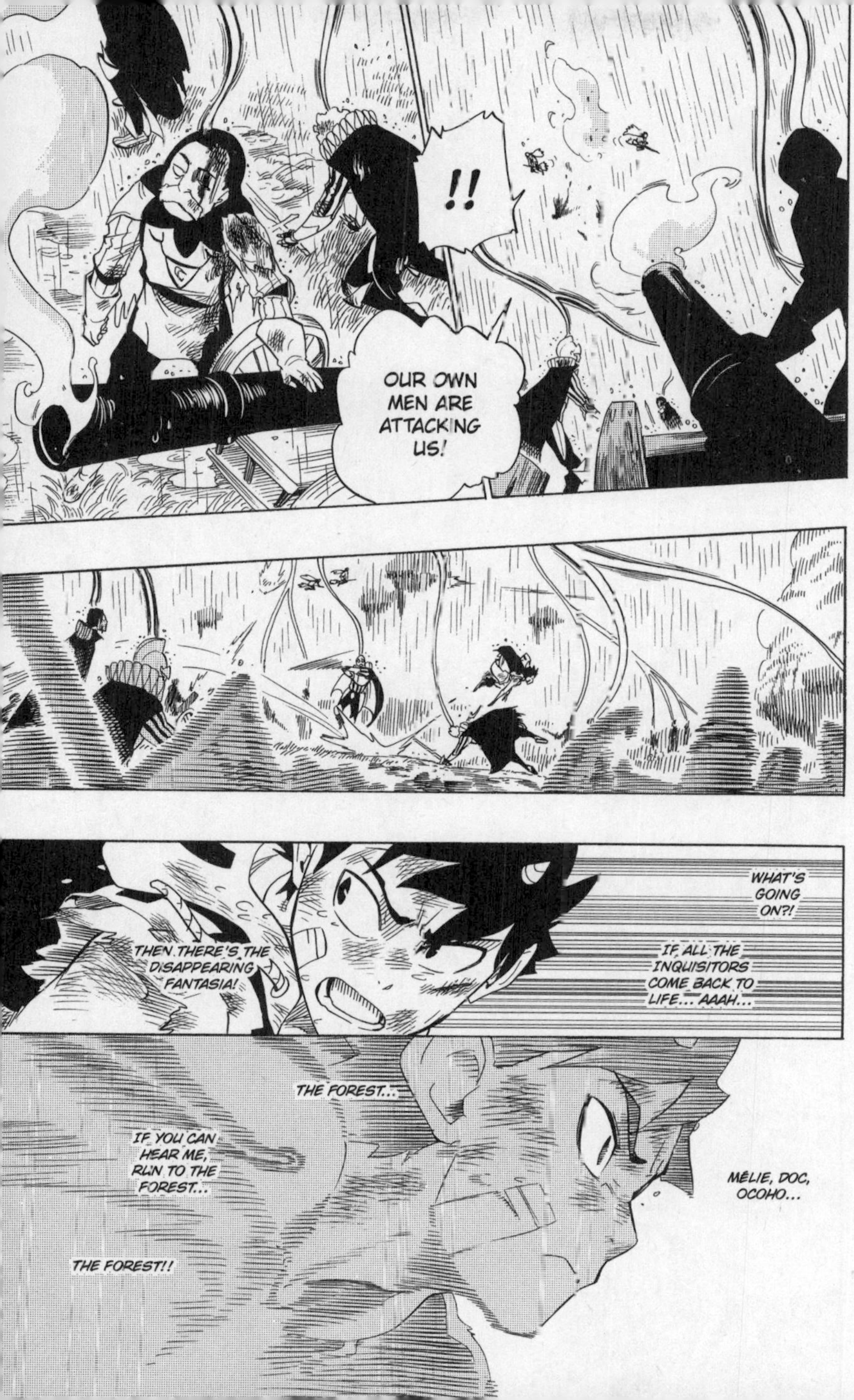
!!
OUR OWN MEN ARE ATTACKING US!
WHAT'S GOING ON?!
IF ALL THE INQUISITORS COME BACK TO LIFE... AAAH...
THEN THERE'S THE DISAPPEARING FANTASIA!
MÉLIE, DOC, OCOHO...
THE FOREST...
IF YOU CAN HEAR ME, RUN TO THE FOREST...
THE FOREST!!

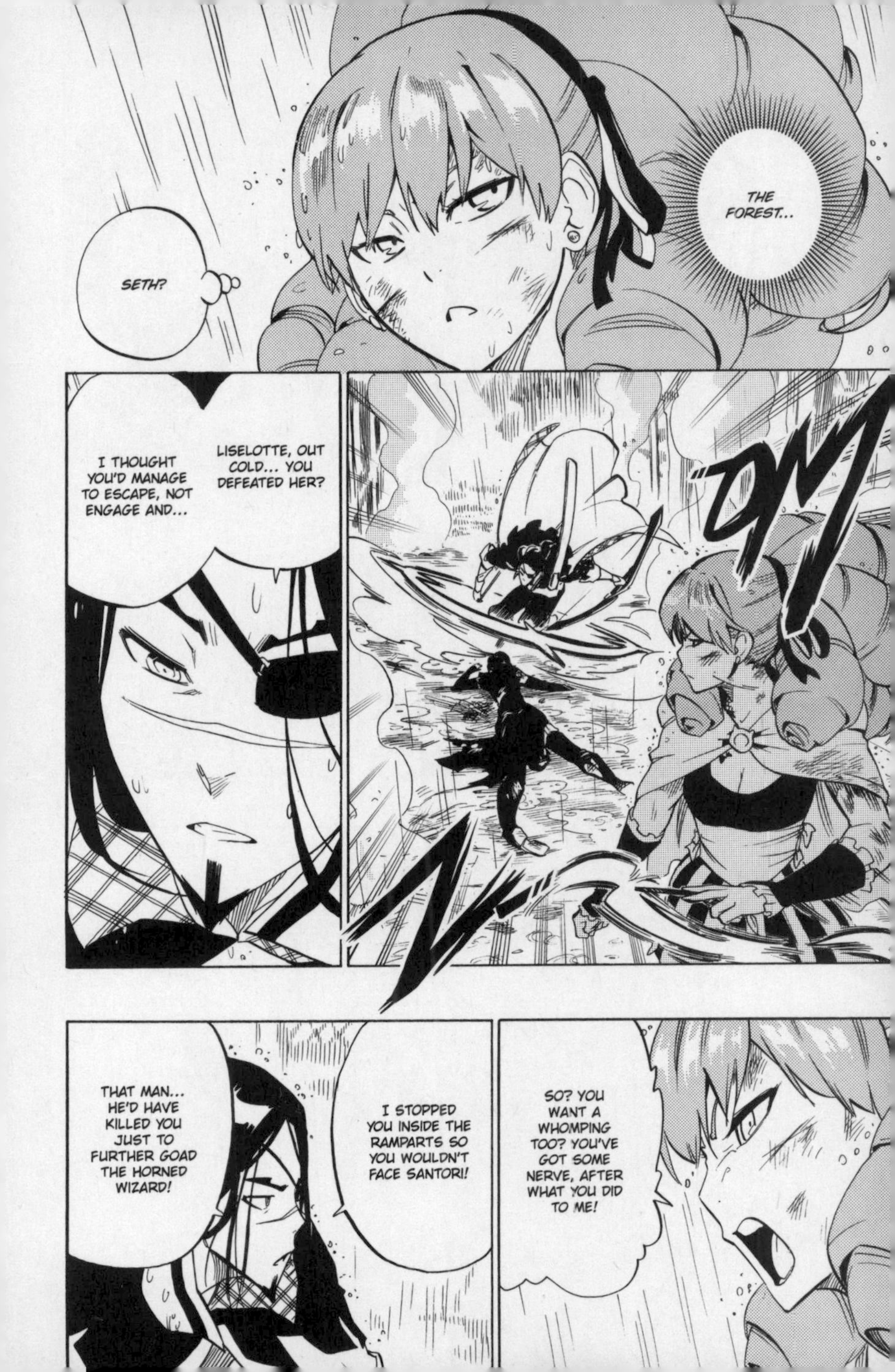
THE FOREST...
SETH?
LISELOTTE, OUT COLD... YOU DEFEATED HER?
I THOUGHT YOU'D MANAGE TO ESCAPE, NOT ENGAGE AND...
SO? YOU WANT A WHOMPING TOO? YOU'VE GOT SOME NERVE, AFTER WHAT YOU DID TO ME!
I STOPPED YOU INSIDE THE RAMPARTS SO YOU WOULDN'T FACE SANTORI!
THAT MAN... HE'D HAVE KILLED YOU JUST TO FURTHER GOAD THE HORNED WIZARD!

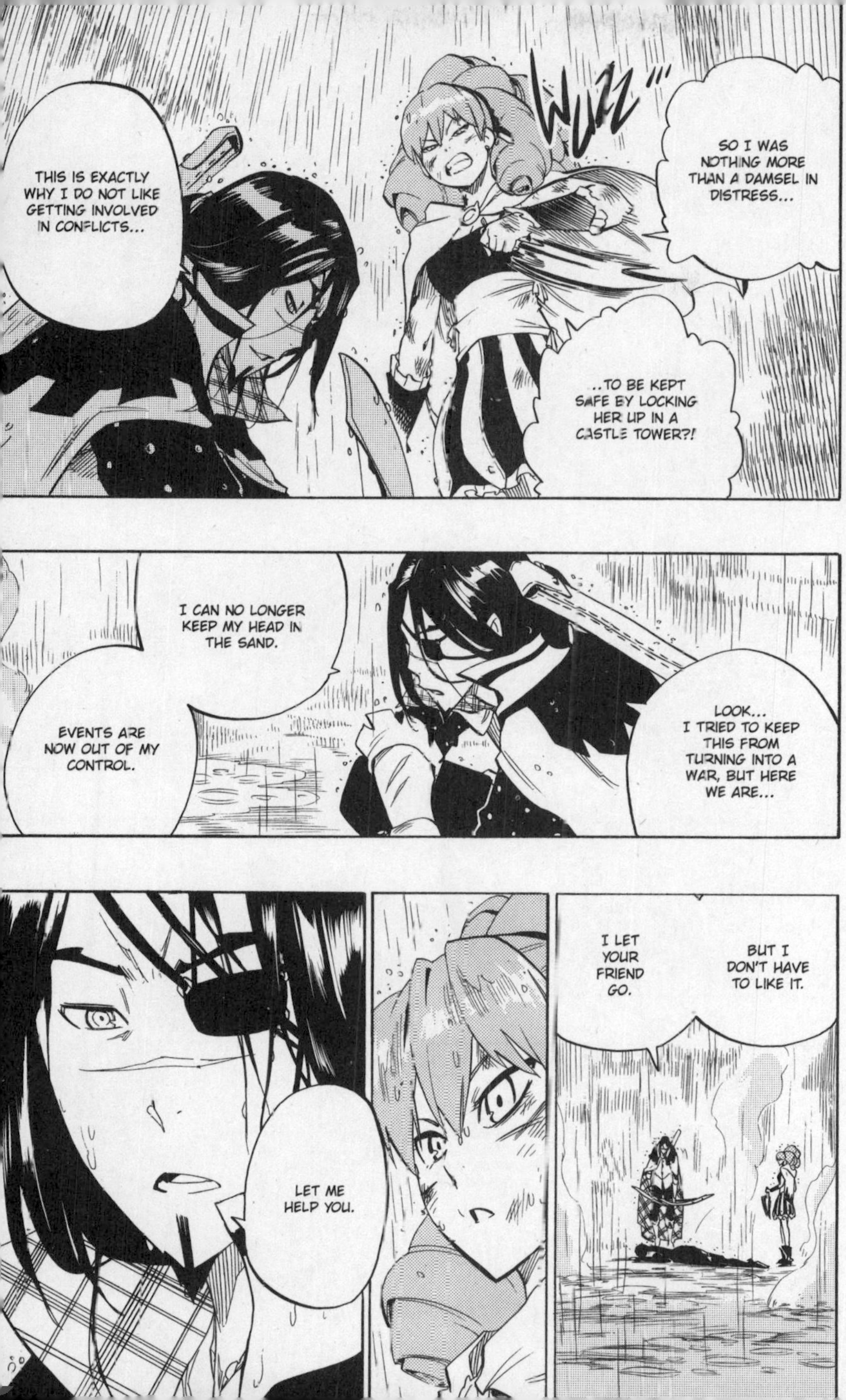
SO I WAS NOTHING MORE THAN A DAMSEL IN DISTRESS...
WUZZ
...TO BE KEPT SAFE BY LOCKING HER UP IN A CASTLE TOWER?!
THIS IS EXACTLY WHY I DO NOT LIKE GETTING INVOLVED IN CONFLICTS...
LOOK... I TRIED TO KEEP THIS FROM TURNING INTO A WAR, BUT HERE WE ARE...
I CAN NO LONGER KEEP MY HEAD IN THE SAND.
EVENTS ARE NOW OUT OF MY CONTROL.
I LET YOUR FRIEND GO.
BUT I DON'T HAVE TO LIKE IT.
LET ME HELP YOU.

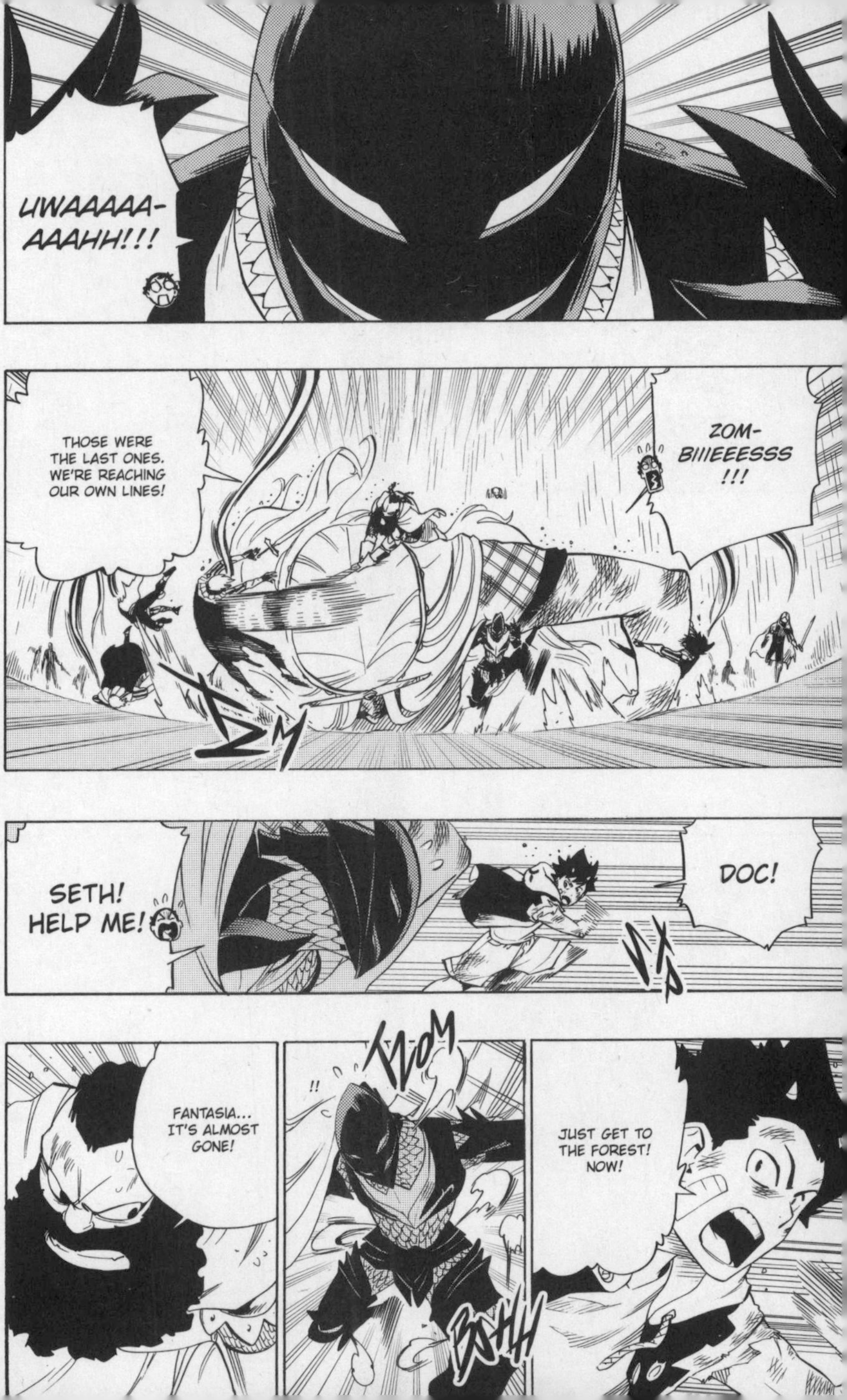
UWAAAAAA-AAAHH!!!
ZOM-BIIIEEESSS!!!
THOSE WERE THE LAST ONES. WE'RE REACHING OUR OWN LINES!
DOC!
SETH! HELP ME!
JUST GET TO THE FOREST! NOW!
!!
FANTASIA... IT'S ALMOST GONE!

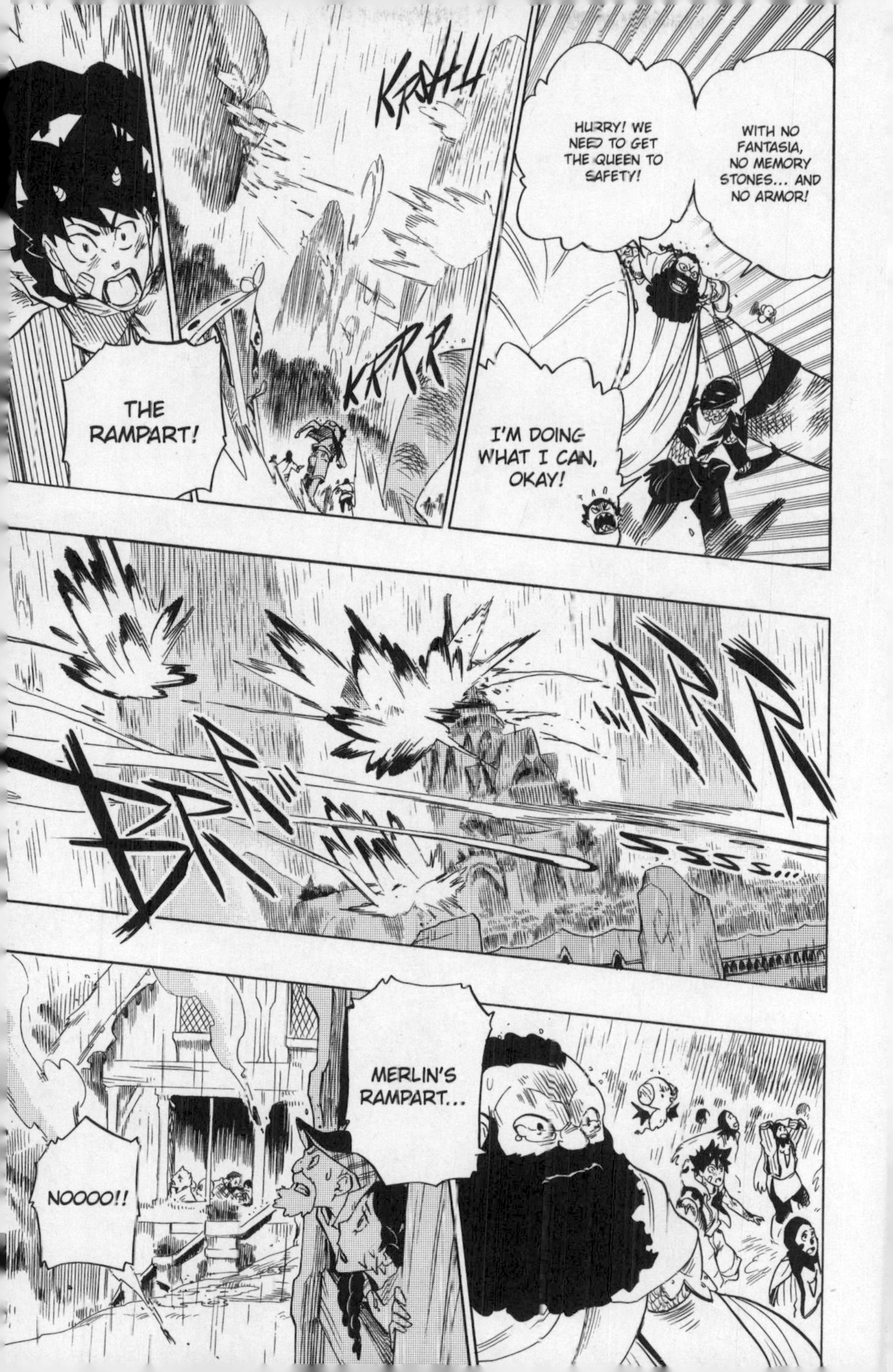
WITH NO FANTASIA, NO MEMORY STONES... AND NO ARMOR!
HURRY! WE NEED TO GET THE QUEEN TO SAFETY!
I'M DOING WHAT I CAN, OKAY!
KRRR
THE RAMPART!
MERLIN'S RAMPART...
NOOOO!!

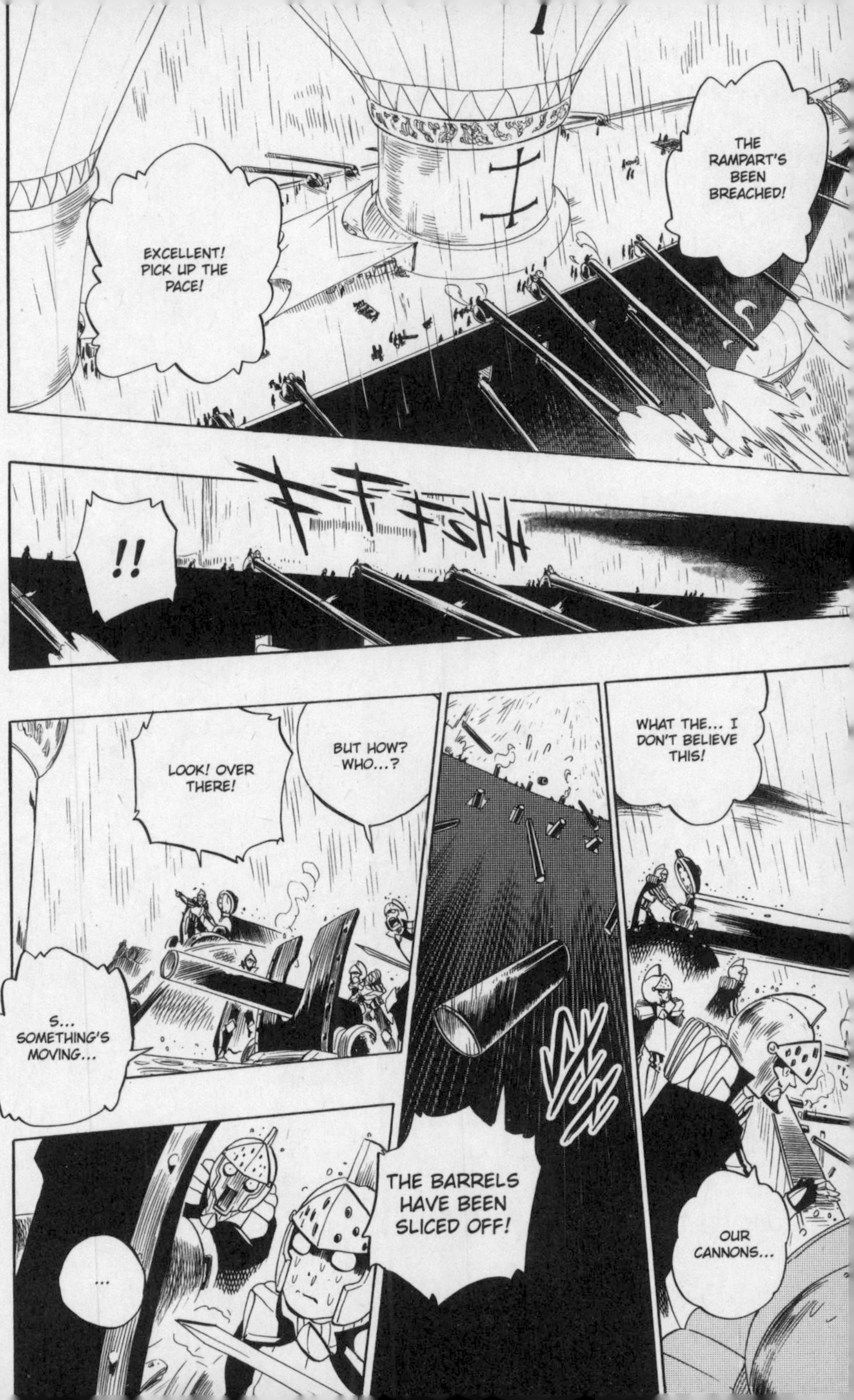
THE RAMPART'S BEEN BREACHED!
EXCELLENT! PICK UP THE PACE!
!!
WHAT THE... I DON'T BELIEVE THIS!
BUT HOW? WHO...?
LOOK! OVER THERE!
S... SOMETHING'S MOVING...
OUR CANNONS...
THE BARRELS HAVE BEEN SLICED OFF!
...

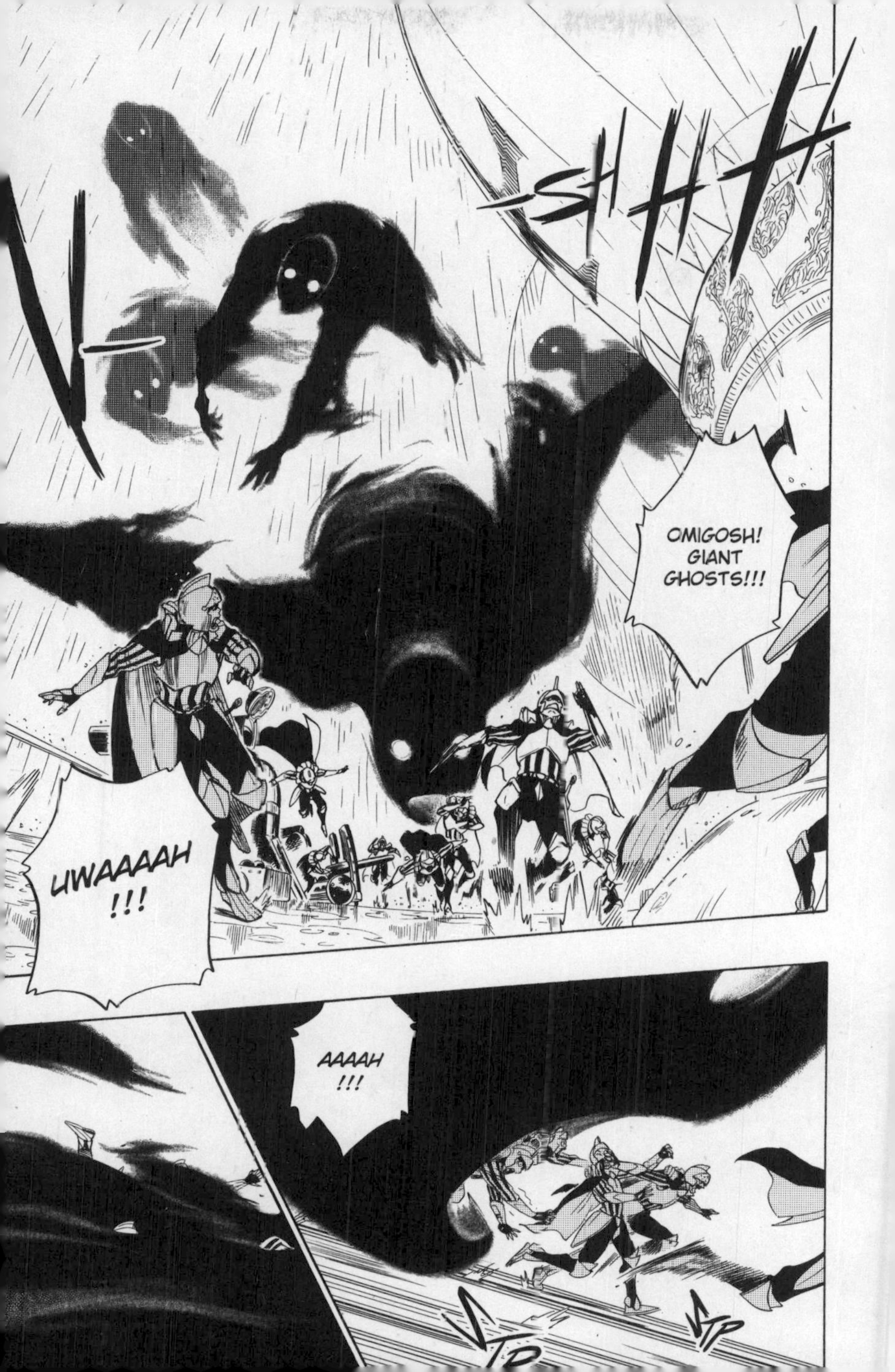
SHHH
OMIGOSH! GIANT GHOSTS!!!
V—
UWAAAAH!!!
AAAAH!!!
STP
STP

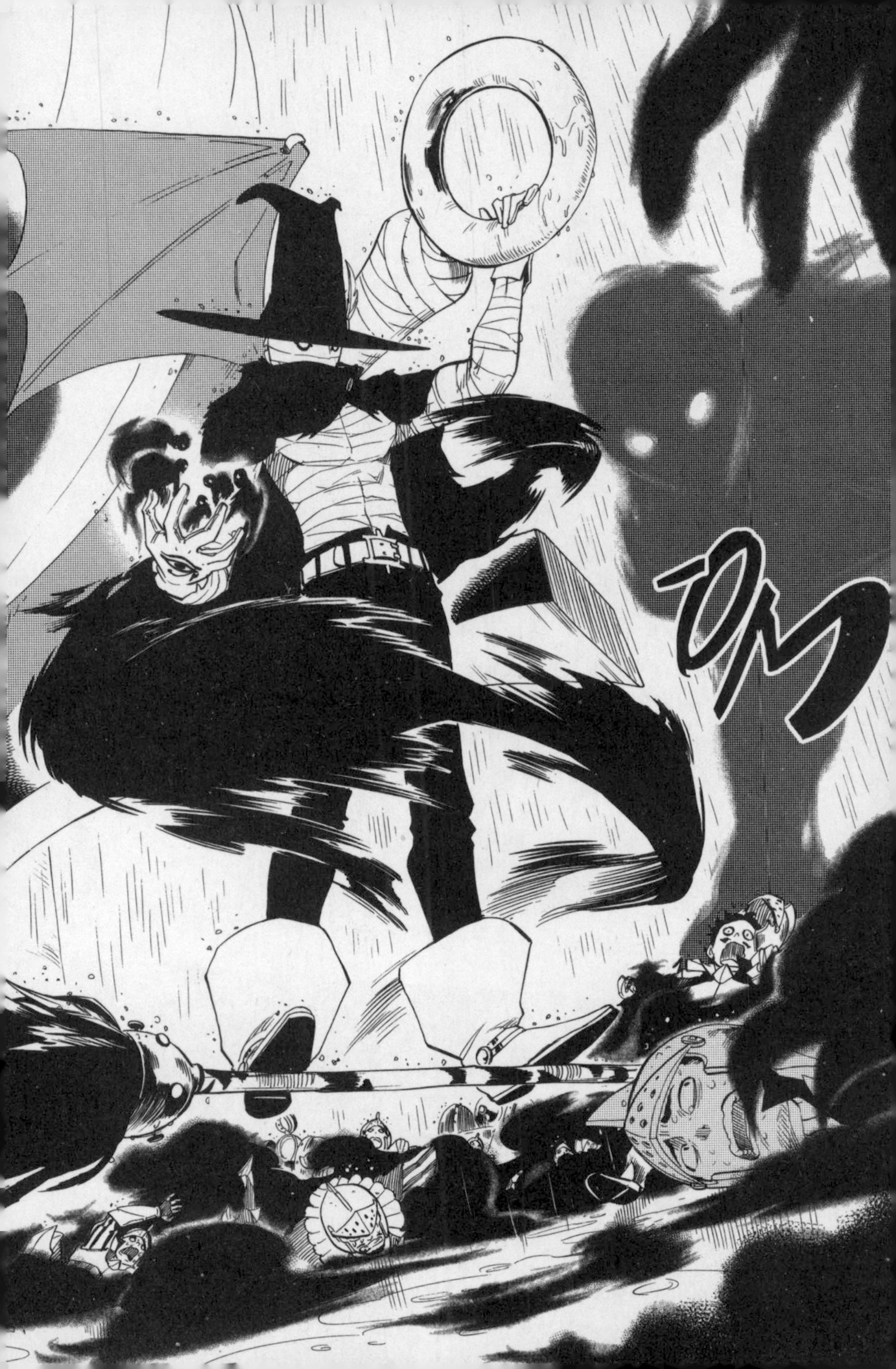

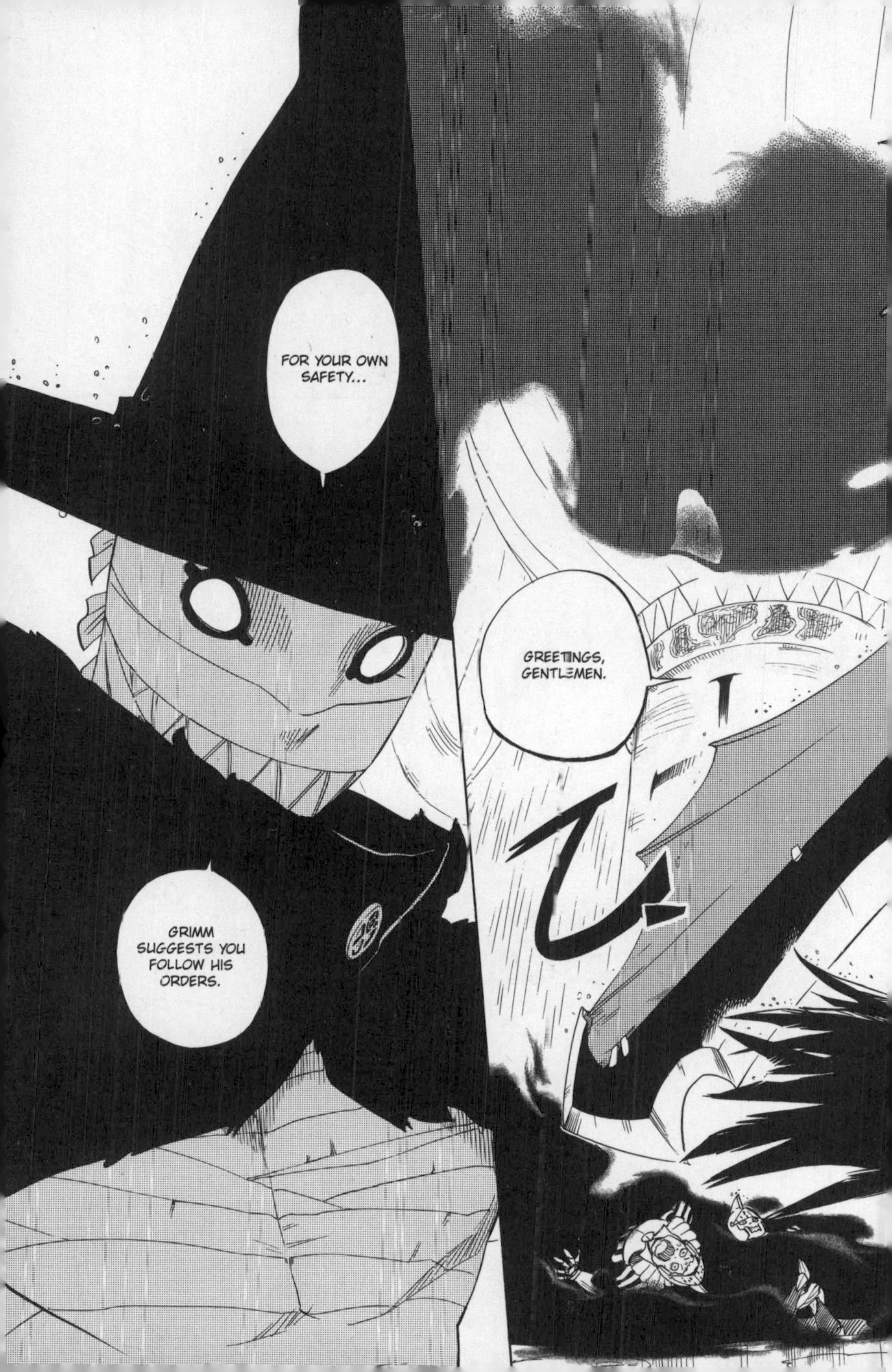
GREETINGS, GENTLEMEN.
FOR YOUR OWN SAFETY...
GRIMM SUGGESTS YOU FOLLOW HIS ORDERS.

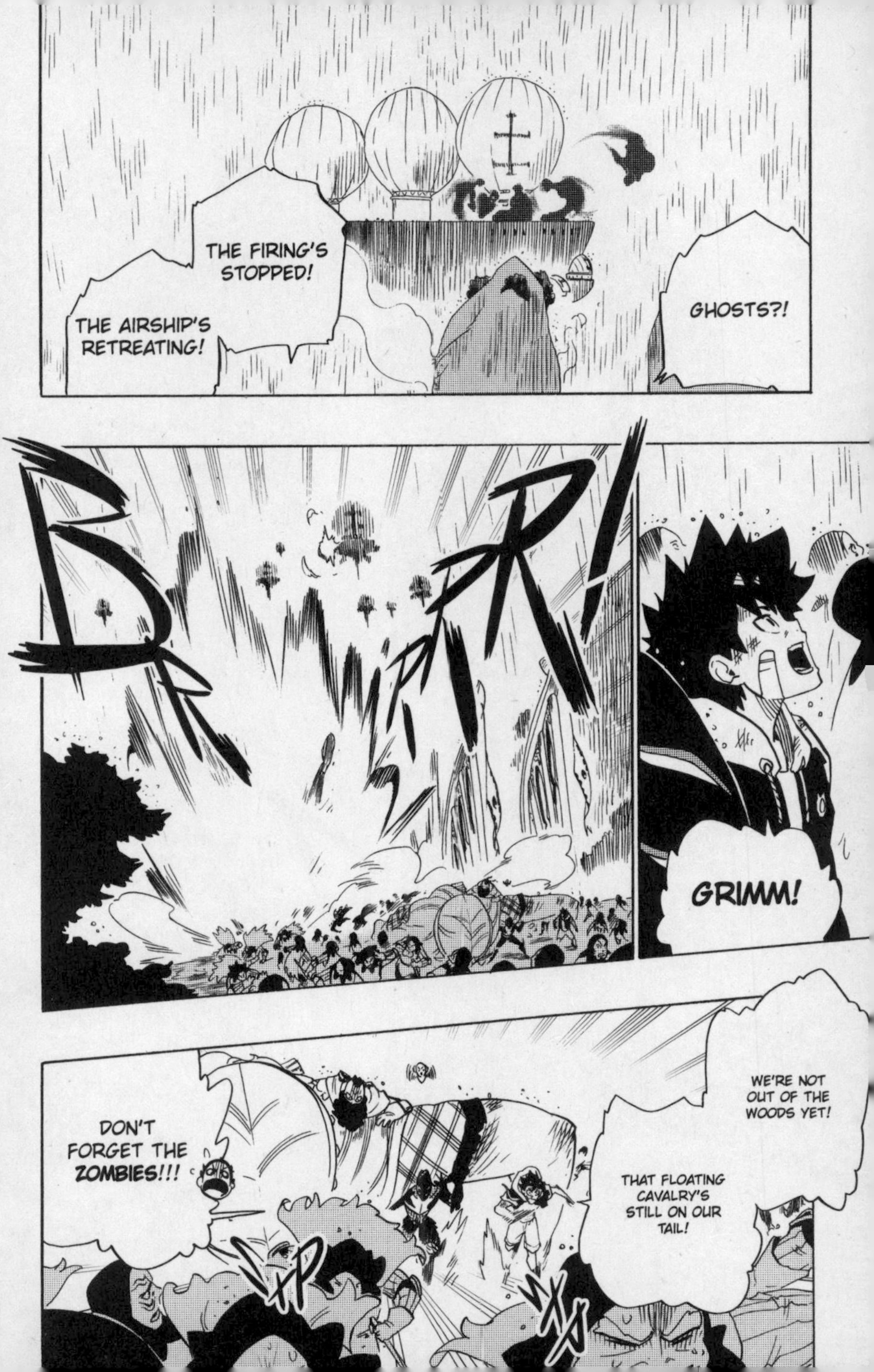
GHOSTS?!
THE FIRING'S STOPPED!
THE AIRSHIP'S RETREATING!
GRIMM!
WE'RE NOT OUT OF THE WOODS YET!
THAT FLOATING CAVALRY'S STILL ON OUR TAIL!
DON'T FORGET THE ZOMBIES!!!

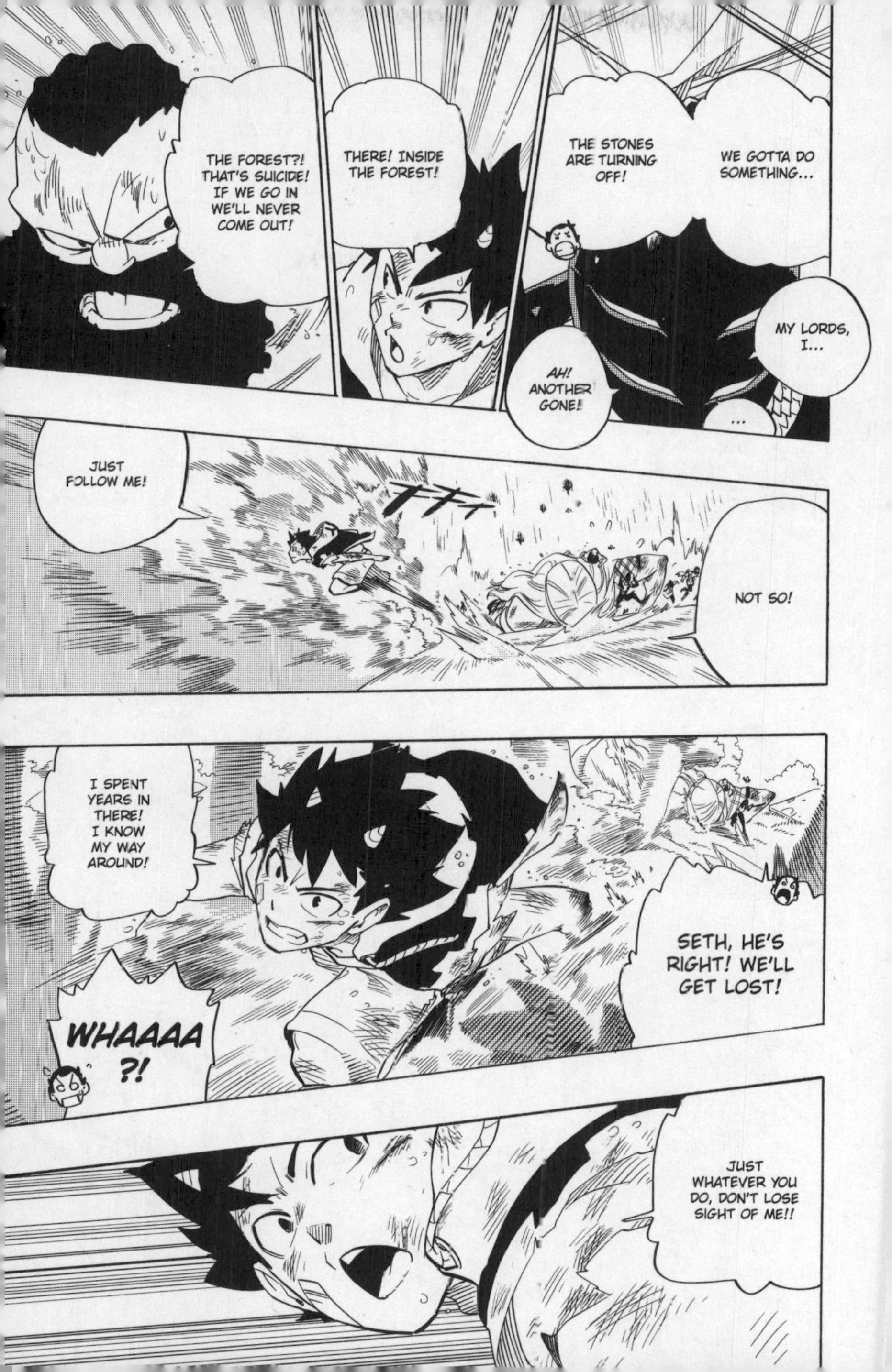
WE GOTTA DO SOMETHING...
THE STONES ARE TURNING OFF!
MY LORDS, I...
AH! ANOTHER GONE!
...
THERE! INSIDE THE FOREST!
THE FOREST?! THAT'S SUICIDE! IF WE GO IN WE'LL NEVER COME OUT!
NOT SO!
JUST FOLLOW ME!
I SPENT YEARS IN THERE! I KNOW MY WAY AROUND!
SETH, HE'S RIGHT! WE'LL GET LOST!
WHAAAA?!
JUST WHATEVER YOU DO, DON'T LOSE SIGHT OF ME!!

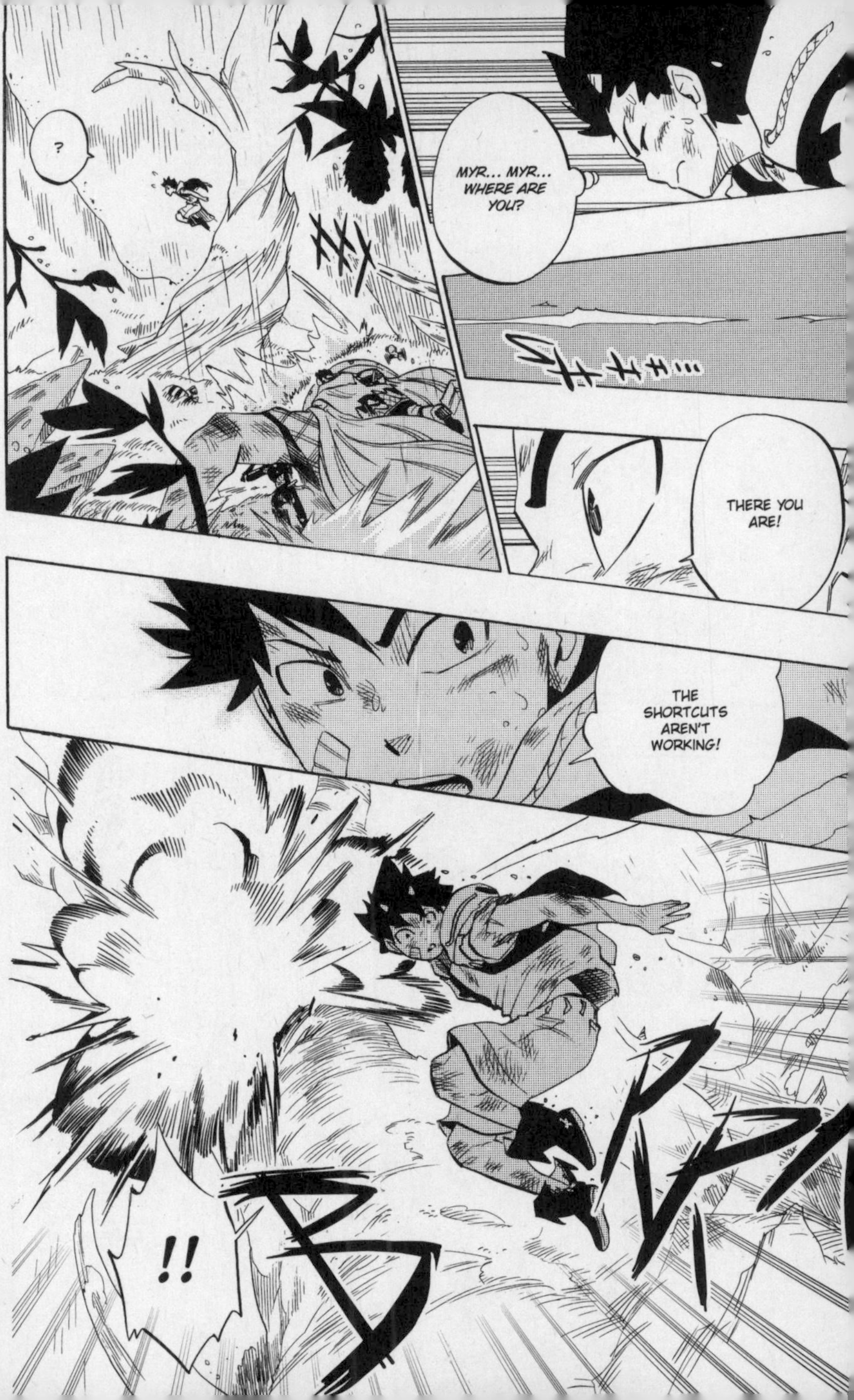
MYR... MYR... WHERE ARE YOU?
THERE YOU ARE!
?
THE SHORTCUTS AREN'T WORKING!
!!

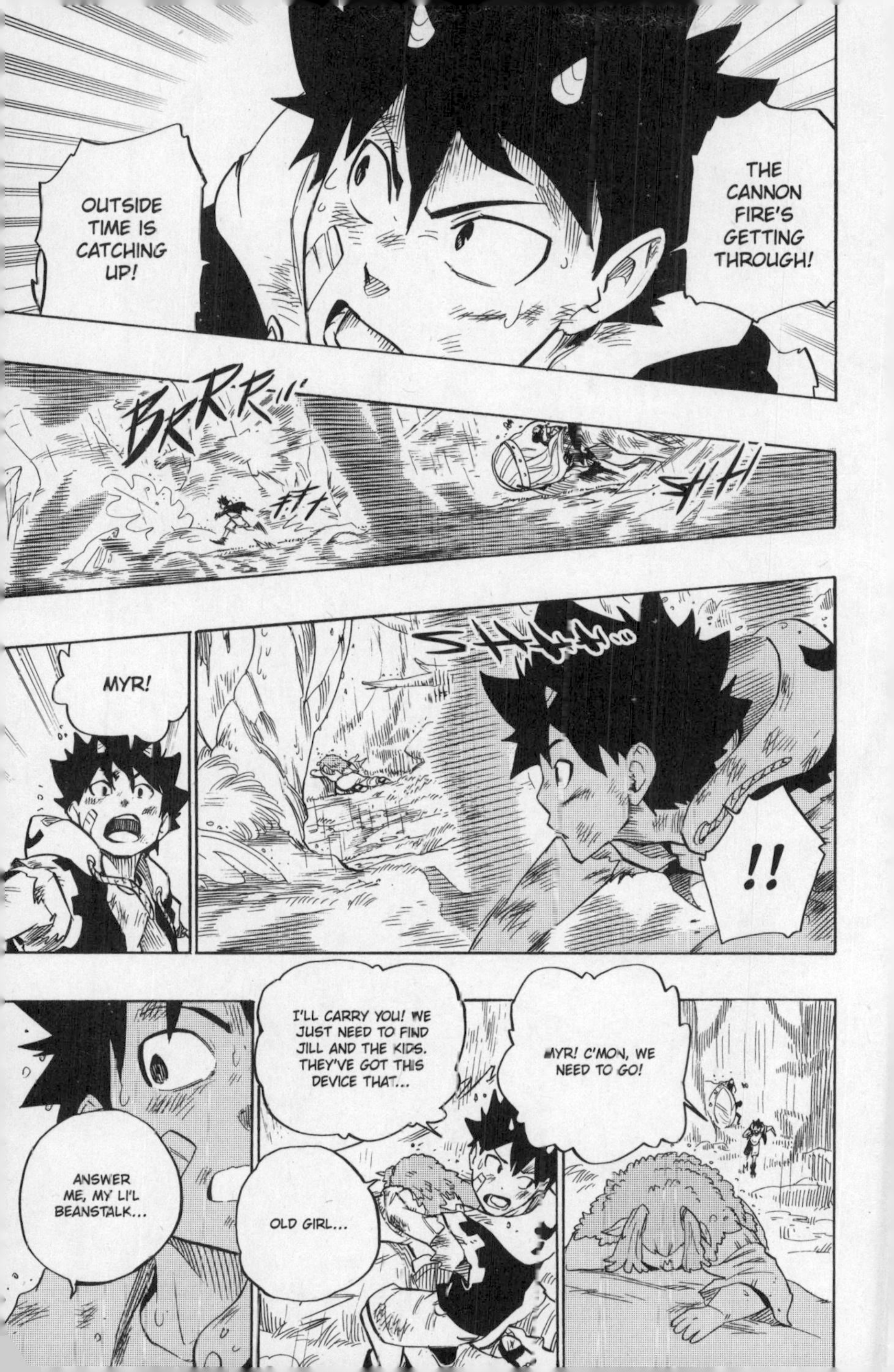
THE CANNON FIRE'S GETTING THROUGH!
OUTSIDE TIME IS CATCHING UP!
SHH
BRRR
SHHH...
!!
MYR!
MYR! C'MON, WE NEED TO GO!
I'LL CARRY YOU! WE JUST NEED TO FIND JILL AND THE KIDS. THEY'VE GOT THIS DEVICE THAT...
OLD GIRL...
ANSWER ME, MY LI'L BEANSTALK...

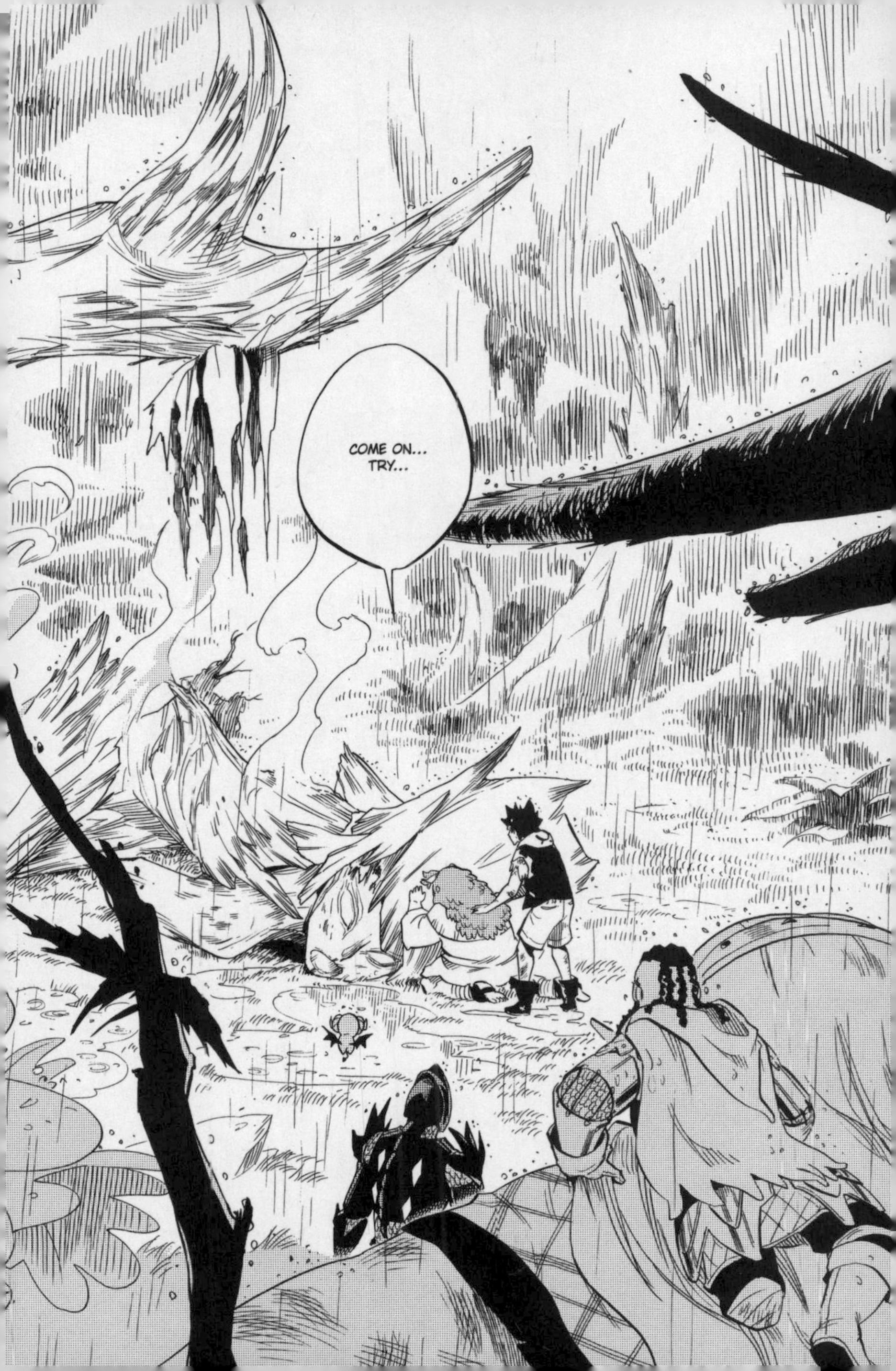
COME ON... TRY...

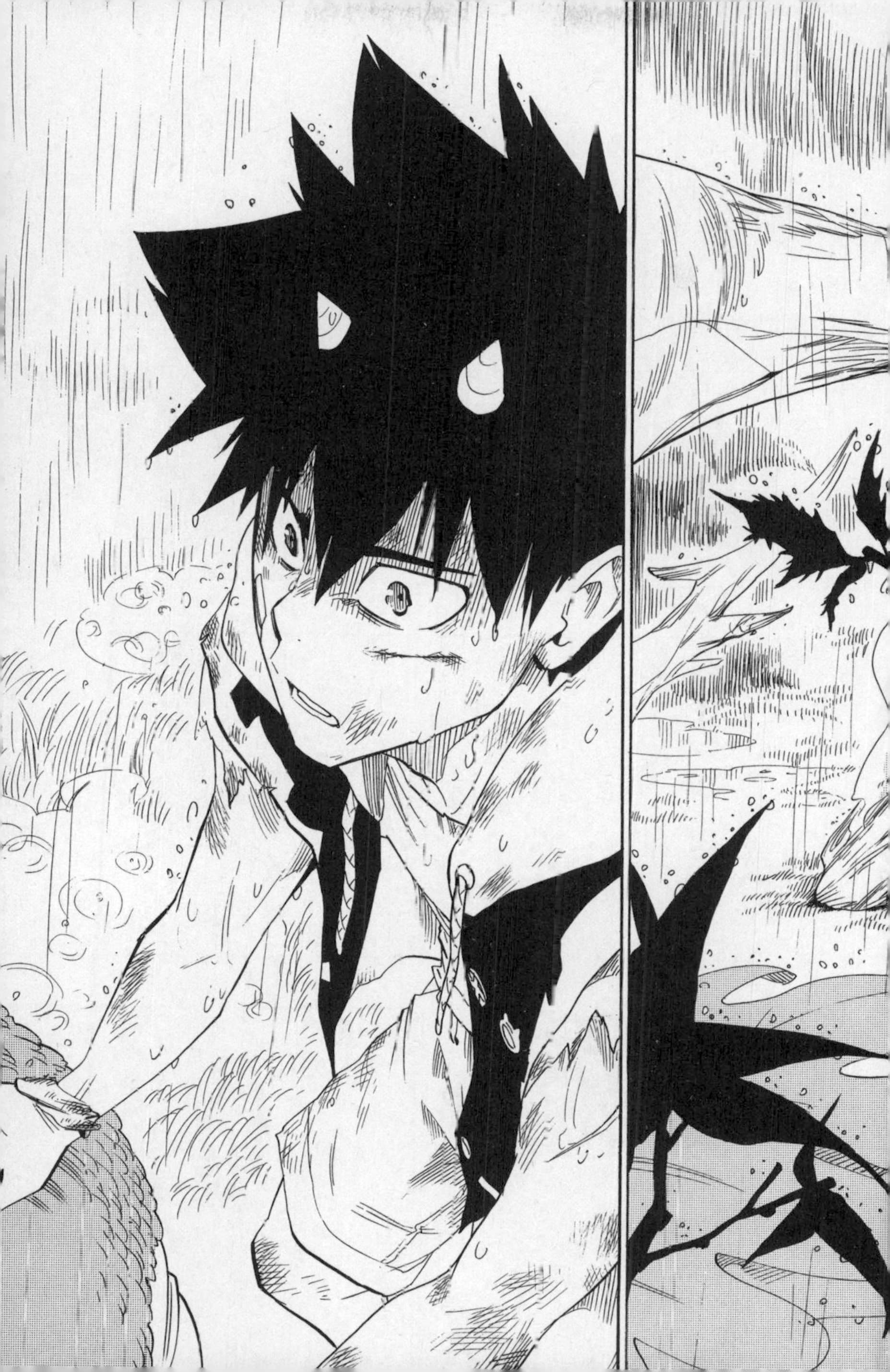

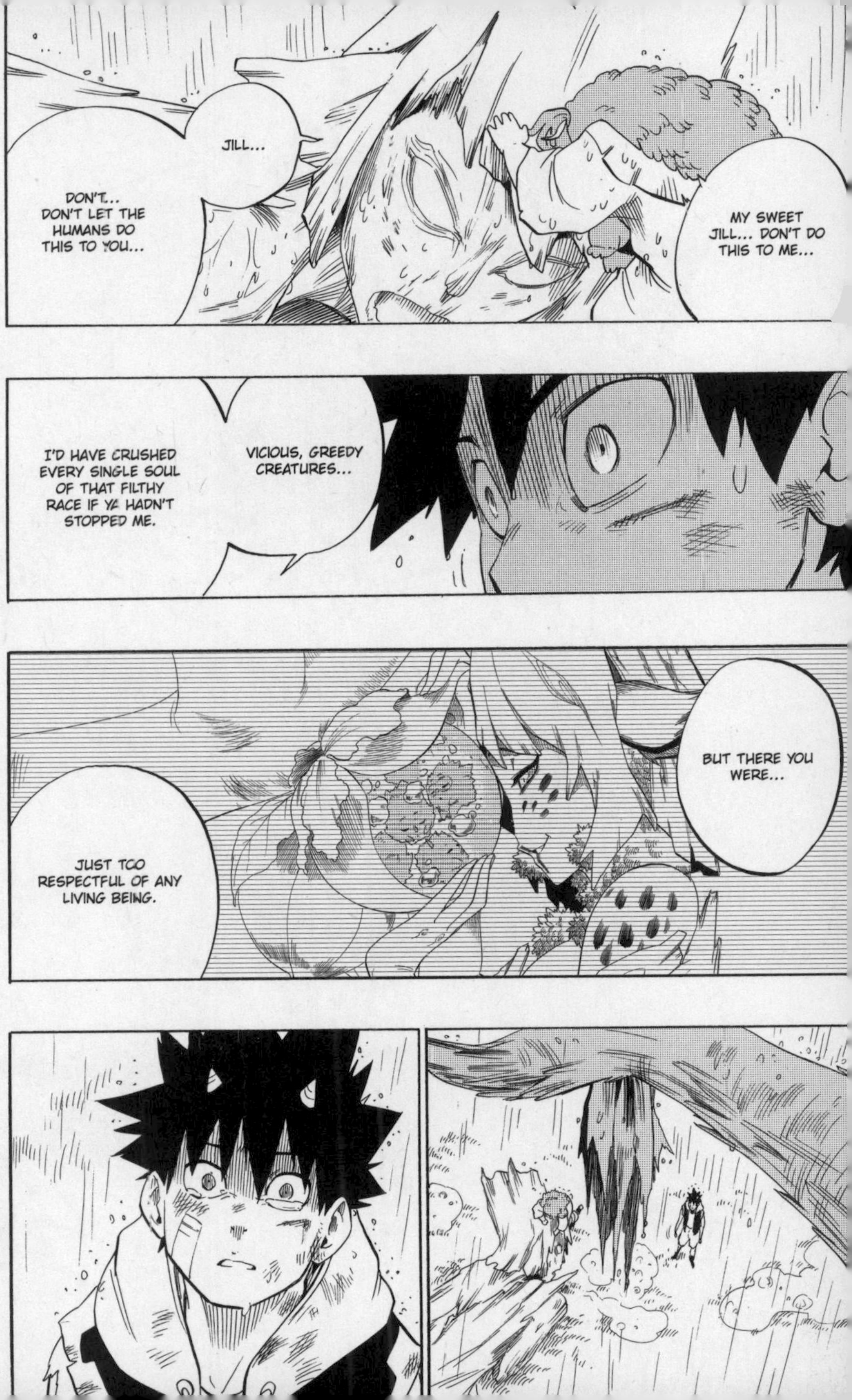
MY SWEET JILL... DON'T DO THIS TO ME...
JILL...
DON'T... DON'T LET THE HUMANS DO THIS TO YOU...
VICIOUS, GREEDY CREATURES...
I'D HAVE CRUSHED EVERY SINGLE SOUL OF THAT FILTHY RACE IF YA HADN'T STOPPED ME.
BUT THERE YOU WERE...
JUST TOO RESPECTFUL OF ANY LIVING BEING.

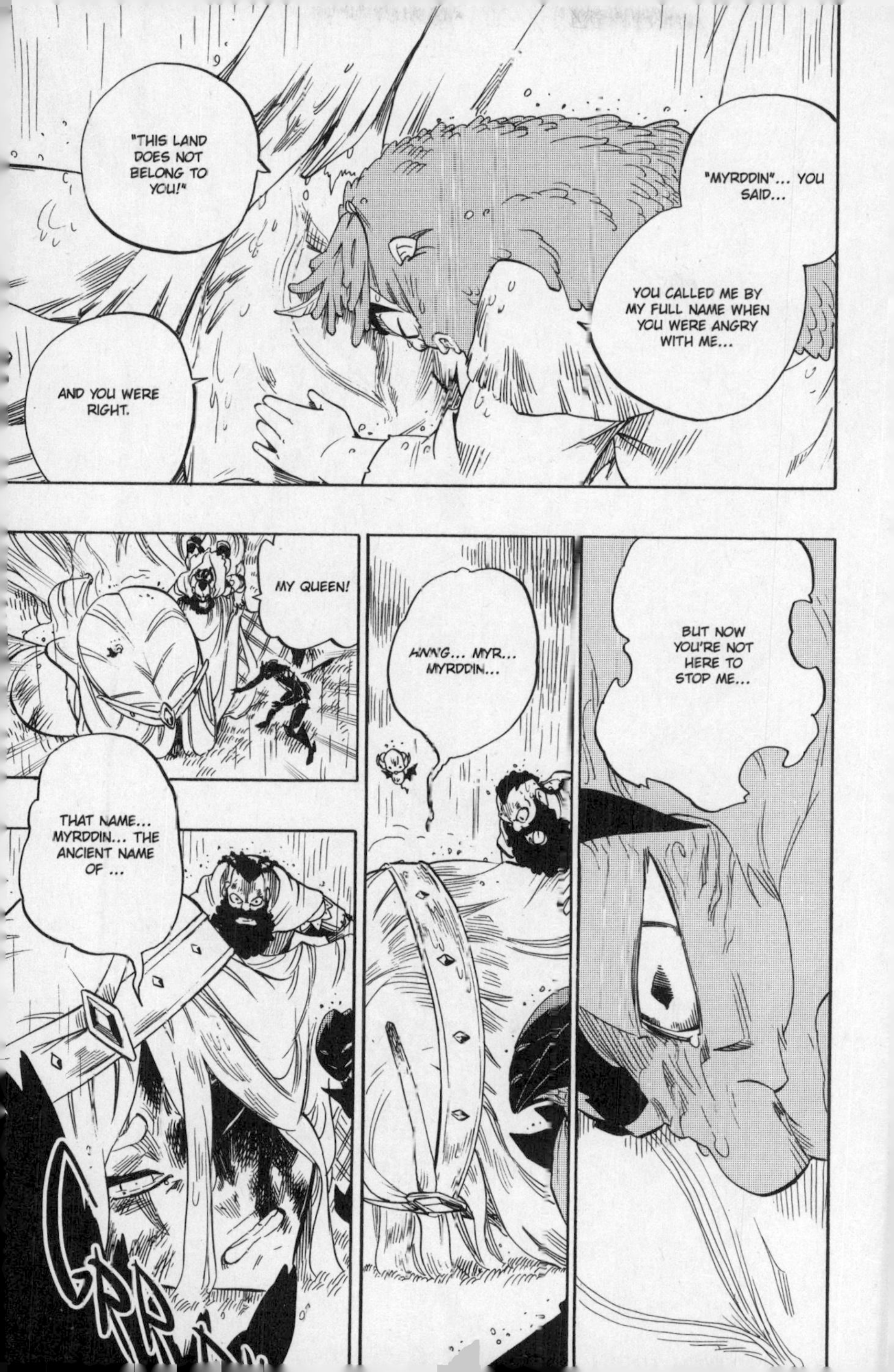
"MYRDDIN"... YOU SAID...
YOU CALLED ME BY MY FULL NAME WHEN YOU WERE ANGRY WITH ME...
"THIS LAND DOES NOT BELONG TO YOU!"
AND YOU WERE RIGHT.
BUT NOW YOU'RE NOT HERE TO STOP ME...
HNNG... MYR... MYRDDIN...
MY QUEEN!
THAT NAME... MYRDDIN... THE ANCIENT NAME OF ...

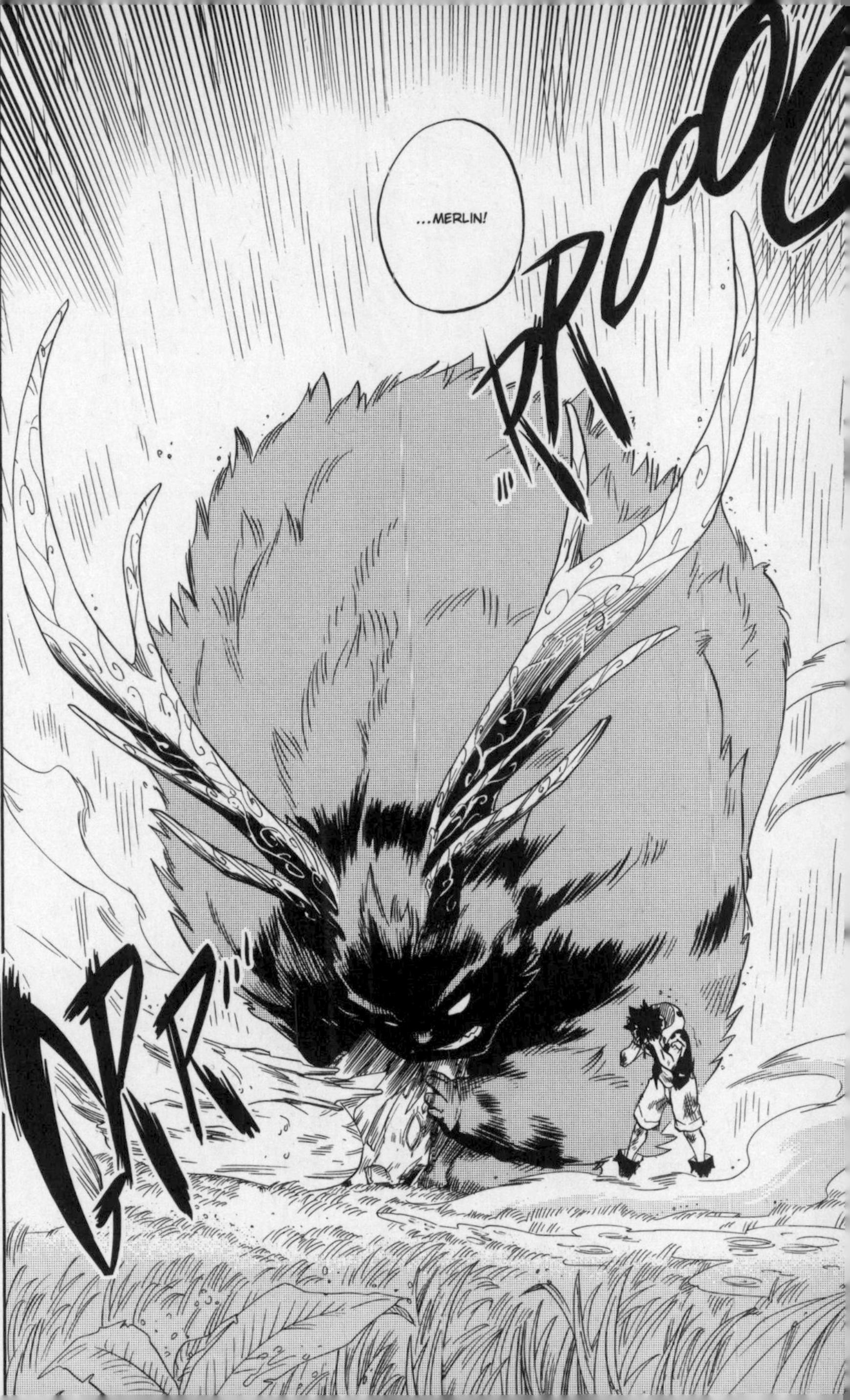
...MERLIN!

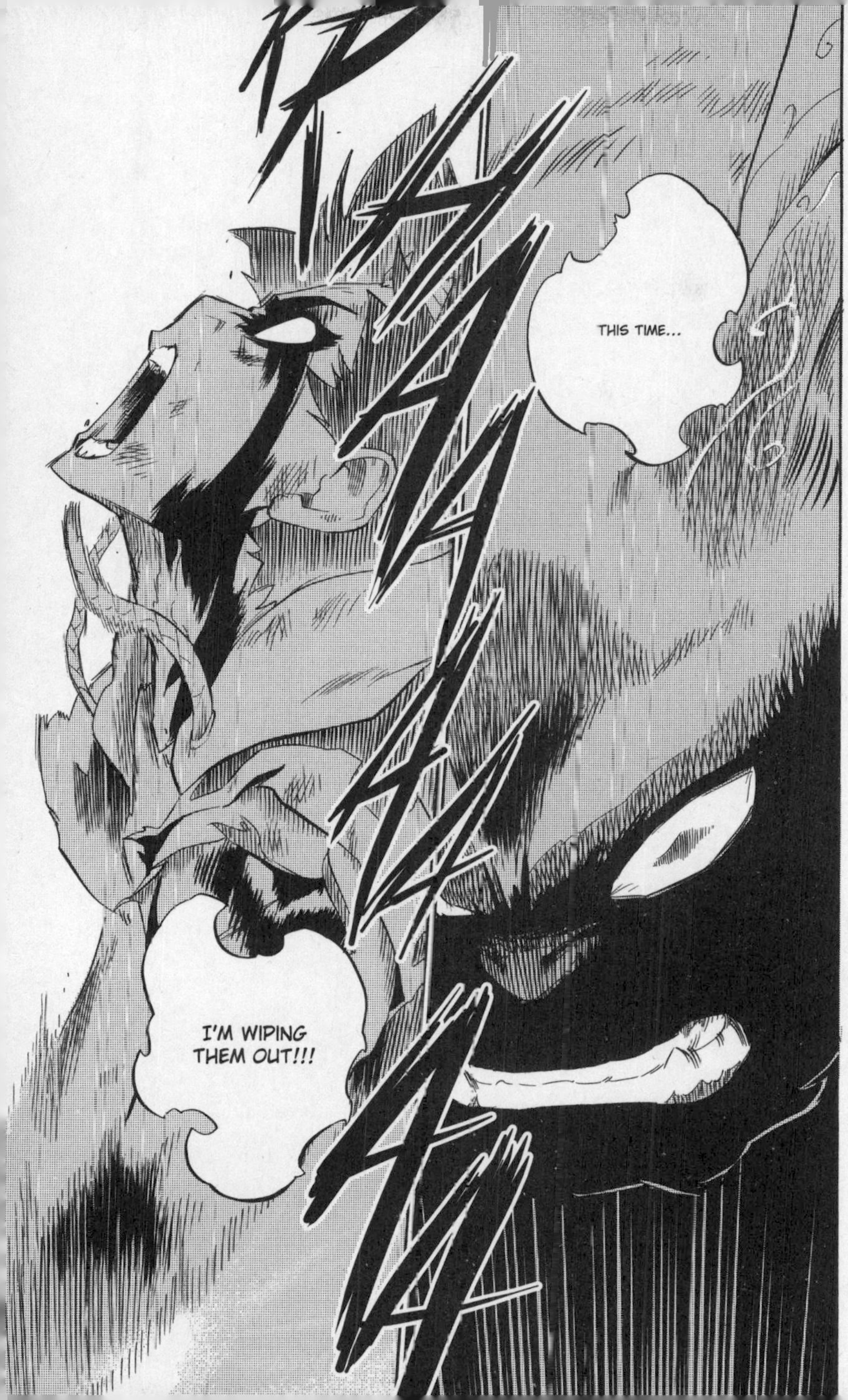
THIS TIME...
I'M WIPING THEM OUT!!!

TO BE CONTINUED...

THANKS FOR THIS AMAZING OPPORTUNITY!

I'LL DO MY BEST!

HERE'S A LI'L DRAWING DONE BY A YOUNG ILLUSTRATOR WHO WAS MY SCREENTONE ASSISTANT FOR THIS VOLUME! I WANT TO THANK HER FOR HER AMAZING HELP! WITHOUT THAT I WOULD HAVE DEFINITELY, ROYALLY MISSED MY DEADLINE!
I'VE BEEN WAITING ALL THIS TIME TO BE ABLE TO DELEGATE SOME WORK TO SOMEONE AND I NOW CAN FINALLY DO IT! AND IT ONLY TOOK NINE VOLUMES -_-

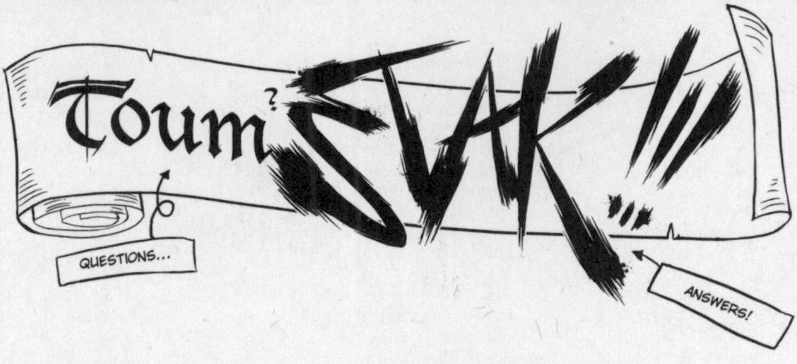
Toum? STAK!!!
QUESTIONS...
ANSWERS!

Baptiste: While Diabal's talking to Seth about the old fight between mages and holders of magic items, we can see a wizard (who reminds me of Darkhell, from the French comic book *The Legendaries*) going up against a silhouette armed with a pitchfork. Is that the Patrem Inquisitor? So are the Thaumaturges' Miracles actually magical items that don't use Fantasia?

Tony Valente: Yup! That's him! That's the Patrem Inquisitor! As for the Miracles, actually it's not... Oh! Wait, no, I see what you did there! You almost got me, sneaky boy! You'll just have to wait for the next volumes in the series!

-I think Lord Brangoire is super cool, in terms of his design as well as his character. Did you have any particular inspiration for him?

You know, I like him too, that Brangoire! And no, no particular source of inspiration. To be honest, he was literally created on the page he first appeared in, no prep work for him... Just like Dragunov in volume 1 for that matter! I actually drew him an afro (on Brangoire, not Dragunov) but I decided I liked it better underneath his mouth so he'd look a little more special. And his character came to me as I was drawing him!

....

Cédrick: Can we get a tutorial on how to tie a double tie like Doc? Because I've been trying to wrap my head around how to do it and I can't figure it out.

Tony Valente: So, first you take the end here like this, pass it over like that, you wrap it around, strap it back and ta-daaah! You've got a... Ah, nope. You were right, this is hard!

....

Erwan: Hi, Tony! My name is Erwan and I've became a HUGE fan of *Radiant*! I was wondering if you had any specific idea for the end of the manga? If so... DON'T TELL ME!!

Tony Valente: Yes, I have an overall idea of the ending, but I'm still missing the details. For example, I'm still hesitating on the color of underpants Seth'll be wearing at that time.

....

Mathieu : Hello hello! I've got a couple of questions related to volume 8 of *Radiant*! According to what Diabal told us, Piodon would have supposedly brought him and Triton to the Inquisition so they could torture them (most likely in Bôme or somewhere else in Estrie since that's the Inquisition's HQ) so how'd he cross a sea of clouds and end up in Caislean Merlin and all that while literally traveling blind?

Tony Valente: He jumped very far in the direction he was told to. Or he got some help...

-Will we see Triton again or did he die under torture?

We'll see him again, dead perhaps. Or not.

-Are there more Thaumaturges than the ones we've seen (Vérone, Santori, etc.) or are there MANY more?

There are more but not maaaany more.

-Will we get another original character contest or any bonuses? Anyway, that's it for me, I hope you're preparing the next volume to come out soon, because I really want to get answers to my questions (°u^)

Bonuses? Sure! But character contests? I don't know! It takes me a crazy amount of time to go through all the answers and unfortunately I don't have any more. Time, that is...

Saïna F.: Hi! First of all, I wanted to say I looooove *Radiant*! The characters, the world, your art style *o* And I also had a question... In volume 7, when Myr is looking at Seth trying to control his inner "guest," he reminded me of Ahmour, the medusa that haunts the roads of Imagination in the French books by Pierre Bottero, Les Mondes d'Ewilan. Also, Myr tells us that "Fantasia," in the tongue of the little people, means "imagination" and that those who master it can create plants... So yeah, I was just wondering if you had been inspired by the world of Pierre Bottero or if I was just a fan seeing connections with his trilogy all over ^^ Thanks for the manga and for your answers!!

Tony Valente: Ah, well, no, I'd heard of the name before, but I've never read it! But you've piqued my interest and now I'm going to check it out^^

....

Jules: Good morning! See how polite I am? I wanted to thank you soooo much for your amazing series that I'm carefully reading. In the middle of a load of manga series that I do not care for very much, yours always succeeds in transporting me into the story and I have to admit that once I start reading it, I can't stop...

So as for my questions, they're pretty simple: considering how detailed the map is, will our hero be traveling the entire world in the future?

Tony Valente: He's gonna be jumping around here and there, yeah, but he's not going to be doing an entire tour of the map, no. Or maybe I'll just draw 100 volumes and there, problem solved!

-And what's that continent on the West? Is that the end of the map or is the world bigger still?

Yes, the map shown in volume 5 is of North-Western Pharenos... Which implies that there's also a Northern Pharenos, a Southern Pharenos, South-East and South-West... So it's only about a quarter of the entire world! But not sure we'll be seeing the other quarters. At the very least not in *Radiant*...

-And there's one thing that's especially been bothering me... In the Caillte Forest, if Myr could stay inside as long as he'd like while staying in the same era, then why is he in Seth's era? (He's clearly saying the temporal loop needs to only move for humans—and he's not human. At least I don't think he is?) Then why did he not stay in his era when the Fantasia was all over the place?

Very good question! Maybe he did want to... But even in the forest he could get caught in the time of someone from the outside! If someone knows how to find him in the forest, then from the time they meet, Myr will be in the time of that person. So, next time he comes out of the forest, it'll be impossible to get back. Myr, even while trying to isolate himself, got a few visits throughout time, people who knew how to find him... Making his time go forward along with them. I hope my explanation was understandable enough. -_-'

-And if someone comes into the forest and their time sets the time for the forest, then why aren't there any people from the future in the forest? Is it because the forest got destroyed or burnt?

If people from the future'd come in, they wouldn't be able to meet any people from the past, like Seth, for example. Seth'd need to stay inside for a long time for that to happen... And after being found, he'd only be able to get out in the future, which would become his present. Yup, not easy.

....

Mé: Hello!!

First of all, I LOVE *RADIANNNNTTT*, the characters, the world and all that 😊 . So THANK YOU SO MUCH for this beautiful manga. As for my questions: will there be any other posters in packs of six (especially thinking of Grimm's illustration and the first few volume covers)?

Tony Valente: Yup!

-Who's the character who takes the most amount of time to draw? And which one takes the least amount of time?

The most: Doc in his armor, the one you can see in this volume!
The least: Boobrie! I don't even do any rough sketches for him anymore!

-How do you become a member of the Inquisition? They're seriously all really weird in that organization!!

You need to want to hunt different types of people and *BAM* you just add a little thing around the neck, a long cape and you're good to go!

-Will we get more information on Queen Boadicée's past? Her persona intrigues me.
Maybe…

-And lastly, will there be a fight between Alma and Torque? I don't know why, but I can see both of them going at it in an epic battle 😊 (maybe because they both have a huge hairdo, but mostly because I want to see Alma fight).
All right then, a hair battle, coming up! I like! But no using your hands!

……

<u>Marc-Olivier</u> **: Hello mister Tony. So, I have a couple of questions. First of all, we can see in the Rumble Town Arc that from the start you talk about some complex themes that don't get talked about a lot in fiction, like immigration (which really interested me because I have an immigrant background). How did you tackle those themes? Is it somewhat like your opinion, an outlet for you?**
<u>Tony Valente</u> : I write about things that have some importance to me whether it's because they interest me personally (I grew up in the French projects and added a little bit of that into Rumble Town), or because they have my characters go through some test. On the subject of immigration and all the debates surrounding it, I thought the parallel with Seth and his band of pariahs was really interesting. And at the time there were also a lot of politicians whose political rhetoric made my ears bleed… That's how I created Konrad of Marbourg, whose worst lines are quotes of things I've read. That's how I deal with my issues: I write stories! Whether it's to share things that I feel passionate about, or make my blood boil: I write!

……

<u>L. Quentin</u> **: Hello Tony.**
I just started reading your comic "Hana Attori" and I was wondering: the character Shifu, is there any chance Doc was based on that character. -_-'?
<u>Tony Valente</u> : That's exactly right! That's him! I liked the character so instead of abandoning him when I stopped working on Hana Attori, I decided to put him in *Radiant*… With some minor changes.

-My dad heard on the radio that there's going to be an animated series in Japan *_*!!! Will it come out in France as well?
Yes, but I don't know yet when and where though!

-Is it possible you're friends with Patrick Sobral (author of the French comic *The Legendaries*) because I noticed that you invited him to do a drawing for one of the volumes in *Radiant* and in one of the volumes of *The Legendaries Parodia*, Patrick Sobral drew Seth from behind… Or is it just a coincidence?!
Well, yes, we are friends ^^ We both started at around the same time at the French publishing company Delcourt and Patrick has always encouraged me as I was working on my various series. So when I started *Radiant* I of course invited him to make a little drawing for volume 2!

-I was also wondering how much time you put in your manuscripts, because looking at how beautiful your drawings are, I wouldn't be surprised if you spent a couple of weeks on just one or two pages?! °O°
Well, I can't spend a couple of days on just one page or the volume would never come out in time. °_° It's more like a couple of pages per day. It all depends, but it could go from three to ten pages a day.

Please send your questions to: radiant@ankama.com

RADIANT

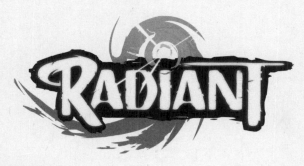

RADIANT VOL. 9
VIZ MEDIA Manga Edition

STORY AND ART BY **TONY VALENTE**
ASSISTANT ARTIST **TPIU**

Translation/**(´・∀・`)ｻｧ?**
Touch-Up Art & Lettering/**Erika Terriquez**
Design/**Julian [JR] Robinson**
Editor/**Gary Leach**

Published by arrangement with MEDIATOON LICENSING/Ankama.
RADIANT T09

Printed in the U.S.A.

Published by VIZ Media, LLC
P.O. Box 77010
San Francisco, CA 94107

10 9 8 7 6 5 4 3 2 1
First printing, January 2020

VIZ MEDIA
viz.com

ratings.viz.com
RATED T TEEN

PARENTAL ADVISORY
RADIANT is rated T for Teen and is recommended for ages 13 and up. This volume contains fantasy violence.

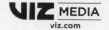

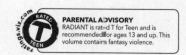

Radiant is being adapted into a Japanese anime!!!! _(°O°)_
Could barely believe it when I was first told about it... And
now... I still can't believe it actually. Nothing yet... Ah! Wait!
Nope, still nothing. So, thank you for getting your hands on this
manga!! If you hadn't read/shared/supported this series from
the start with so much enthusiasm, this wouldn't have happened!
Volume 9 is out, the series is doing well, it's being published in
a lot of countries, the anime coming out... You know what I'd
wish for next? Well... I'm not sure exactly... Maybe a *Radiant*
theme park built in space (it'd be so cool if we could float on
our brooms in zero gravity!), or a life-sized reconstruction of
the *Artemis*! But I'd already be happy if you'd be willing to get
your hands on volume 10... And any other volume that comes
out after that. I'd love that.

—Tony Valente

Tony Valente began working as a comic artist with the series *The Four
Princes of Ganahan*, written by Raphael Drommelschlager. He then launched
a new three-volume project, *Hana Attori*, after which he produced *S.P.E.E.D.
Angels*, a series written by Didier Tarquin and colored by Pop.

In preparation for *Radiant*, he relocated to Canada. Through confronting
caribou and grizzlies, he gained the wherewithal to train in obscure manga
techniques. Since then, his eating habits have changed, his lifestyle became
completely different and even his singing voice has changed a bit!

DEMON SLAYER

KIMETSU NO YAIBA

Story and Art by
KOYOHARU GOTOUGE

In Taisho-era Japan, kindhearted Tanjiro Kamado makes a living selling charcoal. But his peaceful life is shattered when a demon slaughters his entire family. His little sister Nezuko is the only survivor, but she has been transformed into a demon herself! Tanjiro sets out on a dangerous journey to find a way to return his sister to normal and destroy the demon who ruined his life.

YOU'RE RE
THE WRON

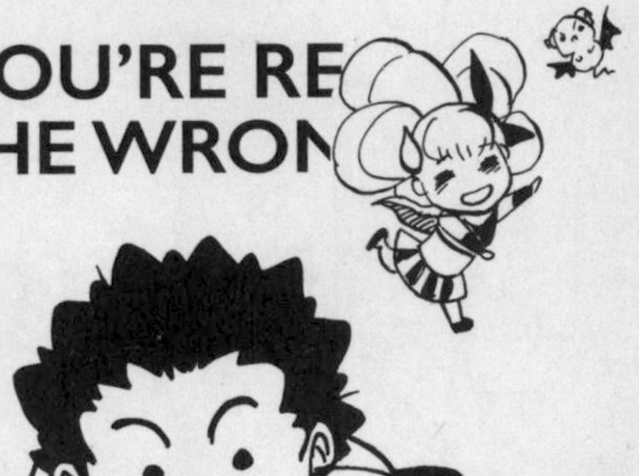

RADIANT reads from right to left, starting in the upper-right corner, meaning that action, sound effects, and word-balloon order are completely reversed from English order.

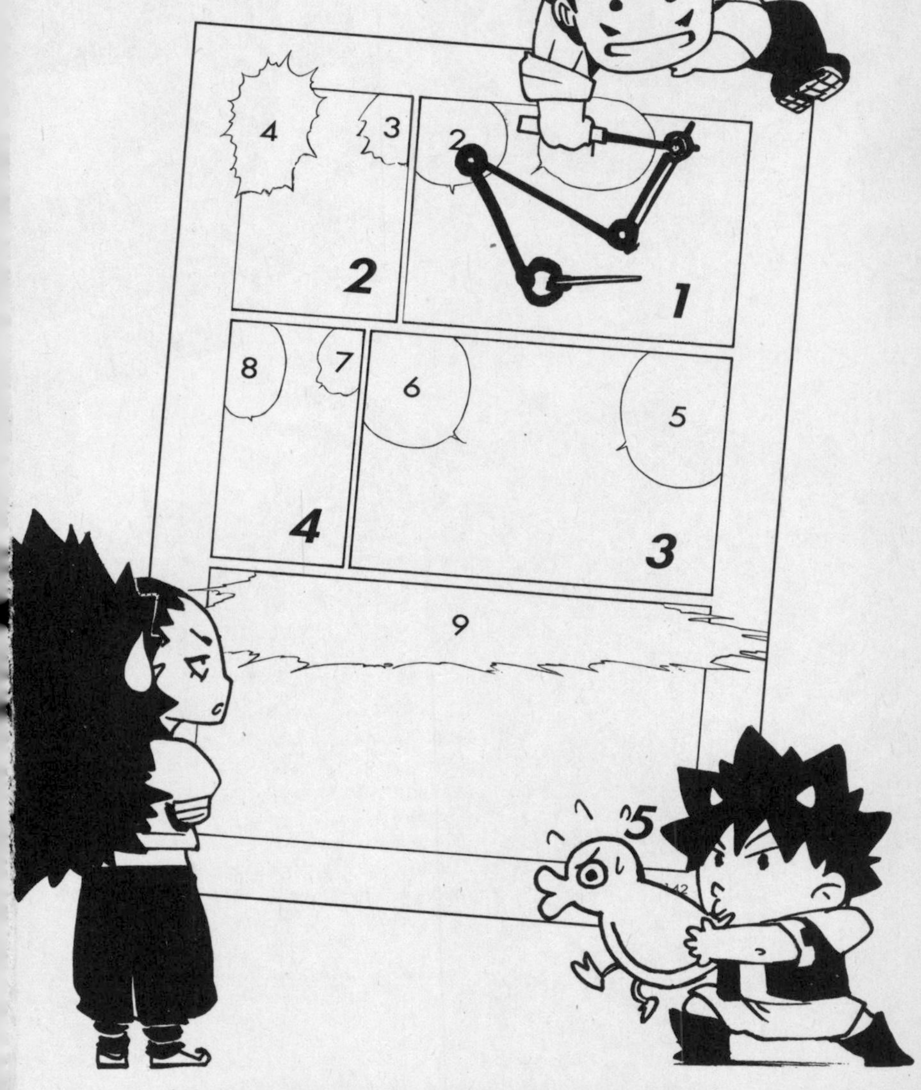

1
2
2
3
4
3
5
6
4
7
8
9
5
142